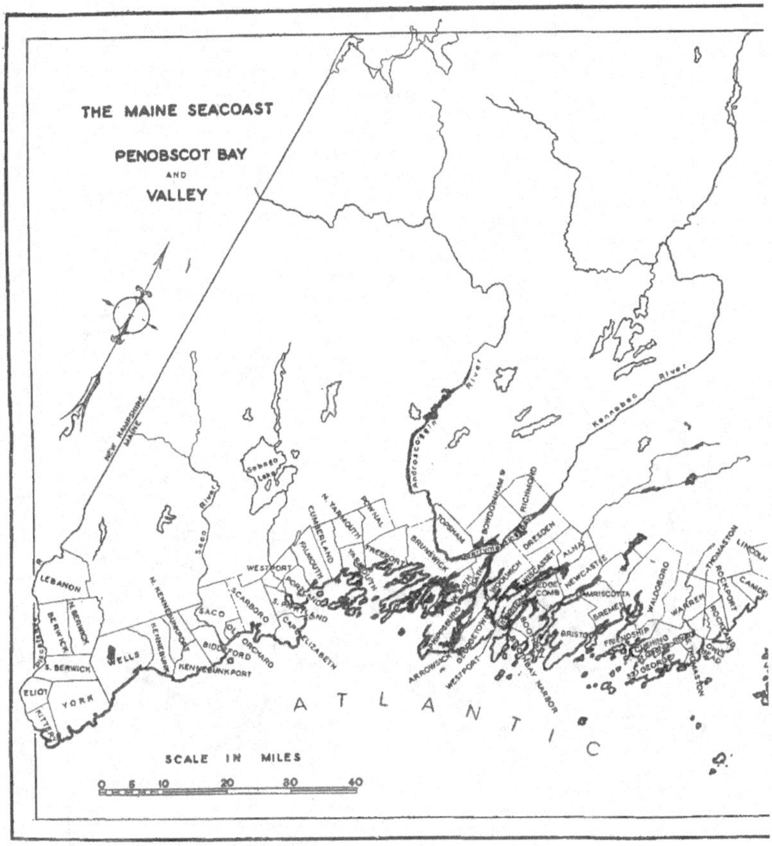
THE MAINE SEACOAST
PENOBSCOT BAY
AND
VALLEY
NEW HAMPSHIRE
MAINE
Sebago Lake
Saco River
Androscoggin River
Kennebec River
LEBANON
BERWICK
N. BERWICK
S. BERWICK
ELIOT
YORK
KITTERY
WELLS
N. KENNEBUNKPORT
KENNEBUNK
KENNEBUNKPORT
SACO
BIDDEFORD
OLD ORCHARD
SCARBORO
CAPE ELIZABETH
S. PORTLAND
PORTLAND
WESTPORT
FALMOUTH
CUMBERLAND
N. YARMOUTH
YARMOUTH
POWNAL
FREEPORT
BRUNSWICK
TOPSHAM
BOWDOINHAM
RICHMOND
DRESDEN
BATH
WOOLWICH
WISCASSET
EDGECOMB
ALNA
NEWCASTLE
DAMARISCOTTA
BRISTOL
BREMEN
WALDOBORO
FRIENDSHIP
CUSHING
ST. GEORGE
THOMASTON
WARREN
ROCKPORT
ROCKLAND
OWLS HEAD
LINCOLN
CAMDEN
ARROWSIC
GEORGETOWN
WESTPORT
BOOTHBAY HARBOR
A T L A N T I C
SCALE IN MILES
0 5 10 20 30 40

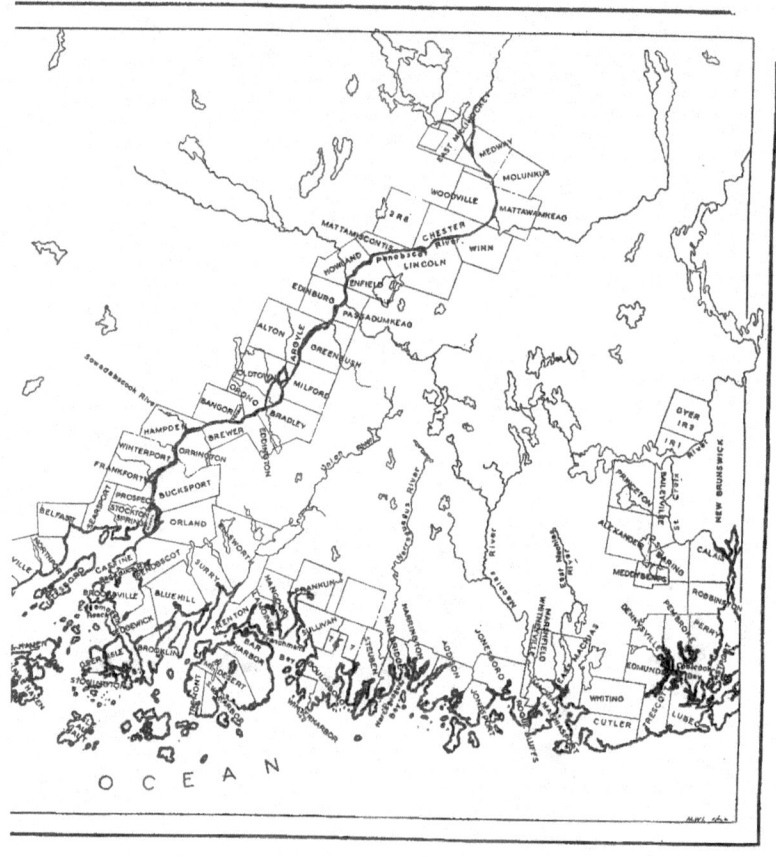

Indian Place-Names
of the
Penobscot Valley
and the
Maine Coast

Fannie Hardy Eckstorm

HERITAGE BOOKS
2025

HERITAGE BOOKS
AN IMPRINT OF HERITAGE BOOKS, INC.

Books, CDs, and more—Worldwide

For our listing of thousands of titles see our website
at
www.HeritageBooks.com

A Facsimile Reprint
Published 2025 by
HERITAGE BOOKS, INC.
Publishing Division
5810 Ruatan Street
Berwyn Heights, MD 20740

Reprinted 1960

— Publisher's Notice —
In reprints such as this, it is often not possible to remove blemishes from the original. We feel the contents of this book warrant its reissue despite these blemishes and hope you will agree and read it with pleasure.

International Standard Book Number
Paperbound: 978-0-7884-4830-0

FOREWORD

When Mrs. Eckstorm consented to prepare for the Committee on the *University of Maine Studies* a treatise on the meanings of Indian place-names in Maine, based upon her extended and painstaking study of Indian lore and historical data dealing with eastern Maine, her original plan was to confine her attention to the names of the Penobscot Valley region, with a supplementary chapter discussing certain of the more common and important Abnaki Indian roots upon which the names were based.

While the study was in progress, however, two events occurred which had considerable effect upon it. One was the death of Dr. William Francis Ganong, who had done a large amount of work on the names of Maliseet origin in Washington County, the easternmost section of the State. This prompted Mrs. Eckstorm to enlarge the scope of her study by adding the Indian names of the entire coastal region, from the St. Croix River to the Piscataqua—a change very gratifying to the committee in charge. The other event was a serious accident which kept the author hospitalized for many weeks and retarded somewhat the handling of her manuscript and the proof sheets. The value of her study has in no way been injured by this interruption, but it is likely that the form of the later chapters, in regularity of arrangement and in the citing of references, may be somewhat less orderly and consistent than they otherwise might have been.

Milton Ellis.

Orono, November 11, 1941.

TABLE OF CONTENTS

		PAGE
Foreword		iii
Preface		vii
Introduction		ix
Chapter I	Penobscot River from Bucksport to Old Town	1
Chapter II	Penobscot River from Old Town to the Great Fork at Medway	35
Chapter III	Penobscot Bay: The Western Shore to Waldoboro	65
Chapter IV	The Middle Coast, from Waldoboro to Brunswick	101
Chapter V	The Southwest Coast, from Brunswick to Kittery	147
Chapter VI	Penobscot Bay: The Eastern Shore and the Coast East to Schoodic Point	187
Chapter VII	The East Coast: Washington County	212
Appendix: Joseph Nicolar's Penobscot Place-Names		237
Bibliography		242
Errata and Addenda		255
Vita		256
Index		257
University of Maine Film Series, 1941-42		273

PREFACE

Because there has been no authoritative source of information about the Indian place-names of Maine, the writer was invited to prepare for the *University of Maine Studies* a treatise on the names of the Penobscot Valley region and the adjacent coasts which would meet scholarly standards and yet be serviceable for ready reference.

The undertaking demanded familiarity with several Indian languages and considerable acquaintance with the Maine dialects, solid grounding in the documentary history of colonial New England, knowledge of the coast and woods of Maine more intimate than mere map acquaintance, and actual contact with living Maine Indians. The field was not overcrowded; better scholars had feared to tread, and those who had rushed in had not distinguished themselves. Conscious of limited knowledge and ready to admit more than probable errors, the writer would have hesitated but for having the encouragement of the best Algonkin scholars of New England and the privilege of going to them for help. That help has been often asked and freely given, and at times it has been a consolation to know that what was unintelligible to the amateur was equally obscure to the real scholars. There remains the hope that the resulting study will be both helpful to Maine students and sound enough to stand the tests of time and of scholarly criticism.

Grateful acknowledgments are due to Mr. William Brooks Cabot and Mr. Harry Andrew Wright, now living, and in memoriam to Dr. William Francis Ganong, the Very-Reverend Michael Charles O'Brien, S.J., Colonel Charles Edward Banks, M.D., and Dr. Lucius Lee Hubbard, whose scholarship and labor planted the field which the author of this treatise has been reaping.

FANNIE HARDY ECKSTORM

BREWER, MAINE

INTRODUCTION

Indian place-names interest three classes of inquirers: intelligent readers, curious to know how a certain place-name is spelled, how it should be pronounced, and what it means; students of history, who find in documents references to places which they cannot locate upon modern maps; and students of philology, archaeology, anthropology, and comparative language, who need more material in their work.

The first ask for definitions—concise, authoritative information. The second need identifications, close references, research. The third want vocabulary, stems, endings, comparative language notes. Each of the three needs a different treatment of the same word.

Ground Covered. The full formula implied above, if carried out for each word, would make either three books or one very bulky, conventional volume. The *via media* seemed best found by gerrymandering the geographical limits considered, so as to include all varieties of place-names—the latest and the earliest; those given by Champlain and Captain John Smith, with many used by ourselves and the Indians of today; words of Abnaki, Maliseet, and Micmac origin; words of historic importance and others of no importance at all except as illustrating roots and endings, sometimes merely petty words, saved because they never have been printed.

By taking the drainage basin of the Penobscot River from the Great Fork at Medway downward, with both sides of Penobscot Bay—roughly speaking, lower Penobscot County, Waldo and Knox Counties, and western Hancock County—and then moving westward and eastward along the seacoast, it is possible for a single bulletin to cover the names within the area specified and at the same time to include all varieties, from fossils to living words, in the three different dialects once used in this region, and to propound, if not to solve, problems of historical and archaeological interest. It is, moreover, a region where Indians still live and one which is intimately familiar to the writer from childhood, so that when

Indian friends have given information there has been comparatively little risk of misunderstanding them and a good chance of eliciting full details. Much about modern Penobscot that is important has been drawn from the notes of that accomplished Abnaki scholar, the Very-Reverend Michael C. O'Brien, whose unfinished work has been available, with great profit, to the writer.

At first it was proposed to cover the whole Penobscot drainage basin; but this area is immense, including parts of eight out of the sixteen counties of Maine; and in the northern regions the woods names not only are little used but have been satisfactorily studied by Doctor L. L. Hubbard and others, while no one had ever undertaken the far more difficult coastal names which appear in all histories. Moreover, the writer has already discussed in W. H. Rowe's *History of North Yarmouth and Yarmouth* the Indian names found in eastern Cumberland County, and those of Washington County have been studied by Dr. William F. Ganong in connection with his Maliseet investigations. Therefore, by filling in the important Penobscot region and the long seacoast, we could have a usable, if not a complete, census of our most used names. To do a thorough job on the territory selected and to make the results available to all the different classes of readers who want them is the objective of this treatise.

Arrangement. An alphabetical arrangement would bring together Indian words which have only a mechanized relation; so it has seemed better to depend upon the Index for quick reference and to present the words in their natural geographical sequence, thus keeping as a background the scene familiar to the casual reader, who is more interested to know the names of places near his own home than of those far away. The Penobscot River is followed up its course from Bucksport to the Fork at Medway, and towns on both sides and on the tributaries are placed as nearly as possible in the order in which they occur geographically. Below Bucksport, where the Bay widens out, the shore-line is followed downward, east shore and west shore independently, next westerly along the seacoast to the Piscataqua, and then easterly to the St. Croix. Though the arrangement is irregular, any word, Indian or English, can easily be found in the Index; and making the list a guidebook instead of a dictionary is considered the most generally serviceable plan.

Many of the names which have a historic background are

given detailed treatment. Knowing the ground, the writer at times does not hesitate to differ from generally accepted and often repeated pronouncements about Indian names, whose only authority is their priority. Indeed, in the Castine region, for example, historical work is at a standstill until localities are better identified according to their Indian signification and a clearer understanding of the essentials of Indian life. Did Baron Castine always live at the old fort, as everyone imagines? An old French map shows that he did not. Where was d'Aulnay de Charnizay's mill, where Wannerton of Piscataqua was murdered? What about Church's forays into this Indian country? Questions like these, often largely topographical, the historians have not answered. There was one considerable battle at the foot of Walker's Pond, in Brooksville, of which they have no record. Journals of the writer's father, dated almost eighty years ago, say that when he was camping on this spot an aged resident told him that many years before, when he was a boy, he used to dig bullets out of the pine trees there, where the whites and Indians had fought a battle. In its place we shall call attention to a bit of history connected with Sears Island, near Searsport, which the historian Williamson, of Belfast, could not locate by its Indian name. The determination of Douaquet as Waukeag of today not only defines Cadillac's bound but brings to light a forgotten "scurmidge" with Dutch pirates. The importance of such historical features has largely influenced the preference for the geographical instead of the alphabetical arrangement of Indian names.

Method. The method of investigation followed was first exemplified by the late Dr. James Hammond Trumbull in his essay "On the Composition of Indian Geographical Names." [1] This fifty-page paper is still our best guide into the methods of the scientific analysis of place-names. Others have done good work since, preeminent among them being Dr. William Francis Ganong, long professor of botany at Smith College. Dr. Ganong's five papers on the "Organization of the Indian Place-Nomenclature of the Maritime Provinces of Canada" set a stiff pace for even the advanced student.[2] Though these are primarily of Canadian inter-

---

[1] Printed in Connecticut Historical Society *Collections*, Vol. II (1870).

[2] Printed in the *Transactions* of the Royal Society of Canada, Third Series, Vol. V, sec, ii (1912-1915). Available at the State Library in Augusta, the Bowdoin College Library, and the Bangor Public Library.

est, many Maine place-names were included in the discussions; but the demonstration was too rigorous to be continued throughout the long list. Dr. Ganong's uncompleted "Monograph of the Indian Place-names of the Atlantic Provinces of Canada," upon which he worked for many years, will, when published, be much more popular and will also contain most of the Maliseet names found in Washington County, Maine. While engaged upon his earlier work, Dr. Ganong taught the present writer his method and discussed many of the points he was taking up—instruction and discussion alike invaluable but impossible to acknowledge in particular instances. It is enough that in five-and-twenty years of friendly intercourse, Dr. Ganong's was always the advice most valued.

A much more recent friend, Mr. William Brooks Cabot, who has developed a method of scientific analysis by comparison of cognates in many languages, has freely given valuable direction.

This comparative analytic method is the only sound way of extracting the meaning from words so old and mutilated that the Indians themselves cannot recognize them. It depends upon collecting the dated forms found in old maps, deeds, wills, and other documents, proving the precise location of a place, comparing the translation deduced from documentary sources with the natural characteristics of the place, collecting other instances of the use of the word, studying cognates in related languages, and, if possible, getting the personal opinions or the inherited traditions of living Indians. Laborious and slow, it nevertheless yields sound results.

Phonetics. There are three valid reasons for not attempting phonetic representation of Indian words; the printer could not print them; the reader could not read them; and the writer cannot write them! So, like Lawrence of Arabia, in a similar case, we pass. Like Lawrence also, in his famous preface to *Revolt in the Desert,* we defend our right to spell any Indian word in any way we prefer; also, if need be, to spell it in different ways. When in a list of less than a dozen place-names an Indian can give us *nargar, knargoog, quanough,* and *nargook* and expect us to spell them all as *-nahge-,* "island," it seems only fair to pass along to the consumer-reader as his share of the high cost of finding out what it is all about, an occasional nut to crack; for until a spelling has been established by use in books of reference or as the name of a town or post office, there is no authoritative spelling of an Indian word, no right and wrong way, but only a better and a worse—and often the government has preferred the worse. Correct accent and intonation must be learned from hearing Indians speaking, and not even an Indian could tell us how our older place-names were pronounced. If we place the syllabic stress when we can and occasionally mark the length of a vowel, it is all we can safely attempt. The nasals must be learned from a teacher; or the French nasal can be used or the vowel broadened to approximate the sound. In printing, the nasal is sometimes represented by two dots over a letter, sometimes by an exponent n above it.[3]

Errors. Upon one point Dr. Ganong was always firm. "In any genuine investigation, it is just as important to expose old error as to expound new truth ... for, on the one hand, errors ... have a wonderful vitality, and, on the other, if ignored, they are sure, sooner or later to be dug out and triumphantly displayed by the superficial student as the real truth overlooked by the investigator! The only logical way is for the investigator to recognize the error as a worthy enemy, and then to proceed to demolish it by the same scientific methods which he used for the demonstration of the truth."

We protest that popular errors are the windmill against which Don Quixote tilted and that life is too short to spend it in reforming superficial students who, with the book open before them, do not

---

[3] The question of phonetic representation is one bound to arise when we have sounds in another language difficult to reproduce in our own. The practice of scholars varies, the practical scholars who have had experience in field work other than phonetics alone inclining to such approximations of sounds as do not hinder rather than help those not technically trained, decrying "diacritical points and marks which convey either nothing or a false meaning to uninstructed Western eyes." Such practical scholars in Oriental studies were Dr. D. G. Hogarth, Lawrence of Arabia, and Gertrude Bell; of the same opinion in American Indian studies was Dr. Ganong. And this point of view almost necessitates differences in spellings by the same writer, according to his own intuition, as circumstances vary. Lawrence insisted upon spelling Arabic words as he pleased, and Lady Bell writes of Gertrude, that she "used often to spell the same word in different ways, sometimes because she was trying experiments in transliteration, sometimes deliberately adopting a new way, sometimes because the same word is differently pronounced in Arabic or in Turkish." There may be reasons deeper than inattention or waywardness for varying the spelling of Indian words in this treatise; it is a right which we shall not abandon.

see "the demonstration of the truth," but with the instinct of a pup for a dead rat, dig out the alluring falsity and parade it to show their smartness. Instead of repeating all the wrong definitions and silly stories made up to account for Indian place-names, may we not blanket the whole class by posting some of the worst offenders as persons whose opinions are not worth repeating except when they are known to be correct?

Authorities. Authorities on Indian place-names are of two sorts —those whom it is safe to quote and those whom it is safer not to quote. Unfortunately the latter kind have printed their opinions, which are easily accessible, while the former, even after two centuries, often remain in manuscript, almost unknown. Even if sought out and consulted, they may be of little use to anyone without a good acquaintance with French, some Latin, and at least a little knowledge of Indian dialects.

In the middle of the last century, William Willis, of Portland, made a praiseworthy attempt to collect our Maine place-names and printed many of them in the Maine Historical Society's publications.[4] His object was "to aid in making a catalogue of all the Indian terms extant, applied to any portion of our territory." Laudable as was his effort, the time was not ripe. There were no Indian scholars then, but there were several enthusiasts who thought the undertaking an easy one and who rushed to assist with results best forgotten. When they went to Indians for information, either the Indian did not comprehend what was wanted or else they could not understand what the Indian was trying to tell them, and sometimes the simple native deliberately fooled them when he found out how easy it was to do so. The wild guesses of the Indians were exceeded by the yet more fantastic results obtained when the enthusiasts "resolved the word" into its component parts.

The method favored by these pundits was to break up a place-name into syllables, quite at random, and then to match the individual parts to anything above the earth that they could find in print, regardless of dialect and of grammatical structure. It was the method of two small children who announced that they were studying Latin all by themselves. "I see a volo!" cried one; "I see another volo!"

---

[4] Maine Historical Society *Collections,* First Series, Vol. IV (1856), 95-117 and 185-193.

exclaimed the other, with a vigorous smack of the fly-swatter. A "volo" was a fly, as they proved by showing in an old Latin book, *"volo, volare,* to fly."

In the same volume with Mr. Willis's list are the contributions of Dr. A. J. Chute and Dr. Chandler E. Potter, pioneers in the *volo-*system of studying Indian. While he was in Missouri, in 1838, Dr. Chute obtained from Delaware Indians there a number of "definitions" of Maine place-names which, on his return, he printed in a local newspaper. Among them was the meaning of Androscoggin— "Great Skunk River." Dr. Potter came forward to dispute this: it was "fish-high-place," whatever that may be. Somewhat later Rev. Eugene Vetromile announced that Androscoggin meant "Andros coming" and referred to the appointment of Sir Edmund Andros as Governor of Massachusetts in 1686! With doctors so disagreeing, one may well ask, "What does Androscoggin mean anyway?" "Plenty of fish" is the answer: it was a wonderful river for migratory fish of all sorts, and words ending in *-mogan, -coggin* denote fisheries.

The mistakes of this kind of "students," as they called themselves, fall into several classes. Some of them had no regard for dialects. *Kennebeck,* said Chute, means "they who thanked"— probably in Missouri-Delaware. Judge Potter said it meant "a snake," apparently making it from the Ojibway *kenabeek* ("serpent") of *Hiawatha.* It is the "long, still water," "the long reach," a long extent of river without rapids, referring especially to that part of the river near Bath. Some of them had no regard for self-evident facts. There is Winnegance, in West Bath, which Vetromile said means "a large body of water." Really it is not a water-word at all. Winnegance is *ounegan-sis,* a "short carry," in reference to the short distance between the heads of two tidal creeks, one flowing south, the other north. Some of them outraged all the possibilities. It was Rufus K. Sewall who wrote that Pemaquid is from *"pemi,* oil, and *quidden,* a ship" (that is, a whaling vessel), and in evidence adds that Capt. John Smith fished for whales here.[5] Pemaquid means "long point" and bore the name centuries before John Smith ever saw the place. Nor does *quidden* mean a ship, even though it goes back to Waymouth's voyage: it stands for *akwiden,* a birch canoe, so named because it floats lightly.

---

[5] Rufus King Sewall, *Pemaquid, its Genesis* (Wiscasset, 1896), p. 2.

Folk Etymology. Many interpretations of our place-names that are found in print are pure folk etymology. For some of these the Indians are responsible; but Indians did not originate such sentimental translations as "the smile of the Great Spirit" for Winnepesaukee, or the home-made, humorous sort beginning "There was an old Indian named Matty," used in accounting for name like Matanawcook and Mattawamkeag, in which we are informed that Matty was no cook; or that Mary was no cook, but Anna was "besser cook," or even worse nonsense. There is also the *ipse-dixit* sort, usually clerical in origin, which offers no proof (and could not get any), like Maurault's "where they persecuted us" for Cushnoc (Augusta), or Vetromile's "I go to hide at a place" for Bagaduce (Castine), or Dr. Ballard's "long deer place" for Piscataqua. Upon this, Dr. Trumbull remarked that by Indian grammar it was the deer, not the place, that must be long. Under his pen-name of "Brunovicus," Dr. Ballard tried to push the matter in Dr. J. G. Shea's *Historical Magazine*[6] and for confirmation of his assertion that *attuck* meant "deer," wrote to an informant whose name need not be mentioned since his answer never was published. The oracle replied, "*Attuck* means 'taken,' hence Connecticut, 'long taken.' I cannot say at present whether it may mean something else." It does!

False interpretations of some place-names arise from misinformation given intentionally by Indians, like Vetromile's "Cowsigan, carrying place for cows" (Vetromile MSS.), the name of the "rough narrows" in the Back Channel near Wiscasset. Indian words are sometimes assumed to be English, as when Sheepscot is called "Sheep's Gut," though it is the Indian *Pashipscot.* There is also the contrary error of mistaking an English word for Indian, as Pleajom (Pleasant) Stream, Miskitor (Mosquito) Mountain, and Pushaw, named for a family that early settled upon the lake.

Among our finest English "boners" is *Squamanagonic* (more correctly *Mskwamanganek*), the old salmon fishery in New Hampshire, which comes from *meskwamikw,* a "salmon" (literally "red fish"), and *amangan,* a "fishing place," with a locative ending. A town history explains it as *squam,* "water," *an,* "hill," *a,* euphonic, *gon,* "clay," and *ic,* "place"—"literally rendered, then it means 'wa-

---

[6] *Historical Magazine* (Boston), First Series, IX, 132. Available in Bangor Public Library.

ter of the clay place hill' . . . a tolerably faithful description."[7] We might ask, "Faithful, how?" The Indian also contributes to the joy of living. A very good Maliseet informant told the writer that Machias means "clumsy," and produced in evidence a long Revolutionary tale of an ancestor who clumsily tried to destroy a British vessel there. Another Maliseet told Dr. Gatschet that Machias means "partridge," mistaking *mutchiess*, "bad bird," their name for the ruffed grouse, for Machias, which really means "a bad run of water," or "falls." It was an educated Indian who wrote: *"Matacheeset, from Methodist. The Pilgrim Fathers borrowed some corn from Methodist Indians in 1620."*[8] Nor can we omit this recent example of folk-etymology given the writer by one of the most intelligent of her Penobscot friends. Lucerne-in-Maine is the rather recent rechristening of the place in Hancock County which we used to know as Phillips Lake. The writer was told that when Governor Brewster was taking part in exercises for popularization of the project, he invited Peter Necola to be present, and this so pleased Peter that he said, "Alloosahneh! Let's go!" This in turn so delighted the Governor that he said it ought to be accepted as the name of the lake! Thus is explained the origin of the name Lucerne-in-Maine, according to the etymology of the aborigines!

Ex pede Herculem!—why, when we have samples like these, should we waste time in demolishing all the trumpery mislabeled "Indian information" which is found in print? Why not leave it to the good sense of those who follow to reject worthless accumulations, made when even the best-equipped had to work without tools? At least they did all they could in their own time, and some of them did very well.

It was the entire worthlessness of much of the information given by Indians which led to the discovery that our place-names have several dialectical origins and often can be interpreted only by languages that now are extra-limital. When of the best half-dozen of one's informants no two agreed in the analysis of a word, it is clear that none of them knew what it meant. Either the name had dropped

---

[7] Franklin McDuffie, *History of Rochester, New Hampshire* (Manchester, N. H., 1892), Vol. I, Chap. 2.

[8] Henry Lorne Masta, *Abenaqui Indian Legends, Grammar and Place Names* (Victoriaville, Quebec, 1932), p. 89.

out of their own vocabulary, or it was older than their tribal occupation of the country. Why do we find Micmac names along the whole length of the Maine coast? We do not know. To explain *why* they occur is to enter the precincts of the archaeologist and the ethnologist. We merely report to these specialists what we find.

Difficulties Encountered. One who undertakes to investigate these old place-names treads a thorny path. Some are very old and much worn down by use; they belong to several different dialects; they were recorded by chance visitors from different nations which had dissimilar phonetics, or by officials to whom the form of an Indian word was of no interest; they were printed by typesetters who could decipher their copy only with difficulty and corrected by proofreaders who could not compare with the originals. Altogether, what is remarkable is that the results were not worse.

In Indian words there is always the possibility of pre-Columbian influences—Basque, Norse, or Portuguese. Basque, in particular, is known to have affected the Micmac vocabulary to such an extent that Nicolas Denys, speaking in the middle of the seventeenth century, declared that half of the Micmac words—meaning, of course, the trade vocabulary—were Basque. French and English also pushed their way into the Maine dialects with the novelties Europeans brought in, so that our Indians adopted many loan-words—such as "horse," "cow," "pig," "sheep," from the English, and "bottle," "salt," "stew" (*ragout*), "handkerchief" (*mouchoir*), "soup," and "nutmeg," from the French—which have to be detected under uncouth forms.

Lack of Dictionaries. To the foregoing difficulties, add that of inadequate vocabularies. The only dictionary in print in a Maine Indian language is the French-Abnaki dictionary left unfinished by Father Sebastian Rasles more than two centuries ago; and since this was intended for missionary use, it is long on theology and short on the terms we need most in place-names. The only Maliseet word-book we have is a brief pamphlet by Montague Chamberlain, printed in 1899. There is no Micmac dictionary except the English-Indian one compiled by Rev. Silas T. Rand, whose great Indian-English dictionary was burned in manuscript in the Wellesley College Library fire. The student either must make bricks without straw or grow the straw himself, which is what the serious student has to do by a large amount of copying and photostating of rare items. Of course, in Maine, he can go to an Indian; but we have had a glimpse of what an Indian may do with his own language.

Errors in Interpretation. A frequent source of error in dealing with Indians is the inquirer's inability to get the point the Indian is trying to make. The name of a Massachusetts lake is sometimes cited facetiously as showing Indian stupidity in definitions—Chaubunagunamaug, "you fish on your side, I fish on my side; nobody fish in the middle." As a matter of fact the explanation is excellent; all that is lacking is the one English word which boils it down for handy use. The lake was the boundary of the fishing rights between different tribes. Not having the English word "boundary" at his command, the Indian had to describe the place. Our Bungomug, in Brunswick, is a contraction of the same word: it was the old town boundary of North Yarmouth.

Some years since, when I was working on the meaning of Cobscook, near the Quoddy project, I asked Mrs. Clara Neptune to explain it. "Well, you see, you put rock in stove, get it hot, then spit on it—that Cobscook." My own experience in canoeing in quick water supplied the picture. She meant a "boiling rock," one far enough under water for the swift current to crown and bubble over, as the tremendous tidal flow of Cobscook does over the rocks in its contracted channel. It is not a waterfall or a rapid, but a boiling tide-current. Old deeds mention the "Boiling Rock" on the Kittery shore of the Piscataqua, where similar conditions are found. Nichols' Rock at Eddington Bend, called Sobscook by the Indians, standing where tide and current fought, must have been another boiling rock.

Again, when asked to explain *Kwaykwaynamayk,* Clara said: "Down Pushaw way; you step long step, *so;* it mean dat." Unable this time to get the picture in her mind, I asked Lewis Ketchum about it. Laughing, he said, "A reach; it means a straight place in the stream." The woman had the correct idea, but no English word for expressing it.

Similarly, Pierpole's often-quoted description of Pejepscot (Brunswick Falls) has been made to mean "a diving snake" by those who could not get his point. He was not analyzing the word, giving its roots; he was picturing the turbulent water below the great falls, twisting through broken, irregular rocks. "Extended-rapids-rock-place" would be a literal translation of the word; but anyone who has seen a large snake swim in swift water can see what Pierpole had in mind. It is at this point of getting the picture that closet students, who know nothing but books, blunder badly when they undertake to interpret a word without having seen the place. Even Doctor Trumbull sometimes errs; his provisional meaning of Cobscook as "Sturgeon-catching place" [9] shows that he had never seen those great tide whirls and did not realize that he was dealing with a language unfamiliar to him.

Lack of Fixed Spelling. A difficult concept for the beginner in Indian study to grasp is that the words are *sounds only;* that they have no set and proper spelling. Any spelling which catches the sound will answer. And the sounds must be segregated into the roots they represent. Once these roots have been determined with accuracy, it does not matter in the least who says what about them— the roots speak for themselves. Historians have declared that Pejepscot and Pashipscot are the same place. They are wrong—the roots in the words show it. Pejepscot was Brunswick; Pashipscot was Sheepscot. No matter what historians have said about where Donaquet, or Douaket, was, the correct Indian form settles the locality beyond question. It was Adowakeag, in Sullivan and Hancock, the ridge that cuts across the tide-river just below the iron bridge. In dealing with Indian words, the printed forms are valuable only as a clue to the sounds behind them.

Changes in Sound. Here again is a difficulty. In three centuries the pronunciation of both French and English has changed much. If, in Captain John Smith's day "chaps" was "chops" and "char" was "chore," if long *o* might be *oo* ("Rome indeed and room enough," said punning Shakespeare), if *er* was *ar* ("clarks" and "parsons"), if they filled their lamps with "ile" and put the "kittle" on to "bile" and swept up the "harth" and called both the seals they shot and their garden soils "siles," [10] how did John Smith pronounce his Indian words? And if, in trying to explain John Smith's Indian, we use the Frenchified Indian of Father Rasles, a century later, we are doubling our troubles instead of halving them. The French also had their own way of pronouncing Indian as well as of writing it. Their

---

[9] Connecticut Historical Society *Collections,* II, 42.

[10] "The *Soile,* or *Sea Calf,* a Creature that brings forth her young ones upon dry land, but at other times keeps in the Sea preying upon Fish" (John Josselyn, *New England's Rarities,* 1672, p. 34 of original). Maine fishermen up to sixty years ago spoke of seals as "siles," just as Josselyn must have pronounced the word.

use of *ci* where today we hear our Indians saying *tch* or *dj* is an impediment, the more troublesome because our best authority on modern Abnaki, Father O'Brien, veered between the two sounds, at one time recording in the English, at another in the French method. Who shall say how some of *his* words should be sounded?—and unfortunately he did not live to revise his work; yet upon the sound he meant may depend the root he used.

Then, too, our modern Indians use *l* instead of *r*, seldom using *r* except where it does not belong. Yet Father Rasles used *r* constantly and often must have trilled it. Three centuries ago William Wood wrote in *New England's Prospect* that the Indians of northern New England not only used *r*, but "rolled it like an unbract drum." They do not do so now.

Indian Grammar. The Indian language is intricately constructed and highly inflected: Greek is simple beside it. Yet fortunately the place-names require little knowledge of the grammatical structure. Dr. Gatschet says: "They are mostly compound nouns and combinations either of two substantives or of an adjective and a substantive, with the substantive standing last. In the first case, the noun standing first is sometimes connected with the noun standing second by the case-suffix ending -*i*, as in *Eduki m'niku*, Deer Island, from *Eduk*, deer." This makes a genitive case, and we call it "possessive *i*," as the simplest name for the connecting vowel.

Most of our place-names end in *k*, and the endings -*ek*, -*ik*, -*ok*, -*uk* correspond nearly to the Latin ablative of place and are translated as "at, in, on, upon." The meaning of place-names is commonly given as "at this-or-that place," making a common noun into a proper noun, which in English we distinguish by a capital letter. Since Indians did not have a written language, they indicated particular places by a suitable ending which would catch the ear, as the capital takes the reader's eye. Occasionally, however, the ending in *k* is not a locative but is -*ak*, the plural of an animate noun; while one in -*ol* or -*al* indicates the plural of an inanimate noun, called respectively "strong" and "weak" nouns. There are also two sorts of plurals in Indian, the inclusive and the exclusive, though these do not affect place-names. The verb is exceedingly complex. The prospective student of Indian who reads Father O'Brien's paper on

"The Abnaki Noun" [11] will find so many pitfalls in his way that he will have little enthusiasm for attacking the far more difficult Abnaki verb.

Inseparable Roots. The peculiarity of the Abnaki language which gives most trouble in the place-names is the use of two sorts of roots to represent the same English word. One is independent; the other, used only in composition, is inseparable from the elements combined with it. They never appear alone, and are so unlike the independent roots that even the best experts have not found all of them. As a word used by itself, an island is *menahan'*, and the *men-* syllable is often combined with other words, particularly in possessive compounds; but oftener in compounds the other, or inseparable, root *-naghe-* appears, coalescing with adjoining syllables so that it is hard to detect, indeed was not even suspected by some of our best students. A hill is *wadjo*, or *watcho*, when we use the word independently, as in Wachusett, "the Hill," "at the hill"; but when compounded, it is oftener the inseparable *-adene-*, as in Katahdin, "the Principal Hill," where we recognize it only by the sound. In Maliseet, an animal's tail, if an independent root, is *usukwun'*; if an inseparable, it is *-ah'le*, which the French wrote as *-añ'ri*, to make it more difficult. A tree, in Abnaki, used alone is *aba'si;* but in composition to denote a particular species, it is *-me'zi-*, *-mi'si*, or *mo'zi-*. *Nahmays'*, a fish, becomes *-mecq* in some fish names, *-am* in others. *Sep'sis*, a bird, turns into *-lessoo* when indicating a special kind of bird. Most of these inseparables the learner has to dig out by himself.

Telescoping of Roots. The inseparables themselves create another hindrance. They are subject to such condensation that from a word of a half dozen letters the root may be pared down to one or two. For example, Katahdin is from the adjective *keght*, "principal," and the inseparable *-ad'ene-*, a "mountain"; but from the first root we retain only the *k* and *t*, and from the second only *d* and *n*, the vowels being inserted for English use. When, in 1736, Capt. John Gyles, who had long been a prisoner to the Indians, wrote "The Teddon" for Katahdin, he gave a good Indian form, and his definite article correctly represented the first root as a translation of it, while "Teddon" caries over the final letter of *keght* and contains only two

---

[11] Michael C. O'Brien, "The Abnaki Noun" (Maine Historical Society *Collections,* First Series, IX (1887), 261-294).

letters, *d* and *n,* of the second root. In 1786, Robert Treat of Bangor and John Marsh of Old Town, interpreters, named "Mount Tadden" on a sketch map. It is the same word as Gyles's, entirely recognizable to an Indian; but when Judge Sullivan misprinted the name as "Mt. Fadder," no one could have recognized it; he had made an impossible word.¹²

Long and Short Vowels in Roots. Words which in print or when spoken by whites appear to be the same may be wholly dissimilar in Indian pronounciation, when long and short vowels are properly recognized. The old name of Fryeburg was sometimes printed Pegwacket and sometimes Pequawkett, which were supposed to be the less refined and more refined forms of the earlier Pigwacket; but Pegwacket, or Pegwocket, has a short *e* in the first syllable, from the root *pĕg-,* something "humped up, swollen," while Pequawkett, with a long *e* in the first syllable, from the root *pīk,* means something broken:¹³ they are not the same word at all.

The Indian Alphabet. Several of the sounds represented by the letters of our alphabet are lacking in Indian. The Maine dialects have no *f* or *v,* and no complete Indian word begins with *r;* thus, a name like Ripogenus, though Indian, is defective at the beginning. Maine Indians generally substitute *l* for *r* and do not roll *r* when they do speak it. They do not, perhaps cannot, distinguish *p* and *b,* saying "Penobscot" and "Bemopscot" indifferently, and the shift from *p* to *b* may occur in almost any word. Sometimes *t* and *d* are interchanged. One would not suppose that Joe Denoque and Joe Temakweh were the same man, but an Indian would know him. *M* is an elusive sound, often at the beginning retained as a mere breathing, perhaps oftener dropped where it should appear; thus words beginning with *mekw,* "red," are apt to drop every trace of the element or at best to retain only *m'*. *H* is often only a rough breathing between doubled vowels,

---

¹² James Sullivan, *History of the District of Maine* (Boston, 1795), 37. The word no doubt was a misprint. Sullivan seems to have known the Treat and Marsh map, now in the Massachusetts Archives (Maps and Plans, 38:8), and probably intended to follow it. His form is impossible because Abnaki Indian has no *f,* and final *n* could not change to *r.*

¹³ The change from one form to the other was made about 1824 by John Farmer (of Farmer and Moore's *Historical Collections*) quite arbitrarily and ignorantly. As the second element shows, this was a mountain name. It must have referred to Jockey Cap in Fryeburg, since it fits so well that unusual hill, "the punched-up-through mountain," which rises abruptly out of the surrounding sandy plain.

but it is aspirated also, often strongly. *G* is always hard. *K* is constantly dropped; wherever there is a double *a*, we may suspect that a *k* between them has been dropped. On the other hand, *s* is so persistent that if a root contained it, it must be accounted for in analysis. There are no silent letters in Indian; in general letters have but one sound; the stress varies but usually is thrown well toward the end of the word.

Using Rasles. To make Rasles' Dictionary useful for modern Indian, one must learn to transliterate his sounds into the modern dialect. This is not hard to do. Where Rasles has an *r*, substitute an *l*. When he gives a dotted letter *ṅ*, exchange it for *h* to broaden the vowel, or use an *m*, or a French nasal. In writing, the dotted n can be represented by a raised *n;* as for *awaṅgan* write *awa^{n}gan*. An apostrophe in the middle of a word usually indicates a rough breathing as in Greek. Rarely Rasles makes us of several Greek letters—chi(kh, rough), theta (th), psi (ps)—but these have no special significance to us, nor does it seem necessary to reproduce the Greek letter in copying such words. The commonest of Father Rasles' unusual letters is a character which stands for our *w*, lacking in French but abounding in Indian. It was shaped much like a figure eight, and before a vowel, can be replaced by our *w*, or before a consonant by *u* or *oo*. (At the end of a word, as in -meckw, or *-mecqu'*, we have an explosive sound.) If Rasles wrote *érérm8et*, "what one wills," pronounce it *el-elm'-wet;* if he wrote *araṅmbeg'8k*, "under the water," read it as *alambag'ook*, and the result will be an approximation to the modern Indian; but one cannot learn Indian by a correspondence course, as Will Rogers said he learned how to use a lariat.

Grammatical Difficulties. There are plenty of them, but the only one likely to give trouble in place-names is in the separation of a root from its possessive adjective. The Indian has no article. He cannot say "a dog"—he says "my dog," "thy dog," "his dog," and he welds the possessive adjective and the root together so that in each resultant person it looks like a wholly new word. The changes run through all possible owners of the canine, varying in inflection until the original dog all but disappears in a maze of grammatical person and number. *Netep, ketep,* and *outep* are all *heads,* but each belongs to a different person; and though we might recognize *antep* as the root of "a head," when it suddenly changes into *wedep* or *outop* we better understand why King Charles's head, in *David Copperfield,* drove Mr. Dick crazy.

Roots and Stems. Though we may speak of *-antep* as the root of "head," in reality we often get only *tp* (just as we got *tn* standing for "mountain"); this *tp* or *tn* we recognize as the *root.*

A root is a primitive and fundamental group of a few sounds which convey an idea; it is the part of a word which cannot be reduced to simpler form and which cannot be used alone; it usually conveys some idea of action.

A root will label classes of words which have to do with giving, or making, or walking, for example; but it will not tell us who gives, or what is given, until a formative element is added to show the agent, the giver, the object, the gift, or some other relation, which in English we represent by separate words called nouns, or names. When the formative element is added, the root becomes a *stem.* Then by adding other syllables, a prefix before or a suffix after the stem, it is qualified to vary its meanings. We make words in English in this way, and we also put them together to form new compounds; but except in chemistry, we do not make words of such inordinate length as the Indian or the Sanskrit language does. Both of these will put together enough words to make a whole sentence and then compress the sentence into a single word. "It is plain that such compounds must tax the ingenuity of those who wish to find out their syntax; and after all they must often be ambiguous, capable of expressing more relations than one" (J. Peile, *Primer of Philology*). There is a limit to what can be done with Indian place-names, because often we cannot loosen up this compression.

Syllabic Analysis. Roots, we found, were very small clusters of sounds representing definite ideas. The sound and the idea progress at equal pace, and the same sound will carry the idea through many languages. In Sanskrit we have the root SPA or SPAN, meaning to draw out or extend; and in English we get "span," "space," "speed," "spin," and other words which carry the idea. The Indian language, which owes nothing to the Sanskrit, for a river has *sepe,* or *sepu,* literally, "it extends, stretches out," the same fundamental SP. The Sanskrit has SIK, to pour out, and SUG, SIG, to cause to flow; and the the Indian parallels it with *sauk,* an outlet, "where the river pours out," and *soglan,* rain, "what comes pouring down." We feel beforehand that *sl* combinations will slip or slide or slant, be slim or sly or slender, while *h* combinations will heave or hump or hop or hurry, or lend themselves to motion with an effort.

In Indian this harmony of sound and sense is particularly marked, and almost any combination of two or more letters will suggest to an expert in language a syllabic meaning. Only the few who have thoroughly assimilated the Indian way of thinking can master this method of analysis; but to one who, like Mr. William Brooks Cabot, has succeeded, a word opens up like the beads on a string, each syllable separate and significant, yet all bound together. To such a one there are pictures in words. Once for a long time Mr. Cabot and I had been discussing the meaning of "Wiscasset." Judging from the historical forms of the word, I had contended that it must mean an outlet of a definite type, one which ran out strong from a basin out of sight around a bend, not visible when the force of the current was first encountered, a "concealing outlet"; that it derived from *wetchi*, "from," *-kask*, "comes out," and not from *wis-* or *whis-*, an ebb-tide word. Later Mr. Cabot wrote: "After we talked Wiscasset and my mind sat up again, it came back that you were quite right, as I see, about the run of water, *wu-ich,* I write it: the *wu* gives a sort of purpose or intention, it *wants* to run; that's the way we work it in Montagnais. The *-kasika* means it scrapes, rubs, wears as it goes." That is, to Mr. Cabot the word itself pictured a place he had never seen. The old Indian deed of Wiscasset proves that the land sold was "at the outlet" of the great inland harbor, and the word itself described just the kind of outlet it was, one where a sharp bend in the river cut off the view above, and one felt the current before seeing the great bay behind the barrier.

The Indian Languages of Maine. Today the Penobscot Indians speak Abnaki, and the Passamaquoddy Indians speak Maliseet, which represents the Etchemin of the old explorers. Indeed the Passamaquoddies call themselves *Skidjim,* "Men" (that is, Indians), the same word as Etchemin. The Penobscots call themselves *Alnanbiak,* also meaning Men. Maine place-names represent both Abnaki and Maliseet origins, and we know that both tribes have occupied the country. Yet many place-names, extending the whole length of the coast, cannot be satisfactorily explained unless we use a third language, the Micmac, or Tarentyn, and no Micmacs have lived dominantly on our coast within historic times except for one brief incursion.[14] Until archaeologists and ethnologists can account otherwise for the presence of these names, we have to assume that at some time the Micmacs, as well as the Maliseets, lived much farther to the westward than they do today. It is, however, not a theory of our own—picking up fossils does not make a geologist of the finder, and our only concern is to show what we have found, not to theorize upon the way it got here.

Arrangement. Once again we call attention to an arrangement of our subject which is unusual but has a reason behind it. The political divisions of today do not coincide with natural topography; we need more than the location of a shire town to determine the order of arranging our place-names. Penobscot County is large and very long; Waldo and Knox Counties are very small and compact; to follow county lines alone would result in unequal divisions of our space and no natural order. The first natural division is the River and the Bay, fresh water and salt water. Salt water begins at Bucksport, where seaweed growing marks the change. Therefore, beginning at Bucksport, we proceed up the river, taking in all towns on both sides of the river and the tributary waters; we stop at Old Town Great Falls, in Old Town city. This is the natural head of the section of the river properly called Penobscot, "the rocky part." Also it includes most of the area settled by the English after 1763 and before 1800, which gives it a sort of historic continuity. This is our Chapter One.

From Old Town Falls up, the river to the Great Fork at Medway gives us quite another terrain and a different background. Here lumbermen and Indians for a long time were more numerous than white settlers and the names are often mint-new modern Indian words. This is a natural Chapter Two. At Medway, we stop. Above that point the river branches widely and drains too large a country to be treated within reasonable limits, and with the exception of a few names found on old maps, such as Chesuncook, Ripogenus, and Matagamock, the place names are well understood.

Returning to salt water, we begin Chapter Three, the western

---

[14] Just before the Pilgrims landed, the Tarentyns, or Micmacs (the Souriquois of the French) invaded the region of Penobscot Bay, conquered the country, and for a few years held it. They left after an occupancy too brief to have affected the place names, many of which, recorded by Capt. John Smith a few years before they came, are still in use; such are Matinicus, Metinic, Monhegan—all of them Micmac.

coast of the Bay, at Stockton, and follow the western shore line as far as Waldoboro, or all of Waldo County except Winterport, Frankfort, and Prospect, all of Knox County, and Waldoboro in Lincoln County. Chapters Four and Five are devoted to Indian names along the coast from the Penobscot westward to the Piscataqua.

Chapter Six starts at the Bucksport lower line and goes down the eastern side of the Bay and along the coast eastward. Verona and Orland are included in this section partly because of historic connections and partly because it brings them closer to the important fish-names treated in the last chapter. This covers all of western Hancock County except Bucksport. It was not intended to carry the list much east of Naskeag Point, but to leave the place-names of the Maliseet country to be treated by Dr. Ganong, who was the authority upon them; but for convenience of readers, to whom Dr. Ganong's work, not yet completed, may not be accessible, the names of Washington County have been briefly considered in Chapter Seven.[15]

Should anyone remark upon a lack of uniformity in treatment of the topics, as that sometimes words are syllabled, sometimes not, some accented, others not, the answer is that often the writer does not know what is correct; often the Indian does not know either. Different Indians place the stress differently: which shall we follow? The same Indian may give half a dozen forms of the same word at different times; he may even give one that is incorrect: we must choose, at our own risk. Therefore stress is marked only when we are fairly sure of it, and the forms of words are sometimes varied according to the source of the information. Syllabification presents problems so awkward that it will be impossible to please everyone, most of all the one responsible. Shall we make it easy for the reader by setting off *cook* and *keag* and such syllables when we know that the *c* or the *k* belongs with the root preceding; or shall we insist upon his learning to use the roots, even though the divisions are uncouth and difficult? It might have been better to repeat each leading word twice, once undivided and then accented and divided; instead we have compromised by hyphenating sections of words easily pronounced without splitting into too many syllables, and

---

[15] Dr. W. F. Ganong died suddenly September 7, 1941, at Rothesay, New Brunswick, without completing his Indian Studies.

sometimes we may have neatly avoided a difficulty by making no division at all.

There are some words in common use which would be in much better form if differently spelled. In most cases the form is too fixed to be disturbed now: it is a town name, a post office, on newspaper headings and letterheads and the name of banks and of business firms. There would be no justification, for example, in urging the use of a single *t* in Mattawamkeag. On the other hand, there may be a name like Mattamiscontis, large on the map perhaps but of little social weight, which is wholly misleading as to its derivation and could well be changed to the correct Madamiscontis. In two particular cases, we have used forms which could be adopted without dislocation of anything but map-names, which are always subject to change. Instead of the ugly Sowadabscook Stream we could easily say Sawadapskek Stream and have a correct spelling conforming to the roots. Instead of Sebasticook Stream we might adopt Sebesteguk, or Sebesticook even, and show the original root. The fact that the poor forms are on maps would make little difference; for the United States Geographic Board changes names when the reasons advanced are good. In many instances it rests with the local community to adopt a form pleasing to them—and put it to work. Above all, the old Indian names of the Maine mountains should be kept—they are an asset whose value is not yet appreciated. We should do well not only to keep Katahdin, as we shall do, but to put back Kokadjo and Sabotawan, Sowanga and Sowangawas for the sake of their primeval wildness.

The day is past when our Indian names were the butt of foolish laughter, to be distorted, mutilated, displaced by trivial appellations. All Indian place-names had a local pertinency; in recovering the meaning and the correct form of the names we enlarge our horizons and make home a more romantic place to live in. These old names are the colored curtains which hang beside the windows through which we look back into the beginnings of human living here; for ages upon ages countless human beings have lived and toiled and suffered here, and have left only—these names.

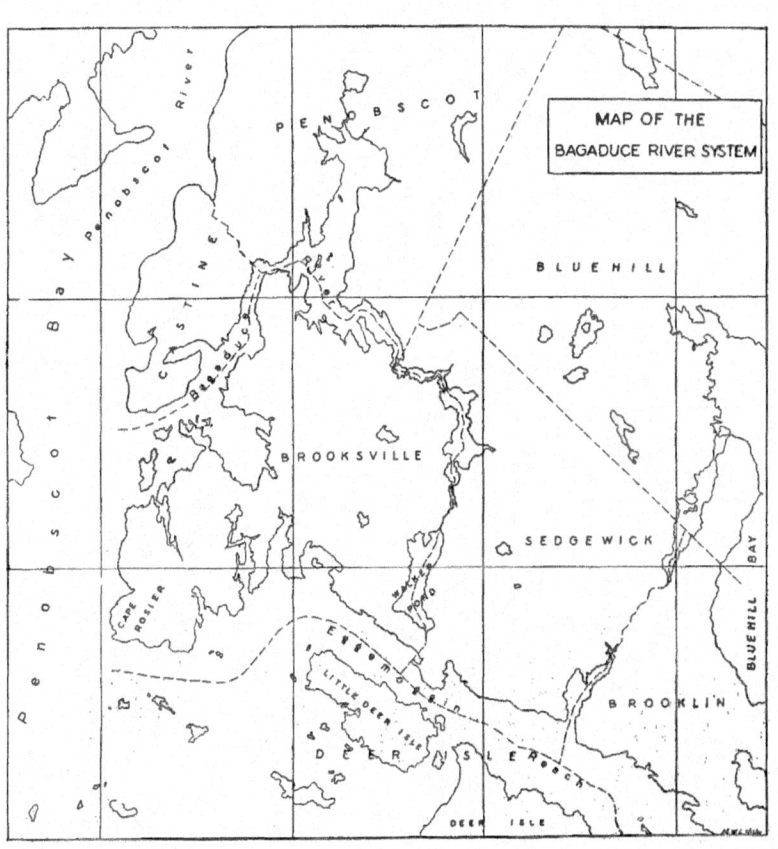

CHAPTER ONE

PENOBSCOT RIVER FROM BUCKSPORT TO THE GREAT FALLS IN OLD TOWN[1]

PENOBSCOT RIVER.

This is a natural division, terminating at the head of the part properly called *Penobscot,* "the rocky place," "the descending ledge place," where are ten miles of falls in close succession. Many of the words are Maliseet or Micmac, and some of them have historic associations.

Penobscot. Originally only the section between Treat's Falls and Old Town Great Falls, "the rocky part," literally "at the descending rock."

The word Penobscot has nothing to do with *Pannawambskek,* which is the open valley above Old Town, or with *Paamtegwetook,* which is the main river below Bangor. We regret having to disagree with so much that has been written about the word, including a great part of the very learned discussion by Dr. Ganong ("Organization of Indian Place-Names," Third Paper, 1913, 94-102); but having spent a lifetime upon the river and knowing it mile by mile for almost its entire length, we refuse to accept explanations which do not fit. Several names, belonging to different sections of the river, after having been very thoroughly mixed up by transient whites and mapmakers, have been explained by students who did not know the river and could not distinguish among the prefixes *pen-, pem-, pemi-, pehem-,* and *panna-*.

Without going into the details of misunderstandings, we should remember that in naming streams and rivers an Indian's point of view was that of a canoeman working his way upstream, concerned only with the set of the current, the river-bed, the carries, the routes by way of entering streams, and the immediate banks. Between Bangor and Old Town, the river was a succession of rapids, falls, and carries, and he traveled up in a rocky trench,

---

[1] Including also the eastern part of the old Short Route to Quebec by way of Sawadapskek and Sebesteguk.

unable to see beyond the immediate banks, which were covered with thick woods. What lay beyond the cut bank on each side did not matter. Therefore the Abbé Maurault's "land that is covered with rocks" does not apply—for the canoeman's whole concern was the river-bed, not farming country. Equally off the mark is Professor J. Dyneley Prince's "rocky territory" (*American Anthropologist,* XI, 1909, 649), and Dr. Gatschet's "where the conical rocks are" (*National Geographic Magazine,* VIII, 1897, 20) —for this never was a country of conical rocks. Better are Williamson's "rock land" (*History,* I, 512), Lorenzo Sabine's "place of rocks" (*Christian Examiner,* 1852), and Thoreau's "rocky river" (*Maine Woods,* 1864, 145 and 324), which are not very close but not misleading; but not one brings out the idea that in dropping a hundred feet between Old Town and Bangor, over transverse ledges, the river is a series of rock-hewn steps, causing the difficult falls and hard carries.

Dr. Trumbull gave a remarkable analysis of the word, considering that it was printed so early and that he confounded Penobscot with *Pannawambskek,* because he did not know the prefix *pen-* was not the same as *panna-.* " 'At the fall of the rock' or 'at the descending rock' is a more nearly exact translation. The first syllable, *pen-* (Abnaki *pa*n*na*) represents a root meaning 'to fall from a height'—as in *pa*n*ntek8,* 'fall of a river' or 'rapids'; *pena*n*-ki,* 'fall of land,' the descent or downward slope of a mountain, etc." (Connecticut Historical Society *Collections,* II, 1870, 19).

The second root of the word is of course *-apsk-,* "ledge," with the locative ending *-ot,* in some forms *-ek* or even *-eag.*

Penobscot was originally the name of about ten miles of the river between Bangor and Old Town; but the name might apply to any steeply inclined ledgy place anywhere.

Pemtegwa'took, the "main river," or the Penobscot, from Bangor downward.

This is a somewhat simplified form of a name no longer in use but preserved in several forms in print.

 1823. *Pem-ta-qua-iuk-took*—Moses Greenleaf, Letter.
 1851. *Baam-tu-guai-took,* "broad river, sheet of water, or more lit-

erally, all waters united"—Springer, *Forest Life and Forest Trees* (New York, 1851), 186.

1866. *Boamtuquet, Boamtuquaitook,* "broad water"—Vetromile, *The Abnakis and their History* (New York, 1866), 48-49.

To this form we believe belong those earliest mentions from Champlain, *Peimtegoüet,* 1604; *Pemetegoet* and *Pemitegoet,* 1632; *Pemetegoit,* 1613 and 1632; Lescarbot's *Pemptegoet,* 1609-12; and Father Le Jeune's *Pemptegous,* 1635. I am indebted to Dr. Ganong for the dates of these occurrences, but do not at all agree with him that the *m* was changed to *n* "under the influence of the easier pronunciation" (*op. cit.,* 94).

These are forms similar to the modern ones given above in which *pem-* "extended," and the more emphatic *pehem-, baam-, boam-* are used correctly instead of the *pen-,* "downward," which later was confounded with the word correctly given by Champlain for the main river Penobscot. It has to be remembered that Indian pronunciation is often blurred and some sounds are hard to catch, while they themselves frequently substitute *m* and *n* for each other. Considering the difficulty that we find today in taking down Indian words from literate Indians who are trying to help, the wonder is that early travelers did so well.

BUCKSPORT.

No Indian name has been found for the site of the town of Bucksport, which for a long time was called Buckstown, for Col. Jonathan Buck, who settled there in 1764. *Buckstown-i-Menahan,* "Buckstown Island," given by Indians as the name of Verona Island, shows that the Indians had adopted the English name before it was changed to Bucksport in 1821.

Edali-q'saga-holdemuk, the ferry to Prospect, now discontinued. *P'sage-sagwanuk* is a bridge.

Alnambi-kweysahwayk, Indian Point (translation of the English name).

The point where the Seaboard Paper Company's mill now is, once a favorite camping ground. There was a fine spring here, whence it was often called *T'kope'suk,* "the spring." The same name was given to a large spring and camping ground on the Prospect shore. Salmon Point is the name on old maps, 1764.

PROSPECT.

Wa-ka-lo'sen, "fort" (Mrs. Clara Neptune, 1916). Fort Knox.
"A fort, the enclosure, not the site, used by all the Maliseets," was Dr. Ganong's comment.
(On December 4, 1923, the United States Government deeded the fort and one hundred and twenty-four and a half acres of land to the State of Maine "to be used for public purposes only." It is now a free pleasure ground at the western end of the Waldo Bridge.)

K'tchi'-peskwahon'da, "big guns" (Clara Neptune). Fort Knox.
Before the fort was dismantled, great black cannon, looking like shining beetles, used to lie on the ramparts—whence the name.
K'chi, "big"; *peskwhañdi,* "gun" (O'Brien). Rasles has *pesk8añdi,* "gun," a weak noun with plural in *al,* so that the form given should end in *-ial* to be strictly grammatical.

Penopsqua'-cook, "just across from pulp mill in Bucksport, where Indians used to go to get basket stuff" (Clara Neptune).
The word refers to the steep, rocky shore.

FRANKFORT.

Kwi-kwi-mes-wi'ticook, "black duck stream." Marsh River.
The name, given by Clara Neptune, confirmed by Lewis Ketchum, is in Joseph Nicolar's list and in Father O'Brien's notes, but not on any map or document examined.
Kwi-kwi-mes'-ook (plural), "black ducks" (*Anas rubripes tristis,* formerly *obscura*), named from their note; *-wi-,* the possessive sign; *-ticook,* "a stream," locative ending.
This broad tidal stream, parallel with the river behind Fort Knox, was a favorite haunt of Indians. It was wonderful hunting country, and with only a short carry from the head of the stream into Beaver Brook, which outlets near Sandy Point, they could avoid the dangerous narrows of the main river near Bucksport while keeping in a food-supply country.

Kinabsk'-atn'-ek, "steep ledge mountain." Mount Waldo.
Name given by Clara Neptune, 1916.
Kee, "high"; *-apsk-,* "rock, ledge"; *-atn-* (*-adene-*), "mountain"; *-ek,* locative.

WINTERPORT.

Catamawawa. The northern branch of Marsh River.

Nothing is known of this word, given by Miss Ada Littlefield (*An Old River Town,* New York, 1907, 37) as belonging to the north branch near Flat Rock Falls. If it were *K'tamaha'ga,* it might mean "very rough" and be well applied.

Eda'li-t'wa'kil-a'muk, "place where you have to run up hill." Bald Hill Cove.

Dr. Frank G. Speck (*Penobscot Man,* Philadelphia, 1940, 190) says: "The old Indians tell of a test that the warriors used to put themselves to when traveling up and down Penobscot Bay. Near Camden, Maine, there is said to be a steep hill of loose shifting sand visible from the water. Here the warriors would land and try to outdo one another in running to the top. It is said to have been very difficult and was considered a great proof of strength to succeed."

This is entirely an error. The place was not within forty miles of Camden. It was the glacial gravel bluff on the upper side of Bald Hill Cove, nine miles below Bangor. The writer's father, whose grandparents lived within sight of the place, has often spoken of seeing the Indians run here and has said that the women took part as well as the men, and upon at least one occasion of which he knew, a woman was better than any man contesting. Lewey Ketchum and Clara Neptune both spoke of the custom of running up the bluff at Bald Hill Cove and Joseph Nicolar describes it at some length (see Appendix).

Et-tah-li-tek-quan-ki-lur'-muk is the name as Nicolar spells it, but it is the same word we give.

Etali- or *edali-* is the copula corresponding to the French *il y a,* "there is," or "place where." *T'kwaki* corresponds to Rasles' *neda'k8añki, je monte la montagne;* the *l* probably is only a glide between vowels, making the ending *-amuk* (or *-lamuk*), the same as *-hemuk, -haymock,* a place-ending. "The place where one climbs the hill."

SOUTH ORRINGTON.

Walini'tuk, "cove brook." Mill Creek Cove.

The brook enters the Penobscot at the head of a large rounded cove.

Walini means "curved," like the arc of a circle; *-tuk* (from *tegwak*), a "stream." "A cove with a river in it as distinct from the ordinary cove, simply a bight in the shore." (Ganong, Letter.)

HAMPDEN.

Eda'la-wi'kek-had'imuk (also pronounced *Edalo'wikek-had'i-muk*), "place where they made markings or writings." Hampden Narrows.

It was the belief of our Indians that in the clefts of the steep sides of Hampden Narrows lived the rock-fairies, only a few inches tall, who made little teapots and kettles and put marks on the rocks to indicate the canoes which passed. These little *Wanagames'wak,* the rock-fairies, though often mischievous, were not malicious, and the Indians liked to talk about them and their larger confreres, the *Mikumwes'sak,* dwarfs, corresponding somewhat to the English Puck or Robin Goodfellow. I recall that when I was a child my father showed me marks—reddish as I remember—on the ledges in Hampden Narrows and told me that the Indians believed they were made by the fairies. "The Indians believed that marks on the ledges told the exact number of canoes going up and down the river," wrote Father O'Brien.

Wanagames'wak Eda'la-wikhegee'dit is the name for Hampden Narrows as given by Father O'Brien. The first word is the plural of the word for a fairy. In the second, *edala* is the copula "there is," "the place where," and *awikhe'gan* is the name of anything written or painted, as a book or a document.

Joseph Nicolar does not include the word in his list.

Sawad-apsk'-ek (officially, but less correctly, *Sowadabscook* or *Souadabscook*) "at the sloping ledge." Western tributary to the Penobscot, entering in Hampden.

    1764. *Sowardebscot*—Chadwick, Large Crown Map (London).
    1767. *Sowerdebscot*—Chadwick, Map for Heirs of General Waldo (Maine Historical Society, Portland).
    1786. *Sowadabscook*—Massachusetts Archives (Town Plans #893).
    1792. *Sowadapscook*—Massachusetts Archives (Maps and Plans #1000).
    1802. *Sawadapscook*—Osgood Carleton's Map: the best early form.

1832. *Sowesdabscook*—Williamson, *History of Maine*, I, 62.
1890. *Sewadapskek*—O'Brien.

The word comes from *sawade*, "sloping"; *-apskek*, "ledge," with the locative ending; *-ticook*, "stream," is understood. "The Sloping Ledge Stream."

The influents to a river were named from some characteristic feature near the mouth by which they could be identified. This name is no longer applicable. When the first settler, Benjamin Wheeler, the writer's ancestor, built his home at the mouth of this stream, in 1768, near its entrance to the river the stream ran over a high, smooth, sloping ledge. Upon this the settler built a mill. Later, wishing to have both a grist mill and a sawmill, he started to make a canal around the other side of the outcrop of rock; but a great freshet took the stream out of bounds and sent it pouring down his ditch and forever changed its course, so that for a century and a half the sloping ledge has been high and dry. Thus runs the family tradition. The name, however, had become fixed in use and is still retained.

After much indecision, I have settled upon *Sawadapskek* as the best form. Some support from Rasles and Nudenans, with the English pronunciation of *a* as *o* (thus accounting for the earlier spellings) outweighs the later recording of Father O'Brien.

Tolb-untb-es'sek, "at the turtle head." Turtle Head.

A high glacial sand bank, now dug away for gravel, but formerly standing boldly just above the mouth of a small brook which enters the Penobscot on the west side about two miles below Bangor, used always to be called Turtle Head. It was just above the site of the Stearns Lumber Company's sawmill.

1887. *Toulbuntbussek*—Joseph Nicolar, the only record in print.

From *tolbeh*, "a turtle"; *antep*, "head" (in *-untb-*, *b* replaces final *p*, and *e* is elided); *-essek*, locative.

By an error, Father O'Brien wrote *Nilbandbessek*, perhaps accidental in the first two letters, the rest of the word being regular.

HERMON.[2]

Nadded Pond. Hermon Pond, on Sawadapskek Stream.

    1764. Joseph Chadwick, Small and Large Crown Maps (London).
    1767. Joseph Chadwick, Map for Brigadier General Waldo's Heirs (Maine Historical Society). *Not* on map in Massachusetts Archives.

Medet (or Meder). Hermon Pond.

    1715. Father Joseph Aubéry's map (Bureau of the Marine, Paris).

These maps show that both Nadded and Medet (or Meder) were Hermon Pond, and probably both were intended to be the same word. Any name for this pond must have been significant, yet we have to guess at the meaning.

The characteristic of Hermon Pond, through which the Sawadapskek Stream passes, is that the inlet and outlet are so situated that the inlet enters from the north, but the outletting stream flows eastward, changing its general direction. It may be that it gets the name of *Nadded* from *Nedethemen,* "I change my course, go around." In Father O'Brien's notes is found the word *N'dedlikangonawak,* given without explanation.

Sewadepskangamisuk, given by Father O'Brien for Hermon Pond, is very late and without interest.

Eda'wi-man'wik, "where one can go both ways, by Kenduskeag or Sewadapscook to Penobscot" (O'Brien). Hermon Pond Inlet.

Though the Kenduskeag and the Sawadapskek come into the Penobscot seven miles apart, at the Hermon Pond inlet there is but a short distance between the two routes (at Chebatigosuk in Levant); thus it was important at this point for the Indian to decide which route he preferred to take.

If this word is not the same as the next, *edawi* is for *edali,* "a place where," and *manwik* is *mañ8i,* "together" of Rasles, with locative *-k*—"there is a together-place" that is, a place where the streams are not far apart.

---

[2] Hermon, Etna, Stetson, and Newport are all on the Short Route from the Penobscot to Quebec by way of the Sebesteguk, or Sebasticook, River and Arnold's Trail. The only names we have for any places on this route are the following, found on ancient maps.

Kwedawi-manwik (O'Brien). For the same place, perhaps the same word. O'Brien says "*kwedawi*, 'down,'" without comment other than "sometimes written *Wenkwedawiwiewak* 'where stream enters, goes down.'"

Pomeg-obs-et. Hammond Pond, formerly Patterson Pond, on Sawadabskek. Given on Chadwick's maps as Pomegobset and Pomegobscook Pond.

A man intimately familiar with the place says that on the right side of the outlet "there was a ledge that dipped under the stream from that side." Since *-obs* clearly is *-apsk*, "ledge," *pemeg-* may stand for *pemi-*, "slantwise," "bias"—"a place where the ledge runs slantwise"; but this meaning is purely conjectural.

A map in the Massachusetts Archives (Maps and Plans #893), dated 1786, shows four houses on this pond and another on the inlet to it.

STETSON.

Nex-a-on-ger'mek. Stetson Pond, now Pleasant Lake.

>   1764. *Nexaongermack*—Joseph Chadwick, Large and Small Crown Maps (London).
>   1767. *Nexaongermeck*—Joseph Chadwick, Waldo Heirs Map (Maine Historical Society, Portland). *Not* on map in Massachusetts Archives.

One of the stages on the Short Route. Name known only through Chadwick, who gives a different form on each map; *-ongermeck* (*-germeek, -germack*) stands for *-gamok*, "lake," leaving *nexa* to be accounted for. If the *x* is soft (*sh*) and not hard (*cks*), *nexa* might stand for *nassawi*, "between," that is, between Etna Pond of the Penobscot drainage and Newport Lake on the Kennebec system.

Necadoram. The Main Stream of Sebesteguk River.

>   1764. Joseph Chadwick, Large Crown Map (London).

The word is known only from Chadwick's using it once; and since in writing English Chadwick could spell "accuracy" as "acqurice," what he could do with Indian passes description. There is no guessing what this word means, though it might come from the root *nik-*, "a fork"—(Rasles has *nikade8a*, "forked") or from *nek-* (with long *e*), "the better of two," which is lacking in Rasles but found in Nudenans, with the comment, *"Net* for *Nit,* in composition, indicates superiority." Perhaps *Necador-* stands for *Nikatow,* "the fork of the river"; or *Nec-adoram* might be a wild stab at *Neek-awangan,* "the better route"; it is probably neither.

ETNA.

Naw-lom-bag-es. Etna, or Parker Pond, at the head of Sawadapsk- ek Stream in Etna.

> 1764. Joseph Chadwick, Large and Small Crown Maps (London).
> 1767. Joseph Chadwick, Map for the Waldo Heirs (Maine Historical Society).

Apparently from *nala-* and *bague,* with a diminutive ending, as if it were compared with the next word; also spelled *Naulombages.*

NEWPORT.

Nala-bongan. Sebasticook Lake, formerly Newport Pond, still earlier the Great East Pond, on Sebesteguk River.

> 1764. Joseph Chadwick, Large Crown Map (London), but not on the Waldo Heirs Map, since it lay outside the Waldo properties.

The two words *Nalabongan* and *Nawlombages* (the *g* hard) occur nowhere else and are hard to account for. In 1932, Francis Stanislaus said they both meant "long, level, still water"; but the meaning does not apply well to either lake. Since they are very unlike in size and characteristics, and upon different river systems, they could not be compared as larger and smaller. The only link between them seems to be that both are on the same travel-route by means of carries.

No other Indian name has been found except the following.

Sagon-dagon. Newport Pond, now Sebasticook Lake.

> 1715. Father Joseph Aubéry's Map (Bureau of the Marine, Paris).

Apparently intended for the same word as the preceding, but what it means is not known. The nearest word in the lexicons is *sakkadegen* of Nudenans, *planus est,* "it is level," which, though approximately the definition of Stanislaus above, is not very pertinent.

It is possible that *Sagondagon* may be explained by Father Pacifique's word *Sageoei onigen,* "an ancient portage," but this is farfetched and wholly conjectural, and on the map the word is assigned to a lake and not to a portage, so that *Sagwai-ahwangan,* "the Old Route," does not recommend itself.

Sebesteguk River, "passage river," "almost-through river." Tributary of Kennebec River in Winslow.

The *Sebasticook,* better written as *Sebesticook* or *Sebesteguk,* was a section of one of the most important travel-routes of ancient times, the shortest way of going *via* Arnold's Trail from the Penobscot to Quebec. Though not a translation of the word, the best English equivalent is "The Short Route."

1719. *Sebestegook*—Joseph Heath's Map ("Pejepscot Papers," Vol. VIII).
1741. *Cebestogoog*—Joseph Bean's Scout Map (Mass. Hist. Soc.)
1754. *Sebestocook*—Johnston's Map of Plymouth Company Claims.
1767. *Sebasstock*—Joseph Chadwick's Map (Maine Hist. Soc.)
1767. *Sebestook*—Plan in Mass. Archives (Ganong).
1790. *Sebesticook*—Map of Lincoln County (Mass. Archives, Roller #978).

These early forms of the word show no disagreement: the roots are *sebes* and *tegwe.* Any difference as to meaning must arise from the translation of the roots. As *tegwe* means "river," the differences must lie with *sebes.*

What is *sebes?* The Indians do not know. Between 1916 and 1930, seven Indians of three tribes, as intelligent as could be found, gave the following meanings of *Sebasticook*:

"Sebattis Stream"—Lewey Mitchell, age 83, Passamaquoddy.

"Sebat or Sebatis, an Indian who lived on the river"—Nicola Soccabesin, age 89, Penobscot.

"River scatters"—John L. Mitchell, Passamaquoddy.

"Might be from *tebascodegan,* a measure, or mark"—Lewey Ketchum, age 82, Penobscot; but he admitted he did not know.

"Level ground, flooded at high tide"—Gov. William Neptune, Passamaquoddy.

"Stream coming from a lake"—Sol Neptune, Penobscot.

"To the empty river"—Henry L. Masta, St. Francis (in his book).

"The short route"—Unknown Penobscot to C. T. Libbey, of Newport.

Large-scale guessing evidently explains these interpretations, of which only the third and the last could have any application, although there was evidently an early tradition of an old Indian named Sebatis—which in turn was perhaps only folk-etymology. In 1856, Judge Potter wrote that the name meant "John Baptist's place. Sebattis was a corruption of Jean Baptiste. They called the word Chebattiscook, or Chebattis' place"—(Maine Historical Society *Collections,* IV, 1856, 191). The list of names cited does not confirm this, yet seventy-five years later old Lewey Mitchell wrote me the same thing, and a hundred years before Capt. Israel Herrick, in his Journal for 1757, mentioned "a large branch of Sabattesses River" (Mass. Archives, 38A, 257-263). The tradition must have been old in Herrick's day—clearly the word comes from a language that the Indians did not understand.

Judge Potter's definition seems to have come from Indians. So also probably did Father Vetromile's "a small branch of a river" (1859, in Vetromile MSS.), and Father O'Brien's fantastic meaning: "*Tchibestekuk,* unexpected, causing surprise; *chibi,* to startle, *e.g.,* jumping Frenchman."

But *chibai* is a ghost, in Penobscot—something separated from the body; the being startled is a secondary meaning. There is, however, a very old word *Tchibatigosak,* meaning "across," which we have found used for the short distance between Sawadapskek and Kenduskeag Streams, which may underlie both the O'Brien word and Potter's *Chebattiscook.*

To appreciate why the Sebesteguk was of such importance in Indian communications we should note the topography of its drainage basin.

The Sebesteguk fans out in wide-spreading branches. The longer but lesser branch, rising in Sangerville and Dover, was known as Main Stream; the shorter and more important branch, with its chief head in Newport, was called the East Branch. Probably originally only the main river and its East Branch were known as *Sebesteguk,* "the almost-through river," because this was the shortest and easiest route to the Penobscot. The Reverend Paul Coffin, in his *Missionary Journeys in Maine* at the end of the 18th century, noted that it was but a mile overland from Penobscot to Kennebec waters by the Sebesteguk and Sawadapskek. By following different tributaries, six important objectives could be reached. One could go

1. by Twenty-mile Stream and Unity Pond to Belfast on Penobscot Bay to get to Castine.
2. by Sawadapskek Stream to Hampden to strike any point on the lower tidal part of the Penobscot.
3. by Kenduskeag Stream to Bangor, to reach any point near the head of tide.
4. by Pushaw Lake to Old Town, entering the Penobscot above the falls section, for the routes to Machias and St. Croix.
5. by Main Stream to Piscataquis River for the upper Penobscot and routes through to Mattawamkeag and St. Croix.
6. by Main Stream and upper Piscataquis waters to get to Moosehead Lake and Penobscot headwaters, keeping in a food and hunting country and avoiding the hard and dangerous route up the Kennebec.

Thus the Sebesteguk was a main highway of aboriginal travel and the principal route by which the French missions communicated with one another in the days when a mission was a palisaded town defending a strategic point in the French plan of occupying the country against the English.

Chebatigo'-suk, a short space of about forty rods in Levant between Sawadapskek and Kenduskeag Streams, which are now connected by a canal dug for lumbermen. It was called "the crossing." The root *chebaht* was often used for "across," meaning a short cut. Maliseets seem to have preferred the sharp *tch* and Abnakis the softer *se* or *ci*. Tchaibayik, Chebeague, Sebascodegan and Sebesteguk are among the names which come under this root used for "narrows," "short cut," "across," or "almost through," even in religion for the Cross, which was *Ci'batek8*. It probably explains the word Dr. Potter used, *Chebattiscook,* an older, perhaps more eastern, form than Sebasticook, which by folk etymology was accounted for by the perhaps wholly imaginary Sebattis.

BANGOR.

Wassam'ki-he'muk, "white sand place." High Head.

Years ago, about a mile below the center of Bangor, a huge drift of glacial gravel followed the shore from a little below Railroad Street almost to the Hampden line. It has now been almost entirely removed for road-building material; once, on the side toward the river, it showed a raw, white bank of sandy gravel higher than the masts of the largest ships tied up along the shore. This was *Wassamki-hemuk*—*wassamki*, "white sand," from *wassa*, "white," "shining," and *amk-*, "sand," with the ending *-hemuk* (*-hamook, -haymock*), not infrequent in Maine place-names. No Indian has been found who could explain this ending, though we find it in Rasles, as in *k8esañ8aañm8* (*kwesahwaha'mook*), a peninsula.

In the form *Wassassumskwemuk* Father O'Brien gives the word as the name of High Head with the meaning "where the pole could not get bearing." There is confusion here which may be accounted for when we recall that Father O'Brien left the words that he took down without any correction unless, in recording them later, he entered a different form, as often occurs. They were jotted down as he chatted with his parishioners in their homes and at their work and do not reflect his scholarly judgment.

One would not pole a canoe anywhere along the High Head shore; and if one did, it offered the very best of pole-hold—fine, packed gravel. Whoever gave that meaning did not know that place or had some other in mind and made the word not from *wassa,* "white," but from *wazawa* (as given by Nudenans), or *8asasse* (as in Rasles), which means "slippery." Slippery ledge was the very worst of pole-hold. Father O'Brien's word apparently belongs to Slippery Ledge Rapids near Old Town (see *Wasassabskek*), but not at all to High Head near Bangor.

Both Greenleaf and Nicolar had difficulty with this word, indicating an old confusion in the minds of the Indians themselves. Greenleaf does not give a name for High Head but enters Marsh Island as *Was-soos-sumps-sque-he-mok,* "Slippery rock I. (Wassous is a bear)." We have received very similar information from Indians, who connected this place with bears by catching incorrectly the first element, "slippery."

Norumbe'ga. This is a word which need not worry us. It is good Indian with several possible meanings; but as the name of a town or city, it has no value and therefore is not properly a Maine place-name. For the satisfaction of those who must have an answer, we may refer to Father Biard and to Lescarbot, the companion of Champlain.

Says Biard, in free translation: "The old geographers speak of a certain Norumbega and give the names of cities and strongholds of which today no trace or even report remains"—*quorum hodie vmbra quidem aut ipsa vox extant.* (*Jesuit Relations*, II:8.)

And Lescarbot, in his *New France,* speaks at some length. He says the Spaniards "have been drawing the long bow" concerning America and "a great and powerful city which they have named (neither I nor they know why) Norombega, which they have placed about the forty-fifth degree.... If this fair town ever existed I would fain know who has destroyed it in the last eighty years; for there is nothing but scattered wigwams made of poles covered with bark or skin, and the name of both the settlement and the river is Pemptegoet, and not Agguncia." (*New France,* Champlain Society edition, I: 31; II: 272ff.)

Agguncia, or *Agoncy,* it may be remarked parenthetically, is not an Algonkin word at all. It is a Huron word which Thevet borrowed, with a list of other words, from Cartier.

Kendusk'-eag, "eel-weir place." The tributary to the Penobscot which flows through Bangor.

    1604. *Kadesquit*—Champlain.
    1616. *Kadesquit*—Father Biard.

Kat, the Maliseet name for an eel (changed to *kad-*); *esog,* or *esogw,* Maliseet for a weir (changed to *-esq-*); and a locative ending.

The name is pure Maliseet. Commenting upon it, Lewey Ketchum remarked, "It seems as if the Quoddies must have named it"—which in fact they did, the Indians whom Champlain and Biard met here being Etchemins, or Maliseets.

The change to modern *Kenduskeag* is accounted for by a nasal in the word *kat-,* or *kaht,* which appears in English pronunciation as an *n*; and the ending has been changed to the more local *-eag* (the *k* belongs with the root). An earlier spelling, used by the first white settlers, was *Condeskeag.* When these came, the

Indian village was near the present Penobscot Exchange Hotel, beneath which used to be a large spring; their planting grounds were on the hillside back towards Broadway and the eel-weirs were on the rapids from State to Franklin Streets.

Lovers' Leap, a steep ledge on the banks of the Kenduskeag, in Bangor. No Indian name has been found, and the story is undoubtedly of white manufacture at the beginning of the 19th century. It is first found in print about 1825, as the name of a romantic walk. Later, Elizabeth Oakes Smith, under her pseudonym of Ernest Helfenstein, wrote in prose the story of the Indian lovers who preferred death to separation. In this story she promised a poetical version later, but killed off Helfenstein before he could do it. Later a long poem, which has become traditional, was written, but we have never been able to locate its first publication and author. Presumably it was Mrs. Smith herself. The poem has been several times reprinted, and in 1937 Mr. Phillips Barry composed a folk tune for it and printed it in *The Maine Woods Songster.* The Indian names in the poem are borrowed or invented.

Ko-chis'-uk, "eel-weir place." An unidentified locality on Passadumkeag Stream where they caught eels.

Though different in appearance from the foregoing, this is substantially the same word. If written *Kat-esok-uk,* the Maliseet roots would appear under the changed pronunciation.

In the fall of the year eels were caught in large quantities in eel-traps as they were descending the rivers, and were smoked and dried for winter use. Passadumkeag Stream was one of the best sources for the fishery, which has been fully described by Joseph Nicolar. Lewey Ketchum said that *Kochisuk* was somewhere on Passadumkeag; he had heard others speak of it. Clara Neptune said that when a child she had been at Kochisuk in eel-catching time, but did not know where it was. As late as 1880 Indians used to trap eels in large quantities at the foot of the Grand Pitch on Passadumkeag Grand Falls. They also caught them at the little pitch at the outlet of Saponac Lake, and Miss Rhoda Porter, who used to live in Burlington, said there was an old eel-weir at Lowell. As a survival of the Maliseet occupation of the country, the word is well worth preserving.

The modern Penobscot name for an eel is *nahurmo*. *Nahumkeag* on the Kennebec is the Abnaki equivalent for the Maliseet *Kenduskeag*.

Pem-jeedg'-e-wock (also as *Pen-jeej'-a-wok* and *Bem-idj'-i-wok*), "current raggedly dropping down" (Joseph Nicolar). The old name of the falls at Bangor, now flowed out by the Water Works Dam.

Pem- or *bem-*, prefix meaning "extended"; *jedjwa-* or *-idjwa-* or *-iji-*, "rapids"; *-ok*, locative ending. (The *w* more properly belongs with the root, but is awkward to pronounce when so divided, since the word has but three syllables as spoken.)

There is no difference of opinion as to the meaning. Clara Neptune said "water going swift"; Lewey Ketchum said, *"Pem-ijw-ok,* pouring down." Though all the forms are acceptable, the most pleasing is *Bemidjiwok*. In Father O'Brien's notes we find *Petchitchwak*, which should have been written *Pem-tchitch-wak*, though probably recorded as heard.

Though Joseph Nicolar assigns the name to the small mill stream near the falls, we have no hesitation in calling this an unconsidered statement. Years before Nicolar's paper on place-names was discovered, Dr. Ganong wrote: "*Bem* always means a *stretch* of something, and *ijiwok* means rapids—hence a stretch of rapids. Now I take it this was Treat's Falls . . . the name being transferred, as so often by the whites, to the brook there. It was 'the brook at Bemijiwock,' 'Bemijiwock Brook,' and the name stayed with the brook after Treat's had got the falls." This is such sound sense that Nicolar's speaking of it as the brook must have been a slip of memory.

The old falls consisted of two small pitches of several feet each with broken water between, but the total drop was not as great as the heavy tide-rise (which at Bangor is from twelve to eighteen feet, depending upon the moon and the season of the year). At high tide, therefore, these falls were flowed out and the head of tide was not reached until it got up to the "first falls" at Eddington Bend, now permanently submerged by the dam at Bangor. In dealing with old documents it has to be remembered that in local speech the First Falls were not those at Bangor, but, as old maps show, those at Eddington Bend.

Though *Bemidjiwok* must have been the name for Treat's Falls, no record of it has been found antedating Nicolar's of about 1887. The place was one of relative importance. It was a natural stopping place for Indians, who by waiting for the tide could avoid carrying or poling over the rapids, and it was convenient for the whites, who at low water could ford the river above the falls. Therefore Treat built his truck house on the west bank near the mouth of the mill stream called Hathorn's Brook, on a site now covered by the railroad embankment, and his name became attached to the falls early, displacing the fine Indian name which has passed out of use and memory.

Matchi-hun'du-pemab'tunk (O'Brien), **Marjee-hondu-bemoptuk** (Ketchum), "The Devil's Footprints."

These were not far above the present Bangor Dam, but are now submerged or covered by the railroad embankment. There were several prints in the rock, "just like someone walking down river," said Lewey Ketchum. Clara said: "This foot one horseshoe; this one *so*," putting down her own foot to show that one was human.

Mahjeehondu was the term used by both whites and Indians for the Devil; from *matchi* (*mahjee*), "bad"; *hunondu* or *awahan'du*, a form of *manito,* a "spirit." The idea of Satan was borrowed from Europeans and is late. The word is only a translation of the name given by the whites.

Matchi-woo'da-da-wa-boodi', "The Devil's Arm-chair."

Not far from the foregoing, a place in the ledge along the riverbank was fancied to resemble a chair. "Devil where he sit down, then you put it your arms *so,* just like chair," said Clara, indicating that it had a back and high arms.

BREWER.

Se-de-dunk'-e-hunk, "rapids at the mouth" (commonly, but incorrectly written and spoken as Se-ge-unk'-e-dunk). A millstream in Brewer, outlet of Field's and Brewer Lakes.

The form Sededunkeunk was given by the Indians to Col. John Brewer, who came in 1771. Colonel Brewer wrote this in his diary, which was read by Brazier Brastow, of Orrington, whose daughter, the late Miss Julia T. Brastow, dictated to me a statement which she took down from her father in 1886:

"He [John Brewer] landed twelve miles below what is now

Brewer Village, and walked up. He selected a site at the outlet of the *Sededunkeunk Stream*. This stream is known as the Segeunkedunk, but *Sededunkeunk* is the correct name, for it is the name given in Col. Brewer's Journal, in which he says that he got it from the Indians themselves."

The incorrect form seems to have got currency through Williamson (*History of Maine,* 1832, I:69), who printed it on the authority of a letter from Hon. David Perham.

Vetromile gives "*Segeundehunk,* it runs into the gulf," which is meaningless. O'Brien has "*Segeundecook,* from *se'gen,* muddy," which does not apply: this was a swift, clean stream of very pure water, used now in pulp-paper work, which needs the best. A Brewer Town Report for 1859-60 has: "B. Fowles for Sedunkeunk Bridge, $167.00."

On a plan of 1779, probably French, Dr. Ganong found the name *Sedydankiou* and suggested that the original may have been *Matasededunkeunk,* "enters the river with rapids." As this is the only stream of importance below Old Town which shows this feature, the suggestion is probably correct. The *-unk,* or *-hunk,* ending shows that it was a rapid stream, with a considerable fall.

Piwan-gamosis, "(round) little pond," given by O'Brien as the name of Field's Pond on the Sededunkehunk.

Gamosis is a pond, the diminutive of *-gamoc*; but *piwa* is not round, but small. As the early settlers called this Little Brewer Pond and the next above it Great Brewer Pond, the word is probably only an adaptation of the English name "the little pond." It is nearly round, but this was most likely a descriptive touch. This should have been a *panna-,* "opens out," pond, since it was an expanse of the stream through which one passed. The name is probably recent or made to order.

"*Pi8i, pavum, pusillum*" (Nudenans) is "small."

Pe-sut-am'esset, "near sighted," that is, "seen only when near by it." Old Indian camping ground in Brewer.

This was just below the present Hardy Street, on land formerly occupied by the Dirigo Steam Sawmill, between the river and a deep inlet at the mouth of the former Tannery Brook, now diverted into the Spring Street sewer.

The word, given by Mrs. Clara Neptune and confirmed by

Lewey Ketchum, is on O'Brien's list, though not as a place-name. It means "near-sighted"; Clara explained it by holding a newspaper close to her eyes and pretending to read. The Indian camps, facing the brook, could not be seen from the river.

Rasles has *pes8t,* "near." Nudenans has *pesi,* "what hinders vision." O'Brien has *pessut,* "near," "approach," as an adjective and *pesutc(h)iwi,* "near," as an adverb. The ending *-esset* indicates "in the vicinity." Mr. Cabot got the word at Old Town as *bestuji.* Found as a place-name only in this instance.

Kaghsk-i-bin'day, "cedars." Old camping ground in Brewer.

Identified as a rocky knoll between the head of School Street and the railroad tracks, where I can remember a growth of small arborvitae. The word was given by Mrs. Clara Neptune, who said that when she was a child her family camped there—"hollow, with little trees," said she.

Kaghskee'suk, "cedars"—in Rasles as *kañkskak* (*bois,* 61, *canot,* 82) "*petits planches de cedre pour faire,* etc." The root has the idea of brittleness, something easily broken, from which our lumbermen got the word *konkus,* used of trees dry-rotted and therefore easily broken.

Manta-was'suk, "inlet" (Ketchum). The mouth of Johnson Brook, very near the Brewer-Eddington line.

This was formerly called Eaton Brook, still earlier Nichols Stream, and farther up, the Phillips Millstream. O'Brien calls it Eddington River, though it is only a brook, heading in Holden.

The name does not apply to the whole stream but only to its distinguishing feature, a large pool near the mouth. In old times the stream had some importance as a route; for a succession of beaver dams probably flowed it enough to make it navigable for canoes to a point about two miles from the route through to Union River. *Muntawassuck,* 1831 (letter of Capt. Mansell to Williamson); *Mantawassuc* (O'Brien); *Madaway-ay'sik, Madaway'-suk* (Ketchum). The word is *madawa,* or *mantawa,* "at the mouth of," with locative ending *-essek.*

EDDINGTON.

Sobscook. Nichols Rock.

Almost abreast of the Brewer-Eddington line there used to be a dangerous rock in the river, called Nichols' Rock from an early settler. The tide flowed up beyond it, making its location uncertain at some stages of water on both ebb and flood.

Moses Greenleaf lists the rock as *Sobscook* and Nicolar gives it as *So-ba-quar-ps-cook,* "sea rock," that is, *Soba-kaps-cook.* Though authorities say that *kapskw* means a "waterfall," we have found it is specifically a "boiling rock," one set in a variable, or reversing current, as in a tide-flow; and *soba-kapskw-k* would mean very literally a boiling rock in salt water, because *s8bék8* (*soobekou,* or *soobago*) is Father Rasles' word for *eau salée,* "salt water." But Nichols' Rock was more than twenty miles from the nearest salt water (that at Bucksport) so that it is hard to see how the name could aptly describe anything so situated.

Greenleaf's word is the same as Nicolar's, the same we get as *Cobscook* at Quoddy, but with that initial *s* which has to be an integral part of the word and must be accounted for in its meaning. These are the only occurrences.

Ak-week'-ek, "steep hill." The high hill on the east bank of the Penobscot at Eddington Bend.

This is the hill up which the Air Line Road to Calais sweeps as it turns away from the river, the same hill on which General Waldo buried the lead plate with which he took possession in the name of England of the land east of the Penobscot, and shortly after dropped dead of apoplexy near its foot.[3] The lead plate was probably buried about where the old Town House used to stand, west of the cemetery. The location is identified beyond a doubt by an entry on Governor Pownall's map of 1759, in London, which marks "the spot where the lead plate was buried."

The word *Akwekek* is found in Nicolar's list, but nowhere else.

---

[3] When Waldo buried the lead plate, he owned land on the east side of the Penobscot; but when Massachusetts confirmed his grant, this was surrendered, and his heirs gave to Massachusetts "all their Right and Title to the Lands lying between the Rivers of Penobscot and St. Croix," retaining only the great region west of the river. The original grant from the Commonwealth to the Waldo heirs, dated March 6, 1762, is now owned by the Bangor Public Library, which bought it in London in 1941.

Waldo's northern bound was not at Veazie Falls, as has been supposed, but at the old "First Falls," now submerged, at Eddington Bend, as is shown on the Chadwick Map made for the Waldo heirs, now in Portland.

It means "at the steep place," the word "hill" being supplied Nudenans has *ak8, altus,* "high," and Rasles uses *ak8,* in composition, meaning "high," "steep of ascent." This word transliterates into *akw* or *akwe,* which by the addition of a locative becomes *akwekek,* or as Nicolar writes it *Ar-quer-kek,* "the steep hill."

Wequ'-agaway'suk, "head of the tide." The old First Falls at Eddington Bend.

An old Maliseet or Micmac name equivalent to the more recent *Mitanganessuk* for the same place, which is now flowed out by the dam at Bangor.

Wequah is an old word found in a few place-names, principally Maliseet, meaning "head" in the sense of termination, as in *Wequahyik,* "head of the bay," for Oak Bay, Charlotte County, New Brunswick, and *Wequash Pond* (later Wigwam Pond) in Meredith, New Hampshire. *Agawasuk* or *agowaason* is "the tide." Nicolar preserved the word in slightly different form.

Mit'an-ganes'suk, "head tide." (The same place as the above.)

Mitan- is *metin-,* prefix denoting the end of something, or something cut-off; *-aness-* is the latter part of *pessanessen, haute mer* (high tide) of Aubéry, or *p'sannussuk,* of Rasles. Literally, the word means "the end of the high tide," its farthest point.

The word, preserved by Father O'Brien, is Abnaki and much more recent than the preceding word, which is Maliseet. It might equally well have been written *Mitangawessuk,* since *angawessuk* is the tide in Penobscot.

VEAZIE.

Wabe'no-bahn'tuk, "white-water falls." Veazie Falls.
Wabeno-bahntuk, "white falls"—Clara Neptune.
Wabena-waghticook, "place which shows white water in coming up the river"—Lewey Ketchum.
Wabenungtacook, "crooked falls"—Moses Greenleaf.

Nicolar does not give the word at all, or any name for the falls. Greenleaf is mistaken in his meaning. If his informant had intended to say "crooked falls," he should have said *walini,* "curving," instead of *wabeno,* "white." The error was no doubt accidental.

The falls at Eddington Bend were in two parts, the lower and the upper falls, each with a descent of about six feet. The lower, or First Falls, were flowed out by the tide twice each day and to them belonged the names signifying the head of the tide. The upper falls, on the site of the Hydro-Electric Dam, were always above the reach of the tide and so always showed quick water, whence they were called the "White-water Falls."

This locality was always a favorite place with Indians. Not only was there a historic Indian village on Fort Point (Negew) after Old Town village was burned in 1723, but in prehistoric times the Red Paint people lived here and fished on the falls; and upon the bluffs on the east side in Bradley, Mr. Walter B. Smith discovered a cemetery of another prehistoric people who used fire in burial.

Negas, or **Negew.** The English fur-trading house, built during Oliver Cromwell's time by William Crowne, "far up ye river of Penobscot, at a place called *Negue;* to which he gave his owne name and called it Crowne's Point." (Maine Historical Society *Collections,* Doc. Ser., X, 27.) The story is a remarkable one, never carefully studied.

"*Negew* was on the Penobscot, west side, between Bangor and Old Town—it is on more than one early map"—(Ganong, Letter, March 9, 1924). The only place where such a trading house could have been established within these limits was in the present Veazie, at Eddington Bend, upon the high point known as Fort Hill.

This is a large triangular point of free soil, early cleared by the Indians for planting ground and affording a clear lookout in every direction except to the west. The flat top stands eighty feet above the water and it was more defensible than any other place on the river above Bangor. For a trading house it was a location unexcelled and also the head of navigation for keeled boats. At high tide, which flooded out Treat's Falls and the "First Falls" at the Bend, English boats could come up to the lower side of the point. Above this place the river was too shoal, rocky, and rapid for boats except on the top of the tide, and just above were the impassable Veazie Falls. The point was Indian camping ground and the Indians once had a stockaded village here, while above for ten miles they had villages and occupied sites, and all about was wonderful hunting country.

By a deed of 12 September, 1657, Thomas Temple deeded to his partner William Crowne all his lands on the Penobscot, and soon after Crowne established his trading post "far up ye river of Penobscot, at a place called *Negue*.... But the said Thomas Temple, hearing there was a *great beavor trade* at Negue ... by violence took from him his fort at Penobscot [Castine], his trading house at Negue, and all his lands" (Crowne's "Memorial to the Lords Commissioners," 1697). It is safe to say that in all of Maine there could not have been a better location for the beaver trade.

The point of this historic resumé is to determine the possible meaning of *Negue*. We find in print:

1662. *Neager's House*—attacked and taken by Mohawk Indians.
1662. *Neagew House*—report by Gardiner of this attack (*New York Colonial Documents*, XIII:224-226).
1692. *Negas*—John Nelson, nephew to Sir Thomas Temple, a prisoner at Quebec, proposes to Madockawando, Penobscot chieftain, to establish a trading house at Negas up Penobscot River—(Joseph Whipple, *Geographical View ... including the History of Acadia*, Bangor, 1816, 70).
1697. *Negue*—John Crowne, son of William, tries to establish his title, as detailed above (Maine Historical Society *Collections*, Documentary Series, X, 79).

Forms are early but meager, and the word appears incomplete, but certainly was of two syllables.

Knowledge of the locality shows that the practical way of getting above this point, except at high tide, would be by landing on the lower side of the point and crossing on foot, a short cut to the camping grounds above, marked on Joseph Chadwick's Large Crown Map of 1764, as "Indian Campts. Strawbury Ground." Just below Veazie Falls he also says "Indian Camping." For the same place, Governor Pownall's map of 1759 says "Clear Land with improvements by Indians." One of Chadwick's maps has a dotted line across the neck, indicating a trodden path.

While *Negew*, or *Negue*, may be a remnant of the word *ounigan*, a "portage," this was not an unavoidable carry, and the place no doubt had many foot-paths, each man going where he pleased. Therefore instead of assuming it to be merely the name of a necessary overland route, we suggest that it may be connected with a word given by Father O'Brien without location—"*Negis-keskami-*

higen, cut across, short cut." He also gives *"keskami,* across" and Nudenans has *"keskamige, via breviora,"* "a shorter way." In O'Brien's word the first part might sand for *ounigan,* whose root meaning is to carry upon one's back, while the ending *-higen,* or *-higan,* is the usual one for anything made by men, as a tool, an instrument, a ditch, and so forth, in this case a shorter, man-made carry, preferred to the longer and arduous water-route around the cape.

It may be added that in the John Hay Library, Brown University, there was a letter file which contained many papers about John Crowne, the heir to this property, and his literary work, evidently material amassed by someone who planned to write about him. Twenty-five years ago this was not catalogued but stored in a side room off the Harris Collection.

BRADLEY.

Mad-a-mis-com′-tis, "plenty of alewives." Blackman Stream, outlet of Chemo Lake (but not the same as Blackman Brook).

Moses Greenleaf gave this word, with the meaning "young alewif stream," to an eastern tributary of the Penobscot between Basin Mills and Great Works. This can be nothing but the outlet of Chemo, since alewives will not go up a stream unless it has a lake upon it in which they can spawn.

The word is from *madames,* "alewife," and *kaüntti,* or *contee,* an occurrence place, indicating abundance of something. The ending is not the diminutive *-sis,* "little," "lesser," or "young," but the softened Penobscot locative, ending in *s* instead of in *k*.

For Blackman Stream, Nicolar gives *Mar-tar-mes-con-tus-sock,* "at the young shad-catching"—the same word. The Indians seemed to regard alewives as small shad and usually so translated alewife words. However, alewives old enough to run up to spawning grounds are not young; therefore the ending cannot be a diminutive.

Just below Blackman Stream Greenleaf gives a stream which never existed; he calls it Patagumkis, "crooked stream," and locates it below Basin Mills. It was probably an erroneous duplication of the Patagumkis above Mattawamkeag.

CLIFTON.

Chemo Lake. Though Indian, the name does not belong to the lake, which was formerly called Nichols Pond and still earlier Leonard's Pond. The original Indian name is lost. Chemo is the old name of the bog upon its outlet, *k'chi-mugwaak*, "the big bog." It was transferred to the lake by means of a popular local song written in 1871 by Mr. James Rowe of Bangor, printed in *The Minstrelsy of Maine*, 1928, p. 70; also, with the air, in Phillips Barry's *Maine Woods Songster*, 1937, p. 11.

ORONO.

O′ro-no. The University town. Named for Chief Joseph Orono, who died in 1801. He was a beloved and highly respected man, said by the Indians to be the son of a French father and a mother half French and half Indian. He was blue-eyed and so light of skin that in his own life time he was often thought to have been a captive white boy adopted by the Indians. No one has been able to explain the name, and some Indians have said it was not Indian.

Nalum-sunk-hungan, "alewife fishery below the outlet." Ayer's Rips at Basin Mills, Orono, below the entrance of Stillwater River. Also, by extension of the name, the whole of Marsh Island, including the grounds of the University.

    1775. *Nerumsuckhungon Falls*—Survey of Elihu Hewes, 24 December, 1775, for Jeremiah Colburn, "who lived there on the spot" (Massachusetts Archives, Maps and Plans, 38:1).

    1784. *Nerumsuc-hangan Falls*—Deed of Joshua Ayer, of Ayer's Island, now Basin Mills (Lincoln County Registry of Deeds, 18:137).

    1788. *Rumfeekungus*—Rev. Daniel Little. Often quoted, though clearly misprinted, a long *s* being mistaken for *f*, not in the Indian alphabet. The initial *R* shows a defective word.

    1838. *Narumsuckhangan*—Captain Mansell to W. D. Williamson (*Bangor Historical Magazine*, IX:14).

    1884. *Nollommuscongan*—Francis Neptune to Hubbard, "where they catch alewives."

    1884. *Nolumsokhungan*—John Pennowit to Hubbard.

    1887. *Mur-lur-mes-so-kur-gar-nook*—Joseph Nicolar, "alewife catching on the way."

Singularly, Moses Greenleaf does not give the word. In Nicolar's word, which is not the same word as the others, the first three syllables stand for *m'aⁿmessoo*, "alewife," and *-kur-garn* represents *-congan*, a "fishing place."

The other names come from *nala-* (*norum-, nerum-, nolla-*), "below"; *sunk*, "outlet" (*-sak, -sauk, sun^k,- suck*), and *-hungan* (*-cogan, -coggin*, etc.), "fishing place." The meaning of "fishery below the outlet" refers to Ayer's Rips being below the junction of the main Penobscot and its Stillwater Branch. Hewes' Survey of 1775 by his map shows this so conclusively that there can be no question about the word.

Arumsunkhungan, the form most commonly seen in print, is regular except for having *r* instead of *l* as the second letter. Either *nala-* or *ahlum-* is correct for "below."

The two words given by Hubbard are variants of the same word; the first carries more of the *aⁿmessoo*, "alewife," in the syllable *-ommus-* than does the other with only *-um-*, but the endings are the same.

The nearest parallel that we have found to this word is *Nallahamcogon River*, or Bennett Brook, in Bernardston, Mass., in an Indian deed dated 1695 (Wright, *Indian Deeds of Hampshire County*), which looks like the same word.

Nutsk-amon'gan. Unknown locality near Old Town, probably identical with the foregoing.

Known only from Lewey Mitchell, of Point Pleasant, who told the writer that it was where the *Mikumwessak*, or dwarfs, warned the Indians that the Mohawks were coming to destroy them. Since the ending shows that it was a fishing place, the probability is that it was *Nalumsunkhungan*, or Ayer's Rips. I had heard the story from others, but no one could name the place.

The *Mikumwes'-sak* (plural) were little people with very narrow faces, rather solitary and distinctly friendly to the Indians; they were much larger than the *Wanagameswak*, or rock fairies, and stayed in the woods. Ordinarily they wore a red cap, with ears that stuck up, like those the Indian men wore in winter. In their last appearance, described to me by a Passamaquoddy, who said his boy saw one about a dozen years before, the Mikumwes wore a black frock coat and carried a red cane, and the hat, if I recall it aright, was broad-brimmed. In the singular, the word is

Mikumwes strongly accented upon the last syllable. They seemed to be all males, or sexless; no one has mentioned a female Mikumwes. They corresponded distantly to the English Puck or the brownies.

Pem-skud'-ek, "the Farm." John Marsh's clearing at the foot of Marsh, or Old Town, Island.

From *pem-*, "extended"; *skut,* "fire"; *-ek,* locative, "the extensive burned place," hence a clearing, or a farm.

When I mentioned the name to Lewey Ketchum, in 1916, he said at once, "*Penskodek,* cleared land on sloping or descending ground," and remarked that though he had often heard the word, he did not know where to locate the name. It was the old Webster Place, at the end of the bridge across Stillwater River, in Orono. (Note that Ketchum used *pen-*, "descending," and others used *pem-*, "extensive," as the name of the same place.)

Edji'da-waskod'ek, "grassy place cleared by fire." (Same as the above).

Edjida- is *etida* or *edali-*, "there is," "a place where," making it definite and limited; *wask* is *-esk,* something "raw, uncooked, green"—in this instance grass; *skod* (the same as *skut*) is *"fire."* (the *-sk,* occurring in two adjoining syllables, is telescoped to avoid repeating the sound.)

Waskodek is a "grassy burned place," that is, a farm.

It is interesting to observe that Abbé Maurault (*Histoire des Abenakis*) explains Damariscotta by this word—*damapskotek,* or *pamapskotek, "il y a plus d'habitations";* thus, instead of making Damariscotta from an alewife word (*madamas-contee,* "great many alewives"), he made it from the word for a farm.

OLD TOWN.

Wa'sass-absk'ek, "slippery ledge." Slippery Ledge Rapids, below Great Works Falls, in Old Town.

These falls, also called Marsh Island Rapids, begin at 7.7 miles above Bangor and end about two and a half miles farther up river. A slippery ledge gave the worst of pole-hold, so that this stretch of rapids was particularly difficult for the canoeman going up stream.

From the debris of several names furnished by Indians long

ago we have had to reconstruct this word, because the Indians had long confounded two very similar and somewhat related words, and so had misplaced the words and misnamed two wholly unlike localities. For other details, see *Wassamki-hemuk,* "white sand place," High Head, Bangor.

Moses Greenleaf, Joseph Nicolar, and Father O'Brien have all given names said to mean "slippery ledge," or an equivalent, though they are only erroneous forms of the old word for High Head, where there is no ledge at all, but a hard beach of fine gravel. Father O'Brien also gives as "slippery ledge" *Wanassabskek,* which would be made from *wanask* and *apsk,* "the end of the ledge." It is clear that to get the meaning given he should have written *Wasassabskek.*

Father Rasles has "*8asasse, cela est glissant, bien poli*" (under *glisser,* 462), that is "slippery." The word is an extension of the meaning of *wasse,* "white," "shining," such objects often being slippery also.

It seems better, with such authority behind the claim, to give the word correctly and regard the forms of Greenleaf, Nicolar, and others as a long-standing confusion of related words which has resulted in the interchange (on paper) of the names of places wholly dissimilar and many miles apart.

Mat′chi-wis′is, "bad falls." Great Works Falls, below Old Town city.

An especially bad fall of about seventeen feet in a third of a mile upon a bend in the river, Great Works Falls well deserves its Indian name.

    1793. *Machewegesuck Falls*—Given by Dr. Ganong as from Hay; otherwise unknown to the writer.
    1793. *Machewegchich Falls*—Capt. Jonathan Maynard, "Plan of the Penobscot from the Foot of Marsh Island to the Forks" (Medway), (Massachusetts Archives, Roller #1012).
    1823. *Macheeweesis,* "bad falls"—Moses Greenleaf, *Letter.*
    1887. *Maggewessusick,* "bad gall"—Joseph Nicolar (see Appendix). Printed as *Wagge-,* clearly a misprint for *Magge-.*
    1890. *Metchwisissuk*—O'Brien, who says "Great Works Falls."
    1890. *Metchwisussick*—O'Brien, without location.
    1917. *Mahjeeweesis,* "bad falls"—Lewis Ketchum.
    1917. *Machechamussick,* "anybody got bad name, *macheewis*"—Clara Neptune.

The two earliest names plainly show the root *-idj-*, "rapids," and the prefix "bad" and might be written *Matchiwidjisuk*, "bad falls." We suspect that some of the later forms are only a softened variation.

However, when so good an authority as Joseph Nicolar goes into purest folk-etymology to explain the word by the story of a great sturgeon taken there which had a "bad gall," it would appear that he did not recognize the root *-wisis* and made it from the Abnaki *8isi*, "bile," which comes from the color *8isa*, "yellow." This points to an earlier language and an obsolete name. Though *-wis* might possibly come from the root meaning to "run out," a tidal word, it is so much weaker than *-idj-* that it ought not to have been applied to this fall, one of the worst on the river. It may be that Clara Neptune was right and *machiwis* is all one word, combined with *essuk*, which so often means falls.

Ounegan'-ek, "the carry." The great carry past Old Town Falls.

This was nearly upon the site of the present main street of the city of Old Town, where the Ounegan Block and former Ounegan woolen mill continue the name.

An *uni'gan* or *8ni'gan* is defined by Nudenans as "*locus ubi non navigatur, sed limbus et res humeris gestandes* [sic] *sunt*"—"a place where there is no canoeing, but boat and baggage must be carried on the shoulders," whence the French *portage* and our Maine "carry."

The Old Town carry had various names, not notable:

On-ne-gar'nuck, "at the carry"—Nicolar.

Edalni'gan (*edali* and *ounegan*), "there is a carry"—O'Brien

Winnigan'ik—O'Brien. The word is the same as *ouneganek;* with us, *winne-* is not "beautiful," as so often translated.

Nekoune'gan, "the better carry"—Mrs. Peter W. Ranco. So named in contrast to one on the left bank of the river. (Note that the first *e* is long.)

Mada-wan-ig'-an-ook, "at the foot of the carry" (Ketchum). The old name for French Island, in Old Town.

This island, crossed by U. S. Highway No. 2, stood opposite the lower end of the principal carry past Old Town Falls, on the right bank of the river. The island was earlier called Treat and Webster Island, and still earlier Shad Island. In the name the element meaning island is understood.

This is a difficult word to divide according to its roots. It is made of two parts, *madawa* and *ounigan,* which coalesce slightly, and a locative ending.

Matawi (or *madawa*) is Rasles' *matañbe,* "*il va au bord de l'eau —à la grève pour s'embarquant.*" Therefore Rasles' *metaⁿbeniganik, au debout de la portage,* "at the foot of the carry," is identical with our word and equivalent to the lumberman's "putting-in place" for the end of a carry. *Mattapan,* in Massachusetts, is the same word.

Ne-gan-o-den'-ek, "old town." The Indian village on Indian Island. Gatschet gives the form *Nganudene,* from *neganie,* something "old, worn out," and *oudene,* a "town" (*Handbook of the American Indian,* II, 118).

Though the name may have been applied after Colonel Westbrook burned the town in 1723, evidence that the Red Paint people had occupied the place for centuries before makes it probable that it was the "old town" ages before the white man came.

It is also probable that the word comes from one of the older languages. Father Pacifique gives in Micmac the word *ngani otan,* "old town," and Lacombe has the Cree word, "*nikan, devant, en avant, premier,*" indicating that this was not a worn out and deserted town, but the *first* town, the earliest. The form we give seems better than Gatschet's.

Someone may ask, Is not this Negas, or Negew? It cannot be; the English trading post had to be on water navigable by English boats, and the head of tide was the highest point to which a keeled boat could go.

Wal-kam-i-gos'sek, "a hollow." "A particular place near Oldtown" —O'Brien.

Father O'Brien did not locate this, but added, "*walkamigek,* an excavation; *waligo,* a bowl; *wali,* hollow."

Wali- means "scooped out," like a dish, having a curved outline. The word is related to the Micmac *oalogogeg* (*walokumkek*) of Pacifique, used for sand holes. It must have been what we call a "punch bowl," that is, a depression in the glacial drift near Old Town, a natural round sand pit.

STILLWATER.

Kwel-bejwan-o′sik, "where the waters turn when they meet." The passage from the foot of Orson Island to the Back Channel, on Stillwater Branch. In this channel at high water the current runs toward Indian Island; at low water, it runs away from it. Word given by Clara Neptune; explanation and meaning by Lewis Ketchum.

Kwel is the rare root *kool-,* or *kul,* "mixed"; *-bedjwan* is the familiar *idjewan,* "strong current, rapids"; the ending is a diminutive locative. As Newell Lyon explained *pemijuanosick* to Mr. Cabot, "pet name for falls, rapids, quick water, not dangerous, canoe all right." The same word as the Micmac *golpitjoig* of Father Pacifique, an "eddy."

Skit′-i-kuk, "still water." Stillwater Branch of the Penobscot.

The usual term for a deadwater. Skiticook and Chimskiticook, or Jimskiticook, are not uncommon terms; the last two have the prefix *k′chi,* "big."

The word would be better divided *Ski-tikuk,* if it could be properly pronounced. In this, *-tikuk,* is the locative for a stream. The first element is not so easy to catch. Hubbard (p. 157) says that *ski,* or *skit,* is "water in a stream 'at rest,' " but gives no authority. The nearest in Rasles is *ske,* "he is standing."

Pitawi-te′guk, "the round-about river" (O'Brien). Stillwater Branch. Often called in English, the Back Way, because less direct than the main river east of the island.

Kwetah-wamk-i′-tuk, "long sandy stream" (Ketchum). The back passage from Pea Cove, not the whole Stillwater Branch.

Kwetah (*kweni*), "long"; *amk,* "sand"; *i,* possessive; *-tuk* (*tegw*), "river."

Ounigan-is′sis, "the very short carry." The carry past the heavy fall under the old covered bridge in Stillwater.

A double diminutive, with *ounigan,* a "portage."

Ouniganissis′-ikuk, "stream with the very short carry" (Stillwater Branch). An occasional use.

The name of the Stillwater Falls is not known; early maps call them Treat's Falls, and Maynard and Holland's map of 1793 called them Jamieson's Falls. (Brig. Gen. Charles D. Jameson, killed in the Civil War, lived in a large house, still standing, perhaps eighty rods from the falls.)

Msku'took, given by Greenleaf, 1823, as Stillwater is an error. The word is only an abbreviated *Pemskudek,* the name of John Marsh's farm.

Pushaw'. Pond and stream tributary to the Stillwater Branch.
Named for an early settler; not Indian as commonly supposed. The old Pownalborough Records have Pochard (1782), Pouschard (1782), Pushard (1791). Pauchard Pond is found in 1790 in Massachusetts Archives (Maps and Plans, #1000) and in 1795 Pooshaw is given by Sullivan (*History of the District of Maine,* 37). The Indian name was *Pigwaduk.*

Pig-wa'-duk, "bent stream." Pushaw Stream.

Pig-wa-duk-gam'ok, "bent stream lake." Pushaw Lake (probably recent).
The name properly belongs only to the outlet of Pushaw Lake. Near its mouth it encounters a long horseback, or glacial kame, parallel with Stillwater River, and in seeking a way through, the stream has to double upon itself in a fish-hook bend, so that it enters the river in a direction opposite to that in which it had been flowing. O'Brien's comment on *Pigwaduk* is "Back, or on one side from the river. Observe: Pushaw Stream goes back in the opposite direction to the main river."

This upward bend at the mouth is so characteristic of this place that Hubbard (whose form *Beegwatook* is only another pronunciation of *Pigwaduk*) would be obviously wrong in calling it "big bay place" and making it from *anbagwat,* a cove, even if there were a cove here. *Beg8* is a cove, but the root here is *pika,* or *bika,* "a crook"; *Pigwaduk* is properly a "turn-off," a bend in direction.

Dr. Frank G. Speck gives the meaning of *Pigwaduk* as "abundance of game," but it is on the very poor authority of Newell Lyon ("Penobscot Shamanism," *Memoirs,* American Anthropological Association, IV, 1919, 280). In *Penobscot Man* (1940, 18), Dr. Speck remarks that "Pigwacket may be a form of *bigwa'kik,* 'abundant game country,' as suggested by Newell Lyon." This is worse than a bad guess. Pigwacket (Fryeburg) got its name from Jockey Cap, "the punched-up-through mountain." The name has nothing to do with Pigwaduk.

Kukunsook, "cedars," Moses Greenleaf's name for Pushaw, is a wholly different word. Clara Neptune's *Poosah-alnay-tequick* for Pushaw Stream is a mixture of Indian and English.

Teg'o-ak, "waves." The small pitch just west of Indian Island commonly called "The Cook"; the plural of *teg8,* a "wave," the same stem which forms the inseparable ending of many river-names. The river here boils over a few deep-lying rocks, at some stages of water dangerous.

CHAPTER TWO

PENOBSCOT RIVER FROM OLD TOWN GREAT FALLS TO THE GREAT FORK AT MEDWAY, WITH TRIBUTARY STREAMS ON BOTH SIDES

These names, kept alive by constant use, are more recent in form than those in Chapter One and show less Maliseet influence. Though they have little historical importance they are interesting as comprising most of the place-names in the State which have the prefix *mata-* and the softened Penobscot locative ending in *s,* usually mistaken for a diminutive, peculiarities which to an ethnologist may indicate some prehistoric occupation of the region.

OLD TOWN.

Panna-wambsk'-ek, "where ledges spread out." The Penobscot Valley above Old Town Falls; also the Indian village there.

This is not the same word as Penobscot, as is sometimes stated. Father O'Brien wrote: "Panawanbskek signifies a wide-spreading place—a broad expanse; a wide valley. It is not the name of the river in that form, which is called Panawanbske-witegwock, or teguk" (*History of Penobscot County,* 1882, 524).

The word comes from *pannawi,* "spread out"; *ampsk,* "ledge"; and *-ek,* locative ending. It refers to the way in which after mounting the long succession of heavy falls and rapids between Bangor and Old Town, culminating in the great rocky barrier of Old Town Great Falls, the voyageur suddenly sees the river opening out into tortuous channels and many islands in an extensive meadowy and bog country.

Some, including Father Vetromile and many Indians, mistake the *-wamb-* element as meaning "white" and say "spread on the white rocks"; but there are no white rocks at Old Town Falls and the *w* comes from the adjectival ending; the *m* represents a nasal.

Citation of forms adds nothing to Father O'Brien's concise statement; but for the historical tracing of the name it is well to add a few dated forms:

1699. *Pana8mske*—Map of Guillaume de Rozier.
1715. *Panaouamske*—"*village scittua dans l'Isle*"—Father Aubéry, Map.
1718. *Pana8apski*—Letter of Father Lauverjat—Massachusetts Archives, 51:302.
1724. *Panouamke*—"*village abandonné situé dans l'isle*"—French Archives, Bureau de la Marine, Map #254.
(The town was burned in February 1722-3 by Col. Thomas Westbrook.)
1724. *Panna8anbskek*—Father Rasles, *Dictionary*, 501.
1755. *Lake Pananke*—Mitchell's Map, and many others (used of the deadwater above Old Town).
1760. *Pana8apske*—"*Lucus amnis ubi velut aperitur alveus propter multitudinem lapidum,*" "A place in the river where the channel opens out, as it were, on account of the many rocks"—Nudenans, "*Radicum Sylva*" (dictionary).
1823. *Penoomskeook*—Greenleaf, Letter. (Indians call this a poor form.)
1917. *Penamskiak*—Ketchum, "where ledges spread out."
1931. *Bahnawampskek*—Mrs. Sylvia Stanislaus, "Old Town."
1931. *Panawamskiak*—Peter W. Ranco, "where ledges spread out."

The differences are superficial. The word is closely allied to the Micmac *panoeg*, "opening" (Pacifique, 205), who also gives *panoanapsgog* (*panawapskek*), "opening out between rocks," which is our word.

The form *Pananke* had much vogue, but only because it was copied from map to map. Though he did not see this part of the river, Champlain gives a lake-like expansion here, which later map-makers increased to a large lake, borrowing from one another. Bellin, 1744, probably misprinted de Rozier's *Pana8mske*, omitting the *s* by mistake, thus originating the form *Panoumke* found on many maps (Ganong).

ISLANDS IN PENOBSCOT RIVER

Between Head of Tide in Veazie and the Forks at Medway.
Many of these names are trivial, some are recent, some are English adoptions, or mongrel words; but such as they are, they are given as nearly as may be in the order of their occurrence in going upstream, on the principle that it is better to save something that is worthless than to risk throwing away anything which might be wanted later.

Ant Island, Ant-Hill Island. The island at Basin Mills upon which the pulp mill now stands.

    1823. *Anaksassis'sak,* "Ant Island," Moses Greenleaf.
    1887. *Ane-quer-sar-sa'suk,* "Ant Heap," Joseph Nicolar.
    1890. *Enikusasis'sek,* "Ant-hill Island," Rev. M. C. O'Brien.
    1918. *Aneksassiss'cook,* "Ant Island," Newell Lyon to W. B. Cabot.

This island, of considerable size, is a low, alluvial island, not much above the river level; in old times it might have been hackmatack swamp. In such places, black ants thrive, and the word *E-nikus-was-is'-sek,* "at the ants' nests," was a fitting name. In Penobscot, *énooks,* or *énikus* (the *e* long and accented was the pismire, or black ant; and *wassis* is the diminutive of *was,* a nest.

Other explanations have been offered. Both Lewey Ketchum and Newell Lyon thought it meant "notch in a ledge." Clara Neptune said "Something put in ground"—"What?"—"Moosehide, anything," and she made motions as if digging with her hands to bury something. Quite likely there was a trace of some tradition about using this convenient spot of soft soil, free from depredations by bears, for burying articles not immediately wanted; but Father O'Brien's form and meaning, in full agreement with Greenleaf and Nicolar, establish the name beyond question.

Marsh Island, on which are the University and the City of Old Town, named for John Marsh, the first white settler; also called by the Indians *Panawambske-menahan,* probably its correct name, since the first comers called it "Penobscot Island." It was also known as *Arumsunkhungan* from the falls just below (*q.v.*) and *Pemskodek,* or *Mskutuk,* "the clearing," from Marsh's farm on the old Webster property at the end of the bridge across the Stillwater Branch.

Ella'la-gwaga-ways'-ek, two small islands in the Stillwater Branch between Highway Number 2 and the Penobsbcot. So named, according to Ketchum, because they were often overflowed in freshets.

Treat and Webster Island, now often called **French Island.** The high, rocky island in Old Town, crossed by Highway Number 2, had several names.

1. *Kee'naht-nas'sik*, "Steep Island"; from *keenaht*, "high," and *nassik*, a softened locative form of the inseparable *-naghe-*, island.
2. *K'tchi-penab'sq'-mana'nook*, "Big Ledge Island." *Mananook* is *menahan* with the locative ending.
3. *Ta-la-la-godis'sek*, "place of painting"—the most interesting of the various names.

   1823. *Ta-la-godissek*, "a painting place for squaws"—Greenleaf.
   1887. *Talalargoodesook*, "a place of painting"—Nicolar.
   1890. *'Tal elagodissuk*, "where they painted"—O'Brien.

   The reference to painting is explained in Mr. Nicolar's article in the Appendix.

   Rasles has *eraghinañs8*, "il le faut peinturer" (336); *nedéraghi*, "je me matache"; *érag8*, "il se matache." In these the *éragh8* corresponds to the *elagoo* of the island name, while the introductory *elala* or *tala* is equivalent to French *il y a*, "there is"—a place where they painted themselves. (*Cf.* also the *Natick Dictionary*, *anogku*, "he paints himself, appears fine.")
4. *Sataylan* is merely the English "Shad Island," because on Shad Rips beside it, the Indians used to catch shad by wading into the shoal water, as well as by other means.
5. *Skeenaylat* is also English, "Skin Island," because the Indians used to leave furs and supplies here to keep them from marauding bears.

In all, we have found seven names for this one island.

Indian Island. In old documents and maps this was generally *Panouamske* in French sources, *Pannawambskek* in English. Recently the Indians have called it *Alnambi-i-menahan*, Indian Island, merely translating the English name. It was occupied by the Indians from times immemorial and by the Red Paint people for ages before the Indians came, because it afforded safety from enemy attack, good soil, and nearness to fine hunting and fishing grounds.

Orson Island. The next great island above Indian Island was called *Assah-i-menahan'*—"Assah, kind o' John name," said Clara Neptune, explaining it. Assah' or Uzzah' (Husah' among the Maliseets) with a very strong accent on the second syllable, is the Indian pronunciation of Jean (John). White influence has changed it to Orson. The island was occupied by an old chief named Orson, and on Maynard and Holland's plan, 1793, it appears as Orson's Island. *Asnela,* in Douglas-Lithgow's list, is plain English—*Asn,* for Orson; *ela* for *"eylant,"* island, the English name.

Another name, *K'chi-mugwack'-i-menahan',* "Big Bog Island," is given by Newell Lyon.

Orono Islands. There were two Orono Islands, belonging to the old chief Joseph Orono. The larger one was in the Stillwater channel, just above the mouth of Pushaw Stream. They are called *K'tol'aqu'-wi-menahd'nook,* "Big Ship Islands," from the nickname of Chief Orono, who was dubbed *K'tolaqu,'* the Big Ship. The Indians cannot explain the name, but it seems to have been given him in the Revolutionary War after he had paid a visit to the French frigates stationed at Newport, Rhode Island, where he was entertained by the officers on board their vessels. A small priming-flask, believed to have been Orono's personal property, and now in the Abbe Museum, Bar Harbor, has on it the crudely scratched likeness of a ship, whose boarding nettings show her to have been a man-of-war. Other pictures, such as a cat, a harnessed horse, a hand-lamp, and a bird in a cage may represent some of the wonderful things old Orono saw on this visit. His nickname may have been given because he talked so much about the big ships; to this day his descendants are called "The Big Ship People."

The large Orono Island was also called *Machlik-nahgook* or *Mach'lik-nuqu',* "hardwood growth island."

Sock's Island. A very small island just off the shore of Orson Island. (There is another Sock's Island west of Olamon Island). At low water this is connected to the large island by a sand-bar. Sock was the Indian pronunciation of Jaques. Ketchum said the island was named "for an old Indian who lived there one hundred and fifty years ago," or about 1750.

The Sock's Island at Olamon was called *Waylumkit'uk,* indicating a rounded sandy cove; from *walini,* a "cove"; *amk,* "sand"; *-ituk,* locative, "river" or "current." Clara Neptune called the first *Sachtahlen,* which is not Indian, but her rendering of Sock's Island.

Black Island. A small island just above Orson Island, identified by Clara Neptune's comment, "Piscataquis cars go that way, cross the island." It was called *K'seusk-i-naghas'sik*, "Little Hemlock Island," from *kessi8sk*, "*épinette rouge*," of Rasles. Clara also called it *M'kaza-ni-kuk-menahan*, "Black Island," translating the English; and Newell Lyon gave it as *Kayzeweshnaghassik*, a poor form of the first name. The word "black" in the name refers to the hemlock growth, evergreen trees being called "black growth" by lumbermen.

Boom Islands, north of Orson Island—*Menahanisis'icook*, "the very little islands." The Pea Cove Islands were perhaps included in these; the Argyle Boom Islands were called *K'noonahgek* (Ketchum).

Twin Islands, *Tagwe'si-menahanol*. *Tagwesswak*, "twins." The final *ol* is the plural ending of a weak noun.

Freese Island. See *No-lat-kee-hee-nungan*.

White Squaw Island. In Argyle. A long narrow island, probably the home of an Indian woman called White Squaw. Indians have told me that her father was a priest who spent a winter with the Indians in the late eighteenth century. This girl, very white and with blue eyes, married a Susep (Joseph) and had seven or eight sons including Sebattis, Francis, Mitchell, Paul, and Susep. They were known as Sebattis White Squaw's Son, Mitchell White Squaw's Son, etc. The mother's Christian name was said to be Sylvia. The writer's father said that when he was a boy, about 1840, White Squaw's Sons were grown men and married.

This may be the island called by Greenleaf *Kah-no-nah-jik* (*Kweni-naghek,* Long Island) which he places just below Thoroughfare Island.

Thoroughfare Islands. There are two sets of islands, one just above Sunkhaze, the other above Passadumkeag, which are doublets, with a channel between the two parts; both are called Thoroughfare Islands by the whites.

It happens that in relatively the same locations, Greenleaf gives two islands with the singular names of Burying Ground Islands. The lower one he calls *Bosquenuguk*, "Burying Ground Island," with an English name of Broken Island; the other he gives as *Bosquenoosik*, "Burying Ground for Mohawks." This Indian name is the diminutive of the first.

Greenleaf's translation is correct. *P8skenan,* "to bury," and

P8skenigan, "a burial ground," are in Nudenans, while O'Brien has *Poskenigan,* "a coffin," and *Poskeniganikek,* "a cemetery." But the derivation from this root sounds like folk-etymology: our Indians probably never killed enough Mohawks to make a burying ground for them necessary, and would not have spent much labor in burying them at all. It seems more likely that *p8sken-* may be an early mistake for *piske-;* that these are *piskenahgek,* "split islands"; for it is unlikely that two islands, miles apart, both with this peculiar feature, should have been chosen as burial islands, when the name occurs nowhere else. The English name of Broken Island for the lower one is confirmatory of the guess that the real root was *piske,* "split."

Hemlock Island. In Argyle. Clara Neptune gave the name as *K'seuskis-menahan* and said it belonged to "Old Neptune." Greenleaf, in 1823, gave the name *Kus-sus-cook,* "Hemlock Island." The ending in *-cook* is accounted for by *K'seuskuk* being the name of Hemlock Stream near by; Greenleaf has omitted the *menahan;* Hemlock Stream Island is its correct name.

Birch Island. In Greenbush, next to Hemlock Island. Greenleaf gives this as *Pem-squam-ku-took;* the channel near he gives as *Beem-squam-kee-took,* which is the same word. Evidently, like the above, the name belongs to the river or to Birch Stream near by, not to the island, and *menahan* must be understood.

Sugar Island. Between Greenbush and Argyle. On Greenleaf's list as *Suga-la-manahn,* "Sugar Island." *Soogah* was a loan word, early borrowed from the English. The island was so named because, from the maple trees on it, the Indians made quantities of maple sugar.

Pimiwamkikatook is a name for Sugar Island found in some manuscript notes of Father Vetromile.

Joe-Beetle-I-Menahan-Point. Near Sugar Island, "jus' cross way" (Clara Neptune); a good example of the mongrel names once in use. Joe Beetle was an old Indian, Beetle his nickname in English.

Eagle Island. Named by Greenleaf as *Sowongun,* the name of the bald eagle. Probably at some time it had a conspicuous eagle's nest upon it.

Olamon Island. A very large island, formed by Olamon Stream dividing near its mouth into two channels which enter the river nearly two miles apart. *Oolamon-oosuk,* that is, *Oulamon-i-suk,* "red paint his place" was the Indian full name of it. *Oulamon* was the word for "vermilion," from *oule,* "good, pretty." Deposits of red hematite, found on the island and stream, were much in demand for pigments and personal adornment. Hon. R. G. Leonard has told me that in paddling up Olamon Stream at very low water, the blade of his paddle was dyed red where he had driven it into the mud in rounding bends of the stream.

White Man's Island. Next above Olamon Island, Greenleaf gives *Wom-be-man-do,* White Man's Island, a name now discontinued. The word is of unusual interest. Wambemando does not mean an Englishman, but "white devil," "white magician or sorcerer," and it happens to be the personal name of an Indian who figured in some documents of about 1750. In 1930, Lewey Mitchell, the best informed Passamaquoddy of his day, wrote me: "Another Indian (Micmac) come to join the Penobscot called Wabimando, meaning 'White Devil' in Micmac." This would seem to have been the man of the documents and this island probably his residence.

This island was below Passadumkeag Stream, one of several named by Greenleaf which we are unable to identify, excepting

Nicola's Island, named probably for Captain Nicola, a sub-chief, who married the daughter of old Chief Joseph Orono.

Tomah Island, probably the residence of a sub-chief, perhaps the Tomah seen by Chadwick in 1764, perhaps the later Governor Tomah.

Saugus Island, "Bad Island," named by Greenleaf; unknown to me, and no explanation of the name.

Man-da-wessoe, "Hedgehog Island," named by Greenleaf, correctly translated.

A-was-soos, "Bear Island," correctly translated.

These seem to correspond to Grass, Fiddler's, and Craig Islands of the topographical map. Greenleaf also has

Bos-que-noo-sik, already commented upon.

Chee-manahn, "Big Island," probably the Long Island of recent maps.

Piks-him-menahan, Hog Island, named by Clara Neptune. *Piks* was a loan word from the English for "pig," a creature for which they had no name. The name is offered as a dreadful example of what Indians can do with place-names!

Cow Island, *Kaoo'si-menahan.* *Kaoos* was another adaptation of English. The island was probably used for pasturage, whence the name.

Mohawk Island. Named by Clara Neptune and said to be near Sugar Island, where she used to live; "Injun kill his brother close there." *Mayquay-menahan* is a literal translation of Mohawk Island. Our Indians called the Mohawks *Mayquays* (cannibals), the same word used by Fenimore Cooper's Mohicans (*Maqua*) and by Roger Williams.

Above this point we have no topographical maps as yet and except in the case of the large islands, identification is difficult. The following are on Greenleaf's list:

Mee-soc-dow-hok, "Burnt Land Island." This was above the Piscataquis and may have been at the mouth of Gordon Brook in Howland. The last three syllables seem to indicate an outlet, like Sagadahoc, where a stream flows out with a strong current; in that case, the first syllable may be *misi,* "big."

Ba-kun-gun-a'-hik, "Crooked Island." This is clearly one of the *pika* or *bika* words, meaning "bent," "crooked." Greenleaf has divided it wrongly: *-nahik* is a locative form of *-naghe,* island.

Ma-num'-kook, "Sandy Islands." Evidently well named, though we cannot locate them; the root *amk,* "sand," is clear; *man* may stand for *mun,* "a heap," something rounded up, like a mound. A better syllabification would be *Man-umk-ook.*

Na-mok'-a-nok, "Turtle-shell Island," so named from its high, rounded shape. (See under Lincoln.)

Matta-na'-cook Island. A large island at Lincoln; name with several possible meanings. (See under Lincoln.)

At-te-beme'-nok, "Cherry Island." So syllabled by Greenleaf but better as At-te-be-men'-ok). *Min* is a berry, or small fruit; *atebemin,* of Rasles, "as big as large peas, red," is the chokecherry. "Choke-cherry Island."

Sku'-ko-al, "Grass Island." Probably originally *'Mskukwal,* Meadow Island.

Man-ask'-oos, "Green Island." Like the above it contains the root *-esk,* "grass, green herbage"; the ending may be the diminutive;

perhaps, by comparison with "Grass Island," a smaller island, also grassy.

The following are merely personal names, hardly worth saving:

Soosunsees-i-nuchkek, "Young Susan her island."

K'chi-Soosun-i-menahan, "Old Susan her island."

K'chi-meesel-louiskek, "Old Mitchel Louis' Place."

Chaquottis' Place, belonging to one of the early Mitchells, who was nicknamed Mitchell Chaquot (from *tse'kwat,* "dawn") because he got up so early in the morning.

Joe Pease Rips, on the easterly side of Indian Island, named from an under-chief, Joe Pease, who lived there in the late 18th Century.

Seguski-menahanikkuk, given by O'Brien without translation or location, means "Broken Island," and may be another name for Greenleaf's *Bosquenaguk.*

MILFORD and GREENBUSH.

Wetchi-san-kas'sek, "concealing outlet." Sunkhaze Stream, which enters the Penobscot from the east a few miles above Old Town.

    1786. *Sunkhaze*—Massachusetts Archives (Maps and Plans, 39:8).
    1795. *Sunkhaze*—Sullivan (*History of the District of Maine,* 37).
    1812. *Sunk Hayes*—Massachusetts Archives (Maps and Plans, 41:27).
    1823. *Sunk-haze*—Moses Greenleaf, Letter. No meaning given.
    1832. *Sunkhaze*—Williamson (*History of Maine,* I, 68, n.). "Sunkhaze means dead water at the mouth of a stream"—an incorrect explanation, repeated by Willis.
    1864. *Sunkhaze*—Thoreau (*Maine Woods,* first ed., 302, 326), with a correct interpretation; see below.

Suñk was pronounced nasally by the Indians, almost like "suck," and approximated the word ordinarily printed as *sauk* or *sahk.* Father O'Brien says that in composition it meant *"out,"* as, *suñkehile,* "he comes out."

This may be the simplest interpretation of *Sunkhaze*—*sunk,* "out"; *kask-,* "to go out"—Thoreau's "see canoe . . . no see um stream."

It is, however, admittedly a very hard word to explain and the only instance of its full form is an entry in Father O'Brien's notes as *Wetchi-san-kassek* (also spelled differently again).

Wetchi is "from"; *sank* is "out," and the ending *-ek* is the locative; but the syllable before must have been telescoped with the second element and stand for *kask-,* "to go out," "to come out." A literal translation would be "from-outlet-comes-out place," which agrees with the Indian explanations. Ketchum could give no translation and no analysis of the word, but said, "Something you could not see at a distance; cannot English it— place where you would come out; place where you might see people come out; a route, might not be seen quite a ways off." To Thoreau, in 1857, Joseph Polis said: "Suppose you going down Penobscot, just like we, and you see canoe come out of bank and go along before you, but you no see 'em stream. That is Sunkhaze." (*Maine Woods,* first edition, p. 302.) So strongly do both these Indians emphasize the "comes out" idea that we may be sure that *"khaze-"* covers the root *kask.*

Wetchi- is an important addition to the idea; it is an emphatic "out"—as if saying, "Out of the outlet he comes (to our surprise)." *Wetchi* is found in Wiscasset and a few other words, all agreeing in one important particular: they are applied to an outlet (probably also to an inlet) with a sharp bend in the stream shutting off a view of what is ahead, a "concealing outlet," not a "concealed" one.

The topography of Sunkhaze bears out the interpretation. The stream runs for a short distance almost parallel with the river, then, just before crossing Highway Number 2, turns almost at a right angle and enters the river very shortly, shutting off any view above this bend. In addition, between the highway and the mouth of the stream are two small, muddy islets which so block the outlet that from the river it looks like a mere indentation of the riverbank.

MILFORD.

Saquaische. Probably a very old word for Sunkhaze.

> 1686. "*Saquaische qui est un fort de sauvages ou il y a encore de fort bonne terre et de beau bois.*"—(Documents collected in France by Ben Perley Poore, about 1844; reprinted in Maine Historical Society *Collections,* Doc. Ser., IV:426).

From the context this seems to be Sunkhaze. The common Indian pronunciation of the word as "Suck-has" or "Suck-hays" is not too far from the French form given, and the name found in the legend intended to accompany a map, in which places were numbered but not named, is relatively at this place.

Marjee-pemsapsk'-ek. Sunkhaze Rips.

The name is rectified from a word given by Clara Neptune, who said, *"Marjeescarskoosik,* just like anything homely." Lewey Ketchum said she meant Sunkhaze Rips; "Bad ledges would go for that." From this hint we volunteer a form which "would go," but has no authorization.

OLAMON.

Olam'on, "vermilion," "red paint." Adopted as the name of the town from either the stream flowing through or the island already mentioned.

The word has the root idea of *oule* or *wuli,* "pretty," "fine," something agreeable to see or useful for adornment. Father Rasles has *8raman,* which transliterates to *oulaman,* "vermilion."

The word is found in a few places in Maine, as *Mun-olammon-ungan,* "heaps of red paint," (*mun* being a word for anything piled up or in quantity) on the west branch of Pleasant River (Greenleaf). Tonomy Hill in York also has both red and yellow ochre, and the name is a defective form of *wunnam-etoneme* in which *wunnam* is the *l*-form of *oulamon.*

ARGYLE.

No-lat-kee-hee-mun'gan, "old settlement." Named by Moses Greenleaf as an island.

    1823. *Nolatheeheemungan*—Greenleaf, as printed by Edgar Crosby Smith, but an evident misprint in third syllable, *hee* for *kee.*
    1918. *Nahwatgehemahga*—Clara Neptune; "when Injuns go there get wild potatoes—*dakeetemook,* wild potatoes."
    1918. *Newatkay-hamockganook*—Lewis Ketchum; "where they dug up lily roots, up at Sunkhaze."

We strongly question the accuracy of Grenleaf's translation of this word—nothing in it means old, nor does it seem to contain the idea of a settlement. It was an old camping-ground, where Clara said they used to go and dig the bulbs of the nodding meadow lily (*Lilium canadense*), which they used for thickening soups. "Stop there for dinner always—dig roots—sweet, oh, sweet!" said she, smacking her lips. Lewis Ketchum gave the same word and the same information, but neither attempted an analysis.

Greenleaf's informant, knowing that the spot was an ancient camping ground, may have connected it with old times through *nañ8at,* "I remove, go far off" (Rasles, 206), also "a long time ago." But *nahla, nawa, nawat* also stands for "between," and the terminal *ka* (*nahwatka, nalatka*) went with words of hunting and fishing (Newell Lyon to Mr. Cabot), while the ending *-mungan* was a gerundive denoting a place for hunting or fishing; so that *-ahmunganek* (Greenleaf's *-heemungan*) would be "hunting grounds." The locality was not far from two of the finest hunting grounds in the State, Birch Stream west of the main river and Sunkhaze east of it; it was the campground from which Indians could make a start in either direction.

Nalatka-ahmangan'ek, "between the hunting grounds," seems preferable to Greenleaf's "old settlement." The interpretation is conjectural, but reasonable.

Maskwa'-i-cook, "birch-bark stream." Birch Stream, tributary to the Penobscot in Argyle.

We have *Maskwi'-sikuk* (O'Brien); *Muskqua-i-cook* (Ketchum); *Masquazicook* (Newell Lyon); *Maskweisikuk* (O'Brien) —to all of which *sibou,* "stream," should be added.

The word is entirely simple. Rasles (30) has *"mask8em8si, bouleau,"* in which the ending *m8si* is the inseparable for a tree.

PASSADUMKEAG.

Passad-umk'eag, "above the gravel bar." A small river entering the Penobscot from the east in the town of the same name.

    1823. Greenleaf, "Stream above falls."
    1832. Williamson, "Where water goes into the river above falls."
    1884. Hubbard, "Falls running over gravelly bed," and other Indian interpretations (p. 207).
    1890. O'Brien, "Over the gravelly place."
    1931. Peter W. Ranco, "Above the rips."

There is entire agreement upon the forms of the name and no disagreement in the interpretations cited, though others given under the root vary widely but without authority.

The last element of the word Passadumkeag is the familiar *amkiak* or *amkeag*, found often in Maliseet words for a gravel-bar or sand-beach. The first part, *passad-* a root rarely used in place-names, is the Englished form of *pansit8i8i* of Nudenans, "*desuper*, above." Rasles' *pansitsi8i* (560) is a misprint of the same word, with *s* in place of *8*, and in his translation "*au de-la du rapide*," he has supplied the *du rapide*. The original Indian word is only the preposition "above."

The topographical peculiarity in this place is that the stream does not take its name from something at or in its mouth, but from rips some distance below it. Passing over these rapids on his way up river, the canoeman knew that he was near this stream, which was one of the most important routes to the eastward—a place he must not fail to identify. By way of the Passadumkeag one could go to the headwaters of Union River, Narraguagus, and branches of the Machias, and through two routes to places on St. Croix waters.

Psinkwand-is'sek, "Scalp Rock." A ledge, still locally called Sculp Rock, in Passadumkeag Stream a few miles above the mouth.

This place got its name because the Mohawks in the old wars of the 17th and 18th centuries at some time murdered two Indian women and left the bodies on this rock in mid-stream where they would be sure to be found.

Psinkwa'lan, "to scalp" (from the roots *p'si*, "split," and *antep*, "head"), with a locative ending.

ENFIELD.

Tekebi'-suk, "cold water" (Ketchum). Cold Stream, tributary to Passadumkeag.

Tekebi'suk-gam'uk (Ketchum). Cold Stream Lake.

Both names may be recent, perhaps translations of the English name; the second must be modern.

Tekebi, "cold water" (Rasles) from *téké*, "it is cold" and *-abi'*, "liquid, drink." *Tekebi'suk* or *Ticope'suk* was the ordinary name of any good spring of water.

Madamas'-wok, "alewives" (plural), *teguk*, "stream" understood. Cold Stream (Mrs. Sylvia Stanislaus).

M'nadagahm'-is (Mrs. Stanislaus). When pressed for the old name,

Mrs. Stanislaus gave this, but whether for the Lake or for the Stream is uncertain. She said it was named for a fish, she could not tell what kind—"they used to stand on their heads to find snails there; they were called *m'nadagah'mis*." Identification of the species must be left to those who know the lake. The word Mrs. Stanislaus gave for alewives was *amaswak* (plural) and for shad *m'nawamswak* (plural), which correspond to *aüms8ak* and *ma8m8ak* of Rasles.

Ammadamast, the name of the Grange of Enfield, whose grange hall stands near Cold Stream, clearly carries with it some reminiscence of either *n'ahmays,* a fish, or *madames,* an alewife. In printed form it is found in 1882 in the *History of Penobscot County* (p. 342, foot of second column): "Cold Stream Lake, called by the Indians Ammadamast."

TOWNSHIPS 40, 41, etc.

Nicatow'-is, "the little fork" (officially, but incorrectly, *Nicatous*). One of the largest lakes in Hancock County, tributary to Passadumkeag Stream.

The name is a misnomer. It was not the name of the lake but of the Fork of Passadumkeag Stream where the Main Stream and Nicatowis Branch of the Passadumkeag unite. This was known as the Little Fork to distinguish it from the Great Fork at Medway; both were the junctions of very important travel routes and needed distinctive names.

Kia-so'beak, "clear-water lake." The old and rightful name of Nicatowis Lake.

Kia-sobee-sis', "little clear-water lake," (variously misprinted as Gassobeeis, Garbeus, etc.) A tributary to Kiasobeak or Nicatowis Lake.

Abam-gam'ok. A lake-like arm of Nicatowis, called West Lake.

It probably comes from the root *aba* (See Abahos Stream). It lies very near to Nicatowis and almost parallel to it.

BURLINGTON.

Sapon'-ac, a corrupted form of *Chibanook,* "the big opening." The first lake on Passadumkeag Stream as one ascends.

It was a common Indian custom to call the first pond through which one had to pass in going up the stream *Pawnook,* or *Bahnook,* "the opening," "the place where it spreads out," from *panna-.*

The old name of this lake was *Chibanook,* "the big opening," because it was larger than most of its kind. Chibanook was corrupted to *Japonic,* which in turn became *Spawnook* and now is the uncouth *Saponac,* which must be endured because it is the name of a post office. A century ago the lake was most commonly called *Pawnook,* or *Bahnook.*

Mada-gask'-al, "meadows at the mouth." A stream tributary to the Passadumkeag in Burlington.

Very extensive grassy meadows mark this stream at its mouth. *Mada-(mata-),* "comes in," "at the end of"; *g,* dividing consonant; *-ask,* the same as *-esk,* "grass"; *-al,* the plural ending of a weak noun, the name of a plant. The root *-esk* means something green, succulent, eaten raw. Rasles has *meski'ki,* "*herbes, le lieu où il y en a,*" that is, "meadows." The stream name is a shortened form. It is often, and equally well, spelled Madagascal.

Skutah'-zis, "brook-trout stream." A tributary to the Passadumkeag in Burlington.

    1815. *Skutarzy*—Massachusetts Archives (Maps and Plans, #1798).
    1822. *Skutarzy Stream*—Holman and Rose, *Survey.*
    1824. *Escutassis Pond* (in Lowell)—Newspaper notice of drowning of Timothy Miller.
    1867. *Escutasis*—Maine *Acts and Resolves.*
    1877. *Escutarsis,* official name of the Grange at East Lowell.

Where the newspaper got the initial *E* is not known; for *escotam* would indicate something which was eaten raw—and so Lewis Ketchum instantly translated the word when it was submitted to him. It may be a prefatory *e* or *a* found in some Maine Indian place names, and as yet unexplained.

Skutahzis comes from *sk8'tam,* "trout" (Rasles, 405), with the diminutive ending *-sis,* "small," meaning what we call "brook trout."

The word was once in general use for any trout stream. We find *Schootarza Rips* on Piscataquis River (*Water Supply Paper,* #279, 162-3) and *Scutarzy Brook* on the same waters, while *Schoodic Lake* on Piscataquis is given on Moses Greenleaf's map as *Scootum Lake,* which is not a misprint, but means "Trout Lake," from Rasles' *skoo'tam,* "trout."

MATTAMISCONTIS PLANTATION.

Mad-am-as-cont'-es, "alewife stream." In Mattamiscontis Plantation.

> 1805. *Mad-am-as-con-tes River*—Massachusetts Archives (Maps and Plans, 44:3).
> 1825. *Mad-a-mis-kon-tis Stream*—Moses Greenleaf, Letter; "young alewife stream."
> 1884. *Matamiscontis*—Hubbard, 200; quotes Trumbull, but gives no interpretation of his own.

Any one of these forms is preferable to the official name of the plantation, which wholly disguises the meaning of the word. This is not a *mata-* word, indicating some feature at the mouth of the stream, but an alewife-abundance word. It comes from *madamas,* "alewife," and *kaïntti,* indicating a place of occurrence, with the softened Penobscot locative -*es* rather than the diminutive -*sis,* "little."

That this is the correct meaning is assured by finding, some twenty-five years since, an old man who could remember that in his youth alewives came to this stream in such numbers that early settlers carted them off by the horse-sled load. This effectually disposes of Dr. Trumbull's labored exposition (Connecticut Historical Society *Collections,* II, 1870, 25) that alewives formerly, but no longer, resorted there. Dr. Ganong also makes too hard work of his interpretation ("Organization... Indian Place-Nomenclature," Fifth Paper, 1915, 400). He distrusted Dr. Ballard's statement that *mahdames* was the Penobscot name for an alewife (*Report of the United States Coast Survey,* 1868, 249) and interpreted it as "Stream that empties at the alewives' occurrence place," disposing of *mada-* or *mata-* as the usual prefix for "at the end of." For once Dr. Ballard was right. *Madamas* means "alewife." The whole word means "plenty of alewives."

The particular difficulty with this word is the ending in -*is* or -*es,* which cannot stand for -*sis,* "little," though whoever gave Greenleaf his translation seemed to think so. There is no reason to suppose that the alewives frequenting this stream were either smaller or younger than those in other streams, and since Greenleaf has another Madamiscomtes in Bradley, with the same apparently diminutive ending, it cannot be that they were Big and Little Alewife Streams. We regard the ending as the "softened Penobscot locative," of which Dr. Ganong says (*op. cit.*, 400): "But on the lower Penobscot, and thereabouts, occurs a curious assemblage, a kind of island, of place-names having the termination S, *e.g.,* Matamiscontis, Patagumkis, Matagoodus, Quakis, Umbazookskus, Molunkus, Piscataquis, with some thirty others. In several of these cases it is possible that the S represents an abbreviated *sis,* meaning little, as it certainly does in Seebois, which means little river, but this cannot be true of them all. . . . It seems pretty clear that in the Penobscot names above cited we have the same phenomenon, and that the final S, probably a relic of the aboriginal Sh, represents a softened form of the locative. . . . But what a problem in the Ethnology-Etymology of the earlier Indian immigrants do these islands of the softened locatives represent!"

Abahos Stream, "a stream that runs parallel with a big river" (Hubbard).

> 1822. *Aberhorse,* "tributary to Madunkaunk"—Holmes and Rose, Survey (Massachusetts Archives).
> 1836. *Eber Horse*—Noah Barker, Survey (Maine Land Office).
> 1884. *Abbahs* and *Abahticook,* as well as *Abahos*—Hubbard, who says it is "a branch of Madamiscontis."

Dr. Ganong thinks that *aba-* means a stream parallel with another.

LINCOLN.

Na-mok'-an-ok, "turtle island." A high island about three miles below Lincoln Center.

The island gets its name from its shape. The full form, given below, is "big-turtle-his-shell island."

> 1823. *Na-mok-a-nok*—Moses Greenleaf, *Letter,* who says "Mohawk Rips"; but the name belongs to the island, which is above the Rips. This is the earliest occurrence found.
> 1838. *Na-ma-ka-nock*—Dr. Jackson, *Survey,* Second Report, p. 9.
> 1884. *Namokanok*—Dr. Hubbard; "high land—kind of a lump" (Francis Neptune).

1890. *Nemakenagek*—O'Brien, "turtle island." (The ending is the inseparable *-naghe-*, "island.")

1912. *Mahockanock*—Barrows, *Water Supply Paper*, #279, plate xiii C (a misprint).

1917. *K'tol'beh-i-ahmik'enaqu'-nagh'ek*—Lewis Ketchum, "big-turtle-his-shell island." *K'tolbeh* was the great snapping turtle. This is the only time the name has been found in full.

For *tortue*, "tortoise," Father Rasles has *t8rebe*, which transliterates to the modern Penobscot *tolbeh*, often pronounced *dolebeh*. Rasles also has *"son écaille, his shell, amikenak8,"* the same word given by Ketchum. It is this which persists in our word *Namokanok*, which is literally "shell island," with the understanding that it is the turtle's shell, or carapace. The initial *N* seems to be a replacement by the English of an original rough breathing with which Indians often prefaced a word beginning with a vowel, *e.g.,* Orono, pronounced "Horno," and *ahkik*, "seal," as *hahkikw*.

Mata-naw'-cook. A lake, a stream, and an island in Lincoln.

Though all three lie very near together and the names are very similar in sound, the lake and the island names come from quite different roots.

To show the variety of forms and meanings assigned by different authorities, we give a list, to be distributed later to the proper features.

1793. *Mordenarcooch Stream*— Maynard and Holland, Survey Map (Massachusetts Archives, Maps and Plans, Roller #1013).

1822. *Matenorcook*—Silas Holman and Daniel Rose, Survey (Massachusetts Archives, Maps and Plans, #1798).

1823. *Mad-a-nau-kook*, stream and island—Moses Greenleaf, *Letter*.

1829. *Mattanawcook*—Moses Greenleaf, *Survey*.

1856. *Metanawcook*—William Willis (Maine Historical Society *Collections*, IV:106).

1858. *Madnaguk*—Vetromile, "full of many small, broken islands" (given in Douglas-Lithgow Dictionary).

1858. *Mat'nahguk*—Vetromile MSS., "the act of going up into a mountain by following a stream."

1882. *Mattanawcook*—Hubbard, 200, "place of bad islands."

1910. *Mat'nahguk*—Dr. J. Dyneley Prince (*Amer. Anthropologist*, N.S. XII, 194), "large hills."

1931. *Mat'nahgook*—Mrs. Sylvia Stanislaus, "lake between hills," "kind of going up between."

1940. *Matna'gak*—Dr. Frank G. Speck (*Penobscot Man*, 25 and 212), "long island."

In 1934, Mr. W. B. Cabot came from Boston to Lincoln principally to determine the meaning of this one word *Matanawcook*. He went away less certain than when he arrived; for he was told that the right word was *Pematina'cook,* "hilly country," "up into the hills." The next year I went myself to Lincoln to see again Mrs. Sylvia Stanislaus and her son Francis and got the same word. Yet the same day in Old Town Mr. Peter W. Ranco gave me another name for Matanawcook Lake, *Mahdagam',* or *Matagam'.* By taking the stream, lake, and island separately, we may yet be able to determine the true meaning of each.

Matanawcook Stream, the outlet of the lake.

In Mordenarcooch Stream, 1793, we recognize the inseparable *-nahge-,* an "island." The first part is the broad Yankee pronunciation of *mada-* or *mata-,* "at the end of." "At-the-end-of-it-an-island" is the idea. Matanawcook Stream enters the Penobscot behind one of the largest islands in the river.

Matanawcook Lake, for which Peter W. Ranco gave the name *Madagam,* with the meaning, "lake which runs way down almost to the river." Its outlet is extremely short, there being hardly a half mile in a direct course between the lake and the river, a feature presented by no other lake on Penobscot waters. *Madagam* has nothing to do with Matanawcook. The first element is the familiar *mata,* "at the end of," and the other, *-gam,* is a short form of *-gamok,* "a lake." The meaning is somewhat forced, but quite understandable: you are at the lake very soon; the stream stops shortly.

Matanawcook Island. This large island near the mouth of Matinawcook Stream has a peculiarity. At its lower end is a trail of small islets, slightly separated from it. They are *metin-,* "cut off," "chopped off" from the large island, "separated." That is the meaning of the *words* as given by Vetromile, Dr. Prince, Dr. Speck, and Mrs. Stanislaus: their interpretations of them have to be disregarded. *Metinahguk* means, as Father Vetromile puts it, "full of many small, broken islands." It is not the name of the large island alone, but of the whole group, though most of them are insignificant, alluvial islets; that is, it is a *feature* by which the large island could be identified and the voyageur would know where to turn off to get upon a route to some place beyond. Always in Indian travel the route was of more consequence than any place upon it, and the names were largely sign-boards, read from natural features of the place, indicating a choice of routes.

Nudenans gives *met-nagek* as *"ad extremitatem insulae,"* "at the end of the island."

Pemat'inek and **Pematina'cook**, given by Mrs. Stanislaus, who lived very near, do not apply to the lake and stream at all: they are route names, "the act of going up into a mountain by following a stream," to quote Father Vetromile, who, however, uses a word which could not mean that. *Pematinek* is from *pem-*, "extended," and *-adene-*, inseparable for a "mountain," a loose expression for seeking mountains at a distance, not for a range of hills. The word *ahwangan*, "route," is omitted.

We have then:

Matanawcook Island, properly *Metinah'gek*, "small, broken islands."

Matanawcook Lake, properly *Madagam'ook*, "lake that ends almost at the river."

Matanawcook Stream, same as the lake, with *seboo*, "stream," added.

Matanawcook Route, properly *Pemadn'ek* or *Pematina'cook*, "the route into the hill country," up Matanawcook Stream and Lake.

Cambolas'-sie. Pond in Lincoln, and stream connecting with the river.

In 1932, Mrs. Sylvia Stanislaus, of Lincoln, aged 97, told the writer that the word came from *ahgobe'la*, "tied up," "closed," and *lahsis*, "a little lake." "Going up stream and closes in"; "going up deadwater, closes in and then opens out a little." She gave the following forms:

Ah-go-be-lo-lah'-sis; Ah-gom-pe-lo-lah'-sis; A-gob-la-lox'-es; A-gu-ma-bo-la-lox'-is.

This word seems to be the Micmac *Amgôpîlasig*, "tied together," of Father Pacifique. It also appears nearly related to *Umsaskis*, on the Allegash, from *Ansaskek*, a Maliseet word, "having opposite points which run out to meet one another" (Hubbard, 212), or, as Moses Greenleaf put it, "tied together like sausages." In old times the name must have referred to the whole chain of small ponds.

The Micmac *Amgôpîlasig* would be written in Penobscot as *Ah-go-be-lah-sik,* very close to Mrs. Stanislaus' forms. The word is related to others meaning "long joints," as "jointed grasses."

No Indian form has been found for Molasses Pond, in Franklin, but it may be related, or it may be wholly English.

Mugaleep'-ahwan'gan, "the caribou trail."

The word was given in 1932 by Mrs. Sylvia Stanislaus of Lincoln as the name of a rather small pond on the left of the road from Lincoln to Calais, not far outside of Lincoln Center. It lies in a valley which crosses the main road and evidently used to be an old caribou route.

Mugaleep' is the Maliseet word for a caribou (which in Penobscot is *mogalibou'*). It means "the shoveller" and was given from the habit of pawing away the snow with its forefeet to reach the reindeer-moss upon which the animal feeds. *Ahwan'gan* (literally "bait," whence a "trap-line") has become the word for a route. The word *mugaleep'* survives in Washington County in Mugur'rewock Lakes, so called, said Lewey Mitchell, because the snow drifted down through valleys, as if the wind were shovelling it into them.

Kassa-num-ga-numk'eag. "Elaware Rips." Given in Greenleaf's *Letter* of 1823, without meaning or location, but below Namokanok Island and Mohawk Rips. (The story of Mohawk Rips is in Thoreau's *Maine Woods,* 1864, p. 299.)

No other occurrence is known and the locality is undetermined, so analysis is theoretical. We may safely assume that the last part of the word, *-ganumkeag,* is *kinamkeag,* a "bed of coarse gravel," while the first part appears to be from *kesso,* "swift," probably in the adjectival form *kessawi.* The whole indicates rapid water over a coarse gravel bottom, not rocky rips.

WINN.

Kessolagessemodik. Five Islands Falls.
 1823. *Sologismoodik*—Moses Greenleaf; no meaning.
 1890. *Kessolagessemodik*—O'Brien; no meaning.

Greenleaf's word is evidently an abbreviation of O'Brien's, showing that it is an old name. O'Brien gives *kessegosso,* "swift water," and the next element seems to be *esseman,* indicating a current, but this being a single occurrence of the word, we can say no more than that we should look for "quick water" where such a word is placed.

Hanol-menahanol. Five Islands Falls.

Another name for the Five Islands, recorded by O'Brien, possibly a late word used by river-men as a translation of the English name.

Menahanol is the plural of *menahan,* "island," a weak (inanimate) noun. The correct form of "five" to agree with it would be *nanenol* (*naïnnen8r,* Rasles, 30), which *"hanol"* probably represents, not too closely.

WYTOPITLOCK.

Wyt-o-pit′-lock, "alder place." A stream tributary from the north to the Mattawamkeag River.

    1829. *Wytopidlot*—Moses Greenleaf, *Survey of Maine,* 1829, 79.
    1884. *Wydop′iklock, Wytopidlot*—Hubbard; "the river is broad and there are no trees on its banks except alders (*wydopi*)"— Indian information.
    1890. *Wedobekkek*—O'Brien.
    1937. *Widoop′ikeag, Widoop′icook*—Mrs. Peter W. Ranco, with the meaning of "alders."

Out of twenty-eight spellings of the word, the above are all worth recording. There is no question about the meaning of the name; Rasles has *8doppi, "de l'aune dont le charbon sert à piquet";* O'Brien gives *wdo'bi.* Indians accent the second syllable, but the town and river names are stressed on the third syllable.

MOLUNKUS.

Molunk′us, "deep-valley stream," "ravine stream" (*tegwe* understood). A stream tributary to the Mattawamkeag River from the north.

    1822. *Molunks Stream*—Holman and Rose, Survey.
    1826. *Mocuncas Stream*—Joseph Norris, Survey (a slip of the pen).
    1851. *Molucas*—Massachusetts Archives (Maps and Plans, 38:8).

1884. *Molunkes, Moluncus*—Hubbard. "High bank on each side of stream" (Francis Neptune to Hubbard).
1890. *Molankessek*—O'Brien.

The early forms are not good. *Molunkus* is official but Hubbard's *Molunkes* is better.

O'Brien has *molanke*, "a ravine," from *mola*, "low," "deep," "between two mountains." The form *Molankes* has the softened Penobscot locative, not the diminutive *-sis*. In O'Brien's *Molankessek*, given without comment, his Indian informant seems not to have recognized the old locative and to have added another.

MACWAHOC.

Mac-wa'-hoc, "bog." A stream outletting into Molunkus Stream.

Rasles has *meg8ak*, "bog," and Pacifique has the same in Micmac, *mgoag*. Dr. J. Dyneley Prince gives *mak'waku*, "bog," and *Mug'wa'kwuk*, apparently the locative Macwahoc (*American Anthropologist*, New Series XII, 1910, 195). The word is the simple word for "bog." The Indian comment was *"Mug'waak*, sluggish water, as running through a bog" (Ketchum).

Nudenans gives the same form as Dr. Prince, *meg8ak8*, (*m'gwakw'*) with the definition, *terra aquosa, mollis, qualis est ubi multae sunt cedri, cedratum;* that is, he makes it specifically a cedar-swamp, which is not the Maine idea of a bog. Rasles, however, defines his word as *"marécage, de l'eau des terres"* (332).

MATTAWAMKEAG.

Mata-wamk'-eag, "at the mouth a gravel bar." This was the mark by which to recognize Mattawamkeag River, tributary to the Penobscot from the east.

The Indian named the affluents to a river by some easily recognized natural feature near its mouth. *Matawamkeag* pictured to him a point of gravel on the upper side of the entrance where the current of the main river had crowded the wash of the smaller entering stream into a pointed bed of gravel. *Matawamkeunk* would be an entering stream with a bed of gravel *inside* its own mouth. *Passadumkeag* was a stream entering *above*, or *beyond*, a gravel bar across the main river. Except at very high water one would never miss locating a gravel bar. Thus the little rivers named themselves.

The word is made from *mata-*, "at the end of," and *-amkiak*, the Maliseet word for a gravel-bed, which has *-amk*, the root for sand or gravel, and a locative. It seems better to revert to this simple, and old, stem rather than to attempt to explain *-keag* as an ending meaning "point," since it does not *mean* a point, though most of our *keag*-words refer to points formed by the action of two confluent currents. O'Brien gives *madaweik* as the Maliseet for "mouth of a stream," thus indicating that in Mattawamkeag *madawa* is the first part and *-amkeag*, "a gravel bar," the second; or, that the whole word is good Maliseet.

The word has a long history and many varying forms; though all are easily harmonized, we may cite some of the dated occurrences.

1686. *Madaham-ouit*—Documents collected in France, in 1844 (Massachusetts Archives, quoted in Maine Historical Society *Collections,* Doc. Ser. IV, 426)—"*grand fort de sauvage quils tiennent estre a moitie de quebec,*" "half-way to Quebec, where the land is very good, there are the finest oaks and the most of them in the world and a great eel-fishery and all kinds of fish." This document seems to be the legend to accompany a map, perhaps the great Franquelin-De Meulles, issued in 1686.

In this, *d* replacing *t* is normal; the *h* is an aspirate which replaces our *w* (probably sounded as *hw* here), and *-ouit* is our *-quit,* substitute for *-keag.* This is the earliest occurrence found.

1690. *Metamkik* River—Memoir of M. d'Iberville on the ways to launch an expedition against Boston (*N. Y. Colonial Documents,* IX, 731): "to river Metamkik which falls into the Penobscot River eighteen leagues from the sea." An admirable form of the word, with every root distinct.

1715. *Mandaouanmki*—Map of Father Joseph Aubéry.
But for lacking the locative ending, this is the form of the word we now use. The two *n*'s are nasals, making the *a* broad; *ou* stands for our *w*.

1736. *Madawamkee*—John Gyles, *Memoirs of Odd Adventures* (during his captivity by the Indians), written of events dating to 1689, printed 1736; "a village which stands on a point of land between the main river and a branch which heads east of it."

1764. *Meddewamcaige*—Joseph Chadwick, Survey and Maps.
1786. *Montawamkeek* River, *Montawawkeektook* River—Sketch Map of Robert Treat and John Marsh (Massachusetts Archives, Maps and Plans, vol. 38, 8). Fairly good Indian, the *n* probably nasalized;—*took* means "river," and needed no repetition.
1793. *Metawaumkeeg* River—Maynard and Holland, Survey (Massachusetts Archives, Roller map #1012).
1826. *Matawamkeag*—Joseph Norris, Survey (Massachusetts Archives).
1832. *Metawamkeag*—Williamson, *History of Maine,* I, 66 n. Indian information; "means the stream running over a gravelly bed at its mouth."
1884. *Matawamkeag*—Hubbard, 200, whose explanation is too labored, and who accidentally says that the bar would be on the downstream side of the mouth. Such bars are necessarily on the upstream side; on the lower side the current of the smaller stream would unite with that of the large river in washing away the obstruction; on the upstream side they crowd against each other.

Some of the meanings offered are wholly irrelevant. Masta, an educated Indian (*Abenaqui Indian Legends,* 1932, p. 88), wrote: "Mattawamkeag from Mattawamkiag means the Indians of the farthest or last settlement. Prefix 'matta' means the farthest or last. Suffix 'wan' for wigwam or settlement, 'ki' means land, the final 'ak' means the inhabitants of the land."

Mata-se-hunk', "rapids-at-the-mouth stream." A tributary from the east to Penobscot River in Mattawamkeag.

1822. *Matasehunk*—Silas Holman and Daniel Rose, Survey (Massachusetts Archives, Roller map #1798).
1824. *Mettaseunk*—W. B. Cabot, MS., List of Maine Names from Documents (Massachusetts Archives, Maps and Plans, 62:8).

The name is found only on this stream, to which it belongs, and on the lake four miles up in which the stream rises, where it cannot belong by aboriginal use. Though the popular form is Mattaseunk, the better one is the earliest recorded, *Matasehunk.* The accent falls heavily on the last syllable.

Mata-, prefix, "at the mouth of," "enters river," "ends in"; *-se-,* the remnant of *kesitchuan,* "rapids"; *-hunk,* "stream," always one with a strong current. "Rapids-at-the-mouth stream." The name is appropriate; between the main highway and the river is a stretch of brisk rapids. Though *Water Supply Paper*

#279 places Mattaseunk Rapids upon the main Penobscot, the name can refer only to those on an entering stream.

Words ending in -*unk,* or -*hunk* always indicate streams with a strong current, entailing work in poling upstream. As Mr. Cabot says, the *h* should be kept in these words because it pictures the exertion which has to be used. These *hunk*-names are very characteristic of Penobscot waters. From the name alone, no Indian would ever confound a *hunk*-stream and a *skiticook,* or deadwater-stream.

Of the middle syllable -*se-,* "rapids," which is all there is left of *kesitchuan* or *kesidjuan,* we may remark that Rasles has *kesit's8ann,* "a swift, rapid river" (444) and *kesi'tann,* "what flows swiftly" (136). In the Micmac, Rand has *kesego,* "flows rapidly," and Father Pacifique, *gesigao,* "flows rapidly." The roots of this are the intensive *kes,* "large" or "much," and *sep-* (radical of *seboo,* "a river") something which flows continuously—let us say a steady current, rather than broken falls and pitches.

Mata-ke-hunk'. A brook, tributary to Mattawamkeag River about three miles above its mouth.

Though the popular spelling is *Mattakeunk,* a much better one is *Matakehunk.* In all these *hunk*-words the *h* should be retained; in them there is a heavy accent upon the final syllable, or at least a secondary accent there. No early occurrence of the word has been found.

In 1935, Francis Stanislaus, of Lincoln, said the word means "runs right straight." Since this did not identify the roots, I asked him if it might not be *mata-,* "at the end," *kes,* "high," -*hunk,* "stream"; and said "quick drop," that is, a stream which very near its mouth comes down suddenly from high land. "Ends-high-brook" is about as near as we can come to the idea in English. This Stanislaus accepted.

Mad-un'-ke-hunk. Stream in Chester, entering the Penobscot opposite Lincoln; said to have a fall of sixty feet in the last half mile.

Stanislaus said the meaning was "pretty near like the other one," that is, *Mata-ke-hunk.* It is, however, an entirely different word; its full form is *Namadunkehunk,* the name of Webster Stream.

1805. *Madunkeunk* (Massachusetts Archives, Maps and Plans, 44:3).

Mad-un'-ke-hunk'. Webster Stream, headwaters of the East Branch of the Penobscot.

Known only from Thoreau's *Maine Woods,* first edition, p. 326. Thoreau gives this for the stream, and *Madunkehunk-gamoc* for Webster Lake, as meaning "Height-of-land" Stream and Lake, thus proving that the full word is *Nemadunkehunk* and accounting for the two *-unk* syllables.

The two foregoing are the same word, applied to places far apart, and neither is a *mata-* word.

Mata-gwad'-is. Stream tributary to Mattawamkeag River, with its source in Carroll; commonly called Mattagoodus.

    1822. *Madaquowoodis*—Holman and Rose, Survey (Massachusetts Archives, Roller map #1798).
    1860. *Mattaguedis, Mattagoodus*—Vetromile, "no good place to land a canoe on account of marshes."
    1866. *Mattaguadus*—Davis S. Libby, Journals.
    1884. *Mategwe-oo-dis*—Steven Stanislaus to Hubbard, "meadow ground." (Word badly divided; Hubbard's mistake.)
    1890. *Matagudis*—O'Brien, who assigns no meaning.

The meaning of "bad landing-place for canoes" is no doubt descriptive: the terrain vouches for it. There is some question as to the analysis of the word, for no known example has *matche,* "bad," and *mata* means "at the end of." The next element is probably from *ahguahassin,* "to make a landing." The ending is the soft Penobscot locative.

It is possible that by the telescoping of roots so common in Indian words, another root is almost suppressed but is indicated in the first and fourth examples by the lengthening of the penult; and this may be a root not yet analyzed out but apparently existing in words like Gaugus, Narraguagus and Quakish, meaning "overflowed." In that case the word would be "at-the mouth, landing-place under water," which would be properly descriptive.

O'Brien's form *Matagudis* is not the same as his word *meta-guidek,* "the end of a canoe." That is *metin-,* rather than *mata-,* and *aguiden,* or *akwiden,* "a bark canoe."

There is more than a possibility that another word in O'Brien's notes may have been intended for this. He has *"madgwendissak,* 'old' tracks of beavers, landing of otters," that is, an "otter slide," making the word related to Agwahassedek, the name of Fort Point, and telescoping the prefix *matche,* "bad." In this case we should have simply "bad landing-place"; but there is no evidence that Father O'Brien associated this word with Matagwadis.

MEDWAY.

Nicatow, "fork of a river." The old name for Medway, which lay at the great fork of the West and East Branches of the Penobscot.

The word is entirely simple—*nik-,* "two," indicating an even division, or branches of equal importance, and a remnant of *-tegwe,* inseparable ending meaning a "river," "stream with a current."

Patagumkis, "the gravelly bend" (Ganong). Stream entering the Penobscot from the west in Medway.

> 1823. *Pata-gum-kis,* "half-circle point, stream, and falls"—Moses Greenleaf (*Maine's First Map-maker,* p. 123).
> 1864. *Paytgumkiss*—Thoreau (*Maine Woods,* first ed., 326); a misprint for Patygumkis. "Petticoat," apparently given as its meaning, is nonsense, probably accounted for by Thoreau's handwriting; this volume was posthumous and some of the Indian names show misprinting.
> 1884. *Patagumkis,* "sandy round cove"—Hubbard, whose analysis is faulty.

The best explanation of the word found was given in 1914 by Joseph Francis, one of the finest of our Indian guides, who said it meant "a sharp turn in the river where the bottom is gravelly." Another informant said that at low water there is a curving sandy beach near the mouth of the stream.

This word cannot be, as Hubbard thinks, from *peteg8,* "round"; *-am,* "sand"; *-ki,* "place"; and *-sis,* "little"—"the little place of round gravel"—because Rasles' *peteg8* refers to something spherical, while the ending *-sis,* as Dr. Ganong points out, is not a diminutive but our softened locative in *s* instead of in *k.* "The first part," says Ganong, "obviously involves the root PET(E)K (which is evidently the same in Micmac, Maliseet and Penobscot) . . . meaning 'back turn,' with which all three explanations, 'half circle,' 'round cove,' and 'sharp turn,' above given are in full agreement."

... The second root is equally clear; it is plainly AMK, a very wide spread root meaning 'gravel' or 'single,' here again in full agreement with the meanings above given. The remainder of the word, that is, IS, appears to be nothing other than the softened locative termination—IS used instead of IK after a preceding k sound ... of which I have found a good many other examples in Penobscot. It cannot well represent an abbreviated diminutive, SIS, because that termination is always comparative and involves a larger PATAGUMKIK, near by, of which there is no trace. The name in full, therefore, would be PETER-AMK-IS, meaning literally 'back turn-gravel-place,' or more generally, 'the gravelly bend.'" (Ganong, *Transactions* of the Royal Society of Canada, Third Series, Vol. VIII, 275-6.)

The spelling *Patagumkis* is greatly to be preferred to Patagumpus, or to the illiterate Paddygumpus of the rivermen. The correct *Petekamkis* can hardly be restored at this late day.

CHAPTER THREE

PENOBSCOT BAY: THE WESTERN SHORE TO WALDOBORO

STOCKTON SPRINGS TO ROCKLAND AND COASTWISE WESTWARD INCLUDING WALDO AND KNOX COUNTIES AND THE EASTERNMOST PART OF LINCOLN COUNTY

The place-names in this section are fairly numerous, most of them are old, and many of them are among the oldest which we find in records. Many of them are beginning to come within the range of territory entered on the York Deeds, which makes the history of the word more important because the word is definitely dated and located.

STOCKTON SPRINGS.

A-gua-has'-si-dek, "landing-place"; also "an otter slide." Fort Point in Stockton Springs. (Usually called *Wassumkeag, q.v.*)

This easterly extension of the great Cape Jellison peninsula was chosen in 1759 by Gov. Thomas Pownall of Massachusetts for the erection of his frontier fort, called Fort Pownall, which commanded all the passages, both of ships at sea and of Indians along the shore, up and down the Penobscot. The fort was stripped by the English before the Revolution and burned by Cargill in 1775. Detailed plans and something of its history are in Dr. Henry E. Dunnack's *Maine Forts* and a fuller history by Dr. W. O. Sawtelle in his "Thomas Pownall" (Massachusetts Historical Society *Proceedings,* 1931).

At the very tip of Fort Point runs out a sharp bar of white sand, exposed at low water, which protects a small cove with a white beach, a perfect landing-place for canoes. If Governor Pownall had asked some Indian what he called that, the Indian naturally would have replied, "A white sand-beach, *Wasa-um-keag.*" And the Governor might easily have taken it for the name of the whole end of the peninsula.

However, the Indians had a very different name for this place. They called it *Aguahassidik,* which might be either an otter-slide or simply a landing-place. The word, says Father O'Brien, comes from *aguahassi,* "to get out of," with the locative *-essik,* that is, "a landing-place." And *agwahassi* is the same as Nudenans' *ag8ane, extraho ex aqua,* "I drag [my canoe] out of the water." Since the otter has a habit of coming out of water and climbing steep banks to slide down them into the water again as a sport, the same word means "an otter slide." Nicolar explains the application of the word to this particular place. "In olden times when the members of our tribe visited there, they only stopped long enough to make the sign of their visit, showing in what direction they were going, the number of their party and canoes, etc. On account of it being a marking place, no one was ever allowed to mar or deface its outline by using it for a camping ground." Nicolar said it meant "stepping ashore."

The word *Aguahassidik* probably serves in explaining several other place-names.

Agguahe'ga. "An island called Agguahega, or Damariscotty" (*York Deeds* VIII, 230). Probably Damariscove Island, which was well situated to be a marking-place.

Aquehadongo'nock, land now in West Bath, surveyed in 1718 by Capt. Joseph Heath (*Pejepscot Papers,* VIII :53). It is in a deed of 1654 from Indians to Thomas Stevens of Brunswick. The location shows that a portage here would save the often very dangerous passage through the Chops of Merrymeeting Bay, so that it was well located for a marking-place.

Aquadoc'tan (The Weirs, N. H.) and **Aquadoc'ta** (somewhere near the mouth of Contoocook River, Concord, N. H.) were probably also marking places.

STOCKTON.

Es'sick, "clam place," if not simply **Es'sak,** "clams."

Stockton, says Nicolar, was the first place on the way to saltwater where the Indians could get good clams. From *ais,* or *es,* a clam; plural, *essak.*

Ooni'gan-is'sek, "the short carry." At Cape Jellison Neck.

A carry of less than a quarter mile across the neck of the peninsula made a safe and short journey into Stockton Bay; thence across the bar of Sears Island into Searsport Bay, an "inside passage" for canoes. The ending *-issek* has nothing to do with *essek,* "clams," in the foregoing word. It is the diminutive *sis,* and locative *-ek,* added to *ounigan,* "portage."

ISLESBORO.

Pitau-begwi-menahan'uk, "the island that lies between two channels." Long Island, part of the town of Islesboro.

This fine, full form of the word was preserved by Father O'Brien, who further identifies the place by saying "Long Island near Searsport."

"*Pitau,* between, bay on both sides," he says; *begwi* is a creek, a tideway, or a channel; *menahanuk,* the familiar locative of an island.

Father O'Brien also has *Pitabeguk* but it is not so fine a form of the word. Nicolar gives *Pitowbaygook,* "inland sea island," not a satisfactory definition. Ballard has *Betowbagook,* which is Nicolar's form, and the excellent interpretation, "between two channels."

It is interesting to note that the Abnaki name of Lake Champlain is very similar. A personal letter of Rowland E. Robinson, the Vermont writer, to my father, dated Feb. 24, 1896, says: "*Petowbowk* is the name that all St. Francis Indians give Lake Champlain; translated by ... Wadso, 'the lake that lies between,'" which is explained by John Watso or Wadsho, the intelligent St. Francis Indian who gave the information, as meaning that Lake Champlain lay between the countries of the Abnaki and the Iroquois. It is also given by Douglas-Lithgow as *Petoubougue.* The last part is *begat,* a "lake," not *begwi,* a "tideway."

SEARSPORT.

We have found no word for Searsport except *Mosemadage,* treated under *M'd'angamek* (Castine).

Was-sum'-keag, "shining beach" (Ketchum). Brigadier's or Sears Island.

This name has usually been applied to Fort Point, though it does not belong there. Governor Pownall first placed this name upon Fort Point in 1759, probably through a misunderstanding of Indian information. As we shall show, it had long priority on

Sears Island, which the Indians have always called *Wasa-umkeag*.

Sears Island got its present name from Hon. David Sears, of Boston, one of the Ten Associates who bought out the heirs of Gen. Samuel Waldo, in whose honor it was, even within the writer's recollection, called Brigadier's Island. Earlier still it was Hazel-nut Island, and through the whole period the white sand-beach has been *Wassumkeag*. It is a round island of considerable size, wooded except for a farm on the eastern side, which was probably the site of Monsieur Gaulin's house two centuries and a half ago. The clean, white sand-beach in front of this house was the landmark of the Indians steering for Stockton Bay and the short carry across Cape Jellison into Fort Point Bay.

War-sumkeag, "bright sand," wrote Nicolar, meaning the beach alone.

Wassampi-menahanik, said O'Brien, of the whole island.

Wasa-umkeag, Pownall's form, though wrongly placed upon Fort Point, is the best form; *wasa*, "bright," "shining"; *-amkeag*, "sand-beach."

Older still and more interesting is the story printed in the *New England Historical and Genealogical Register*, 34 (1880), 90 ff., from original manuscripts of Judge Samuel Penhallow, of Portsmouth, the historian of the Indian wars. Penhallow and Atkinson were ordered to go down to Penobscot in 1703, following an outrage upon the family of Philip Meneer, son-in-law of Baron Castine, then living at Naskeag Point, in which Meneer was killed. They were commanded to embark at once and "make the best of your way to *Awassawamkick* or Hazle Nut Island where you may speak with monser Gaulin and deliver my letter." There follows a report of the journey. The letters were submitted to Joseph Williamson, the Belfast historian, but he could not identify *Awassawamkick* or *Awassamkik* Island although it was within sight of his own home. "The nearest approach to it is Wassaumkeag, a peninsula ... where Governor Pownall built a fort in 1759"—the Governor's mistake, but adopted since by everyone. There was a shining sand-beach at Fort Point, but it was not needed as a landmark and so did not carry the name, which the Indians reserved exclusively for Sears Island.

BELFAST.

Pas-sag-as'-sa-wau'keag, "sturgeon's place," or "place for spearing sturgeon by torchlight." The head of Belfast Bay.

The word is old, but the variations are largely misprint or ignorant abbreviations. It also has two interpretations.

    1757. *Assasawakuk* River—Joshua Freeman's Journal (Massachusetts Archives, 38A, 280-299). Except for lacking the initial letter, a fairly good form.

    1758. *Sackesawakkike*—Capt. James Cargill's Scout Report (Massachusetts Archives, 38A, 300-302); printed also as *Sackasawokkik* (Maine Historical Society *Collections,* Doc. Ser., 24:93).

    1759. *Pauseguse-wa-keag*—Governor Pownall's Map of the Penobscot (The Crown Collection, London). On this excellent map the word is misprinted *Taufegusewakeag;* but the *T* is an evident misprint for *P,* and since there is no *f* in Indian words, this letter is clearly meant for the old "long s"; thus revised, the word is an excellent form, the meaning correct, "Sturgeon River."

    1759. *Pausgasawackheag*—Gov. Pownall's Journal.

    1773. *Passagesswokey*—*Province Laws,* V, 293 (Mr. Cabot's List).

The word is Maliseet, corresponding to the Abnaki *Cobossecontee* (now Gardiner) on the Kennebec. *Pas'ukus* is Maliseet for "sturgeon"; *kebas'sé* is Abnaki for the same.

The word may be made in two ways. *Pasukus,* "sturgeon"; *-i-,* "his"; *-waukeag,* "place"—"sturgeon-his-place," Sturgeon River, or Sturgeon Bay. (*Waukeag* is only "place.")

The objection to this is that *-waukeag* is a land termination; it gives the picture of the encirling bayshore, not of the watery bay. However Soccabesin Swassin, a very intelligent Indian, made no objection, according to Dr. N. H. True (Williamson, *History of Belfast,* 1877, I, 52 ff., which has a long discussion). The introduction of "ghosts," "spirits," into so many of the Williamson explanations is partly a misconception of the *-wassa-* element, partly a recrudescence of an old Indian ghost tale which clung to this region, the fight of old Attean Orson and a ghost.

Lewis Ketchum was of a different opinion. He insisted that there were artificial lights in the word—"Would do for when you go fishing with a light; something about a light in it; perhaps torches." This so well agrees with the Indian custom of driving sturgeons up into bays and spearing them by torchlight when they were blinded by bonfires on the shores and by flaring torches of birch bark in the canoes, that it seems a better interpretation for this place. Nicholas Denys tells of the Micmacs hunting sturgeon in this way and Allen's *History of Chelmsford, Massachusetts* describes how it was done on the Merrimac.

According to this interpretation, the word is *pasukus,* "sturgeon"; *n'wassa, "j'en prends au flambeau"* (Rasles); *-waukeag,* "place"—"the place where they spear sturgeon by torchlight."

Paqua-ta'-nee, "out of the way." Site of Belfast City.

Nicolar, the only one to give the word, says "it was applied to the spot where Belfast City is now located. This place was considered out of the regular course of travel."

The word probably is *Paqu'ouden'ek,* "off the road." Rasles has *pankatsi8i,* "far from us," "aside." *Oudene* is a path or trodden way.

The word was probably the same used by an Indian who worked in my father's haying crew during the Civil War. Sometimes when going to a distant corner of a field, he would say,"Now we go *paquat'amus,*" that is, "out of the way."

Beaver-tail. No Indian word is known for this, but probably it is an old Indian word translated. The *Bangor Daily Whig and Courier,* July 24, 1858, quoted from the *Belfast Journal*: "About a mile from the business portion of our city and just above the upper bridge, a remarkable promontory juts out from the western bank, to a distance of sixty or seventy yards, with an average width of about three yards. From its resemblance to the useful appendage of the Beaver, it is known as Beaver's Tail."

SEARSMONT.

Quonta-ba'-cook. A rather large pond on the old route from Belfast to Kennebec; it outlets into George's River.

> 1764. *Quontabagook*—Letter of Capt. Thomas Goldthwait, commandant at Fort Point, about English hunters who had trespassed on Indian hunting grounds at this place (Mass. Archives).
>
> 1792. *Quantobaycook*—M. Monvel, "Report on Geology of the Knox Lands" (State Library, Augusta).

1797. *Condabaycook*—Plan of the Waldo lands (Waldo Claims Papers).
1797. *Quantibaycook*—Deed to John Braddock (Waldo Claims Papers, II:70).

It is probable that we have here only the last part of an occurrence or abundance word. *Quanti* seems like *contee* or *kaïntti*, and *baycook* is a pond or lake (*begat*). What so abounded there we do not know. It was *not fish;* because the white hunters who were warned off were hunting *furs* there, and they probably went there because some animal was abundant. They were there in March; so muskrat would seem the most likely fur; possibly beaver.

There is a little story here. The men refused to leave and sent Goldthwait a note scratched with a pin upon birch bark defying the officer and signed "Han'l Richardson." Goldthwait, March 28, ordered them out of the country. The original, in the Massachusetts Archives, is endorsed, "An epistolary conversation between Capt. Goldthwait and some English hunters." The men were probably the three Richardsons who the year before deserted a scouting party and ran off hunting on the Kennebec ponds.

LINCOLNVILLE.

Mag-win'-teg-wak, "choppy seas." Lincolnville Beach.

Though the local names about Camden and Lincolnville have been painstakingly studied by historians, a superficial resemblance which has left the best Indian authorities uncertain has been confusing. *Mecadacut, Megunticook,* and *Magwintegwak* are different words.

Mecadacut is the very old Micmac or Maliseet name for the Indian village site at Camden.

Megunticook is the more modern Indian name of Camden Harbor.

Magwintegwak, which the Indians themselves did not seem to distinguish from Megunticook, is the old name of the exposed coast along the Lincolnville shore, dreaded by canoemen in rough weather because there was no avoiding it except by a very long route far inland. For miles it extends, a rocky, harborless coast, exposed to all the prevailing winds. Captain John Smith finely paraphrased the old name when, speaking of the Camden Hills, he said, "against whose feet doth beat the sea." He was not speaking of the quiet Camden Harbor and the mountains as seen from there, but of the stern Lincolnville coast and the high range rising back of it.

The Indian testimony to the word is old, of high authority, and consentient; yet it is incorrect in derivation—or at least the Indians' translations fit more nearly another word than Megunticook, to which they are attached.

In 1887, Joseph Nicolar wrote: "Lincolnville was called *'Markurn-ta-quick,'* 'water ready for waves.' The old Indians assert that the little bay is full of waves from whatever quarter the wind blows." Nicolar's word is only Megunticook, which contains the root for a mountain and therefore is connected with the mountains and not with the waves. Yet in 1798, Rev. Paul Coffin, in his "Missionary Journeys" (Maine Historical Society *Collections,* IV, 1856, 379) says: "Megunticook, waves dashing against each other in an opposite direction." "Great swells of the sea" was the meaning given by Francis Sogabason and Neptune Sogabason for Meguntarcook (Locke, *History of Camden,* 1859, 63); and Eaton, perhaps borrowing from Locke, says the same (*Annals of Warren,* 1877, 134). All these for Megunticook; but we shall give a reason for interpreting Megunticook as meaning "Big Mountain Harbor," that is, Camden Harbor.

The word for Lincolnville Beach was discovered by Father O'Brien, who notes: *"Mahagantegwit*—Lincolnville Beach—'rough coast,' from *Mahaga,* 'hard.'" Elsewhere Father O'Brien says: *"Maagaanteguk,* 'swell of the sea'; *magui,* a swelling; *maguinek,* where there is a swelling." The last element is *teguk,* "waves," (*tegwak, tegoak*) plural of *tegw,* "a wave," the same word used for a river. Thus Father O'Brien's definition is the same as the others', but his word is different.

The idea of a swelling, of waves rising sharply, with the words given, led to finding in Rasles *mag8in,* a "swelling," (*enflure,* 215); in Nudenans, *mag8i, inflatio.* So *maagaanteguk* is literally "swelling waves," which, following Rasles, we simplify to *Magwinteguk,* or *Magwintegwak.*

Indian Place-Names of the Maine Coast 73

CAMDEN.

Mad-a-kam-ig-os'-sek. The modern Penobscot name for Camden. "The name given to Camden on account of its mountains," wrote Joseph Nicolar, who spelled it *Matar-kar-mi-co-suk*. *Madakamigosset* is Father O'Brien's spelling of the same name, with the meaning, "Ridge, high lands."

Kamighe is a very old word for "high land," *-mighe* being the inseparable root for "land" and *ka-* (*kees*) being associated with height, bigness (Gatschet).

The prefix *mad-* is the Micmac *mag-*, "big," not *mada-*, "at the end of," nor *matche-*, "bad," nor yet *mada-*, "homely, poor, worn out," though this same word in some places might mean "land of not much value." "The Big Ridge" is the name of Camden. It is equally well written *Madakamigusset*.

The old names in the early histories of Camden reduce to this word. *Mar-tac-a-ma-coose*, which Lewis Ogier gave to Locke (*History of Camden*, 1859, 62-63), when resyllabled is *Matakamigus*, and James Thorndike's *Netuc-hama-coose* (same reference) easily pronounces as *Netakamicus*. Both are Nicolar's form, lacking the locative ending.

Meg-un'-ti-cook, probably "big mountain harbor." In old times the harbor at Camden; the name later extended to a mountain, stream, and lake, to which it does not belong.

The word was long in coming to a settled form, and we have found no very early instances of its use. Megunticook, Segunticook, and Negunticook seem to have been used almost indifferently, leading to the inference that the word may have been a disintegrating form of an earlier word.

Twenty years ago Professor Ganong wrote: "I think it involves the root *-adn-*, a hill or mountain, as in Ktaadn. I am not so sure of the root *mag-*. If it were Micmac or Maliseet, it would be perfectly clear, for that is their word for *great* or *big*." At that time we did not realize how many of our Maine names were from Micmac roots. Provisionally at least, we assume that *Meg-* is the Micmac *mag-*, "big," that *-un-* stands for *-atn-*, or *-adn-*, the root for a mountain, and that the ending *-ticook*, a water word, is "stream or harbor," the whole making "big mountain harbor." It may be a broken form of *Mecadacut*.

We prefer to assign the name to the harbor, since early usage seems to have placed it there. The Survey Map of 1795 puts the word "Negunticook" upon the large outer harbor, and Locke said: "In 1769 Camden *at the harbor* was known as Negunticook or Megunticook" (*History of Camden,* 1859, 66 n.). The inner harbor, which would have been the one most used in early days of small craft, is so quiet and safe that, if it belonged there, the word could not have had the meaning assigned to it by the best Indians, and it could not have belonged to Lincolnville where there is no stream or harbor, except at the Duck-trap.

Paul Coffin's statement, in 1796, that Camden was formerly called Medumcook (*loc cit.,* p. 336) is an error. Medumcook was the name of Friendship.

Mec-ad'-a-cut, Mec-add'-a-cut. The name for Camden given by Capt. John Smith in 1614.

Smith wrote: "And Northwest of Penobscot is Mecaddacut, at the foot of a high Mountaine, a kinde of fortresse against the Tarratines, adjoyning to the high Mountains of Pennobscot, against whose feet doth beat the sea." (*The Historie of New England,* MacLehose ed. *Works,* II:23; VI:214).

We get the picture if we remember that the Tarratines were not a native Maine tribe, but invading Micmacs frm Nova Scotia who for several years previous to Smith's visit had been coming to harry this region and who later conquered it and held it for one or two decades. The Indian village was where the center of the town now is, and when attacked, the inhabitants had only to run up steep Mount Battie, close by, to reach an impregnable place.

Mount Battie can be climbed on its eastern and southern sides only along the crest of the angle where these sides meet. Even then, the climb is arduous, as the writer knows well from many trips up it by that trail between 1876 and 1892, when summering in Camden. Mount Battie would indeed be "a kinde of fortresse" to any who could flee up this hard, rocky trail, easily defended by rolling down rocks from above. "The high Mountaines of Pennobscot" are Mount Megunticook and the Lincolnville hills, fronting upon Penobscot Bay.

With the situation understood, it is not hard to analyze Smith's word. It is Micmac, or perhaps Maliseet, from *mag-* (*mec-*), "great"; *-ad-* (for *-adene-*), the inseparable root for a mountain;

and a locative ending equivalent to -*cook*—"big mountain place," perhaps the name of the stream upon which the village stood, perhaps of the harbor.

The word is substantially the same as Megunticook. Ketchum suggested that it might be *Magadnicook,* "big mountain place," which was what Dr. Ganong had said years before. Father O'Brien has *megankek* as a "steep hill," and almost a century ago Sogabason Neptune gave Locke the word *Chebogardinac,* a "high hill" (Locke, *op. cit.,* 63 n.), using a late Penobscot form with *k'chi,* "big," replacing the older *mag.*

John Smith's form with the doubled letter suggests that -*adda*- was intended for -*adene*-, "mountain," but the sound was not quite caught. *Mecadnecut* would give the roots.

Mount Battie, Mount Batty, Beatty, or Betty. The steep, rocky hill nearest the city of Camden.

The spelling is very variable. Locke wrote: "Mount Batty ... derived its name from Betty Richards, wife of James Richards, the pioneer settler. She always used to call it her mountain and thus the early settlers used to call it Betty's Mountain, or Mt. Batty" (John L. Locke, *History of Camden,* 1859, 63). The story is repeated by Reuel Robinson (*History of Camden and Rockport,* 1907).

The story is folk-etymology. The mountain was called Mount Betty ten years before Elizabeth Richards, who came in 1768, ever saw the place. In 1757, James Cargill, in his *Scout Report,* said: "Again camped at mouth of little river south of Mount Betty" (Maine Historical Society *Collections,* Doc. Ser. XXIV, 76). This passage was cited by John Tewksbury (*Sprague's Journal of Maine History,* XIV, 1928, No. 1, p. 12). A surveyor's map dated May, 1795, has on it "Mount Betty" (Massachusetts Archives, Maps and Plans, #1350).

The name Mount Betty seems to connect with the numerous alewife names of Knox County, some of which have been misapplied to hills, as the Madambettox Hills of Rockland. Indians were superstitiously afraid of mountains and seem seldom to have had names for those which were not associated with some myth or used as landmarks. This led white settlers to transfer to the hills the names of ponds, rivers, or streams near them which had Indian names, but such ones as an Indian would not have used of a land feature. The outlet of the present Megunticook Lake must have swarmed with alewives which went up into the lake to breed, and very likely it had an alewife name, now lost, which might have been transferred to the mountain. This, however, is conjectural; all we are sure of is that we do not know how Mount Battie got its name.

ROCKLAND.

Bed-a-bed-ek (probably accented on the last syllable). Low land near Rockland, probably the site of the city.

A footnote by Dr. Ganong in the definitive edition of Champlain's works, says: "After Champlain's map of 1632, it [Bedabedek] vanished until 1755, when it appears on the Green-Jefferys map applied to Owl's Head at the western entrance to Penobscot Bay. Jefferys took it directly from Champlain and Ballard followed Jefferys" (Champlain, *Works,* Toronto, 1918, I, 286 n.) *C. Owls où Bedabedek* on a German form and *Cape Bedabedek* on a French form of Jefferys are both intended for Owls Head just below Rockland (Massachusetts Archives, Maps collected in France, II, Nos. 716 and 979).

Jefferys had no warrant for placing the name on Owls Head. All Champlain said was, "On the west is low land, called by the Indians *Bedabedek.*" The contour lines of the topographical map show that the lowest land lies between Rockland and Thomaston, and this low level marked the all-important carrying place by which the Indians journeyed from Penobscot Bay to George's River. When they came into Rockland Harbor they steered for this spot, which needed and would be sure to have a name descriptive of it.

Father O'Brien's notes suggest that *Bedabedek* may be only a form of *Wedebegek,* "the beginning of the bay," probably meaning "of Penobscot Bay." However, there was no pressing need for the Indians to describe Rockland Harbor as the beginning of Penobscot Bay. From the voyageur's point of view it would be much more likely for him to look upon the low land ahead as the end of his journey, the head of the bay, where he would find the carry.

There is a Micmac word for "the end of a sheet of water," *Wekobek,* with the locative *Wekobekek,* which might apply, and

Father Aubéry gives *P8debeg8* (locative *Poudebegek*) for *"golfe d'une rivière,"* which might compete with *Wedebegek*. All end in *-begek,* "still water," a "pond," a "quiet bay," leaving a choice between *weko-, wede-,* and *poude-* for the first stem.

Remembering that the French had no *w* and another letter had to be substituted, we might reasonably account for the change of the initial. Of the three, we should prefer *wede-,* making it from the Maliseet root WET-, WEK-, PAT-, which means the end, the extremity, the "head" of something. *Wet-e-beg-ek'* would thus mean "head of the bay," where was the end of the carry and *Catawamtek,* the "great landing place." In this case the word would be Maliseet or Micmac.

The name *Medombetick Bay* for Rockland Harbor found on an old map (*Pejepscot Papers,* VIII, 76-76a) might cause the inquiry whether Bedabedek and Medombetick were not the same word. On the contrary, it is more reasonable to infer that *Bedabedek* was a word so old and unfamiliar that it was not understood and in place of it someone had substituted a familiar and more modern term from a newer language.

Cat-a-wamt'-ek. The Great Landing Place, in Rockland, later Lermond's Cove, near Crockett's Point of topographical maps.

Cyrus Eaton gives *Catawamteak* and *Katawamteag* (*History of Thomaston,* 1865, I, 8 and 23) from which we should suppose the word meant "the principal sand beach"; but Joseph Nicolar has a better form. He wrote:

"*Catar-gwan-tic,* 'Grand Landing.' Now known as the city of Rockland. This was always used as a landing place for those who were going south. Canoes were generally taken out and carried across, that the 'boisterous White Head' might be avoided, for the way round White Head was considered dangerous, also by carrying across into George's River two miles, a trip of fifteen miles was saved." (Nicolar's distances are too short; this carry was more than three miles.)

Nicolar's form of the word needs some reconstruction. As *K't-angwant'-ek* it would be made from *k't* (for *keght*) "principal," and *angwan'* (from *aguahass'-odi*), "a landing-place," with the locative ending. *K't-aguant'-ek,* "the greatest landing-place," was the old name for the Rockland water front.

In the Indian days, Rockland Harbor was the great traffic center of western Penobscot Bay. From this Grand Landing ran three carries to different points westward, the Lower, Middle, and Upper Trails (Cyrus Eaton, *op. cit.,* 23), and because of this the Thomaston peninsula was an important place in the strategic control of Maine; hence the French claims and the location by the English of Fort St. George at Thomaston.

> NOTE. Some months after the two preceding names were written out, I came upon what may be the solution of *Bedabedek*. In the *Eastport Sentinel* for September 15, 1897, that fine scholar Dr. A. S. Gatschet wrote that the old name for St. Stephen, New Brunswick, was *K'chi medabiaught,* "the great landing." Now *medabi-* is practically the same as *bedabe-,* while the endings *-aught* (probably *-ak*) and *-ek* are easily reconciled.
>
> It would seem that *Bedabedek* was the old Maliseet, or Micmac, name for which *K't-aguantek* (*Catawamtek*) was the Abnaki equivalent, and that both mean "the great landing place," confirming our belief that this was the feature of the place most needing a name.

Owls Head. The promontory at the western entrance to Penobscot Bay. So called, says Nicolar, "from its resemblance to the neck and head of an owl when viewed from the north side."

Nicolar's *Coo-coo-har-want'-buk* and Ballard's *Co-co-cas-want'ep-up* approximate the better form *Ko-ko-hass'-want'ep-ek,* made from *ko-ko-hass',* the Penobscot name for the barred owl, and *w'antep,* "his head," with the locative ending. (Nicolar's *har* is a misprint for *has'*.)

The possessive *i* does not appear in this word, because parts of the body have the personal possessive pronouns, my, thy, his, etc., coalescing with the word, which looks entirely different for each person. In this one *w* is the possessive "his" and *antep* is "head." In English we would write the word *Ko'kohas-wahtep'-ek,* The Owl's Head.

Chick-a-wau'-kee. Lake furnishing the water supply of Rockland, formerly Tolman Pond.

An imported name, meaningless here. "The name Chickawakie," says Locke, "has but recently been bestowed upon Tolman's Pond and is said in the Indian to mean 'sweet water.' The oldest Indians with whom we have conversed are ignorant of the name, which was given, we believe, by certain citizens of Rockland" (*History of Camden,* 1859, 63).

Med·am·bat'·tek, Med·am·bet·tox. Tolman Pond, now known as Chickawaukee Lake, near Rockland. The outlet is Mill River in Thomaston. Also Madambettox Mountain, near the Lake.

Cyrus Eaton said, in 1865 (*History of Thomaston,* etc., I, 3n.), that "Mary, daughter of the old Penobscot chief Neptune," said Medambettox was "from *mad-,* great, *om, am,* or *um,* suckers, which, with the *beses* or *betticks,* according to Potter, would make it Great-sucker-pond-place, implying that the pond was named first and its name transferred to the adjoining mountain."

One could not find a poorer authority than Judge Potter, so that his contribution may be safely discarded. Mary Malt (that is, Martha) Neptune, married a Nicolar and was the mother of Joseph Nicolar, so often quoted. She was a very intelligent woman and lived for some years in Warren; what she said is worth attention. However, her English was not equal to her intelligence, and she seems to have given the wrong English name to the fish she undoubtedly knew well and intended to name. The name of a sucker is *abodumqueh,* "something with a turning-out mouth." She probably had in mind *mahdames,* "an alewife," and the first two syllables *medam-* stand for this word. Mill River was one of the most notable alewife fishing places the Indians resorted to. The fish ran up into the pond to breed, for they were never found on a stream which did not have a pond on it for spawning ground. Therefore it seems likely that the name was given from a fish which it is known was seasonally present in vast quantities rather than for one not likely to occur.

What *battek* or *bettox* means I do not know, possibly *-baygook,* "still water," or "pond." If so, the word means "Alewife Pond."

The Mathebestic or Madebustuck Hills, mentioned by Church, the Indian fighter, in 1696, were in this vicinity. Sibley thinks Dodge's Mountain was Mt. Madambettox (*History of Union,* 1851, 21) and he may be right; but the name was a transfer from pond to mountain, therefore meaningless. There can be nothing in Sibley's conjecture that Bedabedek, Madambattuk, and Mecadacut are the same word (*op. cit.,* 21). An old map in *Pejepscot Papers* (VIII, 76-76a) has "Medombetick Bay" for Rockland Harbor and "Medombetech Hills" for Dodge Mountain.

SOUTH THOMASTON.

Wessawes'keag. A short tidal river confined within the great peninsula now South Thomaston. The place is of importance in history as debatable ground between the French and English possessions. The English built St. George's Fort in the present Thomaston, and a Frenchman was holding Wessaweskeag Creek. Because it was a short route on the line of east and west travel, the neck of the peninsula was of great importance in early days.

When we examine Madockawando's Indian deed of 1694 and certain French papers, we see that they have direct bearing upon the meaning of the Indian word.

Drake quoted the deed carelessly (*Book of the Indian*, III: 108); and Baxter, in printing the abstract of the list of twenty-nine Indian deeds to Maine lands (probably following an early copy) (Maine Historical Society *Collections,* Doc. Ser., XXIII, 204), filled in a blank space in the original deed (*York Deeds,* X, fol. 237) and, no doubt correctly, said "Hatch's Cove Island" where the modern topographical map has "Hatchet Cove."

The deed reads: 10 May, 1694, Madockawando to Sir William Phipps, land "bounded east by *Wessaweskek* River; west by ye West side of [blank] Cove Island ... and so by a straight line as high as ye uppermost Falls of St. George's River aforesd as also a Certain Island laying before ye mouth of sd River called and known by ye name of *Matomquoog,* together with all ye Islands comonly called and known by ye name of St. George's Island."

St. George's Islands were those where Captain Waymouth harbored in 1605; Hatch's Cove Island was Friendship Island. Somewhere between them was Matomquoog, discussed elsewhere. The deed shows that the Indians sold Phipps land on both sides of George's River as far east as the Wessaweskeag, or to about the middle of the peninsula.

The French source, for which I am indebted to Dr. William F. Ganong, is the *Inventaire des Concessions en Fief et Seigneurie,* by Pierre Georges Roy, Archiviste de la Province du Quebec, IV, 178 (Quebec, 1927-8).

This states that to Thomas Lefebvre, interpreter of the Abnaki language, there was granted *"lieu appelé 'Kouesanouskek' ... à commencer du cote du nord à la pointe appelé Meniekec, et con-*

tinuer en remontant au sudouest du cote de la rivière Saint-Georges. . . ." (*"Kwesanouskek* . . . to begin on the north coast at a sharp end called *Menikek* and to keep on up the southwest shore of the Georges River").

This can mean nothing but the whole peninsula of South Thomaston and Saint George, *including* the land deeded to Phipps by the Indians. *Meniekec* (in another place printed *Meniquet*) is the same word as *Moniecook* (Eaton, *History of Warren*, 2nd ed., 1877, 33), though without proof we cannot say it was the same place. The word means Shelter Island, or Harbor Island, and is of frequent occurrence.

We are sure that Lefebvre lived in South Thomaston; for Cyprian Southack's map calls the Wessaweskeag "Lefaver's River." His mill must have been the old tide-mill in South Thomaston. He is the Lefavor of Benjamin Church, the old Indian fighter, and was early on the spot. A document of 4 May, 1707 (*Inventaire*, IV, 178), says that the English burned Lefebvre's buildings, took his furniture, and carried him and his family to Boston as prisoners. Another, in 1708, mentions him as "le feu Lefebure" (the late Lefebre) and continues his grant to his son Pierre, also an interpreter, with shares for his sisters. A document of 1725 speaks of the place as "le fief *Kouesanouskek, ou Pentagouet*"—which it was not, since Pentagouet was Castine—unless this is a literal use of the word, meaning "the falls" (see Pentagoet) for the tide-falls of the Wessaweskeag.

What proof have we that this *Kouesanouskek* was South Thomaston? The Indian name itself, for one thing. Also a letter of October 29, 1724, from Governor Vaudreuil to Acting-Governor Dummer remainds him that St. George's River was the boundary between the French and the English, and reproaches him with building "without leave a ffort on the land of one Lefevre . . . that s^d Lefevre had an habitation at Hosanoueskat."

The only fort Dummer could have built here was the one at Thomaston, known as St. George's Fort. If it was on Lefebre's land, then by the terms of his seigneurie, Lefebre owned the whole peninsula. By the terms of Madockawando's deed, Phipps owned half of it!

The rights and the wrongs of this matter may be left to the historians—the Indian name is our sole concern. We can see that it was essential for the French to *claim* the whole peninsula because that carry from Rockland to Thomaston was the life-line of Indian communication to the westward, just as the carry between New Harbor and Pemaquid (which made it possible to avoid going around stormy Pemaquid Point in bad weather) was their life-line a little farther west. We can see that *Kouesanouskek* must have been the name of the whole peninsula.[1]

Wessaweskeag means a "tidal creek," or in the vernacular a "salt creek." It is the name of the little tidal river where the old Frenchman had his tide-mill, the site of which is just above the road across the peninsula in South Thomaston. But when we have the full name *Kouesanouskat*, the name of his bailiwick, much is added to the picture. The first element in this is the unmistakable *Kwesawayk*, a point of land; the second, *-ouskat*, is the outrunning tide—a point of land, or peninsula with a tidal creek in it—"tide-creek peninsula." Nowhere else in Maine perhaps is so strong a tide-power confined entirely within so limited a space.

Wessaweskeag, the stream, is now called Weskeag; formerly it was Westsouwestkeag, Whisgig, or simply The Gigg. The last is found in the journal of the French geologist Monvel, in 1792. The statement, quoted by Eaton, that it "signified in the Indian tongue, land of sights (prospects, visions, or ghosts), wizard point" (*Annals of Warren*, 1877, 143) is not worth contradicting. The word conveyed a picture of a tidal creek in a salt marsh and the *Wessa-* is merely a corruption of *Kwesa-* explained above.

THOMASTON.

Quis-quam'-ego—Eaton, *Annals of Warren*, second edition, 1877, 23.

---

[1] The original of Vaudreuil's letter is in the Massachusetts Archives, 52:77-84. When I examined it some years ago, I read the word as *Kasanoueskek*. The *copy* in London, printed by J. P. Baxter (*Pioneers of New France in New England*, 343) reads *Hosanoueskat*, not a good Indian form. Trask, reprinting the letters of Col. Thomas Westbrook, has the impossible *kannoveskail* (p. 81). Williamson (*History*, II:40, 42) has the good one *Ques-a-nouskek*. It is only justice to Williamson to call to attention that he knew the unprinted papers which dealt with this affair; as also did Cyrus Eaton (*History of Warren*, 1877, 33), perhaps through Williamson.

Quis-quit-cum'egek—Eaton, *History of Thomaston, Rockland, etc.,* 1865, I, 23.

Squitcom'egek Falls—*Pejepscot Papers,* Map, VIII, 76-76a.

"The present Rockland Harbor was called Catawamteak or Katawamteag, signifying *great-landing-place,* from which they took the trail to Mill River. Of these Indian trails, the principal ones in the territory of Old Thomaston were much used and frequently spoken of in early times. That above named was used in passing to St. George's River for the purpose of fishing at the falls or proceeding to the ocean on their way westward. Another was that from the head of Owl's Head Bay directly across to the bay on George's River, the high intervening land of which they early called Quisquamego, and in later times Quesquitcumegek, or *high-*carrying-place. A third was from the same Head of the Bay to the headwaters of the Wessaweskeag by which they avoided the tedious and exposed passage around Owl's Head. These were known to the early settlers and hunters, as the Upper, Middle, and Lower Trails" (*History of Thomaston,* I, 23).

The form *Quisquamego* was used in 1701 by Capt. Sylvanus Davis in his list of English settlements east of the Kennebec— "On the east side of Quisquamego, Philip Swaden, fifty years ago, besides fishermen 60 or 70 years" (Sullivan, *History of the District of Maine,* 1795, 391).

The later form *Quisquit-cumegek* Eaton must have got from Indians. *Squitcomegek* is the same, abbreviated by English use and applied to the falls on Mill River where there was an alewife fishery not very far from the new Knox Mansion.

The original name did not apply to either a carry or falls and fisheries: it was the name of the long, high ridge which follows the east shore of St. George's River, the highway of today. *Cumegek* is *kamighek,* "high land," from *kes-* or *kees-,* "high," and the inseparable *-mighe,* "land." *Quisquit* is *kweni,* or *kwesah'wi,* "long." "The long ridge."

This is *Kw'seh-kam'egus,* an old word, so said Lewey Ketchum, for a horseback, or glacial ridge. *Kwesah* is also a commonly used word for a point, cape, or peninsula, when suitably modified, as *kwesahweik',* "a point," *kwesahwah'kek,* "a peninsula" (Rasles).

Kwe'-sah-kam'-e-gus, "the long ridge," would be a better form than Eaton's.

Georgekeag, or **Georgekee.** Thomaston.

Cyrus Eaton thought this name was applied by the Indians to the shore at the head of St. George's Bay between Mill River and Oyster River (*History of Thomaston,* I, 1865, 23). He also says that Lt. Gov. John Neptune "says the Indian name of the river was *Joiges,* meaning *delightsome*" (*History of Warren,* 2nd. ed., 1877, 16).

Eaton's explanation and defence of the name is labored and weak, and his tribal distinctions are valueless; nor is Neptune's statement to be taken too seriously, for it seems to have been only one of "Old Governor's" jokes.

Georgekeag is English, with an Indian tag-ending. The fort and trading house here had made the name of *George's* so familiar that it was early adopted and Indianized. Such instances were not uncommon. In Whiting, Washington County, an Indian pointed out to the writer a place which he called *Kennelclin.* Years before, Dr. Ganong had found the word on an old map made by an Indian in 1798, and neither of us could explain it. Because I was on the place itself I persisted in questioning until at last I was made to understand that long ago a Colonel Crane had lived there. When they carried by on their way to Machias waters, the Indians used to stop at Colonel Crane's, which in their pronunciation became *Kennelclin.* Not far away I was given another long Indian word which translated into "small chimes" and was meaningless to me until I elicited the information that a man named Bell used to live there. The Indians called him "Little Bell" and his home "Little Bell's place"; and had translated his name, possessive case and all, very literally into the plural number!

Segohquet. St. George's River.

It has been said that the aboriginal name of this river is unknown. However, it was too important to have escaped record, and we may consider Strachey and Smith as meaning this river, or better, this sound, by the following words:

    1605. *Segohquet*—Strachey, *History of Travaile into Virginia* (which then included New England).
    1614. *Segochet*—Capt. John Smith.

The two words are identical and probably were pronounced alike. If divided as *Se-gohq-uet* and *Se-goc-het,* we see clearly the root *sauk,* an outlet, the mouth of a river, a flowing-out place. Like Saco and Sagadahoc, St. George's comes into the sea as a river, not with a great expanding bay, like Penobscot and St. Croix. *Se-gok-et,* "at the outlet," if not the name of the river, denoted some place near its mouth. Foxwell resided at "Saquid Point"; John Brown claimed land at "Saquid"; and modern Penobscot Indians called Pleasant Point, "Sunkheath," which is very close to the way they used to pronounce *Sunkhaze.* All these words argue a close connection with the early *Segohquet* and point to its being the name of the river.

Tahanock. The Simancas Map of 1610 has this name just east of St. George's River, apparently the name of the river. Dr. Banks suggested that it might contain the root *-adn-,* "mountain," and refer to the Camden or some nearer hills. This, however, is contrary to Indian nomenclature; the name should be something near enough or individual enough for identification of the place, and no one could identify this river by hills so far away, invisible in a thick haze. Either the Simancas Map has the name in the wrong place, or else the word has some other root. We suspect some connection with the Micmac *uktan,* "the open sea," the more so as the Simancas map has Monhegan Island as "I. St. George," an English instead of an Indian name.

ST. GEORGE.

Monie′cook. Barter's Island, in St. George River.

Eaton (*Annals of Warren,* 2nd ed., 1877, 33) says that "Barter's Island, off Pleasant Point in Cushing, bore within the memory of one aged woman, the name *Moniekek,* or *Moniecook,* which name an Indian interpreted as meaning 'land or island joined to an island,' which well corresponds with Barter's Island, described as consisting of two islands with a connecting neck of land, visible only at low tide."

But *Moniekek* is not the word for a "bar island." Instead of translating the word, the Indian was describing the place to which the name was applied. When we divide the word properly as *Mon-iec′-ook,* we see that we have the locative form of the old Micmac *mun-eek′,* "an island," and specifically an island lying out at sea, or protecting against the sea, a "shelter island" or "harbor island." A bar-island, like the one described, would be a good harbor island for Indians, whose canoes were not moored out but drawn up ashore wherever they landed. Such a harbor island is Menikuk at the end of Cape Newagen. Another is Menikoe Island near Portland.

The name is found again, in documents, of some place near Barter's Island. On 7 May, 1703, land in the present Thomaston was granted to Thomas Lefebre, Abnaki interpreter, "nord à la pointe appellé *Meniekec.*" Four years later the word is spelled *Meniquet.* The *word* is the Micmac *munee'kek,* a "harbor island"; but the terms of the original grant make it seem impossible to be Barter's Island.

UNION.

Sen-ni-bek, or **Sun-ni-bec.** A lake in Union, formerly called Sunnybec Pond.

Sibley says that "Governor Neptune and some others of the Penobscot tribe of Indians are not able to give the meaning of the word Sennebec" and adds that David Crockett had recently "made inquiries of the Indian doctor of the Penobscot tribe, who intimated that *soony* meant shady, and *bec* meant a place where other water comes across a main channel" (*History of Union,* 1851, 3).

Sen- is one root for a "rock", *nebeak,* "still water"; "rocky pond." A friend who knows it, says that it is rocky.

Nusalkchunangan. Place and meaning unknown.

The word rests upon a single mention, in a letter from Father Lauverjat to Father Rasles, dated *Nusalkchunangan,* July, 1724, only a few days before Rasles' death. The form (in Baxter's *Pioneers of New France in New England,* 338) was copied by Mr. Baxter from the original in the London Public Records Office, and the list of documents says "the fight at Winslow." Lt. Winslow and men were killed May, 1724, at St. George's River; and as Lauverjat speaks of seven men killed and two boats burned, probably this is the Winslow engagement. The place from which Lauverjat was writing was probably somewhere about Penobscot Bay, and the last part of the word, *chunangan,* might be *k'tchiamangan,* "the big fish-weir."

The nearest word to this that we have found is *Nutskamongan* (*q.v.*) where the Mikumwessak warned the Indians. Both evidently were fishing places and must have been villages, at least seasonally.

WALDOBORO-THOMASTON.

Matomquoog, Madomcook, and *Medumcook* are three names, substantially alike in meaning, which may, however, refer to different places.

Mat-omqu-oog. An island at the mouth of St. George's River.

The Indian deed of Madockawando to Sir William Phipps, 6 May, 1694, names an island called *Matomquoog.*

The word is from *mata-,* "at the mouth of"; *omqu'* (*amk*), "sand"; *-oog* (*-ook*), a locative ending generally associated with water, often indicating a harbor. This was some sandy island near the mouth of George's River; identification could be made only by someone familiar with the locality.

Mad-omc-ook. The word is the same as the above and the place is probably the same. The old map in *Pejepscot Papers* (VIII, 76-76a) which contained this name placed it upon an island, apparently near Waldoboro.

Med-unc-ook. The roots are the same as in the two words above. Willis says that Medumcook was Sandy Harbor in Friendship (Maine Historical Society *Collections,* IV, 104), and a modern Penobscot translated the word as meaning "blocked by sand," which is correct. Others call it the tidal river between Cushing and Friendship; but this is probably a late transfer, since it is not a river word.

Sibley says: "Me-dum-cook, by some said to mean 'a sandy, gravelly, poor place, or poor country' " (*History of Union,* 1851, 64). His division of the words fails to catch the first root, *med-, met-,* or *mat-,* "at the mouth of," "at the end of," which shows that the sandy country is near the mouth of a stream or river, which is indicated by the ending *-ook.*

WALDOBORO.

We have a bewildering variety of Indian words in the vicinity of Waldoboro, most of them apparently connected with fish and fishing. The names appear in documents of unquestionable authenticity, chiefly early deeds, which go back to the original Indian conveyances. Yet even then, several wholly different names were sometimes used for the same place, and often the variety does not contribute to the clearing of the problems they create. These Indian names may be taken one by one, as they appear in deeds, and the derivation and meaning given in a summary of the usage.

It should be explained that though the Muscongus and the Medomac are both called rivers, only the latter is properly a river. Muscongus is a sound. It is sheltered from the sea by Muscongus Island and other islands and receives only a small fresh-water inflow. It was a favorite Indian resort and had a very old Indian town, which was visited by Capt. John Smith, located probably at the tiny basin just on the Bremen-Bristol line.

The Medomac, on the other hand, was a considerable river, rising in ponds in Liberty and opening into a great sea-bay of the same name. It was a notable resort of alewives, a great fishing ground for Indians.

The term *Muscongus,* says Johnston, the historian of Bremen and Bristol, who is our best authority, was applied to "the whole territory from Round Pond to Medomac Falls." Therefore we might expect to find it not only upon the large island and the sound called Muscongus, but along the coast for about eight miles, where the contour lines of the topographical maps show shores that are steep and ledgy. Dr. Johnston, who was a geologist as well as a historian, speaks of the "barrier of rock" which runs N.N.E. and W.S.W. "on nearly the whole eastern shore from the lighthouse at the point (Pemaquid) to the northern limit of the town" (of Bremen)—(John Johnston, *History of the Towns of Bremen and Bristol,* Albany, 1873, 4). Therefore we might expect to find some connection between the name *Muscongus* and this rocky shore. What we do discover is interesting and sufficiently curious: the Indians kept the rock-name; the English called it by a fish-name!

BRISTOL.

Mus-cong-us. An island, a large bay, and a sound (formerly called Muscongus River) in Bristol, Lincoln County.

Old deeds give Muscongus as the English usage, the Indians preferring other words and limiting Muscongus to a tiny bay almost upon the Bristol-Bremen line. The following list of dated occurrences, most of them being from deeds, can be located today with exactitude:

1614. *Nuskoncus*—Capt. John Smith (*Description of New England*). From its relative position in his list of places, this must be Muscongus; his *Muscoucus* is a misprint.

1625. *Mescombe* or *Meecombe*—Purchas (*Pilgrims*). Considering how open to errors by copyists and printers was Purchas, we feel sure that this word was intended for the then important place later known as Muscongus.

1625. *Muscongus Island*—Deed of Samoset to John Brown. It should be remembered that although the authenticity of this deed has been challenged, the Indian word need not be considered as late as the deed.

1641. *Remobscus*—Deed of Samoset and other Indian sagamores to Richard Pearce of Remobscus—(Johnston, *History of Bristol*, etc., 63). The name preferred by the Indians is used here.

1694. *Mesconkes*—Deed of Indian Sagamores to Sylvanus Davis, 10 May, 1694, of land "Called and Known by ye name of *Mesconkes*, beginning at a Point of Land Comonly Called and known by ye name of *Madaamok* Point to ye fresh falls called *Magasewannussuck*"—(*York Deeds*, X, fol. 258). We see that a slight error of a copyist would have made Purchas' *Mescombe* from this word.

1716. *Masconks*—(*York Deeds*, VIII, fol. 177.)

1717. *Muscongus*—Pearce of Marblehead to Ewen, 400 acres "which was *by ye Indians called Penobscott* and by ye English Muscongus"—(*York Deeds*, X, fol. 265.)

1726. *Musconasht*, "near Pemequid" and "land up ye river in sd *Musconasht* and *Musconcush*"—Pearce to Barnes (*York Deeds*, XVI, fol. 47).

1730. *Misconques*, "a place called Pemiquida or *Misconques*" (*York Deeds*, XVI:46).

1731. *Miscongas*—(*York Deeds*, XVI:97.)

1731. *Miscongus*—(*York Deeds*, XVI:296.)

1731. *Miscoges*—(*York Deeds*, XVI:359.)

1733. *Miscongus River*—(*York Deeds*, XVI:349.)

1733. *Miskonkas Bay*—(*York Deeds*, XVI:597.)

1734. *Muscongus*—(*York Deeds*, XVI:420.)

Here is the record of more than a hundred years. The most we can gather is that Capt. John Smith could spell better than

"Pears of Mavilhead"! *Musconasht* and *Musconcush,* by the same person, are only soft endings of the regular *Muscongus*. *Mesconkes* is perhaps the most helpful of all: it may contain the secret of the word. We know that John Smith gave the word *Nuskoncus* as the name of an Indian town. We know that old deeds speak of "Injun town" at the little bay called Muscongus. We know that this was a remarkable place for catching smelts which ran up the stream leading from Webber Pond above. And here in the first syllable of *Meskonkes* we see that fish-word, *mes-* for *anmessoo,* while *-konk-* is a strong reminder of *-congan,* "a fishing place." While the ending might be a diminutive, *sis,* it is more likely the peculiar Penobscot locative *-s*.

Personal inspection of the little harbor shows it to have been remarkably well adapted to Indian occupation and without doubt a fine fishing place where countless numbers of fish could have been scooped up with the hands or small nets as they tried to ascend the steep brook. Also in O'Brien's notes appears the entry, "*Anmessokantisis,* Muscongus," showing that he had made a similar connection through the slightly different word *kannti,* indicating an occurrence, or abundance—"small plenty-place for alewives."

Muscongus is a fishing word, originally probably limited to the little bay to which the name Muscongus is attached on topographical maps—(this, however, because there was once here a post office by the name, now discontinued). Except for this one small place it seems not to have been used by the Indians, who preferred *Arramobscus, Seremobscus, Amobscot,* and even *Penobscot,* all made from the root *obs-, ops-,* "ledge," for the long rocky shore which the whites called Muscongus. Follows the history of the Indian usage:

> *Remobscus.* Found in various entries between 1717 and 1724.
> *Remobsquis Stream.* Between Round Pound and Broad Bay. On an old map, not dated, in *Pejepscot Papers,* VIII:76-76a.
> *Remobsey.* Variant in another deed (*York Deeds,* X, fol. 27).
> *Penobscot.* Deed of Pearce to Ewen, 400 acres, definitely of land at Muscongus; no connection with Penobscot River or Bay.
> *Penobseese* River. Deed of Pearce, 1724, of land at Muscongus, "fronting on Penobseese River" (*York Deeds,* XVI:694). "By ye Indians called *Penobscot* and by ye English Muscongus," reads another deed (*York Deeds,* X, folios 265 and 271).

Remobsquis and *Penobseese* are apparently diminutives of *Remobscus* and *Penobscot*—which are the same word!

To the casual reader this will not be apparent; to the Indian student it is clear without further comment except to note that the place-ending *-scus* is found on Penobscot waters in some words still in use, like *Umbazukskus.*

Amobscot. Another variant, in 1719, in the deposition of John Pearce, who says he was born there in 1652 and until he was eighteen lived "on the eastern coast called by the Indians *Amobscot* and by the English Muscongus" (*York Deeds,* XII, pt. ii: fol. 323).

Arramopsquis. Again that apparent diminutive, equivalent to *Remobsquis.* Named in deeds of Pearce to Smith, 1733 (*York Deeds,* XVI :250) and of Smith to Lewis (*York Deeds,* XVI :533) of land on "the west side of *Arramopsquis or Miscongus River* below the falls comonly called *Medomock Falls"* (*York Deeds,* XVI :533).

This fully identifies the place with the main Medomack River, a very considerable stream, leaving us much in doubt whether the ending is really a diminutive. The word also has the singular prefix *arra-* which we find often in the names of large falls and so far have been unable to explain. In this deed it is definitely connected with the important Medomak Falls. It appears again as *Arrimobscus* (*York Deeds,* XVIII:259).

Seremobscus. Yet again we find, in 1720, *"Seremobscus* by the Indians, by the English Muscongus" (*York Deeds,* XVII, fol. 6).

And here we have it!—the clue to the word. *Seremobscus* gives us more than *Remobscus,* which, by beginning with *R,* showed it was a defective form; yet even now we have not the whole word, which must be close to

Meselipemapskek, the modern Penobscot for "much-extended-ledge-place," that long stretch of ledgy coast between Pemaquid Point and the Medomak River.

In the modern Penobscot dialect *meseli* is the *mesairi8i* of Rasles, "much, many." The *8i-* is dropped; *r* changes to *l* and *mesai* becomes *mese; -pemabskek* is the familiar "extended ledge" in the locative form. *Seremobscus* follows the same pattern, dropping the *me-* of Rasles' word, changing *-sairi-* to *-sere-,* "much," shortening -*pem*- to a connecting *m* and closing with the antique -*obscus* instead of -*apskek*.

We are now able to align our various forms and to announce that *Meseremobscus,* "the long ledge place," was the aboriginal name of the coast of the mainland from Pemaquid Point at least as far as Bremen, while *Muscongus* was originally primarily the small harbor near the Bristol-Bremen line, where was a very old Indian village; also quite likely, by extension, waters adjoining toward Waldoboro, where the fishing was good.

WALDOBORO.

Med-om'-ac—a point, bay, and river in Waldoboro, and falls and ponds on the river, a noted resort of alewives. Always pronounced by residents with a strong accent on the second syllable. The word has a number of forms, but since there is no question of the roots involved or the meaning, it is needless to give details beyond the point of clearing up possible confusion.

Madahum'uck—bay, point, and falls on the eastern branch of a river, presumably in Waldoborough. The name found on an old manuscript map in *Pejepscot Papers,* VIII : 76-76a. A carry is marked from these falls to Ammacongan Falls on St. George's River, which, if the scale is correct (as it probably is not), would be only two and a half miles distant. Also, on the same map, the form *Madahunnuck.*

The word is the same as *Madoamok,* the *h* being inserted only to hold the vowels apart, or, more likely a rough breathing (which held the roots apart in Madoamok), omitted by the English.

Madoam'ok Point, "up to ye falls of Magesemanussuk" (*York Deeds,* VIII, fol. 177)—deed of Sylvanus Davis's executor, 13 Sept., 1716, land bought of Indians in 1696.

Medom'ock Falls—Pearce to Ralph Smith, 1732—(*York Deeds,* XVI :250).

The three, the principal, forms are not difficult. The root *am-* in *Madoamok* shows that they are alewife-words. *Mada-* or *med-,* "at the mouth of"; *am-,* "alewife"; -*ok,* locative—"alewives at the mouth" (of the river) is the meaning; we know that the first falls, which would be the place for an alewife fishery, was nearer the river mouth than on other rivers. As Indians named streams from some characteristic near their debouchure, the name is a good one for this place.

The Medomac River was noted for its alewives which crowded up it in inconceivable numbers to spawn in the ponds at its head. Though the Penobscot Indians told Cyrus Eaton that the word signified "a place of many suckers," it is clear that they lacked an English equivalent for the root AM, and by mistake took the English name of sucker instead of alewife. These Indians, Gov. John Neptune, his daughter Mary Malt Necolar, mother of Joseph Nicolar, and some others, spent several years, in the late forties probably, in the neighborhood of Warren and Rockland, knew the country well, and were trustworthy. Errors like this of suckers for alewives were due to lack of understanding English and were unintentional. We have no hesitation in saying, upon the authority of Lt. Gov. Neptune and Cyrus Eaton, that Medomac means "a place of many alewives"—those were the fish found there, that is the root found in the word, that is what they must have meant to say.

In the Muscongus deeds several minor place-names occur which can be located.

Stocemouo Point. Mary Pearce, wife of Richard, disposes of land at Muscongus—"Hog Island . . . in Muscongus River, another small island, Mussel Ridge Island, lying from Hog Island about N.N.E. and from *Stocemouo Point* about N.E." (*York Deeds*, X, fol. 256). This identifies the small island as Oar Island of the topographical maps, and Stocemouo Point as the end of the present Keene Neck.

With only this single occurrence of the word *Stocemouo,* no meaning can be suggested; but there is a possibility, not too remote, that the word is a misreading of Hockomocko, the ancient capital H having been read as two letters and the last *c* printed as *o* from a script which did not contain the second *k;* for thus "Pears of Mavilhead," or whoever did his writing for him, spelled.

Hogamockock Point. "Pears of Remobscey" deeded to Perry of Falmouth land "beginning at *Hogamockock Point* and running westerly to Ed. Ewens Point laying upon Greenland River; and upon the westwardly side to the *Indian Town,* likewise one half of an island lying on the easterly side of the Indian Town and one half an island on the east side of Hogamockock Point, bearing the name of Hog Island" (*York Deeds,* X, fol. 271).

Perry to Cowing, 1731 (*York Deeds,* XV, 554), in a deed names Hogamockock Point, Ingin Town, and Hog Island; and Pearce to Dumaresque (*York Deeds,* XVII :fol. 6) speaks of "all that stream of water called the Mill Stream in Smelt Cove which emptieth itself into the middle of Miscongus, alias Marytown."

Greenland River is still on the map, but if what the modern map calls Oar Island were Hog Island, instead of the large island before Muscongus, the old deeds would read perfectly. Hog Island may be only a short name for Hogamockock, which was most likely Keene's Neck (and this the island near it), sometimes called by the not Indian name of Stocemouo.

But for Capt. John Smith and Purchas, this bit of local topography would have little interest for us, but we see the Indian Town at Smith's Nusconkus becoming Marytown at Smelt Cove and the brook from Webber's Pond the Mill Stream, and the white occupation taking over the country and the old fishing grounds.

Magasewanussuck Falls. In Waldoboro, on Medomac River, the "great fresh falls."

In Waldoboro there were the salt tide-falls, then two sets of falls of about 10 to 15 feet and an 8 to 10 foot fall in the village, and the great fresh falls of 30 to 40 feet a third of a mile above the village (Wells, *Water Power of Maine,* 1869). The last were the ones known by this name, which appears in old deeds.

> 1694. *Magasewanussack.* On May 10, the Indian chieftains Madockawando and Edgeremet conveyed to Sylvanus Davis a tract of land at Maskonkes (Muscongus) "beginning at a Point of Land comonly called and known by ye name of Madaamok Point and so up by ye river or bay to ye fresh falls Called *Magasewanussack,*" etc. (*York Deeds,* X, fol. 258).
>
> 1716. *Magesemanussuck Falls.* Sylvanus Davis's executors sold this land "lying eastward of Masconks, beginning at Madoamok point up to ye falls of *Magesemanussuck"*—(*York Deeds,* VIII, fol. 177).

An abstract of title of this land "from Madamock Point up River to Fresh Falls called *Magesewanusock*" is in Maine Historical Society *Collections,* Doc. Ser., XXIII, 204.

The references show that both *-sewan-* and *seman-* were early used (or else there is a typographical error).

In *Pejepscot Papers* we find both *Magosomanussuck* (I, 88) and *Magessemanussuck* (I, 134); and Ballard, quoting the same, but possibly a different entry, says *Magowmanussuck* and *Chegewunnussock Falls.* The original deed is in *Pejepscot Papers,* X, 371, at the Maine Historical Society in Portland.

Chegewunnussock is a modernized form which proves that in the earlier forms the *g* was hard and stood for the Micmac and Maliseet, *mag,* "big," and not for *mahjee,* "bad." The second element therefore is *-gewun,* which is *-idjiwan,* "rapids." The last part is the element *-ussuk, -esuk* so often found in the names of falls. "Big rapids falls" would seem to be the name, indicating that this was not a cataract, or "pitch," but falls extending over some distance.

Chigewannuskuk Falls are on an undated map in the *Pejepscot Papers,* VIII, 76-76a, showing that it is not a recent name though modernized as to the language.

FOX ISLANDS.

Hahkik'-watpuk, Seal Head—the name given in 1931 by John Soctomer, a Passamaquoddy living at Machiasport, for all the Fox Islands. The word is the aspirated Maliseet form corresponding to a suppositive Penobscot *Akik-outop,* "seal-his-head," meaning here a "headland."

In Father O'Brien's notes is found the entry *"Akikwamandehek* (apparently for *Akik'-wandepek)* s'c head(?),″ probably intended for the Fox Islands.

Akik' or *akik'w* is a seal in both Penobscot and Passamaquoddy. *Antep'* is the word for a head, but always with the personal possessive pronoun (*netep,* "my head," *ketep,* "thy head," *wtep* (or *outep* in French forms), "his head"). In Soctomer's form the *w* is the possessive pronoun "his," and the root *antep* is reduced to *-atp-*. The last syllable is the locative.

In O'Brien's notes occurs the word *ulakikw,* "bull seal." This does not mean the male of the common harbor seal, but the great hooded seal, once common on the Maine coast, not infrequent up to eighty years ago, but now exterminated. Mr. Cabot gives *ulwakakik* for this in Maliseet and Rand has the Micmac *goolwaagook*. Dr. Spek (*Penobscot Man*, 1940, 110) has *"aolwakik, overgrown seal, said to have been common formerly on the rocky islands off the coast,"* and asks if it could have been the walrus. It was the Hooded Seal, and Soctomer said that the Fox Islands were its resort, so that it is possible that the initial *H* in his form, slightly hindering the utterance, stands for the lost preliminary syllable, *ul* or *aol*.

VINALHAVEN.

Vinalhaven. For this Nicolar wrote *See-bur-essek*, "at the sea thoroughfare," meaning Fox Island Thoroughfare. The name would have been spelled differently by a white man, but whether as *Sebayessek* or as *Tchaibeyessek* would depend upon the root selected. If the root preferred was *sebagoo*, "the ocean," then we have Nicolar's word *Sebayessek;* but this seems not very suitable for a narrow passage between islands, far removed from ocean influences. We should prefer the Maliseet *Tchaibayik*, "the narrows," as properly descriptive. The roots *tchaibi-*, "narrow," and *sebe-*, "spread out," are not always easy to distinguish.

NORTH HAVEN.

Kaskoonaguk, "crane island" (O'Brien). Mark Island, off Camden.
  Father O'Brien did not locate the name, but Joseph Nicolar gave the form *Kas-cu-nar-cook* and said it was Mark Island. *Kasq'* is the name of the great blue heron; *-naguk* is the locative of *-naghe,* "an island" (in composition).

MONHEGAN.

Mon-he'-gan. The high island off Pemaquid Point, a landfall for sailors, the resort of early fishermen.
  Apparently a simple word, Monhegan has presented some of the greatest difficulties we have encountered in elucidation. For years Dr. Ganong, Mr. Cabot, and the writer have worked on this name, with different theories, to which the best Indians con-

tributed little but confusion. Finally Dr. Ganong gave a demonstration so completely satisfactory that we need not review the early history of the word.

Mun-a-nook' is the Maliseet, *Menahan'* the Penobscot word for an island; the Micmac is *Mun'-ego.* Nudenans says that the word comes from *moni8i,* "in one place," meaning something off by itself. It is the first syllable alone, says Dr. Ganong, which means "island," leaving the rest to be explained.

"As to this there is ample evidence that the -AN, -AAN, -AHAN mean 'sea' or 'out to sea' (from the land). It is an abbreviation of the root evident in the Micmac word UKTAN 'the (open) sea,' which in composition becomes condensed in the various Algonkin dialects and modified to -AGON-, -EGON- and other forms, and finally, by dropping the consonants, to our -AAN and -AN-. Thus, *Manan, Menanouze* (Petit Manan), *Monhegan* (with its near-by *Manana,* or *Mananis,* islet) all well out to sea from the land; and there can be little doubt that these names are all local divergents from one and the same aboriginal prototype." (*Grand Manan Historian,* No. V, 1938, 43-47.)

Mon-he-gan is simply the Maliseet word for "The Island," the "out-to-sea island." Penobscot Indians gave Cyrus Eaton the name *K'tnagook,* Grand Island, better translated as "the principal island," "*the* island," from *k't* (*keght*), "principal," and *-naghe-,* "island," in composition. (*History of Thomaston,* 1865, I :23). The word is wholly correct and very modern.

Man-an'-is, "little island," diminutive of *Manan.* The small island which makes the harbor at Monhegan.

MATINICUS. METINIC.

Mat-in'-i-cus. The largest island of a group well out to sea from Isle au Haut.

Met-in'-ic. An island of another group adjacent to the above.

To the early voyageurs these outlying islands were important as landfalls and fishing stations. Capt. John Smith's map of New England gives their dedicatory English names, but his text has the old Indian names, which they still hold. "The highest Ile is Sorico in the Bay of Pannobscot," wrote Smith, meaning Isle au Haut. "But the three Iles and the Iles of Matinack are much further in the Sea: Metynacus is also three plaine Iles, but many great Rocks:

Monahegan is a round high Ile and close by it Monanis, betwixt which is a small Harbor where we rid."

1611. *Emmetinic*—*"une isle appelé Emmetinic, a 8 lieuses dudit Kenibequi."*—Biard, *Jesuit Relations,* Thwaites ed., II, 30.
1614. *Metynacus*—Capt. John Smith, *History of New England.*
1675. *Montinicus*—John Josselyn, *Two Voyages,* 205.
1686. *Martinique*—John Palmer, Commissioner for Sagadahoc (a blunder for *Matinic*).
1701. *Mentinicus, Montinicus*—Sylvanus Davis, deeds.
1746. *Mintinicus*—William Vaughan, will.
1752. *Montinicus*—Indian Conference.

All these forms (the first two excepted), with many others which might be cited, show that the form was associated with the root *men-, min-, mon-,* thus making the word from *menahan,* "an island." But the earliest of all, Smith's *Metynacus* and Biard's *Emmetnic,* distinctly make it from the *metin-* root; and *metin-,* says Mr. Cabot, "carried a 'cut-off' or 'cut-up' idea—something obviously cut off from something, or 'end of' something." This probably gives the correct meaning: the islands are those farthest out from shore. Perhaps Champlain's *"Isles jettées,"* "scattered isles," translates the *metin-* idea. They are the *Isles basses,* "low lslands," opposed to *Isle haut* of the Simancas Map of 1610.

Except for the ending, *Matinicus* and *Metinic* are the same word. It has been suggested that the final *-us* of Matinicus is a diminutive, but it is the larger island of the two, though nearer the mainland.

The prefix *em-,* in Biard's *Emmetinic,* seems to be the same introductory vowel often used by the French with tribal and geographic names—as Aghenibeki for Kennebec, Amahingan for Mahingan, Amalicite for Maliseet. Biard's *Emenenic* in New Brunswick is different; Dr. Ganong identifies it as Caton's Island, the modern *Ah-men-hen-ik-mun-eek-wol* (*Historic Sites in New Brunswick,* 1899, 268).

O'Brien has preserved an important modern form, *Metenaghe'nek,* which clearly is *metin-,* "cut-off"; *-naghe-,* "island," in composition; locative *-ek*—"the cut-off island," "the far-out island." From this it would seem that Smith's two last syllables stand for

-naghe-, with the final *s* possibly representing the softened Penobscot locative which often replaces *k*.

Men-asqu-as'-i-cook, "a collection of grassy islands" (Lt. Gov. John Neptune, for the Matinicus group).

This name occurs nowhere except in Eaton's *History of Rockland* (1865, I, 23) and in Father O'Brien's notes. The latter gives it as *Men-usk-us-sis-i-kak* with the patently wrong derivation from *menaasku,* "a rocky island" (no doubt the uncorrected statement of his Indian informant).

Neptune's is only a modernized form of Rand's *Munescoochk,* "little grassy islands," and O'Brien's is the same word in Penobscot dialect.

Mun or *men* for *menahan,* "island," is easily recognized. The second element *-asq* or *-usk* is *-esk,* which means something raw, green, uncooked, which may be anything from a watermelon to a greenhide, but in place-names usually stands for "grass." The third syllable in each form probably stands for the plural ending. To this O'Brien adds the diminutive *-sis,* "little," and the locative.

Menask- or *munesk-* is not uncommon for a treeless, grassy island; we have Menascook, Menaskek, Manashoak, as island names in other parts of Maine (See *Arowsick*).

Raggertask. Ragged Island, the Criehaven of today, is given by Williamson (*History,* II, 63) as Raggertask, "an Indian name." Probably so, but the word is too much corrupted to warrant a guess as to its original form and meaning.

ISLE AU HAUT.

Sol-i-kuk, "shells" (O'Brien).

Father O'Brien, who says this is the Isle au Haut, may have got the word from Capt. John Smith, who wrote: "The highest Ile is Sorico in the Bay of Pannobscot" (*History of New England,* II, 27). Ballard says "The Indian name is *Soolecook,* which is translated 'Shell Place.' J. Smith called it Sorico" (*Coast Survey Paper*). Smith's name would transliterate into Ballard's, and O'Brien's is the same, and the identification of the place is perfect; for Isle au Haut is the highest island in the Bay.

The difficulty is to see how *Solikuk* applies to Isle au Haut; why was that called "Shell Place"?

A Micmac or Maliseet origin is possible. In Pacifique we find *sigoeg* (*sigwek*), "empty," and *ess* or *ais*, a "clam"; Nudenans has *sigwessek*, "dried clams," and Aubéry has *sighessak*, "seashells," while O'Brien gives *cig8essanuk*, "a heap of empty shells." These words all refer to shell heaps such as are found in many places along the Maine coast; but not one of them explains *Solikuk*, for which we suspect John Smith was the only sponsor, and we do not know of any great accumulations of shells upon Isle au Haut.

CHAPTER FOUR

THE MIDDLE COAST, FROM WALDOBORO TO BRUNSWICK[1]

Exceptional difficulty has been encountered in finding the meaning of many of the place-names in this chapter. Documentary sources are abundant and of great age; but when the words were submitted to modern Indians their interpretations were so diverse and often so absurd that it was clear they were only guessing wildly at words which either had come from older and now forgotten languages, or had dropped out of their own. Other races might have inhabited these regions and left the names. If so, these tribes passed eastward in their migration. Using this as a working hypothesis, the writer discovered that many place-names which Penobscot Indians could not translate were easily interpreted by Passamaquoddy and Micmac Indians. Some places had two names, one modern Abnaki and the other an older form readily explained by words still current among the tribes farther east.

It is not maintained that these names are the survivals of Micmac occupation—that is a problem for archaeologists and ethnologists to solve,—but it is certain that many of these words are much closer to Maliseet and Micmac than to Abnaki. We believe that the present paper is the earliest attempt to explain our Maine place-names by working from east to west, and that by so doing we get sensible explanations which fit localities while those who have proceeded in the opposite direction have not been able to interpret the difficult names.

Prepared some years since but not printed, this chapter has had what the others lack, a careful revision by Dr. William F. Ganong, whose corrections and suggestions have been adopted, with, it is hoped, proper acknowledgment. The references to *York Deeds* have been quoted fully because so much local history is locked up in these volumes, which cover all land transfers (including the old Indian conveyances) between the Penobscot and the Piscataqua, from the earliest settlements almost to the Revolution. References to French documents may enable students to identify and locate

---

[1] Including Lincoln, Sagadahoc, and Kennebec counties.

unfamiliar forms. The arrangement is not so simple as that in the earlier chapters, because the country is so cut up by arms of the sea and by meandering rivers. Names have been grouped by their relation to the rivers oftener than by their location in towns which adjoin one another; and the rivers are taken, as before, from the mouth upward, the islands being disposed of as well as may be for easy finding but in no set order. No attempt has been made to follow the Kennebec River much above Merrymeeting Bay, though a few names of historical importance are mentioned briefly.

BRISTOL.

Pemaquid Point. This stern, rocky point, extending many miles into the sea, was one of the first places upon our shores where Europeans came for fishing and trading. In more than three centuries there has been little variation in the name.

    1607. *Pemaquid*—(Strachey).
    1614. *Pemequid*—(Capt. John Smith).
    1623. *Pemaquid*—(Christopher Levett).

Pemaquida and the modern Abnaki *Pemaquideag* show the extreme range of variation. The French usually wrote it as *Pemcuit* or *Pemacouet*. Williamson's *Pemkueag*, obtained from an Indian, is an excellent form (*History of Maine,* 1832, I, 241).

The meanings assigned do not vary much; *Pemaquideag,* "long point" (O'Brien); *Pemequid,* "a point of land running into the sea" (Rev. Paul Coffin, 1798); *Pemaquid, à la terre qui continue"* (Abbé J. A. Maurault).

Trumbull is in error in calling it "the place where the land slopes" (Connecticut Historical *Collections,* II, 250). In the Maine dialects the prefixes *pem-* and *pemi-* have a number of meanings, and here we have clearly one of extent; for, once we are above the rocky shore line, the land does not slope noticeably. On the other hand, between the tip of the point and Round Pond we have about eight miles of the sternest coast in New England; even in the calmest weather there are very few places where a landing can be made.

Doctor Ganong's comment should be quoted in full. "If this

were in Micmac territory, we could say confidently that the -*equid* is the common root *oogwit*, meaning *rests*, or *is situated*, e.g., *Kespoogwit*, Cape Sable, Nova Scotia, 'it rests, or is situated, at the end (of the Micmac country).' The *Pem-* would be *extending*, i.e., long, or far—'it is situated far out,' that is, the Point is."

Doctor Ganong's explanation is so much better than any from Abnaki elements that it seems best to regard *Pemaquid* as of Micmac origin and one of our oldest words. If we use the Micmac -*equid*, the spelling Pemequid is preferable to the official Pemaquid.

The strategic importance of Pemaquid in early times can be understood only by knowing that instead of coasting along this dangerous shore the Indians took out their canoes at New Harbor and carried across about two miles to Pemaquid Harbor on the western shore, where Fort Frederic commanded the end of the carry and controlled all crossing and thereby all travel and trade along the coast.

Monhegan Island.[1] The landfall for Pemaquid. It was an early and favorite resort of European fishermen on account of its small but safe roadstead in the deep cut between Monhegan and the little island of Mananis.

No word has proved more difficult to analyze than this apparently simple one. On the supposition that it was Abnaki, Mr. Cabot and I, after long discussion, agreed that it meant a "passage"; from the root *mun*, which in several Algonkin languages carries the idea of digging, and the ending -*hegan*, which implies something wrought by tools, as if the deep cut between Monhegan and Mananis were artificial.

However, the total disagreement of seven of the best Indians to be found indicated that the word was too old for them to recognize; and the cropping out of other very old words best explained by Passamaquoddy or Micmac roots has brought me to accept the opinion of Dr. J. Hammond Trumbull and Mr.

---

[1] When the comment on Monhegan was written, some years ago, Doctor Ganong had not made his perfect demonstration of the Micmac origin of the word. This has been already given in Chapter Three, but for the sake of its historical sequence the discussion as first written is here included.

Lincoln N. Kinnicut (cited in Judge Charles Francis Jenney's *The Fortunate Island of Monhegan* (1922), p. 5-6), that it comes from *munegoo,* the Micmac word for "island—the principal island of the region—as we say, *"the* island." If an explanation of the ending is demanded, it may well be from *-egon,* "a ridge" in Micmac, according to Ganong. From Port Clyde I have seen it showing as a long, high island, in sharp distinction from the rounded hump of Seguin.

If the word is Micmac and means simply "the island," then it is the equivalent for Governor John Neptune's Abnaki *K'tnargook,* "the principal island," which becomes the modern translation of the name. Early forms are:

    1614. *Monahigan*—(Capt. John Smith).
    1619. *Monahiggan*—(Thomas Dermer).
    1622. *Moratiggan*—(Mourt's *Relation*).
    1622. *Munhigin*—(Phinehas Pratt).
    1623. *Monhiggon*—(Christopher Levett).
    1676. *Munhegon*—(Thomas Gardner's Petition).
    1717. *Mun-Hegan*—(Rev. Joseph Baxter's *Journal*).

To the south and westward, practically the same word in other dialects has, as Mr. Cabot has shown, the meaning of a "passage," which would be the meaning here if the word were Abnaki instead of Micmac (see also Monhegan in Chapter Three, above).

Mananis, "the little island." The small island across the roadstead at Monhegan, which forms one side of the harbor. It is the diminutive of the Micmac *manan,* an island.

Damariscove. A hard problem confronts us in the words Damariscove and Damariscotta. Are these words Indian, English, or a mixture of the two? From many occurrences of Damariscove we will cite a few, with the dates:

    1616. Damerils Isles (Capt. John Smith).
    1621. Damarins Cove (Bradford MSS.).
    1622. Damarins Cove (Winslow, *Good Newes from New England*).
    1645. Dammarills Cove (Massachusetts Historical Society *Collections,* 2nd Series, IV, 6).
    1649. Damarall's Cove (Will of Isaac Grosse).
    1650. Damirell's Cove (*Suffolk Deeds,* III, 49).
    1657. "Island ... called Damerells Cove" (*York Deeds,* XVIII, 114).

Indian Place-Names of the Maine Coast 105

> 1658. "Island ... by the name of Damarels Cove" (*York Deeds*, XVII, 331); "Island of Damariss Cove."
> 1685. "Damerel Cove lying and being an Island in the Sea" (*York Deeds*, IX, 229).
> 1717. "Island called Agguahega or Damaris Scotty" (*York Deeds*, VII, 230).
> 1737. Damaris Cove Island (*York Deeds*, XVIII, 144).
> The *Arcano del Mare*, 1647, shows "I Damar Elscoue," that is, Damarelscove Island.

We see from the evidence that this island had another Indian name (see *Aguahega*); that the whole island took its name from a cove upon it; and that the cove took its name, even before Captain John Smith came here, from a man who lived on it, whose name was English. Colonel Charles E. Banks, our best antiquarian, wrote me that Damerell was a well-known English name and that one Humphrey Damerell was very early in this country. Either Humphrey Damerell or someone of the same surname, coming as a fisherman, occupied the little harbor on the island with a fresh pond upon it, easy of access and safe from Indians, long before the Pilgrims came here.

Damariscotta. A long tidal inlet, a river, a salt pond, and a fresh pond bear this name.

To which of these does the name belong? Is the name Indian, English, or a mixture of the two?

The occurrences do not begin as early as Damariscove, and the variations are not great. The following represent fairly some seventy noted:

> 1659. Damaris Cotty River (*York Deeds*, XVI, 113).
> 1665. River of Damariscotta (*ibid.*, XVI, 113).
> 1694. Damaris Scoty river, "oyster river in" (*ibid.*, VIII, 177).
> 1730. Damaris Scota (*ibid.*, XVI, 1).
> 1732. Damuscottee (*ibid.*, XV, 221).

The earliest of all shows that to the writer, at least, the river was known by the name of the island near its mouth, for he wrote, "Damirescove River" (*Suffolk Deeds*, I, 24).

We also have, in 1717 and 1722, "Damaris Scoty River called by the Indians the Wineganse" ("Wenegans" in 1722). Now Winneganse is not the name of a body of water (see explanation below) but of a land portage. In this connection it refers to

Hodgdon's Mills at the present East Boothbay, where a little carry led across to Linekin Bay.[1] That is, Damariscotta River then, as now, was a salt river from the sea to the oyster beds in Newcastle.

The certainty that the name Damariscotta was applied to the very mouth of the tideway, the close proximity of Damariscove Island, which has been shown to be pure English, and the confusion which might result from other English names in the vicinity have combined to give an impression that the word is English. It must be admitted that English names in the region closely resembled the final syllables. An Indian sagamore called John Cotta sold land here (*York Deeds,* XVI, 344), and *Pejepscot Papers* records Peter Cotter, a barber, in 1728, selling land at Long Reach, and Mrs. Sarah Cotter, of Brunswick, in 1731, disposing of her land. If Humphrey Damerell gave his name to Damariscove, it is conceivable that he and the various Cotters might have been linked together in the name of Damariscotta. And so at one time thought Doctor Ganong, who wrote "it seems to me, that the name is not Indian at all" (*Transactions* of the Royal Society of Ottawa, 1915, Vol. IX, ser. iii, sec. 2, p. 434). "It may possibly prove to represent a corruption of *Damariscove Outer River,* in application to the outer tidal part as distinct from the inner freshwater stream." Had he known the locality, he would have understood that the Fresh Pond, which he conceives as the "Inner River," has an elevation of more than fifty feet above the Salt Pond at the head of the tide river. Its outlet is only a quarter of a mile long and here is the notable "fish ladder" up the falls, by which the alewives ascend from pool to pool to reach their spawning ground.

Thus much for or against the English derivation, which modern Indians have seemed to support by giving the place a quite different name and by always agreeing upon it. They call Damariscotta *Madamescontee,* from *madames,* "an alewife," plus *-contee,* or *-kanntti,* an ending signifying "occurrence" or "abundance." In 1798, Sabatis, an intelligent Indian, gave Rev. Paul Coffin the word "Madamascontee, now Damarascote, many little alewives" (Maine Historical Society *Collections,* IV, 379). In

---

[1] Named from an English family which lived here.

1893, Joseph Nicolar wrote substantially the same in *The Life and Traditions of the Red Man* (p. 146). More recently Indians have given me the same word with the same meaning, "a place of abundance of alewives."

Now Madamascontee and Damariscotta are not the same word. The latter has the locative ending *-scot.* The former—one of those "occurrence" words which rarely take even the weak locative ending *g* or *k*—has in it the letter *n,* never found in any of the fourscore occurrences noted for Damariscotta.

In attempting to harmonize the two words, I would call to attention that Damariscotta begins not with *madames,* but with *n'mays,* a more general word for a fish, and that our Indians have a curious tendency to substitute initial *d* for *n* in the word *nahmays,* or *n'mays.* Initial *m* and *n* are vague sounds, often omitted by Indians or else so faintly sounded that they can be caught only by close attention. In the particular word *nahmays,* which very often lacks any initial consonant (as in Androscoggin), the *n* is often replaced by *d.* An Indian letter, dated 1677, speaks of the "damrallscogon Engens" and the "damrelscoging Engens," instead of the Androscoggin Indians (Massachusetts Archives, Vol. 30, 241a and 242). On his fine map of Maine, dated 1715, Father Aubéry gives *Dan-mira-kangou* for the Androscoggin River, and another French map of a little later date (#253 of the Bureau de la Marine, Paris) has *Damni-kangan* for the same, indicating a fishery. With the same underlying idea of plenty of fish, Ammesoukanti, or Farmington Falls, is called *Damisokantik* by Baron de Portneuf (Charlevoix, *History of New France,* J. G. Shea edition, V, 167 n.); and Abbé Maurault (*Histoire des Abenakis,* pp. 285-289) applies the same form to Megantic Lake. (Our Nahmakanta Lake is the same word.) In each case the meaning is "place of occurrence, or abundance, of fishes." Now Damariscotta falls into this class, with initial D instead of N for a fish-word. I asked two Penobscot Indians for their name for Damariscotta, and while one replied *"Nahmayskontik,* plenty of fishes," the other, with equally good enunciation, said unmistakably, *"D'amaswakkontee,* plenty of alewives"—the same word precisely, only in the plural and using initial *d'* for *n.*

The commonest word for Damariscotta is *Madameskontee,*

which uses *madames,* the specific name of an alewife instead of the general *n'mays,* a fish, particularly a migratory fish, for Indians say that the initial *n'* means "going up." This also is the oldest form found in documents. Purchas' *Pilgrims,* in the list of rivers, towns, and chieftains, gives the town *Matammisconte* on the river Apponick. Damariscotta is later in appearing, and the peculiar ending *-cotta* (instead of *-cot*) is hard to account for; we should suppose that in the many instances noted someone would have slipped in the *n* from *-contee* if it were an abundance ending, or have added a locative *k,* if it were not. But *Damarescot* would have been good Indian, and Heylin (1658) has *Tamescot,* which may be that. We cannot see how the purely English Damarell's Cove could have affected the word. There appear to have been two different words, both of which survived.

Aguahega. An unidentified island, perhaps Damariscove Island. The name is found but once (*York Deeds,* VIII (1717), 230), "an island called *Aguahega,* or Damariscotty." The name probably indicates a "landing place." (See Chapter III.)

Kananaghetne. A point of land in Damariscotta between Day Cove and the Salt Falls.

On an old town plan in the Massachusetts Archives (Town Plans, 1794, Vol. X, 24), Mr. William B. Cabot found this name, now obsolete. He gave me a tracing of the locality with the comment, "a *kenegh-* name which it is interesting to find so far to the eastward." Mr. Cabot noted its similarity to *Quoneneghtuc,* the name of the fall on the lower Connecticut River, "which implies some sort of a crook, or twist, such as you get in the Hudson, Thames and Connecticut near the coast." The twist in Damariscotta River is very evident at this point.

The root *kana-* is not found in the Abnaki of Rasles; but Eliot's Bible has *kenai, keneh,* as "sharp, keen." For the words for knee-cap, big toe, and thumb, Rasles has *neghet-* in composition, implying a bend, since these are the joints of the body which can be bent at the greatest angle. Hence the word refers to the "sharp bend" the river makes at this place.

The reason for preserving the name in 1794 is not clear; most of these town plans are devoid of Indian names. From the head of Day Cove, then Brown Cove, is indicated a road running

Indian Place-Names of the Maine Coast   109

about due east to Bristol which no longer exists unless a short street in Damariscotta represents the end of it. It may be that the name was kept to indicate where the road started.

Ped-coke-gowake. This is commonly supposed to be the old Indian carry between Damariscotta and Sheepscot waters; in reality it is not the carry but a feature near the end of the carry, which, singularly enough, is found at both ends of this ancient route and thus gives a name to the road, although it is a river feature.

In the Indian deed of Wittinose and Erledugles to Walter Phillips in 1662 (*York Deeds,* XVIII, 235), the word is found in four different spellings, *Ped-coke-gowake, Pedcocegowake, Pedcotogowake,* and *Pedcotegwake.* Of these forms the best is *Pedcotogowake,* while the accepted form with its bad syllabification is unrecognizable. The word cannot be interpreted by Abnaki roots. Strange as it is to find it here, the word is pure Micmac, a relic of former occupation by that people or else the survival in the old Etchemin dialect of roots once common to both. The latest archaeological indications point to waves of migratory occupation of the land by several different Algonkin cultures, of whom the Micmacs could have been one. We owe the interpretation of this old word entirely to the masterly demonstration given by Professor Ganong (*Transactions,* Royal Society of Canada, Third Series (Ottawa, 1914), Vol. VIII, pp. 269-274) of its modernized and deformed equivalent, the Micmac *Peticodiac.*

Professor Ganong shows that the first root of Peticodiac, *epetk,* or *petk* (*pedc,* as spelled in our word) "applies to places in which the distinct feature is a bend or turn sweeping around to the reverse of the original direction." The second part of our word Pedcotogowake, *-otog-* (in the Micmac *kutog*) means "around, in a number of combinations meaning to go, or turn, or flow around" (p. 271). Our final *-wake* (which should be pronounced *oo-ak* now that we have removed the *g* to the preceding root) corresponds to Ganong's *uya* or *aya* in words meaning "to bend," plus the simple locative *k*. Thus rectified, the deformed Peticodiac becomes the pure Micmac *Epetk-kutog-oye-k,* which means, literally, "back turn-around-bends-place," or a place where a river makes a reverse turn around a point. Now this Micmac word is essentially our *Pedc-otog-ow-ak* (Pedcotogo-wake), a place where the river makes a reverse turn, only in this case there are several reverse turns.

In Damariscotta the reverse turn comes a little above the bridge at the Salt Water Falls, where the waters of the Salt Pond make a long sweep around Glidden's Point, flowing first easterly and then westerly. On the Sheepscot to the westward, there are three such turns, two of them unimportant; the third is around the Great Neck, where the right-hand fork of Marsh River, coming down from the north, turns sharply westward, and then, as Crumbie's Reach, flows directly north, parallel to its first course.

With this understood, we may turn to the deeds, bearing in mind that Walter Phillips' first house was near East Boothbay, his second at rivel level about a mile below the Salt Falls, and his last home, from which he was driven in the Indian War, on a sightly knoll in Newcastle about a half mile below the Salt Falls. The site is easily located by the contour line of hundred-foot elevation surrounding the top of it. The Indian Carry started from the gully just below this spot.

It has been commonly supposed that this carry was the *Pedc-otog-ow-ak*—which makes the deeds unintelligible. The obligation of Wittinose and Erledugles, Indian sagamores, 19 January 1662 (*York Deeds,* XVIII, fol. 235, p. 537), grants Walter Phillips land "beginning at *pencotogwake* one half upward to the salt Pond," that is, from the bridge, around the bend above, to the southern bay, and "the other half from *pedcocegowake* down to the voke below the house of Walter Phillips which the natives uses to carry their canoes over to Canesix River." This means from about the present bridge down to the gully below Walter Phillips' house. Mrs. Chase has shown that "voke" is only a misprint for "noke" or "nook": it is not so much as a cove, just a gully and indentation of the bank, where it was easiest to take out canoes and carry them up the hill.

How the old carry ran from here depends upon conditions at the other end. Not having seen the place to know about shore conditions and the tidal-waters, I cannot say whether the carry ran due west into the northerly branch of Marsh River or whether it followed very nearly the course of the road which now is the state highway between Newcastle and Wiscasset. Though longer, the latter looks, from the map, to be the better course.

Professor Ganong's prediction that "it is possible the name Ped-coke-gowake ... involves roots identical with those of Peticodiac" is proved by the topographical facts; but R. K. Sewall's derivation as "place of thunder" is a wild fancy, for Rasles' word, from which he makes it, means only "it thunders" and does not include a single one of the roots found in *Pedc-otog-ow-ak.*

NEWCASTLE.

Cowesiseck River. Now called Mill River, in Newcastle.

The name occurs in many forms, such as *Cauesisex, Canessissex, Canesix, Canasixet,* and oftenest of all as *Cavissex* or *Cavessissix.*

The last two forms are spurious—there is no *v* in the Abnaki language. On the *Can-* forms I may quote Mr. W. B. Cabot in a letter, November 23, 1935: "The *n* in Canesix has always offended me; it seems to have started as a *u.*" Undoubtedly it did so start, as the *Cauesisex* form shows. But *Cau-* and *Cow-* are the same in sound, so that *Cowesiseck* and *Cauesisex* are the same word, with the former preferable as a printed form.

The word can be worked out by the Indian deeds to Walter Phillips of Newcastle. His first deed of land down the Damariscotta to East Boothbay does not concern us. The second is an obligation of Sagamore Josle and his son, dated February 16, 1661 (or by the new calendar, February 26, 1662), of land from "the lower end of the Salt Pond ... at Damascotty as tending right over to *Cauesisex* Due West Nor West," and so nine miles up into the woods north, on the west side of Damariscotta Fresh Pond, a long, narrow strip between the pond and Mill, or *Cauesisex,* River (*York Deeds,* XVIII, fol. 235, p. 536).

The third obligation is that of Sagamores Wittinose and Erledugles, dated 19 January, 1662 (by the modern calendar 29 January, 1663), of land from the foot of the Salt Pond at Damariscotta down to the cove a little below the present Newcastle bridge," which the Natives uses to carry their cannoes over to *Canesix River"* (*York Deeds,* XVIII, fol. 235, p. 537). Here we see that *Cauesissex* and *Canesix* are the same place, though not precisely the same word.

The fourth obligation, mentioned only to show the extent of Phillips's possessions, is the deed of Erledugles, dated 28 December, 1674 (modern calendar January 7, 1675), of all the unallotted land "on the Ester side of Damrascotty Fresh Pond as Hy as the Head of the Pond" and back six miles east.

In six months King Philip's War broke out and Walter Phillips was obliged to abandon all his possessions (*York Deeds,* XVIII, fol. 235, p. 538). In 1702, being an old man living in Salem, Mass., he sold, on November 10, to the Rev. Christopher Toppan of Newbury all this land, describing the second piece as "running right over to *Cowesiseck River"* (*York Deeds,* XVIII, fol. 236, p. 538-9).

Therefore *Cowesiseck, Cauesisex,* and *Canesix* are the same place, and the *n* is but a copyist's error for a *u,* the equivalent for a *w* in the first word.

In analysis, the last word *Cauesix,* is *kowa,* a "white pine tree," and *-essek,* or *-issek,* a terminal, meaning "in the vicinity of." It means "near the white pines." The longer word has an extra *s* which must be accounted for. It seems to stand as the remnant of the diminutive *sis,* "little"; hence the word would mean "near the young white pines," merely adding something more by which to distinguish the particular trees. That there were pines near is proved by the Indian deed to John Mason, 1652, of Sheepscot Farms, whose north bound was "over a cove, *to a parcel of pines,"* etc. (Wm. Willis, Maine Historical Society *Collections,* First Series, II: 233).

Nassoemek. Dyer's Neck in Newcastle.

Deeds give the location, very nearly, as just above Sheepscot Farms. "Dyer's Neck or *Nassoemek*... Called by the natives Nassoemek near unto Sheepscot, alias Dartmouth, alias Newcastle," runs the deed of 1712 (*York Deeds,* XV, 225).

Nassoemek has the same root as Nassouak and means the "land between," meaning between the two rivers named in the deed, Dyer's River and the Upper Sheepscot. An Indian at once said, "*Nassokamigek,* a horseback between." The land in question is the narrow ridge, about eighty feet high, just above the Sheepscot Bridge on the Old County Road from Newcastle village to Alna. As *k* is a letter which very often drops out of Indian words when it stands between vowels, it seems reasonable to suppose that the ending *-emek* is what is left of a former *-kamigek,* which means not only a "horseback" but a limited area, a plot of land, like this between the rivers.

Masso-emek. Same as the preceding.

The Indian deed to William Dyer, recorded May 26, 1666, conveys land, "beginning at Masso-emek, as high up as the Head of ye River upon ye Eastward Side Massoemek and the Little Island adjoining to Massoemek Likewise right over the sd Neck of Land from the Head of the River above-mentioned to Kemboeskiseck, so likewise downwards after the sd River as low as the lower end of sd Massoemek" (*York Deeds,* XV, fol. 223). The word is only a variant of Nassoemek. Mr. Cabot, to whom it was referred, was of the opinion that Massoemek is so near a Massachusetts word for a peninsula that this is the meaning.

Kemboeskisek. The word occurs only in *York Deeds,* XV, fol. 223, just cited, which places it at Dyer's Neck.

The last part of the word is clear— *-esk* is a root often found in words referring to marshy places or grassy land; *-isek,* equivalent to *-essek,* combines a locative *k,* which indicates some definite spot, just as a capital letter does with us, and an interposed *s,* which denotes proximity to some place; so that *-eskisek* means "near to the grassy place." From this single occurrence *kembo* cannot be satisfactorily determined.

Sheepscot. The bay and river, confluent at the mouth with Sagadahoc, but trending inland to the land-locked harbor of Wiscasset and above that, in shallow tidewater bays and creeks, to its eastern branch, Marsh River, and its western branch, the narrow stream known as the Upper Sheepscot.

The name appears to be defective, lacking one or more initial syllables. It must have been given from some feature near its mouth. The local explanation that it was "an English word which signified a place for beasts or sheep" is groundless: the name was used before there could have been any sheep there, and the ending -*scot* is pure Indian. The form Sheepsgut, which semes to be English, is more likely Dutch: it occurs as Schipsgut on an early map in the New York Public Library (#281 of the Bureau of the French Marine, Paris), but as this map has many names from Champlain and Captain John Smith, it must have been made after their maps, probably from some Dutch source.

The English traveler E. A. Kendall, whose comments on Indian names are usually judicious, says "Sheepscot is apparently a corruption of some Indian word as that from which is obtained Pejipscot" (*Travels in the Northern Part of the United States*, III, 129).

This is a discriminating comment. The confirmation of it is in a passage which does not appear in Strachey's account of the Popham expedition as printed in Maine Historical Society *Collectons*, III, but which was in a paper discovered in the Lambeth Palace Library, in 1875, by Rev. B. F. Da Costa, and printed by Dr. Burrage in *Gorges and the Grant of the Province of Maine, 1622* (printed 1923). This says, p. 90:

"Satterdaye the 22th Auguste Capt. popham early in the morning depted in his shallop to go for the ryver of pashipskoke. . . .

"Sondaye the 23th our presedent Capt. popham retorned unto us from the ryver of pashipscoke.

A footnote by Doctor Burrage says this was "the Pejepscot or Androscoggin"; but anyone can see that Captain Popham could hardly go in his little shallop from his newly selected site on Cape Small up the long and difficult Sagadahoc, unknown to him, through Merrymeeting Bay and up to Brunswick, returning the next day, and yet accomplish anything. And anyone acquainted with Indian roots would at once perceive that *Pashipscoke* and *Pejepscot* do not contain the same roots. They are not the same words.

In both words the last two syllables are the same, -*scot*, or -*cook*, terminal of place, and *ips*, indicating "rocks." The first part of *Pejepscot*, however, consists of *P'*, indicating "extent," "continuity," and -*idge* (eje), "strong rapids."

Pashipscoke, on the other hand, has nothing in it to indicate water except the terminal, which most often denotes a harbor, or a stream. We do not find the root of the first part in Rasles or in any Abnaki vocabulary consulted, but the idea is a general one in the Algonkin tongues. In Ojibway (Baraga, *Dictionary*), *passa-* has the idea of breaking, splitting; in the Micmac we find equivalents meaning "a split in a rock," and in the Natick (Trumbull, *Dictionary*) we find *pashishau,* "it bursts," *papishau,* "it breaks through," "blossoms," *passipskodtut,* "a cleft in a rock," and other words from the root *pahshe,* "broken," "divided." Not finding it in Abnaki is merely a matter of defective vocabularies. The word, then, is *pahshe,* "divided," *apsk,* "rocks," *ook,* "water place, channels"—a place where the river is split up into many rocky channels, which precisely describes the tortuous byways of the Sheepscot.

As for Dr. Ballard's *Sipsaconta,* "aboriginal for Sheepscot; means little birds flock or rush" (*Memorial Volume of the Popham Celebration,* 1863, p. 171 n.), there is nothing to warrant such a meaning. The word was evidently obtained from some Indian who knew nothing of the old language and probably did not know the place. As we showed in *Damariscotta,* we do not find the *-scot* ending equivalent to the *-conta* ("abundance") ending. Moreover, Dr. Ballard (p. 147) translates the word *Sipsisconta* as "Duck River." Here he is mixing Abnaki and Passamaquoddy. In Abnaki a bird of any sort is *sips;* a little bird is *sipsis,* as in his first translation; but in the Passamaquoddy usage *sips* or *seeps* is not bird in general, but "a duck." Two different languages are used in the translation.

Not to let the meaning and location of *Pashipscoke* rest on a single occurrence of the word, I quote the deed of Pateshall Perkins, grandson of the early Richard Pateshall, who in 1737, a hundred and fifteen years after our first citation, sold Joshua Townsend, "Parcels of Lands in Kennebeck River, *Pesheepsgut* and Damariscove Island" (*York Deeds,* XVIII, fol. 144, p. 351). Here is a fine instance of that initial syllable combined with the recent form supposed to be English and clearly enough identical with the very early *Pashipscoke.*

This decision was adopted by Doctor Ganong, who commented on the margin of the paper: "I have always been tormented by the thought that they might be the same word belonging independently to the two places! But now I see that you are right."

Mountsweag. Bay and Brook in Sheepscot River, a back passage westward of the main channel.

The forms that I have are not good and not precise in location.

    1664. *Mountsweck* Bay—(*York Deeds*, II, fol. 8).
    1684. *Monsiocage falls*—(Petition for New Dartmouth).
    1734. (circa). *Montswads* Bay, *Mount Sege* Bay, *Monsweag* River.

I suspect that, since the Monsweag River is a continuation of Cowsegan Narrows, this is a parallel; *Monsegan* has as its root *cici* or *sege,* "narrows," with *mun,* indicating something "dug out"—a trench-like channel, with sheer, though not necessarily high, rock walls for a space below Cowsegan. This, however, is conjectural.

Cowsegan. On the maps, given as Cowseagan Narrows, at the upper end of the western side-channel of the Sheepscot; but the word "narrows" is tautological, a repetition of *Cowsegan,* which means the same thing.

The earliest instance I have is William Willis's abstract (in Maine Historical Society *Collections,* II, 1847, p. 236), of the record in Massachusetts Archives of Land Claims in Eastern Maine, in the beginning of the eighteenth century. Willis was both lawyer and historian, so that his notes are dependable. John Tucker, heir to John Tucker, fisherman, of Sheepscot River, in 1662 bought of Robinhood, "all the land on the north side of Monsweag great river, up along the main river as far as Cowsegan, being as far as Thomas Cleaves lease runs down the river, and so to run four miles due north from the main river of Cowsegan. Recorded in Sheepscot records."

The Sheepscot records were destroyed by fire, but it is clear that this tract adjoined that deeded to Thomas Clives by Robinhood, December 28, 1662, and that the "lower narrows" of Sheepscot River was called Cowsegan (see Wiscasset, below). This fully establishes *-segan* as meaning "narrows." The first part, *cow,* is not, however, the same root we found in Cowesiseck, though in a roundabout way they derive from the same radical. Here *cow* is the modern Abnaki *kah,* which denotes something spiny, thorny, prickly, as a quill, a splinter, or a thistle. (Thus, the leaves of the white pine are *kah,* hence *kowa,* according to Trumbull.) The Abnakis apparently did not use *kah* of rocks; but the Etchemins did use it, and eastward we find the root in place-names of rocky places or falls, as "rough rocks." The root of *-segan* is *si, ci, tsi,* denoting constriction—as a knot; hence the narrows in a river—especially when it is reduplicated. Thus, when Mr. Cabot wrote, October 26, 1932, "Cowseagan was given me at Old Town as 'rough narrows'," we may accept the definition as accurate. Here clearly is another of the old Etchemin words underlying the place-names of this region as testimony to its former occupants.

The Indian who told Dr. Ballard (*Coast Survey,* 1868, p. 7) that the word meant "fortune-telling" succeeded in an impudent deceit, though hardly so great an one as in telling Father Vetromile that Cowsegan meant "carrying-place for cows"! This last I have found in the well-known handwriting of Joseph Polis, who was Thoreau's guide, among the correspondence of Vetromile and Ballard.

Chewonki Neck. A long narrow headland on the western bound of Wiscasset.

Professor W. F. Ganong analyzed this as meaning "the big ridge," which fits perfectly. *Che* is "big" and the terminal *wonki* he judged to be an abbreviated form of *adowakeag,* a horseback or ridge of glacial gravel. Ballard's "great neck" (*Coast Survey,* 1868, p. 7) is a correct definition, but his derivation is wrong. The final *onki* is not a locative but the main root of the word, which has no locative ending. The local interpretation, "the birds' home," is without foundation.

Chevacobet. The word is known to me only through Alexander Johnston's history of Sheepscot Farms (Maine Historical Society *Collections,* IX, 1887, 133), written in 1873. He says, "The Sheepscot here sends off a branch between these islands—the Nichols River (anciently *Che-va-co-bet*), with triple mouths, flowing easterly about eighty rods—and then uniting in one stream, bends northeast. . . ." The locality is entirely clear on the modern topographical maps as the narrow tidal strait at the foot of the Little Neck (Lehman Island and Cunningham Point on modern maps). Since the Indian has no *v* sound, the form of the word is not a possible form, and beyond allowing that *che* means "big," one cannot get. I surmise that *-vaco-* is an error for *-saco-*, derived from *sauk,* an outflow, or outlet, mouth of a river, and that, to those who named it, Marsh River and its tributaries seemed more important than the attenuated Sheepscot River flowing down through Alna.

WISCASSET.

Wiscasset, "the outlet." The county seat of Lincoln County, on Wiscasset Harbor, at the head of the main Sheepscot salt river.

Above this great landlocked harbor, deep enough for the largest ships, the river shoals and divides into tortuous tidal channels with extensive salt marshes. Below the harbor the Sheepscot, making a double bend where the tide runs deep and strong but unobstructed, flows down a straight main channel between high, ledgy banks which even make rocky palisades much of the way.

The problem is to determine what is the dominant feature which gives the locality its name and what are the roots entering into that name. The historical sequence of the forms of this word is important.

1662. *wichCasset*—This earliest form is found twice in the obligation of "Mr. Robinhood," Indian sagamore, to Thomas Clives, fisherman, December 28, 1662, who sells a tract "on the westward side of Shipscot River *the place caled wichCasset* from the hier end of the upper narowes downe to the lower end of the lower narowes fower mile in length"—that is, the site of the present city.

1663. *Wichcaseege Bay*—(*York Deeds,* XVI, fol. 185), Indian deed.

1664. *Whichacasecke Bay*—Indian deed to George Davies, 15 December, 1664, recorded 11 August, 1666 (*York Deeds,* II, fol. 8).

1718. *Wichcasseck*—Witt to Frost (York Deeds, IX, fol. 188).

1719. *Wichcasseck*—Frost to Tyler (*ibid.,* IX, fol. 189).

1720. *Wichcasseck*—Clark to Frost (*ibid.,* X, fol. 179).

1733. *Wichasseck*—Winslow to Lewis (*ibid.,* XVI, fol. 179).

1733. *Wichaseege Bay*—Clark to Waldo (*ibid.,* XVI, fol. 185).

1733. *Wichasset Bay*—(Same document).

1758. *Whiscassick*—James Cargill's Petition (Maine Historical Society Collections, Doc. Ser., XXIV, 92 and 93.)

1762. *Witscasset Bay*—Settlement of Plymouth Co. (*ibid.,* XXI, 91).

1785. *Witchcasset* Company—(Report on Indian Deeds).
1786. *Wiscasset*—Petition to make a port (Maine Historical Society *Collections,* Doc. Ser., XV, 210).

From this list of occurrences it will be seen that the sharp sound of *ch* or *tch* is universal for almost a century, Cargill in 1758 being the first to use the soft *whis,* while the still softer *wis-casset* did not emerge for much more than a century.

The probabilities are that Whisgig to the west and Wessaweskeag to the east, both with the idea of marshy tidal creeks, have attracted the original *Wichcasset* into a similar form, thereby changing the root of the word. The sharp *ch* or *tch* seems an essential part of the original word. Certainly we found the word first applied to the high western shore of the bay where the town stands, a place which, with its deep-water anchorage, would not have been called a place of tidal marsh. The *Wis*casset of today is a misnomer.

The old word *Wichcasset* seems to have been derived from the roots *wetchi* and *kask,* with the locative ending -*et* and may be translated "at the outlet," that is, of the bay.

The root *wetchi-* or *whicha-* is a rather uncommon root of peculiar significance. Indians hesitate, then give up trying to put it into English and say "it is hard to explain." The idea is "comes out from—but you don't see where," that is, a concealing outlet, one where you meet a strong current but do not see the river on account of a sharp bend in it. This, at least, characterizes the few places in Maine where the root is found. It differs from the *sauk* or *sañk* of Sagadahoc because there the outlet is clearly seen; at Wiscasset, one does not see what is around the bend just ahead, yet both words mean "outlet."

Wetchi- is "from," "this way," "coming towards one"; *kask* is "to go out." One remembers in Thoreau's *Maine Woods* the explanation of Sunkhaze Stream, "See canoe come out; no see um stream" (1864, 302 and 326). Rev. M. C. O'Brien's notes give the full form of the word, *Wetchi-sañkessuk,* which he defines as "where one comes out." A very sharp bend in the stream within two hundred feet of the river entirely shuts off any view into the stream; a canoe coming from it seems to have started out from the riverbank itself.

The word *Wech-ko-tetuck* was given me in 1930 by Lewey Mitchell as the name for Union River, and here we find a somewhat similar feature—the river entering the bay around a bend with another sharp bend at the head of a high fall not far above, which cuts off any view of the stream or the valley it lies in. "Coming towards" is the Indian explanation.

Wichigaskitaywick is defined by Dr. J. D. Prince (*American Anthropologist*, New Series, XII, 206) as "the outlet of a river." He does not locate it. It is the same word as Wichcasset, with *tegwick,* "at the river," added.

The original form of our word would seem to have been *Wichicas-ek,* "at the outlet," referring to the land conveyed by Robinhood's deed of 1662.

There have been several other explanations, which have not appeared in print and therefore do not need to be discussed. Professor Ganong, being unfamiliar with the place and having no form earlier than Cargill's, used the root *esk* for "marsh" and proposed the meaning "at the little tidal creek," which would be the meaning of *Wis*casset, but not of *Wich*casset. Mr. Cabot obtained from an Indian a beautiful form of the Indian word *Wich'ka'sik,* but his Indian seems to have confounded the meaning with another word *waskiaso,* "a landslide," when he gave the meaning "at the wearing banks," for the name does not apply to the place. When Rev. Alden Bradford in the 1790's said it was "the meeting of three waters," he was describing the place but he did not have the analysis of the word; no doubt some Indian gave him the interpretation. Chief Joseph Laurent, of the St. Francis tribe, near Quebec, wrote: "Wiscassut is said to mean at the yellow pines"; but he used the root *koa,* "a white pine," with the adjective for yellow, and no Indian would speak of a "yellow white pine"; he would use a different word.

I believe the list of occurrences given is sufficient to settle the meaning of Wiscasset as purely descriptive of a location near the *outlet* of the harbor, with the implication that a bend in the river concealed it from one coming up the river.

BOOTHBAY.

Epituse. Apparently Fisherman's Island, lying east of Southport, but known to me only by the indenture of Moxes and Edgeremett, Indian sagamores, to Richard Patishall, 3 August, 1685 (*York Deeds,* IX, 229):
". . . a parcel of land comonly called by ye name of Damerel Cove, lying and being a Island in ye Sea, bounded with Seguin on ye West, Wood Island and Pumpkin Island to ye East, Cape bonawagon and *Epituse* on ye north . . ."

If Epituse lay north of Damariscove it could be nothing else than Fisherman's Island, a long, low, narrow island, lying between the eastern and western passages into Boothbay Harbor.

The name has been a puzzle, intriguing to Doctor Ganong, who, however, could come to no conclusion. At Point Pleasant I talked with Benedict Francis, one of the oldest Indians, trying to get a Maliseet interpretation, and he cited *Eptiduke* on the outside of Grand Manan, which Doctor Ganong identified as "old maid rock," a remarkable pillar rock, and cited Montague Chamberlain's *epit,* a Maliseet word for a woman. Dr. Ganong also named *Epidesk* or *Epitesk* as Carlow's Island "at the tip of Pleasant Point," but could not interpret beyond suggesting that there may once have been a standing rock here.

On the other hand, there may be something in this island's lying in the way of entering the harbor; for we have at Passamaquoddy, Harrison's Island, called *Epukunikek,* "something you have to go around" (Cabot); and Rasles gives us *nega epit* (p. 558), "he is there." A number of words for islands contain a very similar root. *No-epi,* Nantucket Island, was translated by Tooker as "in the midst of the waters," an appropriate name since four tides meet there (Dr. C. E. Banks). *Epagwit,* "it lies on the water," is one name for Prince Edward Island, and *Ebaghuit* (the same word) was given me by John Soctomer as the name of Campobello Island, to which Lewey Mitchell gave the translation "lies between (the passages to Passamaquoddy Bay)." We should surmise that the word Epituse meant that the island lay between the two passages into Boothbay.

As for the root, we note that in 1625 Purchas gave the name *Epistoman* as that of the country west of the Bashaba's dominions, and in 1658 Gorges' *Brief Narration* speaks of *Apistama* as "that part of the country which *lay between* the Sockhigones and Moasham," or the country near the Kennebec.

Hypocrites. Two ledges eastward of Fisherman's Island are known as The Hypocrites. The name has never been explained. That it does not belong to the ledges is shown by the earliest reference found, in 1674, when a tax of five pounds was levied on the inhabitants of Damariscove and *Hyppocras*. These ledges could never have had inhabitants.

That Fisherman's Island is the place meant is shown by the petition of William Sturt to Governor Andros, about 1688. Sturt wrote:

> "Whereas yor Petticon^r being Possest of a Small Island comonly caled *hypocrist* where yor Petticon^r is building an house, in ord^r to A Settlement But the sd Island being voyd of Wood Either for ffire or otherwise: And there being A small Rocky Island wth Woods Cloase by Caled Squirill Island which is Noe wayes Comodious for the fishery, & never have been taken vp, or Disposed of to Any as Yett the Which yor Petticon^r humbly Prays yor Excelency to Confirme to him," etc.

The island "cloase by Squirill Island" must be Fisherman's Island. We have seen that the Indian name of this was Epituse, which a man who could spell like Sturt could easily make over into Hypocrist. This was meaningless; so it was transformed by folk-etymology into The Hypocrites and transferred to the two bare ledges; because in the meantime Epituse was a forgotten name after William Sturt's house was built and the island was generally called Fisherman's Island. The only proof of this is the way it explains all the facts.

Abonegog. The Back River in Boothbay beyond the Oven Mouth.

> 1719. *Aboneisg* River—(*York Deeds*, IX, 188), "Land at Wichacassek Bay.... Marsh at ye head of ye Oven Mouth and from thence to ye head of *Aboneisg* River south" (Witt to Frost).
>
> 1720. *Obonagog* River—(*York Deeds*, IX, 156), "Land... thence to the head of *Obonagog* River" (Clark to Frost).

The description leaves no doubt about the two Indian words being the name of the long "Back River" behind the Oven Mouth. The first form is a clear mistranscription, the old *c* having been mistaken for an undotted *i* and *s* having been written in place of an *o*. The word is from *apanna-,* "spreads out"; *n'bi (ne),* "water"; and *-ook,* locative suffix indicating water— "spreads-out-water-place," referring to the way the long bay is enlarged behind the narrow Oven Mouth. *"Abonnebog,* open-wide-river," said a Penobscot Indian to Mr. Cabot.

Though the same word, this is not the same place mentioned in an Indian letter received in Boston July 1, 1677, regarding the exchange of prisoners, which says, "we would have you come with your vessel *Abonnegog"* (Massachusetts Archives, Vol. 30, 241a and 242). This is Ebenecook Harbor.

SOUTHPORT.

Cape Newagen. Southport is a large island, separated from the main by Townsend Gut, so narrow a stream that the whole town is more like a peninsula than like an island. Modern maps put the name "Cape Newagen" upon the very tip of the great point. The question is whether the name did not properly belong to the whole island; for it is Indian, not English, and has nothing to do with English capes.

The early forms are numerous and vary much, many of them being freaks which need no special consideration. The earlier examples are all in one word, indicating that the recorders of them understood that the word was Indian. Examples, out of more, are:

> 1623. *Capemanwagan*—(Christopher Levett, *Voyage*).
> *Capmanwagan*—(*Ibid.*).
> 1672. *Capanawhagan*—(John Josselyn, *Two Voyages*).

In these forms the initial syllable seems to be the Indian *kep,* which means "closed up," as by a stopper. *Kepahigan* is the word Rasles uses for a cork stopper. The last part of the word appears to be *ahwangan,* the word for a route, a general line of travel, but not a path or a road. *Kepan-* is used in composition, and Josselyn's form seems to be *Kepan-ahwangan.* Does it mean a "closed route"? If so, why?

A visit to the place with a cursory examination showed that off the tip of the point lie three islets which make a tiny harbor, sufficient for the old time fishing vessels from Europe and for modern small craft—Cape Harbor, it is called. This does indeed provide a refuge, but the place offers no attraction to Indians except occasional safety; they would not make a route around that rocky coast, exposed to the full sea, when there was something better. They would hardly call it a "closed route."

The word *kepan* is composed of two elements, *kep,* "plugged," "corked up," and *-an-,* "an opening" (Dr. William Jones, *Algonquin Word Formation,* p. 410), and to this Father Rasles contributes an idea. He gives *kepanousesek "l'endroit où on traverse les terres p'r se rendre dans un lac v. rivière, v. p'r aller en qq [quelque] endroit"* (478), a place where one crosses land to get from water to water or to get to some place. It was not a carry, *ounigen,* nor a road, *anudi,* for one could go or not, and as one pleased, but a place from which one was shut out unless he interrupted his course by water and went over land. Thus *kepanahwangan* would be a route across country.

The conditions at Newagen are these: there were three ways of getting along on a journey east and west—around the tip of the point, exposed to the sea; by the narrow Townsend Gut to the north; and across the land from side to side. Now on the west side of Southport was Ebenecook, the pleasant harbor beloved of Indians, where they could stop and camp and have social life and then stroll across the land to the other shore by any path preferred. Who would not choose this way? I think Capanawagan meant "where one crosses the land" (from preference, not from necessity), "an interrupted route."

Ebene'cook Harbor. On the western side of Southport Island, a favorite home of the Indians and a fine harbor.

Save for James Cargill's Scout Report, which in 1757 mentions *Abbenecook,* I have no early occurrences, though I believe it to be the *Aponeg* of Purchas. The meaning of the word is the same as that of *Abonegog,* though the two places are entirely different. No one can criticize the Indians for using the same name twice for places not far apart when today we have *four* Back Rivers there on our latest maps! "The entrance is narrow," says the *Atlantic Coast Pilot,* "but it is a fine harbor." "Opens-out-behind-entrance" is the idea, the word coming from *apanna,* "spreads out wide," and a locative ending.

Doctor Ballard's "bread-place" and "high-bush cranberry place"

Indian Place-Names of the Maine Coast 125

have no standing. The latter *ibimin* has the roots *n'be,* "water," and *min,* "berry," describing its preference for wet ground, and neither root appears in Ebenecook. The former is only the English loan-word, *abaïin,* "bread," from the English "oven," something baked in an oven.

Menikuk. Cape Harbor at Cape Newagen, Southport.
This has already been described, as one of the small harbors made by shelter-islands, often called harbor-islands. It is from the Maliseet and Micmac inseparable *meneek,* "an island," with the locative *-ook.*

A parallel name is *Menikoe* Point in Portland, where a small island makes the shelter, also *Moniecook* (now Barter Island, St. George's Bay). It should be remembered that Indians named these spots with reference to canoes, not to keeled craft; they needed no depth of water to find good harborage.

Aponeg. One of the nine rivers ruled over by Bashaba, the great sagamore of the Etchemins, according to Purchas.
Sheepscot River seems the river meant. The Indian headquarters were in the vicinity of Ebenecook Harbor, so Aponeg is most likely only a form of Abonegog (Ebenecook). In Indian words *p* and *b* were interchangeable, so that *Apon-* and *Abon-* are the same, while *-neg, -neag, -cog,* and *-cook* have the same value as endings. Some early explorer who had gone as far as Ebenecook probably understood that as the name of the river. The idea is of something spreading out, widening, from *apanna.*

Appowick. On Purchas's list of rivers this is the one next east of Apponeg. He says it had on it a town called Matamisconte. This can be nothing but Damariscotta; hence we take Appowick to be Damariscotta River.

Moasham, Mavooshen. The name given by Purchas to the country between the Kennebec and the rivers eastward over which Bashaba ruled. Our modern Indians make havoc of the word, yet they seem to associate it with a thickly settled country, so perhaps Father O'Brien's *pemabañsin,* "it is settled, can be traveled," has a bit of tradition behind it.

Hendrick Head. A headland, with lighthouse, standing out on the western shore of Southport Island.

Mrs. Fannie S. Chase could find no clue to this name. It is possible, however, that it was named for Hendrick, a prominent Mohawk chief, who in 1722 was a delegate to a conference in Falmouth (Portland).

Nekrangan. The only time this word has been found was in R. K. Sewall's *Ancient Dominions*. Sewall said it was the mouth of the Sheepscot River and meant "a gateway," from Rasles' *nekrangan*, "corrupted into Newagen." Sewall seems to have no authority but himself for either the word, the meaning, or the location. The word has nothing to do with Newagen, Rasles has no *nekrangan*, and his *kerangan* means a "door."

GEORGETOWN.

Erascohegan. Parker's Island.

Rascohegan, Rasthegan, and *Reskhegan* Island are the principal forms. Doctor Ganong thought that *eras-* might be the Micmac *welas* (Abnaki *oule*), "good," "goodly," expressing the comparative degree, while *sko* or *skwa* means a "watching place." We note that Treat and Webster Island in Old Town has the same name *Erascohegan,* "a watching place" (O'Brien), for which Father Vetromile in his correspondence gives the more modern form *Elaskahegan.*

> *Skwahegan* (modern Scowhegan), a "watching-place for fish," that is, a place where they watched to spear salmon as they passed up over the falls (Abnaki).
>
> *Skwazodic,* at Machiasport, a point where the Indians in the Revolution kept watch for British ships. The Machiasport pictographs are on the ledge here (Passamaquoddy).
>
> *Eskumunaak,* Nova Scotia, "a watching place," says Rand (Micmac).
>
> *Eskinwobudick,* Burnt Church, Nova Scotia, "a look-out" (Rand).

This shows that the root was common to the three languages and leaves no doubt as to its meaning. *Eraskohegan* must mean a watching-place, a look-out, regardless of which race named it. It would probably be applied only to some special spot at the tip of Parker's Island from which a sentinel could observe ships or canoes passing up or down either the Kennebec or the Sheepscot.

Malaga Island. A small island lying near to the western shore of Phippsburg.

Though it appears English, this in reality is a true Indian word, not much distorted. It means Cedar Island, if cedars ever grew there. The evidence is wholly circumstantial.

The St. Francis Indians of Canada, who were largely emigrants from the Kennebec, have kept the word *Môlôdagw* for the white cedar ar arborvitae, which is precisely the same word that Father Rasles gave in the form *mañrañdak8*, as *cèdres*. This was pronounced *maladag'w* and could easily become Malaga.

Now it happens that this word Malaga also occurs as the name of one of the Isles of Shoals. Though Celia Thaxter said very positively, "This name Malaga, by the way, is a very distinct token of the Spaniards" (*Among the Isles of Shoals* (1873), p. 35), she names both Cedar and Malaga as small islands connected at low tide with Smuttynose and says that on the latter island she herself had found a piece of the root of a very old cedar tree in a cleft in the ledge (p. 10). We may be quite sure that both Cedar and Malaga originally had the same name, "the cedar isles," and since we read in *York Deeds*, II (1667), 101, of "*Malligoe Ysland*" at the Ysles of Shoales," we may safely banish the Spaniards. The word is surely Indian.

If Malaga Island of the Shoals is Indian, the chance is remote that Malaga Island of Phippsburg is anything else.

Seguin. A high island off the mouth of the Kennebec River, important as a landfall for vessels. It is 145 feet above the sea (*Atlantic Coast Pilot*).

    1607. *Sutquin*—(Strachey).
          Satquin—(*Novi Belgii*).
    1616. *Satquin*—(Captain John Smith).
          Sodquin—(Captain Brawnde).
    1622. *Setquin*—(Council for New England).
    1647. *Zedguin*—(*Arcano del Mare*).

These forms of the name, collected by the late Dr. Charles E. Banks, would suggest very little as to the meaning of the word if it were not for a remark by Champlain, who says that in their explorations they arrived *"à la rivière du Quinibequy, où à l'ouverte d'icelle il y a une isle assez haute, qu'avons nommés la tortue"* [the tortoise] (Biggar's definitive edition of Champlain's *Works*, Toronto, 1922, I, 313).

Dr. William F. Ganong, editing the New England portion of this edition, explains in a footnote how Champlain's name is a translation of the Indian name. "From the east it does resemble a tortoise, whence evidently its name from the Indian, *che-quenocks,* called Siguenoc."

If it were not for the high authority behind this interpretation, we should say that it was farfetched and that more might be said for the suggestion of Doctor Banks, who wrote: "It seems to have in it the word used by the Algonquins, *segunau* (alone), in reference to its being the last one, alone out at sea. It is four leagues from land."

Against Doctor Banks, we might say that a Micmac name would be more likely than an Algonquin, unless the same root is common to both; and against Champlain's "tortoise"—though he has the name "La tortue" on his map of 1607 and on that of 1612, not only the same name but a picture of a big horse-shoe crab swimming lustily with its hind feet—we may cite another Seguin Island far to the eastward in Washington County. Can this, too, be explained by turtles or by horseshoe crabs? Though Champlain calls the island Turtle Island, yet his huge king-crab swimming so near it suggests an association of ideas. We suspect that the Indians, unable to translate the name for him, illustrated it by showing him a king-crab, while he himself recognized the resemblance to the rounded shell of a tortoise, and that what both he and the Indians were trying to express was a rounded mass, a hump. Now in modern Abnaki, we have a word *sigan,* meaning a hump; *ahassi-siganal* means a horse's withers. In the locative we should have *siganek* for a place resembling a hump, which is not far from Siguenoc, cited by Doctor Ganong. Until we know the Maliseet and Micmac equivalents for *sigan,* a "hump," it seems best to say that we have no satisfactory translation for Seguin; and we should take notice that all the earliest forms are *Satquin,* with a *tqu* cluster, not a *gu* combination.

Sagadahoc. The lower main channel of the Kennebec River, from a little below Bath to the sea.

As Mr. W. B. Cabot says, "Sagadehoc is the undifferentiated name for the mouth of a river." It comes from the root meaning "to pour forth," used especially of liquids and found in the name of rain, *soglan,* "what pours down."

The name is finely characteristic of the Kennebec as distinguished from the Penobscot, for example, which does not "pour forth" into the sea, but has a great bay at the mouth.

The name was early used and varies somewhat, but the forms are of no particular interest, since neither the name nor the location was ever in doubt. Yet it was also an old name for the Androscoggin River, "so called by Mouns[r] Bellin and also by most or all the Antient Plans" (Johnston's *Map of Plymouth Purchase,* 1754). A very similar form was sometimes used of the Saco (see Saco).

No better authority can be cited than Captain John Gyles, official interpreter, who said in his deposition, sworn in 1753: "I also understood by the Indians that the word Sagadarock in their language (and is the same with the word Sagadahock English make use of) means no more than the mouth or entrance into a river" (Suffolk Court Files, Vol. 450, case 74326).

Chegony. "East side of Sagadahoc, being an island comonly called by the name of *Sagosset,* alias *Chegony* by the Indians" (1661, *York Deeds,* XI, 139).

Beyond this note furnished by the late Colonel Charles E. Banks, I know nothing of this unidentified island. Chegony seems to have been the Indian name, and if it is connected with Machigony, it is important.

Sagosset. The word seems to be made from *sauk* and *esset,* in which case it would mean "in the neighborhood of the outlet," meaning of the Kennebec River.

Bombazine Island. A small island in Sagadahoc River.

This is given on modern maps and probably is recent. It may have been conferred in memory of Abomazeen, often called Bombazeen, a chief killed at Norridgewock in 1724, perhaps under the impression that he was the same as Damazee, who deeded land in this vicinity in 1640.

Robinhood Bay. A large backwater in Georgetown, named for a sachem who signed many land deeds in this region.

Sabino. An early chief whose name is kept near Small Point. "His name that Came unto us ys Sabenoa. he macks hemselffe unto us to be Lord of the ryver of Sagadahoc," wrote the author of *The Relation of a Voyage to Sagadahoc,* setting down the events of September 26, 1607 (Burrage, *Gorges and the Grant of the Province of Maine*).

Sasanoa. "The tidal river to which there is an entrance opposite Bath," says Doctor Burrage in a footnote to *The Relation of a Voyage to Sagadahoc.*

This is now called Back River, one of several of the same name. It is mentioned by William Strachey, in 1607, who says that Captain Gilbert, of Popham's expedition, "returned homeward, in the way seeking the by river of some note called *Sasanoa.*" The river was named for Sasanou, the great chief whom Champlain saw. Later John Smith named what is now called Mount Agamenticus "Sasanow's Mount," for the same chief. Elsewhere he is spoken of as "the chief commander to the westward" under the great chief Bashaba, who ruled by his own right to the Kennebec River and by sovereignty over other tribes as far as Saco River.

That there was trouble between Bashaba and some under Sasinow—(the final *a* was added only after a person had died, so that Smith's and Champlain's forms are correct)—is shown by Popham himself. In 1607 he met the Indians at Sheepscot (Pashipscoke) "who delyvred unto them that they had been att wars wth Sasanoa and had slain his Soone in fyght." And Popham says that "skidwares and Dehanada wear in this fyght."

Now Skidwarres and Dehanada were two of the Indians whom Waymouth kidnapped at George's River in 1605. They had been in England two years, but had come back with Popham to act as guides and interpreters. They were landed August 7, fresh from abroad and apparently with no quarrels of their own; yet by August 23, they had been on a raid to Casco Bay, had engaged in a bloody battle in which a great chief's son was killed and were back at Sheepscot again. It was not easy to civilize an Indian.

Arrowsic Island. A large island which blocks the channel of the lower Kennebec River. The accent is on the second syllable; the meaning of the word is unknown.

    1717. *Arousick*—... "called *Arouscag* by the Indians" (Rev. J. Baxter's Journal, in *New England Historical and Genealogical Register*, XXI, 50 ff.). This is the only instance of the ending in *-keag,* a water ending.

    1721. *Arusuk*—(Massachusetts Archives, 51, 357).

    1795. *Arrowseag*—"The lands on Arrowsike, or as the savages called it *Arrowseag* Island, were sold in the year 1660 to Roger Spencer and Thomas Clarke" (Sullivan, *History of the District of Maine,* p. 145).

The resemblance of the first part of the word to the as yet not understood *arra,* so often found in names of falls and rapids, suggests some connection with *arantsoak, nanrantsoak,* "rapids," and that this was the name of the swift channels past the island, while the French *Menaskek* may have been the island itself. The only explanation of the word available is the contemporary one in Hubbard's *Narrative of the Indian Wars in New England* (1676, Vol. II), which says: "This island (called Arowsick, from an Indian so named that formerly possessed it, and of whom it was purchased by one Mr. Richards, who sold it to Capt. Lake and Major Clarke) lies up ten miles within the mouth of Kennebeck River." Careful search of the eighteen volumes of *York Deeds* has failed to disclose any transfer which might trace back to this Indian deed, and it is not among the Indian deeds summarized in the transfer of Kennebec lands to the Kennebec Company. Sullivan remarks that Sir Bibye Lake inherited it through Indian deeds but gives no details (*District of Maine*). Nothing is known of the chief referred to by Hubbard, and we have no clue to the meaning of the word. The interpretations "flint" and "place where arrow heads are made" are fictional.

Manashoak. A name for Arrowsic Island found in the Journals of Rev. Joseph Baxter for 1721, the year he visited it (*New England Historical and Genealogical Register,* XXI, 58). We should like the word better if he had written it *Menaskoak* (as perhaps he did!), but it must be the same as the French *Menaskek* or *Menaskous.* The root is not *man,* but *men,* "island," from *menahan,* and *ask,* "grass," indicating probably an island with cleared fields rather than the common usage for a treeless, or grassy, island.

Menaskek. Arrowsic Island.

This good form was found in a letter from Father Rasles, dated 28 July, 1721. It is printed in French in Massachusetts Historical Society *Collections,* 2nd Series, VIII, 261.

Menaskous, "*le Fort Anglais de Manaskous,*" that is, Fort Frederic on Arrowsic Island (Report of Vaudreuil and Begon to the Ministry, in Baxter's *Pioneer of New France in New England,* 110-113 and 117).

Menaskoux, "the English fort of Menaskoux" (*New York Colonial Documents,* IX, 895).

Manaskong, "fort on the island of Manaskong" (Begon, in *New York Colonial Documents,* IX, 944).

Menaskonkus (Rasles, letter, 1720), probably same as the above.

Father Rasles, at Norridgewock, in 1720, wrote Governor Shute of Massachusetts that the English carpenter "Jebis," who is building his church, "departs to go see his father at Menaskonkus, saying he would return in eight days." We know that "Jebis" was Capt. Jabez Bradbury of Fort Richmond; for we have his deposition under oath that he "assisted in building a house of worship at Norridgewock where I resided among them for a considerable time" (Suffolk County Court Cases, Vol. 464, pp. 94-95, no. 7662b).

Kekepanagliesek. A French name for Arrowsic Island.

This name occurs once only, in connection with the fight there in 1723, when French and Indians attacked the English, killed one man and fifty head of cattle, and burned twenty-six dwellings. "We told you after the fall fight of *Ke-ke-pen-agliesek* that the English would come with the Nation of the Iroquois to revenge themselves," wrote Father Rasles in that long letter which he never signed, because as he was writing the English were all around him, and it was the last hour at Norridgewock. The reference must be to that attack made September 10, 1723, when four or five hundred Canada and Cape Sable Indians descended upon Arrowsic as described by Judge Penhallow in his contemporary account of *The Wars of New England with the Eastern Indians* (pp. 93-94, 1859 ed.) Judge Penhallow's son was the captain in command of the English.

As Father Rasles writes it, the word is not divided to show the roots. Written as *Kekep-nagliesek,* it is easier to extract the meaning. Even here, since the original letter no longer exists and J. P. Baxter had to make his copy from a certified copy in the Public Records Office of London, it may be questioned whether the *l* was not originally an *h,* which would give us *-naghi,* the inseparable root for an island. The first part is the root *kep,* "closed, stopped up," reduplicated as *kekep,* "very much stopped up." What Rasles seems to call it is "the island which almost closes the channel" of the Sagadahoc. Doctor Ganong wrote December 20, 1932: "*Kebaniktak* occurs more than once in New Brunswick for an island lying in a river so that it seems to close the passage, which is divided around it." At first we both thought the word contained the diminutive, that *-naghies* meant "the little island"; but Arrowsic is not a little island. The ending might mean "in the vicinity of" the island (*-esek* standing for *-esset*); but the facts forbid—the fight was upon Arrowsic itself. In a copy of a French letter of that date anything might happen to an Indian word, and the best we can say is that we cannot analyze it entirely satisfactorily though the general signification is clear.

Hobbomocca Point. The point in Arrowsic Island marked on the map as Hockomock Point.

The word means much more than Hockomock, and an old deed reveals the story. The deed of William Phipps, son or grandson of Sir William Phipps, to Andrew Bordman, October 5, 1734, conveys one half of the peninsula of Jeremysquam, with as its southern bound, "a river commonly called the Little River that runs between the Land of a Point of Land [*sic*] called *Hobbomocca Point* and the said Cheremessequame Neck," etc. (*York Deeds,* XVII, fol. 190).

Now Hobomocco was an Indian word used by the English as a cant expression meaning Hell. The epitaph of John Bonython of Saco, current about 1650, readily comes to mind,—

Here lies Bonython, the Sagamore of Saco;
He lived a rogue and died a knave and went to Hobomoco.

A little above this spot modern maps have the name Upper Hell Gate, which implies another place of dangerous currents, which would be Lower Hell Gate, and must be off Hobbomocca Point.

BATH and WEST BATH.

Whiskeag. A creek a little west of Bath, running north into Merrymeeting Bay.

The name has numerous forms, chiefly corruptions by the English settlers—Whisgeag, Whizgeag, Whisgig, Wesquag, Worsqueage, Weswick, and others. The meaning "rapidly running water" is pure folk-etymology, from a supposd element "whizz." The map shows that it is a tidal creek which can have no great current.

Wisqueg, the earliest form, is found in 1677 (*York Deeds,* III, fol. 80) in the deed of Camer's Island, formerly Purchase's Island, in Kennebec River, "with plantation *Wisqueg* westerly and with Merremeeting northerly and the river southwardly." In 1728 we have "the cove or creek called *Weswick*" (*Pejepscot Papers,* VIII, 54), and in Joseph Heath's survey of 1718 (*ibid.,* VIII, 53) we find *Worsqueage.*

The root is the one Professor Ganong found "in all cases applied to tidal creeks, usually if not always bordered with salt marshes. The tidal idea involves, apparently, the idea of the tide running out, as in *8si'kkat (wheshikat)* of Rasles' *Abnaki Dictionary,* p. 493, though it may involve the root *esk,* the stem for many words meaning hay, grass, etc. In any case, the idea of a creek that runs dry (or nearly) with low tide, and is commonly if not always bordered with salt-marsh, offers a consistent interpretation of the main root."

Aquehadongonock. A tract of land at Whiskeag, west of Bath, surveyed in 1718 by Joseph Heath (*Pejepscot Papers,* VIII, 53), who wrote: "This Plott of Land called in Indian *Aquehadongonock* ... to the head of Weswick Creek and from said creek to Sagadahock River and Merrymeeting Bay." This apparently includes the upper part of West Bath and most of Bath, with Aquehadongonock the point at the head of it. Other occurrences:

Aguahadonaneag, "aboriginal name of Whisgeag" (Massachusetts Historical Society *Collections,* 2nd Series, IV, 245).

Aquehadongonock Point (Douglas-Lithgow, *Dictionary of American Indian Place-names*). The meaning is given as "smoked-fish point," which is manifestly wrong.

Aguahadongoneek, in the Indian deed to Thomas Stevens, of Brunswick, December 9, 1654, described as land near Kennebec River called Aguahadongoneek from Grape Island to Wigwam Bay, etc., and the whole neck to Merrymeeting.

The last is the earliest reference and clearly refers to the tract later surveyed by Heath, the large point between Kennebec and Androscoggin Rivers.

The first part of *Aguahadongonek* is from *ag8ama, extraho ex aqua* (Nudenans), meaning "I drag my canoe out of the water," that is, "make a landing." It is substantially the same word as the Penobscot name for Fort Point, *Aguahassidek,* "a landing place." The last part of the word has to be accepted on faith in the mutability of Indian words; but *-adongon-* appears to be *ahwangan,* "a route," as we found it in Newangan, and the terminal syllable is the locative. "Landing for portage" seems to be the meaning, or, as we say, "end of the carry."

The map shows that the Chops of Merrymeeting Bay are very narrow and must have strong tidal currents, dangerous at times to a canoeman. At the head of Butler Cove is a narrow neck of low land which leaves only a short distance to carry in order to get into the Kennebec well below the Chops. *Pejepscot Papers* places the name *Aquehadongonock* upon Chops Point, indicating that here was the portage place.

Wigwam Bay, Wigwam Point. Named in the Indian deed to Stevens just quoted. Wheeler (*History of Brunswick,* 1887, p. 6) places Wigwam Point on New Meadows River. Wigwam Bay may have been the "head of the bay" and the Point may have taken its name from the Bay, apparently Middle Bay and Howard Point on modern maps. In early names like this, the Micmac *wekw,* meaning "the head of," sometimes gets changed to Wigwam, and this looks suspiciously like one of the very old words.

Seogogguanegabo. Robinhood and Derumkin deeded to Thomas Stevens land near the River Abbacoggin (Androscoggin) "at a place called Seogogguanegabo," one mile square (Maine Historical Society *Collections,* Documentary Series, XXXIII, 206). Stevens lived on the Stevens Carrying Place from Androscoggin to New Meadows, and this tract must have been near. The name has been barbarously mistreated, but the *Seo* may stand for *che,* "big," *ogoggua* might have been hazed out of *aguaha,* and *negabo* would not in those days have seemed far-fetched from *dongonek,* a transformation of the word for a landing place considered just above. All that would lend any weight to such a conjecture would be that Stevens's location offered remarkable facilities for Indian travel in different directions, so that, like Katawamtek on the Penobscot and Medabiaught on the St. Croix, it might have been a great resort for Indians coming and going to fishing and hunting grounds, and a grand location for an Indian trader.

WEST BATH.

Winnegance. A bay making up from the south and a creek flowing north, about on the town line between Phippsburg and West Bath, both bear the name Winnegance, which belongs to neither but to the short space of dry land between the two. This was the ancient *wunnegan,* or *ounegan,* the portage between the two waters. Because it was short, the diminutive *sis* was added. *Winnegansis* means "Short Carry."

In 1660, in the Indian deed from Robinhood to Robert Gutch the *Wennigansege* tract is named; in 1684, the Winnegance marshes —"so fare as the carrying place into Weñeganse marshes" (*York Deeds,* IV, fol. 34); also *Winiganse* Cricke (*York Deeds,* IV, fol. 17). In 1693 the Gunnison to Pepperrell deed speaks of "ye narrow of s^d Neck known by ye name of *Winagance,* or carrying place" (*York Deeds,* VI, fol. 58). The name was used frequently in deeds for this particular place, but undoubtedly the same word was applied to a score or more of the short carries across the attenuated necks of land which stretch south into the sea. It is one of the commonest and simplest of all our place names and would not have acquired any prominence where it is now placed, had it not appeared in deeds as the boundary of lands.

Towessic, Tuessick. According to Doctor Ballard (Coast Survey Paper, 1868, 9), this is "a point in Woolwich that lies over against the upper end of Arrowsic Island. The Indian explanation refers the meaning to 'breaking through.' Perhaps it may be translated 'The Broken Passage.'"

Doctor Ballard locates the land where we have previously found the name of Nasket. In a land location, *York Deeds* must be correct, and the deeds put Tuessick not in Woolwich on the east side of the Kennebec, but in Bath on the west side. *York*

Deeds, XVIII, 236, names land, formerly belonging to Robert Gutch, on the west side of Long Reach, from Tuessick Rocks to Winslow's Rocks, and three miles back. In 1734 Mary Soper sells to Donnell land formerly belonging to Gutch "over against Tuessack," mentioning the rocks at the lower bounds and also Winslow's Rocks "right over against" the northern bound (*York Deeds,* XVII, 106).

Several forms have been found. Two old French maps have *Tesies* and *Teouies,* and Joseph Heath the surveyor gives *Towess* (*Pejepscot Papers,* VIII, 54), which is Towessic without the locative ending. We know too little of the history of the word to be able to comment, and we are little helped by finding the word again as *"Tuessick Neck* alias Merriconeage Neck" in a deed from Mountjoy to Penn Townsend, dated 1722 (*York Deeds,* XI, 265).

WOOLWICH.

Jeremysquam. Now a part of the town of Woolwich.

Though Sullivan (*History of the District of Maine,* 144) calls this an island, the Phipps to Bordman deed gives the bounds precisely and shows that it was the great peninsula between Mountsweag Bay and Nequasset Stream.

Sullivan says it was sold in 1649 by Indian deed to John Richards, but I have not seen the original form of the word. In 1664 it was called "land known by the name of Jeremisquome River" (*York Deeds,* II, fol. 8). In 1672 it was mentioned as Jeremesequems Bay (*York Deeds,* II, fol. 127). The name is an impossible one, because no Maine Indian word of native origin can begin with the letter *j*. Only foreign words, like Jesus, have initial *j*, and this was pronounced like an *s;* thus Jaques became Sak, and now is Sock—"James Vincent" becoming "Sockbasin."

However, the Phipps to Bordman deed of 1734, previously mentioned, gives not only the form *Jeremesquame Neck,* but *Cheremessequame Neck.* We know that *misquam,* farther west, meant a "great neck," which leaves the two first syllables unaccounted for; thus far we have found nothing that explains them. The meaning given by Douglas-Lithgow, "the island of Jeremy who lives by the water," and R. K. Sewall's "the island of water creeks" are absurd; the deed proves that Jeremesequam was a great neck and not an island at all.

Nasket Point. Said to be in Woolwich.

This should be the long, narrow point opposite Bath. It is the same word as Naskeag, on the Penobscot, and means "at the end," "the extremity," "the tip," from *anaskwi* or *wanasque*. The place probably is Captain John Smith's *Nassaque*.

Nequasset. A pond, stream, and a tract of land in Woolwich.

This would seem to belong to Nequasset Pond; for *nequassebem* means a pond, and this is the only large one in this region.

MERRYMEETING BAY.

Merrymeeting Bay. The enlargement of the Kennebec River where it receives the Androscoggin, before narrowing to Sagadahoc.

There are no less than three explanations of the name. Doctor Wheeler has two in his *History of Brunswick* and John McKeen Esq., has a third. All sound apocryphal when we recall that Lake Winnepesaukee also has a Merrymeeting Bay, in a place which could not so well be explained, as the meeting ground of convivial persons or of tribal rendezvous. "Anyway, no doubt not Indian," comments Ganong.

Chisapeak. An unusual name for Merrymeeting Bay, found in the journals of Rev. Joseph Baxter, who was there in 1722 (Allen, *History of Dresden,* 281).

The name analyzes easily as *che,* "big"; *sepe,* "river"; *-ak,* locative ending—"at the big part of the river."

Nassouac, or **Naxoat.** Merrymeeting Bay.

In 1648, according to Dr. N. T. True ("Uncle Felix," in *Portland Transcript,* November 21, 1874), Father Druillettes used this name for Merrymeeting Bay. He had founded a mission a few miles from Augusta and knew the region. Dr. True wrote, "It seems to mean 'the halfway place' or 'the land between,' from *nashue,* 'midway,' and *auke,* 'land.' " With this interpretation the name would apply to one of the points of land between the Kennebec and the Androscoggin—above and below their point of meeting— not to the Bay. While the ordinary word for "between" would be *nawiwi,* or in composition *nawi* or *naw,* a Penobscot Indian gave me *nassau* as "center" and *nassoway* as "middle," thus verifying Dr. True's definition.

Quabacook. Another name for Merrymeeting Bay.

This occurs in the deposition, taken July 19, 1793, from Perepole, an Indian. "From *Quabacook* what is now Merrymeeting Bay," is his statement (Maine Historical Society *Collections,* III, 333); but he does not say that it means "duck-water place," as stated by Wheeler (*History of Brunswick,* p. 5, citing this deposition), and by Dr. N. T. True (*Brunswick Telegraph,* 1864).

Quabacook cannot mean "duck-water place": it has no root which means a bird of any sort. The first part of the word appears to be defective. It might be *m'qua,* a shortened form of *m'gwak,* or *mugwock,* "bog," "swamp," "sunken land," and *bague,* "still water," in the locative. Dr. Ganong suggests that it might come "from the Micmac *wekw,* 'head of a bay,' in allusion to the head of the salt water on the Kennebec, the part where the current begins."

The interpretation "duck-water place" is probably the Indian way of describing a place instead of analyzing its name; which a questioner, who does not understand them, accepts as the meaning of the word. Doctor Ganong's comment is: "A very common trait among Micmacs and Maliseets, causing much trouble until one 'gets on' to it." This bay was notable for its flights of game birds. Judge Penhallow says that in 1717, soon after he was there, during the fall moult when the birds could not fly well, the Indians organized a drive and forced them into the muddy creeks, "where without either powder or shot they killed at one time four thousand six hundred," which they sold to the English for a penny a dozen (*History of the Indian Wars in New England,* 1726, p. 85, 1859 ed.). From such an incident, which Penhallow said was an annual custom, we can see how the place was associated with ducks.

Psazeske. Muddy River. A small tributary of Merrymeeting Bay.

The word is rare, but the meaning is clear. *Ps* is the root *pesk,* something that is split off, a "branch," and *asesk8* is Rasles' word for *boue,* "mud." Muddy Branch is the translation.

Cathance River (pronounced Cat'-hance). A tributary to Merrymeeting Bay. Doctor Wheeler quotes Doctor Ballard as saying it was pronounced *kat-hah-nis* and meant "bent or crooked." It certainly is crooked, but we find no word which would give that meaning from these roots. The pronunciation probably was given by an Indian and is closely similar to that of *K'the'nis,* or *Kethen'isq',* the name of Denny's River in Washington County, now also called Cathance. Lewey Mitchell, the Maliseet, told me that this was from *keght,* "principal," and *-nik,* "fork." The words appear to be the same, and Cathance in Bowdoinham, like the other, has two branches, the so-called West River being much the smaller.

Swango Island. In Merrymeeting Bay. Said by Allen (*History of Dresden,* p. 113) to be shortened to Swan Island.

In 1671, Sylvanus Davis bought by Indian deed dated April 22, two hundred acres "over against Swan Island" (*York Deeds,* VIII, fol. 178). This is too early for the name to have been changed from Swango. It may be that Swango stands for *sowangan,* the bald eagle, which might well have nested in the trees of this island near such good fishing ground. The name may mean Eagle Island, and we are not sure that it was the same as Swan Island.

Kebec. The old name for the Chops of Merrymeeting Bay. (The word "chops," by the way, in the older English signified "jaws." The Chops were the jaws where the bay closed in below Merrymeeting.)

The location of Kebec, or the Narrows, is given very precisely in *Pejepscot Papers,* VIII: "Acquehadongonock, a point on the west side of the Chops, Kebec, where the Kennebec leaves Merrymeeting Bay."

Kebec contains the root *keb* or *kep,* something that is closed in, contracted, plugged. It is the same word as Quebec and Doctor Ganong comments: "Hamel, 1833, a fine Indian authority, gives for Quebec, 'which looks closed (as you first see it).' "

Memeeneesitt. A creek a little below Merrymeeting Bay on the east side; found in a map of 1795, copied from a plan of 1750 in *Pejepscot Papers,* VIII. The form of the name uncertain; it might be Memeoneesett; nothing known of it.

Nagusset. Doctor Wheeler places this at Abagadusset Point, the upper point between the Kennebec and the Androscoggin (*History of Brunswick*). In making it from *naiag,* an "angle," "corner," "point," Doctor Ballard is probably correct (*Coast Survey,* 6). This would tend to throw the name Abagadusset to the stream, where it seems to belong. It is probably the same land as Druillettes' *Nassouac,* or *Naxoat.* Pejepscot Papers show that this is not the same place as Nequasset (Cozzen's deposition in *Pejepscot Papers,* I, 105, and Capt. Heath's map, 1719, *ibid.,* VIII, 50 and 50a).

Abagaduset Point and **River** at Merrymeeting Bay, in Bowdoinham.

Though the same document may spell this name in a half dozen ways, they have no special significance. We have, for example:

    1716.   *Abbacadusset Point*—(*York Deeds,* VIII, fol. 167).

    1719.   *Abagadassic Point*—(*Ibid.,* X, fol. 23).
            Abegadesset Point—(*Ibid.,* fol. 68).

    1719.   *Abagadusett* River—(Joseph Heath's map, *Pejepscot Papers.* Heath called the point Point Agreeble.

Which was named first, the point or the river? The word itself must largely determine the question. Though Doctor Ganong has said that *abag-* means "curved in a bow," he adds, "a more general expression for it, applicable everywhere, is 'following a shore parallel.' I think *parallel* is a better meaning; may, or may not be curved, though the *abe* root implies a curve. At all events of the near a dozen cases in Micmac territory with this root, the place follows parallel or concentric with the main shore or land." In this case, the name would belong to the small stream west of the point, parallel with the Kennebec River; its use for the point would have been secondary. "Little-parallel river" (Ganong).

Trumbull gives the meaning "at the cove or place of shelter." Sullivan (*History of Maine* (1795), 30) says "so called from a Sachem of that name who lived there one hundred years ago." We find the man signing deeds in 1649 and 1653, but Mr. Cabot thinks it probable that he took his name from his residence.

Kennebec River. There is little fundamental difference in the forms, which have come down in a perfect series. Among them are:

    1609. *Kinibeki*—(Lescarbot's map).
    1610. *Cinebaque*—(Simancas map).
    1611. *Kinibequi*—(Father Biard).
    1613. *Quinebequy*—(Champlain's map).
    1614. *Kenebecka*—(Captain John Smith).
    1616. *Kenebeke*—(Captain John Smith).
    1626. *Kenebeck*—(Bradford, *History of Plymouth*).

The only point here that is noteworthy is that only the last example shows the locative *k*. The French were apt to omit it from Indian words which they adopted, but the English usually kept some form of the locative.

The word is entirely simple. It means "long, quiet water," in reference to the long stretch without falls or rapids below Augusta. *Kine, kini,* and *quine* are all forms of the word for "long," and *-bague,* in Abnaki, is a very common root in composition for quiet, or still, water. It does not mean "dead water," without a current, but "level water," without rapids or falls. It is a common word for ponds and lakes. However, the root *-bague* was unfamiliar to both those eminent students Trumbull and Ganong, who tried to make the word, the one from *n'be* and the other from *-pac,* a less simple process.

Those who have tried to interpret the word Kennebec have made sad work of it. Dr. J. A. Chute, going to the Delawares of Missouri, announced that it meant "They who thanked!" Judge C. E. Potter made it from the word for "snake." Abbé Maurault said, "which leads to the lake"—a rather far-fetched meaning for the traveler who started from the Chops! Some say it was named from the old chief Kenebis, but he was signing deeds in 1653, almost fifty years after Lescarbot's map. Trumbull says "long water region," though nothing in the word means land or region. Our Indians do no better. Joseph Nicolar gives "long blade." Chief Laurent wrote "large lake" or "deep river." H. L. Masta says, "a river full or nearly full up to its banks." And an old Indian friend of mine said, "Kennebec, named for people—all dead now."

The question whether the name Kennebec applied only to the

part of it above Sagadahoc was answered in the legal review of the Plymouth Purchase Case, 1755. John Phillips, who deposed that his father came to Parker's Island about 1664, declared that the "river Kennebec retains the name not only from Merrymeeting Bay upwards but also down to the sea or Ocean" (Suffolk Court Cases, Vol. 449, p. 122, No. 73396). Others, including Capt. John Gyles, give the same testimony. But it is to be understood that this is only an extension of the *name;* the *meaning of it* applies only above the Chops.

Long Reach. The Kennebec at Bath. Here for some miles was a straight stretch of water where a vessel did not need to trim her sails but could make a "long reach" on the same course. It is a good translation of the word Kennebec, dating back to 1662.

DRESDEN.

Mundoouscootook, or **Munduscoottook,** Eastern River, Dresden. "Devil's rush river." "So called from the rushes of a singular species which grow upon its banks" (Rev. Jacob Bailey, clergyman at Pownalboro, 1760-1779, quoted in Allen's *History of Dresden,* p. 15).

Presumably the rush meant is *Typha angustifolia,* described by Gray as "Southern Maine to North Carolina, less frequent than the Common Cat-tail and mainly near the coast." The cat-tail figures in certain Indian myths as having magical powers when used against an enemy. The name shows plainly enough that this plant was so regarded, for the first part of it means "the Devil." The second root is the familiar *esk,* for a "green, growing thing"; the ending stands for *-tagook—tegwe,* "river," *-ook,* locative ending. The name may be translated, "river where the Evil-Spirit's-rush grows," for the Indian *matsk8* or *matsihannedo* (here *mundoo*), "devil," is not so concrete an image as the Puritan Satan.

PITTSTON.

Nehumkeag or **Nahumkeag.** A stream, pond, falls, and island in Pittston.

The second word is the better form: it comes from the Abnaki *nahurmo,* an "eel," and the locative ending *-eag,* best interpreted as from the Maliseet and Micmac *-eak,* "runs out," not a stream or the point at the junction of streams. Doctor Ganong translated Nehumkeag as "at-an-eel-place-runs-out"; that is, there was eel fishing at the mouth of the stream, to which alone the name applies. It is the equivalent of the Maliseet Kenduskeag on the Penobscot, just as Cobossecontee is replaced to the eastward by the Maliseet Passagassawaukeag at Belfast.

Nehumkeag, in its various forms, has to be carefully distinguished from *Negwamkeag,* six miles below Waterville, because both words rose into prominence during the Plymouth Purchase settlement in 1755, when even the Indian interpreters most experienced upon the river gave somewhat contradictory testimony as to the places because both were insignificant. There are many depositions in the Suffolk Court Files, in Boston, about the words. On the 1790 map of Lincoln County, Maine (Roller #976, Massachusetts Archives), *Nahungig* in Pittston is Nehumkeag and must be distinguished from *Nahumkeek* in Vassalboro, the latter an error for the quite different *Negwamkeag,* which has no reference to eels at all.

Hallowell, often formerly called "The Hook" by an abbreviation of *Bombahook,* supposed to be its Indian name. But Colonel William Lithgow, in his deposition of 1767, said "that it was called by the Indians *Kee-dum-cook* and the Indians, when asked why they so called it, said it was 'because the river was very shoal there and from the gravel and sand that appeared almost across the river at low water,' " (*New England Historical and Genealogical Register,* Vol. 24 (1870), 23).

GARDINER.

Cobossecontee. A name now applied to a stream, and the pond above, near Gardiner. Properly it was neither, but only the place at the mouth of this stream very near the present railroad station. It comes from *kabasseh,* "a sturgeon," and *kañtti,* denoting occurrence or abundance—the place where sturgeon were to be found. The name is too well known in print and the variations of either form or meaning are too inconsequential to need comment. It was pre-eminently the place on the Kennebec where the Indians fished for sturgeon, or, speaking more properly, where they lured them with torches and then speared them.

The name *kebasseh* refers to the habit of the sturgeon of leaping out of water.

AUGUSTA.

Cushnoc. The old name for Augusta.

Not far from here was the head of the tide, which was stopped by the falls, and the name indicates that above this point one met the current. Acushnet, in Massachusetts, is a similar name. Most of the meanings proposed may be disregarded, but we cannot pass by Colonel Lithgow's statement in his deposition of June 6, 1767, in which he says: "On the eastern side of Kennebec is a point of land called *Cusinock* by the natives, who say they give it that name because the tide runs no higher up Kennebec. On said point of land is Fort Western." The idea is not so much "head of the tide" as that here the current overpowers the tide—as Ballard says, "the running down place." After great efforts to get a correct definition from the pundits, James W. North summed up what they had said: "As we have no peninsula, or river point of prominence, nor Indian burying ground, we are at present compelled to adopt the interpretation which gives to Cushnoc what appears to be its probable meaning— 'the head of the tide' " (*History of Augusta,* 1870, p. 452).

Negwamkeag. The old limit of the Plymouth Company lands, about six miles below Taconic.

The depositions referred to previously give information of interest, but it would take too much space to give details. Nagwamkeag was a place between two islands, still to be seen, where at certain stages of water there was a great boil, over sunken rocks or a bar, dangerous to navigation. It seems to have been somewhat similar to The Cook at Old Town. The ending *-amkeag* is a recognized Maliseet word for a sandbar.

WATERVILLE.

Taconic. The great falls at Waterville, just above the mouth of the Sebesteguk.

One of the most difficult words we have encountered. Though the form Taconic is found as far back as Guillaume de Roziers' map of 1699, it seems incomplete. Father Aubéry's, and other

French maps, have *Katakouan,* which gives the impression that the initial T of our Taconic is only the last letter of *Keght,* or *K't,* "principal," "the biggest." Of course the last syllable is the locative *-ic,* or *-ek,* leaving *-akouan* to puzzle over. We suspect a close connection with Captain John Smith's *Ketangheauyoke,* which he places upon the main Kennebec River.

Among the place-names secured for J. W. Hanson's *History of Gardiner and Pittston* (1852) from Gov. John Neptune of Old Town, is *Taconnet,* given as "a place to cross." There could be no better authority at that time, and it is well understood that often there is shallow water, in certain seasons, just above waterfalls. In Bangor the old fording place was above the present Bangor Dam. While in time of freshet the falls of Taconic pour down an overwhelming torrent of water, in time of drought I have seen the ledges below the bridges so bare that, but for a single channel, one might walk across the river, and the channel might almost have been vaulted with a leaping pole. "The great crossing" may have been the name, but we do not yet know.

The strategic importance of Taconic in early times was great. All traffic had to "take out" and carry past the great falls (just beneath the railroad bridge at Winslow and Waterville), so that the position of the fort at Winslow, built in 1754 by Governor Shirley (one corner blockhouse still standing in view from the trains), commanded the traffic up and down the Kennebec, over to the Penobscot, and by the Short Route (Arnold's) to Quebec. Indians going from Penobscot to Quebec did not follow the Sebesteguk to its mouth, but took out some distance above and carried across to the Kennebec at a point above the falls. A blockhouse on the high land above Fort Halifax commanded this carry.

CHAPTER FIVE

THE SOUTHWEST COAST, FROM BRUNSWICK TO KITTERY[1]

In this section, as in the previous one, the names are old, and often they are much worn or disguised by illiterate spellings; but the documentary sources, which are abundant, include the earliest forms. Our modern Indians have much difficulty with the words, and since little is known of the language of the Indians who lived here before war and pestilence swept them away, we lack facilities for translation of names which we find recorded in early deeds and travels. Yet here, as farther east, in the case of important words we often get the most satisfactory results by using Maliseet and Micmac roots and combinations. We are not assuming that these tribes occupied this territory within historic times, for Champlain says that the language of his eastern Indians was different, so that they had to have interpreters; but lacking vocabularies, we find unexpected help in the more eastern dialects. So many words are found only once or twice that no attempt is made to interpret them.

Androscoggin County is small and offers little of importance except the name of the river and "Pejepscot"; Cumberland County, with its extent of coastline, is rich in good names; and York County yields many more. The interior affords few names of importance within these three counties, that of Sebago Lake being the most notable.

Androscoggin River. The name— -*nahmays*, "fish," and -*coggin*, "place for preparing, curing"—indicates the abundance of migratory fish, principally alewives, but also salmon, shad, and bass, which passed up this long river.

The word is found in almost innumerable forms, which need not be assembled except as an assurance that they are all the same word, however much they differ in appearance. The following examples are taken chiefly from men who knew the Indian language and the place.

    1616. *Aumoughcawgin*—Capt. John Smith.
    1639. *Androscoggin*—Thomas Purchase's release to Massachusetts (Massachusetts Records I, 272—Trumbull).

---

[1] Including Androscoggin, Cumberland, and York counties.

1676. *Amascoggan*—Treaty of Mogg, Indian chief (Sullivan, *Maine*, 410).
1677. *Damroscoggin*—Francis Card, Declaration (Maine Historical Society *Collections,* Doc. Ser., VI, 177).
1677. *Damrallscogon Engens* [Indians]—Indian letter to Mrs. Hammond, *ibid.,* VI, 177).
(These Indian forms show clearly the presence of *nahmays,* their word for fish. D and initial N were often interchanged by them, or dropped.)
1684. *Androscoggan*—Indian deed (*York Deeds,* IV, fol. 15). This says that Thomas Purchase settled at Brunswick nearly threescore years before, or about 1624.
1715. *Dan-mira-kan-gou*—Father Aubéry, Map (French Archives, Bureau de la Marine, #254). Falls are marked.
Dammik-kangan—Map #253 in French Archives. Probably Lisbon Falls.
1719. *Amoscogg, alias Pejepscott*—Capt. Joseph Heath's Map (*Pejepscot Papers,* VIII, 50). Clearly Namaskeag, "fishing place," same as Amoskeag in New Hampshire.
1724. *Amuscoggin*—Capt. Thomas Westbrook (Massachusetts Archives, LI, 394).
1741. *Ameroscoggen*—Capt. Joseph Bane (Bean), Scout Map.
1755. *Amerscogging*—*Ibid.* (Suffolk Court Records, Doc. 76624b).
1793. *Amascongan*—Perepole (Pierpole), Deposition in *Pejepscot Papers,* quoted in Maine Historical Society *Collections,* III, 333, and Wheeler, *History of Brunswick,* 504. "Perepole said this was the original word." Probably true; it means simply "a fishery."

To anyone unacquainted with Indian these forms do not look like the same word, but they demonstrate beautifully, and entirely exclude most of the meanings in print. There can be nothing in Douglas-Lithgow's "fishing-weir place, or beaver dam," or in Vetromile's "fish coming in spring," which is a gloss rather than a translation. Potter's "high fish place" and "the great skunk river," quoted by Willis, and Doctor Ballard's "fish spearing" (from *skaughigan,* "a fish spear") are all distanced for first place in improbability by a writer, whom we need not name, who wrote, "still it is believed that the word may have come from the Abnaki 'Am-a-ra-skah-gin' meaning 'the turbid, foaming, crooked snake.' " The Marines should be informed!

Pescedona. Apparently a name for the Androscoggin River, found in "Documents Collected in France" (Massachusetts Archives, printed in Maine Historical Society *Collections*, Doc. Ser., IV, 425 *seq.*). The date is 1686, and it is given for the southern end and again for the passage from the head waters to the St. Lawrence. It seems to be from *peske*, "a branch," from the way the Androscoggin splits off from the Kennebec at Merrymeeting Bay.

Amirkangan. Lisbon Falls. (For the modern name, substitute *l* for *r*.)

Amitgonpontook. Lewiston Falls. (The first *t* probably an error for *l* or *r*; the word is the same as the preceding, with the addition of *pontook*, "falls.")

Unless we go to the bottom of the subject, as we had originally planned, it is useless to expand the treatment of the innumerable forms of these fish names. They present no great difficulties of interpretation, though to the amateur they look hopeless, and to local historians they have caused much grief.

Definitions of "much fish," "plenty of fish," are not strictly grammatical unless the word ends in a form like *-kanntti* or *-contee*, meaning an occurrence-place. Yet the localities would not have received the name unless the fish could be taken there in abundance. The ending *-kangan*, *-congan*, or *-coggin* indicates a fishery, the gerundive ending implying something made by, or used by, man; but in springtime all falls were fishing places and all of them had abundance of fishes, so that the interpretations hardly need to be meticulous for common use.

The word *amilkan* used in the names of these falls is something more than a fishery; it is a factory-word, used of places where either fish or meat was dried by smoke or sun, and even the place where such products were stored. *Amilkesk* is still used by both Penobscots and Passamaquoddies. As late as 1922, Governor William Neptune of the latter tribe gave Mr. Cabot the word as "a place where you smoke meat or fish without salt." The form Amirkangan, for Lisbon Falls, transliterates into *Ahmilkangan*, which we find in modern Penobscot in *Ahmilkangani-pantegu* as the name for Lewiston. *Dan-mira-kangou*, under the preceding word, is the same word, probably intended for the falls instead of for the river. The word is the same as Perepole's *Amitgonpontook*, given in 1793 for Lewiston Falls (Deposition, *loc. cit.*). Whoever called it "clay land falls" blundered.

The word *añmirkañn* (*amilkan*), *"on fait sécher poisson v. viande au feu, soleil,"* is given by Rasles (459), who also has *añmangañn* (*ahmangan*), *"on pêche là, il y a pêche"* (392), from *anme*, "he fishes" (20), in which we see the root of *n'ahmays*, "a fish."

Amirganganeque is the form of *Amilkanganek* used by M. Pasquine in a letter from Versailles, in 1688 (Wheeler's *Castine*).

Amilconganticoake (*Amilkangan-ticook*) is used by Dr. N. T. True (*Portland Transcript,* January 2, 1875) of Brunswick Falls, "place [but literally 'the river'] where they dried fish."

Ahmelahcognetercook is given by Willis, evidently an Indian's form, as "a place of much game." The word occurs in Kendall's *Travels in the Northern Parts of the United States,* 1809, III, 142-5, "banks of the river abounding in dried meat; that is, in venison," and his form is *Amilcungantiquoke*. "This word," says Kendall, "is certainly the etymon of Amariscoggan, and the rest." His comments are still worth reading.

BRUNSWICK.

Pejepscot, "long rocky rapids part." The lower section of the Androscoggin, commonly the portion in the immediate vicinity of Brunswick, but according to Perepole (Pierpole) the whole section from Merrymeeting Bay to Twenty-mile, or Lewiston, Falls (Deposition, July 19, 1793; in Maine Historical Society *Collections,* III, 333).

The forms vary much, and the earlier ones were confounded with the name of Sheepscott, given by Strachey, in 1607, as *Pashipscoke,* a wholly different word. Purchase certainly was at Brunswick, and the fact that James Phinney Baxter says the Bradshaw grant of 1,500 acres was there (*Trelawny Papers,* Maine Historical Society *Collections,* Doc. Ser., III, 207 n.) is evidence enough that the first settlers no more distinguished the names of two entirely different places than do many today who cannot tell the difference between "accept" and "except." Yet Mr. Baxter noted that Bradshaw's home was at Spurwink; and Dr. Henry Burrage, late State historian, went further, saying this was "an error in carelessly substituting Pashippscot for Spurwink in re-

Indian Place-Names of the Maine Coast 151

cording the grant" (*Beginnings of Colonial Maine,* 1914, p. 210).

1628. *Pechipscott*—Patent granted (Maine Historical Society *Collections,* IX, 367).
1632. *Peshipscote*—Grant to Thomas Purchase.
   Bishopscotte—Ibid.
1635. *Bishopscott*—Way and Purchase.
1636. *Pechispcote*—Grant to Purchase (Jenness, *Early Documents,* p. 23).
1636. *Peckispcot River*—Grant to Richard Bradshaw (Jenness, *ibid.*).
1639. *Pashippscot*—Grant to Bradshaw (Baxter in *Trelawny Papers*).
1639. *Pagiscot*—Indenture between Purchase and John Winthrop.
1648. *Mengipscot*—"at Mr. Purchase's house" (Boade to Winthrop)—a freak.
1683. *Pejepscot*—Deed to Richard Wharton.
1684. *Pegipscot*—Land on Androscoggin River (*York Deeds,* IV, fol. 15).
1684. *Pejeepscot*—(*Ibid.,* fol. 18.)
1715. *Poutsepskai*—Father Aubéry, Map.
1719. *Pejiepscut*—Letter of Capt. Joseph Bane (Bean) (Maine Historical Society *Collections,* Doc. Ser. IX, 448).
1793. *Pejepscook, Pejepcook*—Deposition, Perepole.

Most of the earlier forms are more or less confounded with the full word for Sheepscot, or are decidedly "off form." It is 1680 before the name becomes fairly regular and shows its roots, *pem,* "extended," *idge,* "rapids," *apsk,* "rock," *-(sc)ot* or *-ook,* locative—"the long, rocky rapids." Father Aubéry's name is a different word, made from *pontook,* "falls," *apsk,* "rock," and the French locative *ai,* equivalent to our *-wayk,* "rocky falls."

Perepole introduces a new idea, that of crookedness, in his description, "like a diving snake," perhaps momentarily thinking of the initial *P'* as standing for a *pika,* or *bika,* "root," instead of for *pem,* making it "bent" instead of "long"; but his statement that the word covered twenty miles or more of the river shows that *P'* must be "extended." Perepole's word-picture has proved so attractive that it has quite generally been adopted as the translation of the name instead of a description of the place. Springer (*Forest Life and Forest Trees,* 1851, 234) says it "is strikingly expressive of the zigzag course of the stream, and the numerous pitches in its channel, giving it the appearance, or at least suggesting the idea, of the movements of a diving eel." However, nothing in the word supports the analogy, which is pure imagination.

Bungamug Brook, "boundary brook." Brunswick and North Yarmouth.

> 1735. *Bungomungomug River*—"flowing into Maquoit Bay... Town bounds [of North Yarmouth] at Bongomog River" (*York Deeds,* XVIII, 119).
> 1738. *Bunganumgamok*—"a brook or rivulet called *Bunganumgamok* running into Maquoit Bay"—Belcher Noyes, Map of North Yarmouth, Dec. 9, 1738 (*Pejepscot Papers,* Vol. VIII).
> 1795. *Bungonuck*—"line between Brunswick [torn] carrying place"— Stevens, Plan of Brunswick, 1795 (*Pejepscot Papers,* VIII).

Ballard says of this brook that it is a small stream at the bottom of a deep ravine, with high, steep banks on both sides. It is clearly a natural boundary in the open sandy plains roundabout. The word is one common in Massachusetts and Connecticut in various forms, indicating a bound mark.

Pogamqua River. The same place as the preceding, according to Hon. Josiah Drummond (*Oration at the Hundredth Celebration of Freeport,* 1889), who cites the following deed:

> 1684. *Pogamqua River*—Grant to Richard Wharton of land "westward of Macoyte beginning at the mouth of Pogamqua River." (*York Deeds,* IV, fol. 23).

The word is good Indian and means a "shoal, sandy river," probably describing conditions at the mouth.

Puggamugga River. The same as the two foregoing, according to Mr. Drummond.

> 1686. Sept. 16. A petition by the proprietors of North Yarmouth, signed by Jeremiah Dummer and other trustees, "that the *Puggamugga* River be made the east bounds of the township" where it joined Brunswick (Drummond, *Oration*).
> 1688. *Pugganumna*—"Between two creeks *puggunumna* and *maquoite.*" (*York Deeds,* X, 211).
> 1713. *Puggy Muggy River*—"beginning at the mouth of Puggy Muggy River" (Grant to Wharton, *ibid.,* VIII, 137).

Maquoit Bay. Near Brunswick on the seaward side.

>   1662. *Musequoite, Musquequoite.*
>   1684. *Maqcooit, Maquoit* (*York Deeds*, IV, fol. 15).
>   "*Macoyte,* beginning at the mouth of Pogamqua River" (*ibid.,* fol. 23).
>   1754. *Muckquit, Muisquit.*
>   1774. *Mussequoit*—(Jeffery's Map).
>   *Magawok Bay* "near Maquoit" (Willis).

The name offered nothing of interest until we found it connected with a marsh and with a creek. Then it appeared as if it were the familiar *Mugwaak,* "a bog, swamp, lowland." The first word *Musequoite* might then be explained as from *mus* or *moos-,* an Abnaki word for "wet" (as *musabayso,* "a wet thing," that is, a mink); *-quoite* is clearly *-cook.* Thus our oldest word means "a wet place," probably a marsh at the mouth of a creek. As the name of a large salt bay, we would not undertake an explanation for it, but it looks as if the word had been transferred from some small spot along the shore to the bay. The meaning "bear-place," "bear-bay," is fictitious, apparently from the Ojibway *mokwa,* borrowed from *Hiawatha,* like several other Maine place-names, as Opeechee Stream in Searsport and Onawa Lake in Piscataquis County.

TOPSHAM.

Sawacook. A name found in Perepole's deposition (*loc. cit.*), which Dr. Edward Ballard and Dr. N. T. True locate in Topsham. Dr. True made it from "the same root as Saco, Sawquid, and signifies the discharging place"—which may be so, though it hardly seems necessary to have more names for the point where the Androscoggin merges in the Kennebec. Doctor Ballard calls it "burnt pine place"; Doctor Potter, "the place to find many cranberries"; another writer, "a tree forking in many branches." One hesitates to add more confusion, but it seems more likely to be from *sawe,* "sloping," the place where the land slopes down gradually; however, we have found neither the original form nor the location of the land in question.

Skeag. "A place where they find fish," wrote Dr. N. T. True (*Portland Transcript,* November 21, 1874), who said it was an island in the Androscoggin River above Brunswick, shortened by the English to Skeag. Clearly the word was *Namaskeag,* "fishing place."

HARPSWELL.

Merriconeag (now Harpswell). "Lazy carry."

Merriconeag is a long, narrow peninsula with a sound of the same name to the eastward, which, however, must be a recent extension of the word, since the name is a land-name.

    1683. *Mereconage, Mereconeeg*—Shapleigh to Wharton (*York Deeds,* III, fol. 128).
    1683. *Mericaneeg*—Deposition of Francis Small, Sr. (*ibid.*).
    1684. *Merecaneeg, Mereconeag*—Indian deed (*ibid.,* IV, fol. 15).
            This deed says that nearly threescore years before Mr. Thomas Purchase came to Pejepscot and settled there; therefore this probably represents the oldest form.
    1686. "*Merriconeag Neck* in Casco Bay" (*ibid.,* VI, fol. 10).

"This name was originally applied to mark the carrying place on Harpswell Peninsula, or Neck," says Doctor Ballard, who says it is from *merru,* "swift, quick," and *ounegan,* "a portage"—meaning "the quick carrying place" (*Coast Survey,* p. 8 of reprint). The application of the name is correct, but Doctor Ballard has lost the pith of its meaning. Francis Stanislaus gave me *Mollineagan* (with the *l-r* interchange of the old name) "lazy carry," from *molli-yoo* [*koo?*], "lazy." It is only a form of the Maliseet word we find at the outlet of Lower Dobsy Lake (*Sekledobskus* Lake) as *Mollicooniganus,* used of a short place where canoes were not unloaded in carrying across. Doctor Ganong contributed also *Malecuniganus,* found on a map of 1797 for Point of Rock Falls on the Magaguadavic in New Brunswick. "Lewey Francis, one of the best of my Indian mentors, once told me that *malec* meant 'lazy'—making it 'lazy portage,' because it was one that the Indians *could* drag and lift canoes up without unloading as they should—a lazy man's way, often entailing more trouble than carrying."

Sebascodegan Island. In Harpswell.

This is a great, irregular island, sprawling over a large space, but with small actual acreage because it is so split up into long points and deep, ramifying bays. There could be many passages across it by portages too short to be regarded as worth naming, because the water went "almost through."

Though numerous and uncouth, the forms of the name present no perplexities after we get the main roots, but with these there is much trouble unless we go to the eastern dialects.

1683. *Sebasco, alias Sequascoe Diggine*—Shapleigh to Wharton (*York Deeds,* III, fol. 128): "a Certen great Ysland which men call *Sebascoe Diggen* for which this Deponent payd the Indeans a considerable sume of Wampompeage, several Gunnes and a Parcell of Toba"—Deposition of Francis Small, Sr.

1684. *Shebiscodego*—"An island called *Shebiscodego*"—Attested copy of court record of grant to Thomas Danforth (Wheeler, *History of Brunswick*).

1684. *Sebascoa Diggin*—Indian deed (*York Deeds,* IV, fol. 15). *Sebasqua Diggin*—(*Ibid.,* fol. 19).

1790. *Gebasthegen Island*—Map of Lincoln County.

The best that Doctor Ballard could do with the word was: "Great Island in Harpswell, Chebascodeggon—*K'tchi,* "great," *t'bascodegan* in Penobscot is a measure. This solution of the name shows that the natives had some means of *measuring* the island and found it great" (*Coast Survey,* 1868, p. 17). But why should the Indians wish to measure that particularly irregular island and no other? Fifty years after this was printed a Penobscot Indian gave me the same explanation: *If* it was *t'bascodegan,* it would mean a measure." But it was *not* that, and the only inference to be drawn was that Penobscot Indians did not know what it was.

Suspecting that here was one of the fossil words we had been finding occasionally, I tried Lewey Mitchell of the Passamaquoddy tribe, a particularly well-informed man. He wrote: *"Sebasconhegan* —carrying place"; also, *"Sebascodnigan*—through, or passage." To this Doctor Ganong added: "The Passamaquoddy name for Bliss Island, near Latete, New Brunswick, is *Sebeskook,* which according to two of my very best informants, Noel Lewey and Lewey Francis, means peninsulas, or 'nearly through,' i.e., nearly cut by passages. It is true of Bliss Island which is almost three islands. The same root occurs elsewhere in New Brunswick with the same meaning and would apply extremely well to your Sebascodegan."

The root is *sebes*, "almost through," used frequently in Maine place-names, its most notable instance being Sebestiguk, or Sebasticook River. Sebascodegan Island has many of these "passages," which are "almost through."

Sebasco Harbor. Off the west shore of Phippsburg and about opposite Sebascodegan Island. The name is probably a recent one, as it seems to have no meaning at this place.

Quohoag Bay. In Harpswell.

The deed of Alexander Emery to Rev. Samuel Veazie, September 30, 1768, conveys "land on Sebascodegan Island... joining easterly on the common road and... westerly on *Quohoag*."

In the Des Barres' *Atlantic Neptune* we find *Cohauk*. Occasionally the modern Quahog Bay appears.

The name comes from the round clam, abundant farther south but very local in the latitude of Maine.

NORTH YARMOUTH.

Wesgustogo, "mouth of the river." Royall River.

In 1673 William Royall deeded to his sons "land lying between *Wesgostucko* and Chesquissicke Rivers"; but though the earliest reference found, this seems not to cover the whole of it, for other deeds mention land on the west bank as well as on the east.

> 1683. *Westquostuggo*—"bounded with a gutt of water on the west side of it and ye river on the east" (*York Deeds*, IV, fol. 37).
>
> 1684. *Westcostuggoh*—"the place called Westcostuggoh" (*ibid.*, fol. 24).
>
> 1719. *Wesgoostuckett*—"land lying between Wesgoostucket and Arasicket River" (*Essex* (Mass.) *Deeds*, XXXVI, 103).

There is no lack of references to this place, many of them freak forms not worth recording unless for identification; such as *Swegustagee* (Hon. Josiah Drummond), *Usquestuckqua* (*Maine Province Records,* I, 225 n.), and *Eusquastyqua* (*ibid.,* I, 195).

The last element is plainly *tegwe*, "river," and we are inclined

Indian Place-Names of the Maine Coast 157

to put weight upon Kendall's remark much more than a century ago when he was getting his information from Indians, "probably the same word with Wessagusset and Wiscasset" (*op. cit.,* III, 151), which would make it "the outlet of the river." On the other hand, Mr. William Brooks Cabot, for whose mastery of Indian we have great respect, thought that Wessagusset (Weymouth, Mass.) meant "wearing banks," and after inspection of the place, in 1936, seeing the clay banks deeply cut by entering stream beds, we adopted Mr. Cabot's opinion and called it "Gullied-banks river" (Rowe, *Ancient North Yarmouth and Yarmouth* (1937), 387). However, noting that William Wood, in 1634, had two forms for Weymouth, Mass.—"Wessaguscus" on his map and "Wichaguscusset" in his text (*New England's Prospect*)—and that "Weechagaskas" is also given for Weymouth, I have changed my opinion. It seems to be a straight outlet word, quite local in application. Dr. N. T. True was not satisfied with his solution of "clear water" (*Portland Transcript,* October 24, 1874), and Doctor Ballard's "pine-stream-trout-place" is atrocious. O'Brien's surmise of *Kesstegosso,* "is swift water," for *Custogo,* will not work.

Pumgustuck. The first falls on Royall River, in Yarmouth.

    1673. *Pumgustucke*—"ye first falls pumgustucke, or called by the Inglishe *Westcasdogoe* in Cascoe Bay" (Indian deed, *York Deeds,* II, fol. 191).

    1674. *Pungustuck, Pumgustacke*—"alias Westcustogoe" (*ibid.,* II, 185, 191).

    1721. *Pongustock*—"alias Westcustogo, but now called by the English Royall's River" (*ibid.,* X, 272).

The last form suggests that *pontook,* "falls," is the first root. We would revise a former opinion (Rowe, *op. cit.,* 386) that the last element is *tegwe,* "river"; it looks more like *auke,* "place." The troublesome *-cust, -gust,* may be only a form of Abnaki *kask,* "to go out," and the whole idea that of the river ending with a fall near its mouth—"falls-goes-out-place."

YARMOUTH.

Chusquisak. Assumed to be the same as Susquissugg and Sisquisic in Yarmouth, but we know the locality only through the deeds, and the Indian word is very variable.

1643. *Chusquisacke*—Grant of Thomas Gorges to William Royall of Casco, land at Casco Bay where he lives and island of twenty acres, "also a poynt of land lyeing between the River Westgustuggo and the River of Chusquisacke ... the wester end from the ffalls of Westgustuggo to the pteing of the river of Chusquisacke lyeing near north and south"—250 acres (*York Deeds*, I, ii, fol. 3).
1646. *Shusquisacke River*—(*ibid.*, fol. 61).
1650. *Cusquissacke River*—Cousins to Bray, Rigby, and Royall (*ibid.*, 637).
1673. *Chesquissicke River*—Ryall to Ryall (Royall) (*ibid.*, fol. 62).
1678. *Chusqussecke River*—Bray to Pearson (*ibid.*, III, fol. 35).
1684. *Sysquisset Creek*—(*Ibid.*, IV, fol. 35).
Ehusquisack—Pell to Royall, a misprint (*ibid.*, XII, fol. 9).

The land conveyed evidently is the point in Yarmouth between Royall River and Cousins River, the latter being meant by Chusquisak. The topographical map shows that the river had two branches, Cousins River of the map and a smaller stream unnamed, which met in a large tidal marsh. The form for 1673 confirms the opinion that the *chus* stands for *k'chi*, "big," and therefore that both branches were called *susquiset* and the 1684 entry refers to the smaller one, which will be considered under Susquisic or Susquissugg; we note that it is called a creek, not a river.

Susquissug. Cousins River, in Yarmouth.

In 1679, John Cousins of Westgustuggo (Yarmouth) deeded to Mary Sayward land "known by ye Indian name *Susquissugg* or Cousins Place ... in Casco Bay ... 300 acres by ye North River that runs to certain Falls Called *Susgussugg* or ye little River" (*York Deeds*, VIII, 233).

This means that the creek or Little River, not the falls, is called *Susquissug*. Remembering that tract of marsh at its mouth, we would make the word from the Micmac *susqu'*, "mud" (Ganong, *Monographs*, Vol. 7, p. 35), which he says covers more than our word "mud," being "muck, marsh, or wet bog." It is the same as our *aseskw*, which we find in Aucocisco. Indeed, it may be a diminutive form of that word "little muddy place." It would be entirely Indian to speak of Chesquissak as "the big-little-muddy-place," the word for a stream being understood and the final syllable perhaps having at one time stood for *suck, sauk*, "outlet," indicating that the mouth of these streams, big and little, opened in a muddy place smaller than some other marshy spot not too far away.

Presumpscot River.

This secondary, but yet important, river, with its principal source in Sebago Lake, 262 feet above sea level, comes leaping down in a succession of falls to enter Casco Bay in Falmouth. In Standish and Gorham we have five sets of falls—Steep Falls, Great Falls, Whitney, Island, and Dundee Falls. Gambo Falls are in Gorham and Windham, Saccarappa Falls in Westbrook, Ammocongon Falls at Cumberland Mills; and there is another considerable fall not far from the mouth. The river furnishes a tremendous water power, and we should expect the name to indicate its rocky character. The historic sequence is:

1636. *Pesumpsca*—Grant of Gorges to Cleeve "to the falls of Pesumpsca, being the fresh falls in y^t River."
1643. *Pesumscatowitt*—(*York Deeds*, I, part i, fol. 94).
1657. *Passumschaa*—Cleeve to Phillips (*York Deeds*, I, part i, fol. 122).
1698. *Premuscat ffalls*—(clerical error?)
1740. *Pasumscut River*—Capt. Joseph Bane's Scout Map (in Massachusetts Historical Society Library).
1751. *Pasunscot River*—Hutchinson's Map.
1795. *Presumpscott*, "formerly called Presumpsca or Presumpskeag" (Sullivan, *Maine*, p. 26).

Inspection shows that the early forms do not begin with *pre-* but with *pes-* or *pas-*, prefixes which denote something split up, or divided. The second root looks like a mixture of *amk*, "sand," and *-apsk*, "rock," if Abnaki, in which we find no *-umpsk*. But the Natick of Eliot's Bible has the inseparable root *-ompsk-*. "The primary meaning seems to be an upright (*ompae*) rock or stone (*p'sk*)" (Trumbull, *Natick Dictionary*, 106). We find in Eliot, *passompskodtut*, "in the cleft of the rocks," which, dropping the locative *-ut*, gives us our *Pasumpsco(d)t*. The first part is *pahshe* (*pohshe*)—our *passa*, "broken," "divided," which we found in Sheepscot, and *-ompsk*. When Governor John Neptune interpreted the word as "rough places river" (Ballard), he gave an apt characterization and evidently understood the roots although the modern Penobscot would be more likely *Pissapskek*, "ledge with a channel" (O'Brien), or "split-up ledges."

Ammecungan River. The Presumpscot River. A fishery word. The same word as Androscoggin, but not the same place.

> 1657. *Ammecungan.*—Deed of Scitterygusset, Indian, 27 July, 1657, to Francis Small of Casco Bay "all that upland and marshes at Capissicke, Lijing up along the northern side of the riuer; unto ye head of yt and soe to reach and extend into ye riuer side of *Ammecungan* (*York Deeds,* I, part i, fol. 83).

The specific place was the falls of Ammecongan, in Westbrook, the terminus of an Indian route from Casco Bay, later nearly followed by "the King's highway" and the railway.

As is usual with fish-words, the name has many forms, such as *Amiscoggin* and *Amon-coggin,* so near to the Androscoggin names that they can be distinguished only by careful location. The Amoncongan Falls were those at Cumberland Mills. The name indicated an alewife fishery there and we know that it was the planting ground of the Indians, who used alewives as their fertilizer.

FALMOUTH.

Skeecoway. A creek near the mouth of Presumpscot River.

> 1663. *Skeecoway*—Cleeve to John Phillips, "200 acres of upland lijing and adjoining to the falls of Pesumsca and neare the little river of *Skeecoway*" (*York Deeds,* I, part 1, fol. 134).
>
> 1722. *Shecoway*—Mountjoy to Penn Townsend, "land at Capessic... over to Amuncongan and 50 acres on River Presumscutt, 40 acres of this at lowest falls next salt water... also 200 acres adjoyning sd Falls and near to little river of *Sheecoway* (*ibid.,* XI, 265).

The place is insignificant and the word occurs but this once. Quite likely it is the name of some Indian who lived near; but recalling how often Indians, particularly women, were named for birds, we are reminded of the word which Thoreau wrote as *shecorway,* the name of the American merganser, or sheldrake. A better form is *ussikawai,* probably given on account of its rough, shaggy crest. The true history of this word is unknown, and much depends on whether Skeecoway is not a misprint for Sheecoway.

Scitterygusset. A creek near the mouth of the Presumpscot.

The name is said to have been that of Squidrayset, a sachem of Lynn, Mass., who deeded land here. It survives in many uncouth forms in deeds, varying from Squidraysit to Squethequinset (Creek), but none are of any interest, historic or philological. The deed of Scitterygusset was given 27 July, 1657, to Francis Small of Casco Bay and covers land in the 1722 deed of Skeecoway quoted above, a considerable tract (*York Deeds,* I, part i, fol. 82).

Menikoe. Mackworth's Point and Island.
>   1634. Vines to Arthur Mackworth, land on Casco Bay on the northeast side of Presumpsca River, "comonly called or known by the name *Menikoe*"—five hundred acres, one small island (*York Deeds,* I, part i, fol. 1).

Menikoe would have been the name of the island only. It was one of those Micmac *muneeks,* the shelter, or harbor islands, found all along the coast.

FREEPORT.

Harraseeket River. An enclosed salt bay of considerable extent off Casco Bay.
>   *Harrickissecke*—(*York Deeds,* III, 130).
>   *Harrysickett River*—(Cyprian Southack, *Sea of New England*).
>   *Harrakeket*—(*York Deeds,* V, 11).

We have no clue to the name, which may be personal.

Sebago Lake. The great lake in Cumberland County, source of the Presumpscott River.
>   1673. *Sebug*—John Josselyn (*Two Voyages to New England,* 203).
>   1715. *Mesebigou*—Father Aubéry (Map #254, French Archives).
>   1723 (*circa*). *Mesibegat*—Map (#252 French Archives), maker unknown.
>   1724 (*circa*). *Mesebegou*—Map (#253 French Archives), maker unknown.
>   1741. *Cebagog Pond*—Capt. Joseph Bane (Bean) Scout Map in Massachusetts Historical Society Library. (Actual date February, 1740/1.)
>   1800 (*circa*). *Sebagook*—Morse's *Geography,* p. 356 text.

The finest form is *Mesibegat,* which shows perfectly that the word means "great lake," from *mese, mesi,* "big," and *begat,* "still water," "lake." The map may be dated as of 1723, for it states that Old Town is an "abandonned town." It has been burned by Westbrook in February, 1722/3. The next map is not more than two years later, because it does not mention Norridgewock, destroyed in August, 1724.

Our friend John Josselyn was speaking of Sebago Lake but seems to have confounded it to some extent with Moosehead Lake. He wrote: "Twelve mile from Casco-bay, and passable for men and horses, is a lake called by the Indians *Sebug,* on the brink thereof at one end is the famous Rock shap'd like a Moose-Deere, or Helk [elk], Diaphanous and called the Moose-Rock." This seems to be Kineo, which the Indians took to be the body of the moose slain by Glusgehbeh; but Kineo is not "diaphanous."

We may note that upon Sebec Lake, in Piscataquis County, Father Aubéry places the same name *Mesebigou* "big lake," and the name of Moosehead is the same, *K'ci sebem,* on early maps. In 1823, Moses Greenleaf wrote in his *Letter:* "The town next to this [Sebec] is from a pond and stream of the same name, but it is properly called *Sebagook* (a great water) and is the same with the Indian name of Sebago pond in the county of Cumberland. When I first came to Maine Sebago Pond was called *Sebaycook*."

Colby's *Atlas of Pisataquis County* (1882) is not in error in saying that the original name of Sebec was Sebecco, but would have done much better by using Greenleaf's Sebagook.

WESTBROOK.

Saccarappa Falls. Meaning uncertain.

This great fall has no very early annotations and the numerous references in *York Deeds* are principally between 1730 and 1735, when mills were going up and land was changing owners. Thus, though the spellings vary much, there is little difference in the root values of the forms from which to extract a meaning.

> 1730.   *Saccerapey*—"at the third Falls up Persumscot River known by the name *Saccerapey* so called by the Indians" (*York Deeds,* VIII, 595).

Indian Place-Names of the Maine Coast 163

1730. *Decarrabigg*—"Ammocongan River at yᵉ great Falls yᵉ upper Part of them called Decarrabigg" (*ibid.*, XII, 123). (Three deeds of the same year have Secarrabigg, so probably the initial *D* is an error.)
1731. "*Saccerapey* on Persumscott River" (*ibid.*, XVI, 50).
1733. *Sacarappa*, "being the third fall from the mouth of the river"—Joseph Mallison to Samuel Waldo (*ibid.*, XVI, 502).
1735. *Secarrabigg*—Pearson to Waldo, described as in second citation (*ibid.*, XVI, 491).
1745. *Sacaribig, Saccarapig*—Rev. Thomas Smith, *Journals* (ed. 1821, pp. 46 and 48).

There is a tendency to use a locative ending—if it is a locative; and the word contains the elusive *-arra-* found in the names of falls; while the initial *sac* seems like *sauk,* though it is not the outlet of anything. The word has more affinities for the mysterious Ripogenus than any other we have found. Certainly Willis's "towards the rising sun" does not explain it; nor Dr. True's " 'the place where the still water is poured out,' or outlet of Sebago Lake" (*Portland Transcript,* August 22, 1874). With six sets of falls above it before Sebago Lake is reached, Saccarappa can hardly be called the outlet of a lake. Mr. Cabot went purposely to look at the place and reported two pitches with a run between them, which might almost be called a pool; "a fall and a run," was his comment, adding only that "a final *-pa* might stand for *pontook,* 'falls'; verbs with a *p* toward the end have much to do with motion."

The official spelling of the word seems not so good as Sacarrapa, which shows the root *-arra-,* whatever it may mean.

PORTLAND.

Machegony, Machegonne. The Indian name for Portland. The meaning is still conjectural, but we believe it to be Micmac, "shaped like a great knee."

The word is so important that space must be given to its history and to the opposing opinions concerning its meaning.

In 1930, Dr. W. F. Ganong, Dr. C. E. Banks, and the writer united in a three-point endeavor to settle the meaning of the word *Machegonne* or *Machegony*. Dr. Banks, working under the wing of Dr. Trumbull, thought it meant "the big, palisaded town," and over the signature of "Antiquary" printed his conclusions in a Portland paper of date unknown to the writer. Dr. Ganong, using Micmac roots and equivalents, suggested that it might be "the big ridge." The writer tried cognates and felt that Machegony bore a resemblance to Michigan, with the underlying idea of a "big point." No one of us agreed with the earlier opinions of Ballard, Vetromile, and O'Brien.

Doctor Ballard called it "bad clay"; Father Vetromile said "ugly, bad town," and Father O'Brien, "bad or worthless camp or camping ground," all based upon the supposition that the name Machegony was applied only to the end of the peninsula, as in the later deeds, or to the Eastern Promenade, as Goold says (*Portland Past and Present* (1886), 359).

In a letter to Doctor Ballard (October 18, 1859), Father Vetromile made Machegony from *madzigannek* (*matchi,* "bad," and *udenek,* "town") regardless of the fact that you cannot make *udenek* into *annek.* (Upon the original letter is a pencilled note, "*Matchi-egan?-ek*—N.T.T.," showing that Dr. Nathaniel Tuckerman True had examined the paper and had not quite agreed with the writer.) Doctor Ballard, in his reply to Vetromile (December 16, 1859), wrote "[Machegony] which I have interpreted for Mr. Willis as *Bad Clay*: very descriptive of the part of the city to which the name has been attached for more than 200 years. The syllable *gon* I translate 'clay' from Schoolcraft's *List of Primary Terms,* Vol. 3, pp. 504-5, and I doubt not that your form of the word was the original Machegonak and the same would be Bad Clay Place, which embraces the part still called Clay Cove." Unluckily, though in Micmac -*gon* may stand for "silt," "sand" (Ganong), the Abnaki word for "clay" is quite different. *Ar8nesk8* (*alooneskw'*) is given by Nudenans as *argilla,* "white clay," and *manzarunsk8* (*mazaloonskw*) is another form. We find this in *Messalonskee* Stream, near Waterville. Dr. Banks's proposal comes under the same stricture as the others. An imaginary explanation will not stand against a hypothesis with facts behind it. We do not know of any palisaded town at Machegony.

Against these others, Doctor Ganong and the writer advanced interpretations which fitted the background. "The striking feature of the place," wrote Dr. Ganong in 1930, "is the high land on

Indian Place-Names of the Maine Coast 165

a neck in a low country immediately around, and this peculiarity would naturally be expected to appear in the name." The first element he thought was "great," not "bad." "The remainder of the word *-egon* I think involves a root meaning *ridge*—a ridge like an animals's back. ... The Micmac equivalent is *-ogun,* found in various names as *Aspatogun,* a high hill near Halifax ... 'great ridge place' rather describes it, I think." But *mag-ogun* would not account for the *tch* sound.

My own contribution was that it was rather more than a ridge; that the Micmac *chegon,* a "knee," would even better describe it—a great high peninsula, standing out from the main like a thigh and leg, bent at the knee. I did not then know that "according to Bliss, great knee or elbow, from Algonquin *mach,* 'great,' and *chegun,* 'elbow' " (*Trelawny Papers,* 225 n.), had been suggested, and do not yet know who Bliss was or where to look for his statements.

Thus we come to the history of the word. The first settler in Portland was George Cleeve, a squatter, who had his choice of land. In 1640 he deposed that "he hath been for these seaven yeares and upwards possessed of a tract of land in Cascoe Bay, knowne first *by the name of Machigonney, being a necke of land* which was in no mans possession or occupation and therefore the plaint[iff] seized on it for his owne inheritance ..." (*Province Records,* edited by Charles Thornton Libby, I, 62).

The grant of Ferdinando Gorges assigned Cleeve land "beginning at the furthermost poynt of a necke of land called by the Indians Machegonne ... and so along the same westerly as it trendeth to the first fall of a little river [Capissic] issueing out of a verie small pond and from thence overland to the ffals of Presumpsca, being the first ffals in y^{tt} River ... (wch together wth the said necke of land that the said George Cleeve and the said Richard Tucker have planted for Divers yeares already expired) is estimated in the whole to be about fifteen hundred acres or thereabout" (*York Deeds,* I, part i, fol. 4).

In 1636, the whole neck of land, now the city of Portland, was called Machigony. Cleeve, says Goold, lived not far from Longfellow's birthplace.

Dated forms of the word do not vary much. We have *Machigonne* (1636), *Machigonney* (1640), *Muchagony, Majegoneck*

(1731), and, most distinctive of all, *Magegunnuck* (1734/5)— "that certain Neck of Land comonly called *Magegunuck,* alias *Machegony,* sometimes known by the name of Mountjoy's Neck (*York Deeds,* XII, part i, fol. 71).

Compare *Magegunuck* with *M'cheegoon,* the Micmac word for a knee (Rand, *English-Micmac Dictionary*) or with *Cheegooncook,* "a knee," the name of Table Island, Nova Scotia (Rand, *Micmac Reading Book*) or with Father Pacifique's *Tjigonegeg* (*Chigone-kek*), "shape of a knee," as present-day Micmac place-names.

Machegony seems to be only *mag,* "great," plus *chegoon,* "knee," with a locative ending.

Maxigannée is a French form found in a letter from Bigot and Vaudreuil to Louis XV, dated 8 October, 1721—("when the French destroyed [the fort of] *Maxiganée*" (*New York Col. Docs.,* IX, 906).

Stagomor. Georges' grant to Cleeve, 1636, says "a Necke of Land called by the Indians Machegonne and now and forever to be called Stagomor" (*York Deeds,* I, i, fols. 95 and 96). "Stagomor (the modern Stogumber), in Somersetshire, England, was the birthplace of John Winter and Richard Tucker" (Burrage, *op. cit.,* 228n.). It would have been no compliment had Gorges named his grant for the mere tip of the Portland peninsula, a place so small that it was known only as a "bad camping ground."

Semiamis. Given by Strachey, in 1607, and as *Cape Sineamis* on the Nova Belgia Map, as a headland, supposed to be Cape Elizabeth; but nothing is known of the word.

Moshoquen. Given by Capt. John Smith as the name of a place between his unidentified Wawrigwek and Wakcogo. It seems to be intended for the same word we find as *Mavooshan* and *Moasham* of other travelers, but nothing is known.

Perpoodic. The old name of South Portland.

The numerous spellings do not much affect either the meaning or the identification of this word. The first syllable is usually *Pap-, Pep-,* or *Pur-;* the second *-pud-,* or *-pood-;* and the last a locative, *-ick* or *-uck,* sometimes *-ing.* Fair samples are:

1669. *Papuding,* "in Falmouth" (*York Deeds,* II, fol. 69).
1687. *Papocodek* (freak form) (Maine Historical Society *Collections,* Doc. Ser., VI, 301).
1720. *Papuduck, Pappooduck, Purpudock* (*York Deeds, passim*).

The place is spoken of as "Pappooduck side," or "Perpudick Point," indicating that it was removed from the more settled part of Portland.

Inspection of the word suggests that the first syllable is reduplicative, intensifying the second, as "much" or "very," and that the second is *poo-,* "sticks out," still used in modern Penobscot. It is a place which sticks out noticeably and, identified as the present "Spring Point" in South Portland, it is fitting. Moreover, Ruttenberger makes *Podunk,* in Connecticut, from *p'tuk-ohke,* "a neck or corner of land" (*Hand-book of the American Indian,* II, 270), something which sticks out.

Now the southern *Podunk* and the northern *Perpoodic* have one curious detail in common which is not expressed in the Indian roots. Both were used by the whites as meaning obscure places, or places far out of the way. Bartlett's *Americanisms* lists "Go to Podunk!" and in the writer's childhood nicely brought up children, whose fathers did not swear, could say, "You go to Poodic!" with all the fervor of a stronger expression. There is little question but that Perpoodic was a point or headland which jutted out noticeably but was not much frequented.

Capissic. A small stream in Deering, tributary to the Stroudwater River.

Though short and small, not bearing any name on the modern topographical map, this was important to the Indians as a part of the shortest route from Fore River to the fishing station at Ammecongon on the Presumpscot River. It is also a part of the bound to Cleeve's patent, the stream "issuing from a little pond," not named in Gorges' patent, now used as a skating place (*York Deeds,* I, i, 83).

1657. *Capissicke*—"marshes at Capissicke" (Deed of Scitterygusset).
1683. *Capessick Falls*—(*York Deeds,* VIII, 373).
1688. *Capesseck*—Edward Tyng, Letter (Maine Historical Society *Collections,* Doc. Ser. VI, 373).
1729. *Capipissoke Falls*—(*York Deeds,* VIII, 362).

Capesseck Falls—(*Ibid.*, VIII, 364).
Capisseck Falls—(*Ibid.*, VIII, 364).
1728. *Kepiseke*—(*York Deeds*, XII, ii, 311).
1687-8. *Keppisich Stream*—Edmond Andros, "Land Warrants," p. 25 (Cabot).

The last forms show clearly the root *kep*, "closed," "stopped up." Father O'Brien notes, "Capissic—*kebigen*, narrows up." In another place he suggests *te'kebisuk*, "a spring," but this is guesswork.

On October 18, 1925, I went to the place in company with some women who used to skate there when girls, who called it Capizzik. The highway crossed a long narrow flowage held by a stone dam, based upon natural ledge falls, a very old structure, broken where the current fell over the ledge. The stream below is short and small. To an Indian coming up the river, this little branch of the Stroudwater seems stopped up, corked up, by the falls; the word is the one used of a beaver dam, an obstruction. It seems to be from *kep*, "obstructed," *p's*, "a branch," and the locative—"the dammed-up branch"; for above the falls the flowage from earliest times must have made the little pond which is there today.

Casco. The great bay before Portland and formerly that arm of the sea now called Fore River, in early times Casco River (see Map in *Trelawny Papers*, by James Phinney Baxter); but not the Presumpscot River, as Cleeve tried to make it appear (*Trelawny Papers*, 231-232). Yet Christopher Levett in 1623 may have included the Back Bay.

There is no need to cite forms until we consider *Aucocisco*. Though *Casco* is not very modern, it is made from the Abnaki and is generally taken to mean the great blue heron, whose Abnaki name is *kasqu'*. The bird always abounded on the extensive mud flats, but Dr. Ganong upholds Dr. Trumbull's objection that "a heron is not a bay." No form of the word found has anything indicating a bay, river, or any body of land or water; therefore it seems better to consider it only a clipped form of a longer word. (See *Aucocisco*.)

Marchin Bay. Casco Bay. Lescarbot (*Works*, Champlain ed., Toronto, II, 276) says that "beyond Kinibeki one reaches Marchin Bay, from the name of the Captain who was chief there. This

Marchin was killed in the year that we left New France, 1607."

Marchin means "the Wolf"; it is the modern Abnaki *malsum*. This is on Champlain's Map of 1607 as *Baie de Marchen*.

Aucocisco, "muddy bay." The Back Bay, Portland.

In 1614 Captain John Smith wrote of "the Country of Aucocisco, in the bottome of a large deepe Bay, full of many great Iles." The bay with its large islands is Casco Bay; but Aucocisco is "at the bottom of it"—that is, it is the "head of the bay," where now we have the vast mud flats of the Back Bay.

It was Doctor Ganong who suggested that *Auco* might stand for the Maliseet and Micmac *wakw,* "the head of a bay," which occurs often in place-names eastward. The suggestion and the location were proved by entries in *York Deeds*. We find *"Westcostogee at Wackquigut"* in the deeds (XII, i, 14) and again (XII, ii, 282), "near the *Head* or North East Part of Casco Bay ... called by the Indian name Westgastugo." There can be little doubt about the first half of our word being *wakw,* "head of a bay."

The latter half, *-cisco,* is the Micmac *sisgog,* "mud," of Father Pacifique (which he uses as a place-name of a river in Colchester County, Nova Scotia), or *seskoo,* "mud," of Rand (*English-Micmac Dictionary*). We have the same in Abnaki, *asesk8, boue,* of Rasles (68) and of Nudenans; but from the Micmac we make the word with no change whatever,—*Aucocisco,* "head-of-the-bay, mud," Muddy Bay. No name could better fit the place than this when the ebb-tide has drained it.

Is Casco only a clipped form of Aucocisco? We can not say that it is; not unless John Smith made his second *c* hard, like *k*; and the Micmac root would not become *k*. Moreover, Casco seems to have been Fore River rather than the Back Bay, a different location despite similarity of conditions. It seems more as if later Indians had substituted an Abnaki word of somewhat similar sound for an older one and that Casco was a *post hoc* explanation, accounted for by the numbers of herons seen there; for, as Trumbull says, " a heron is not a bay"; the connection does not seem Indian, even though we know it antedates the coming of white men.

Quack. The place near Portland where Christopher Levett obtained a grant from the sagamore's wife and built a house, supposed to be upon House Island, and Quack to be "the region lying between Casco and Cape Elizabeth" (Baxter). The name looks like the remnant of some longer word, nor do we incline to Baxter's remark (*Trelawny Papers,* 4 n.) that it may be a shortened form of *quahaug,* meaning "the clam place." One must first show that the round clam, the quahog, ever abounded there. It is limited in occurrence north of Cape Cod, and had it ever been in quantity in Maine, the shellheaps would show it, and our Indians would not have been buying shell wampum from southern New England (Willoughby, *Antiquities of the New England Indians*).

SCARBORO.

Spurwink. A salt creek in Scarboro, outletting at the eastern end of Scarboro Beach.

The name is early, Dr. Banks citing six spellings in 1634. In 1643 the land of Thomas Cammock went "to Spurwinke on its westerly side" (that is, the west bank of the river), according to the deposition of Francis Robinson in 1670; and in 1633, Capt. Walter Neale "bounded and marked" land "with a brook caled Spurwincke eastward."

There seems to be no Indian origin behind it, and the best Dr. Banks, our ablest historian of that region, could do was to report, October 6, 1930: "As a sidelight I found a Captain Spurwink in England, which seems to be a possible answer to the supposed Indian name of that marshy creek in Scarboro. I believe it has been carefully analyzed by some of the pundits and baptized with a fancy name. Poor Spurwink River!"

Nonesuch River. The eastern branch of Black Point River.

The word is English. We find the name as early as 1678 in the will of Robert Jordan—"a farm called Nonsuch." Sullivan says, "Nonsuch gets its name from the goodness of the land on the west side" (*History of the District of Maine,* 1795, p. 214).

Owascoag River. A small marshy stream, largely tidal salt creek, influent to Black Point River, Scarboro.

1659. Deed to Andrew and Arthur Alger of land at Blue Point, "up along with the River called *Oawascoage* in Indian" (*York Deeds*, II, fol. 114).

On September 19 of this year, Jane Uphannum, an Indian woman, deposed that *Owascoag* meant "place of much grass." The great Scarboro marshes are widest along this stream.

In analysis -*wasco* is *ashq'*, something green, unripe, specifically "grass"; the -*ag* is the locative, and the initial *o* is probably the as yet unaccounted-for initial *a* which we find prefixed to many Abnaki place-names; perhaps it is nothing more than the hesitant -*er* used by our own people in speaking; even Dr. Trumbull could so little account for it that he regarded *Aghenibeki* (Kennebec), as a different word from Kennebec.

Piggsgut River. Now called Mill Creek, in the Scarboro marshes.

Dr. Banks collected ten forms, dated from 1648 to 1730. Most of them are variations of Piggsgut; the earliest is *Pigstie* (1648) and we get *Pigsty* (1685) and *Piggsty* (1713). The most helpful form is the latest, *Piscot River* (1730) (*York Deeds*, XII, p. 257).

Piscot plainly means "a branch," from the root *piske*. This is borne out by *York Deeds*, II, fol. 52: "eastward end of a marsh joyning to the *piggscutt* Riuer and the southward end Joyning to the Mayne Riuer and so to run upp in the marsh," which shows that the Piscat, or Piggsgutt was only a branch stream. It was called Mill Creek as early as 1726 (*York Deeds*, XII, 67). On the Portland topographical sheet it is misnamed Oriocoag.

Saco River. *Saco* is a word so simple that it has given trouble to even good students. Saw-co, as we in Maine pronounce it, is only *saⁿg8k* (*sahcook*) of Rasles, "an outlet," lacking a locative *k*. For the outlet of a river he gives *sañghedé'tegwé*, adding the word for a river. But for Sagadahoc, *"un lieu assez proche d' ici sur le mer"* (under *Noms,* 358), he says *Sañkedé'rañk* (*Sahkedé'lak*).

This last is considerably more than a mere outlet and is specifically the name of Sagadahoc, the outlet of Kennebec River. The first part is the root for "flowing out"; the last syllable -*rañk*, or in English usually -*hoc*, is the root so often given as -*hunk*, "a swift stream," which we thought (see *Machias*) was connected with the

Micmac, -*iak,* "a stream of water"; the whole word indicating a place where a strong current flows out. The mouth of the Kennebec is a blind entrance, the river not in evidence, hence the outflow is emphasized. The historic sequence is:

1608. *Sachadehoc*—Strachey.
1616. *Sagadahock*—Capt. John Smith.
1690. *Sakatahak*—Truce with Indians (Massachusetts Archives, Vol. 242, pp. 209-210a).
1715. *Sanghtderrank*—Father Aubéry, Map #253.
1723c. *Sangherank*—French Map #252.
1724. *Sankderank*—Rasles, *Jesuit Relations,* Vol. 67, p. 197.
1755. *Sagadarock*—Capt. John Gyles, Deposition (Suffolk Court Files).
1755. *Sunkadanock* (for *-hock?*)—Capt. Joseph Bane, Deposition (*ibid.*).
1755. *Sagadahock*—Capt. Jabez Bradbury, Deposition (*ibid.*).
1809. *Schunkadarunk*—Kendall, *Travels,* III, 143-144.
1923. *Sankede'lak*—"where the river flows out"—Dr. F. G. Speck (*Wawenock Myth Texts,* 43rd Report, Bureau of Ethnology, p. 170 n.).
    (And we observe that Dr. Speck's is precisely the form used two hundred years before by Rasles, even to the accent.)

The use of Sagadahoc for the Androscoggin does not seem native. It is a mapmakers' use—"so called by Mouns^r Bellin and also by most or all of the Antient Plans"—Johnston's Map of 1754.

Opposed to these words with the idea of a strong current flowing out, the Saco series presents an almost uniform meaning of "the outlet of the river." This is only "outlet" plus "river," and instead of the nasalized *sa^{n}k* we get what may be a slightly different idea in *sawah.* Instead of a prefix meaning "it pours forth" (*sohkeu,* in Natick), we may approach the milder *sak,* used in Cree, *"sorter, commencer à paraitre,"* even applied to the sunrise, *sakottew,* "it walks forth" (Gerard). At least our series takes a different slant.

1614. *Sawacatuck*—Capt. John Smith, *Description of New England.*
1616. *Sawacotuck*—*Ibid., General History* (Lib. VI, p. 203).
1618. *Sawaguatock*—Rocroft, in *A Brief Relation.*
1619. *Sawaquatocke*—Thomas Dermer.
1622. *Sawwaguatock*—President and Council for New England, *A Brief Relation.*

1623. *Sawahquatock*—Grants to Lenox and Arundel by New England Council.
1623. *Sawco*—Christopher Levett, who was *there* that year, *Voyage*.
1629. *Swackadock*—Grants to Oldham and Vines (*York Deeds*, I, ii, 8).
1629. *Swankadocke*—Grants to Lewis and Hawthorne (*ibid.*, II, 111). (The *n* probably a misprint for *c*.)

The grant to Oldham and Vines, of four miles by eight, reads, "pte of the Mayne land in New England aforesaid comonly called or known by the name of Swackadock . . . between Cape Elizabeth, south side of the river Swachadocke". . . .

In the variations here we probably see only the carelessness of professional copyists. Taken as a whole, the list shows that the place was called "the mouth of a river," shortened to Saco, "the outlet." In 1688, an Order in Council speaks of *Swackadock alias Saco*.

Was there anything special about the mouth of the Saco River by which it could be recognized?

There was. It was a river subject to freshets from the mountains in which it rose and it carried a large amount of silt, which the steady current did not have the strength to clear away; therefore there was a bar of sand across the outlet. Champlain noticed this and took soundings, reporting fully the depth of water at different stages of the tide. In 1700, Colonel Romer, the engineer, wrote: "Saco River is but small and its Navigation interrupted by a Sandy Bank at its mouth almost dry at Low Water" (report in Maine Historical Society *Collections,* Doc. Ser., IX, 88). Oddly enough the old name does not note this peculiarity, while the modern name does, though today jetties make the river scour its own outlet.

Sakadamkiak is the name given by Lewey Mitchell, the Maliseet, as the name of Saco River. It is composed of two roots— *sauk*, "outlet," and *-amkiak*, "sand-bar." He also said *Sakdiamkik*, with the same signification.

Chouacouet of Lescarbot (*Works,* Champlain ed., *Toronto.* II, 276) and of Champlain (*Works,* same ed. I, 327 n.) is only Saco with a locative ending. *Chevacovet* is an error.

KENNEBUNKPORT.

Cape Porpoise. Though presumably an English name, there is a possibility that this may be of Indian origin. Place-names now called "capes" may have been made from the root *kep, kepan,* as Cape Newagen. For "Cape Ann," Father Druillettes wrote *Kepam.* The earlier they are found, the less likely they are to be of English derivation, and the less neatly they fit the spot, the greater the chance that they may be corrupted from the Indian.

There is no particular fitness in calling a projection of the land for a porpoise. The name is found too early for Englishmen to be hunting them—(they were good only for their oil)—and if it was Indian hunting ground, the name would have been given long before in an Indian form. The place is not well adapted to the porpoise, is not a typical cape, and *is* a typical *kep* or *kepan,* "stopped up" location, having a number of islands to seaward. Moreover, it is not the locality for which the name was first used. The old Cape Porpoise River, now called the Mowsam, discharged in Kennebunk several miles to the westward of the present village of Cape Porpoise in Kennebunkport. A low, flat island outside also bears the name Cape Porpoise for no obvious reason. There seems to be reason to question the origin and meaning of the name.

1610. *C. Porpas*—Simancas Map.
1623. *Cape Porpas*—Christopher Levett (*Voyage to New England*).
1625. *C. Porpus*—Map, *Purchas His Pilgrims,* III, 852.
1629. *Cape Porpus*—Gorges to Oldham and Vines, deed to "Mayne Land called Swackadahocke ... lying and being betweene the Cape or bay comonly caled Cape Elizabeth and the Cape or bay comonly caled *Cape Porpus*" (*York Deeds,* I, i, fol. 8).
1631. *Cape Porpus*—"2000 acres on the south side of the river or creek called *Cape Porpus*" granted to John Stratton, December 1, 1631, by the Council for New England.
1649. *Porpos* ("no C. for Cape"—Dr. Banks's note)—Dudley, *Arcano del Mare*

More source material is needed before any opinion can be given about this name.

Kennebunk. The beach of the town of Kennebunk and the river, which outlets in the village of Kennebunkport, the old Arundel.

Forms of the word Kennebunk vary too little to make citations necessary, but the interpretations in print differ much. Doctor Ballard said "long water place, and properly so called"— indeed, the whole Atlantic Ocean is before it. Father O'Brien proposed *kini-paugwauk,* "long shoal," but this takes no account of that persistent *n* in the final syllable. H. L. Masta (*op. cit.,* 84) made it from *kini,* "very," and *b8ke,* "rough ground," which not only involves the preceding objection, but is contrary to the facts, while *kini* is not "very," but "long."

The best suggestion is that of Doctor Ganong, who wrote in a letter, June, 1938, that if the word were Micmac, Kennebunk would mean "long bank"; from *banek,* a bank behind a beach having a raw side, a "cut bank."

When we consider that all Indian traffic with cargo of any weight must pass by canoe outside these ocean beaches, which stretch from York River east to Cape Porpoise (with others beyond it), it is apparent how important it was for the Indians to know where to find the entrances to the creeks and marshes behind them. From the sea, all beaches look much alike. If one of them presented the feature of a cut bank of clay or gravel, even if not very long or high, it would mean as much to an Indian as a lighthouse does to us—near there would be a harbor and an escape from the sea. To get confirmation, I wrote Miss Bertha M. Hadaway, then staying at Cape Porpoise, who replied, August, 1938: "Kennebunk Beach is about four miles away. From Kennebunk River to Great Hill is *level.* Great Hill is a *cut bank.* Much of the land is a sloping, grassy level to the sea, but there are also ledgy shores."

Though the Biddeford topographical sheet does not show a special rise along this shore (meaning that it is less than twenty feet), it would be the *character* of the cut bank rather than its height or length which would be the valuable landmark. Also we must allow for encroachments by the sea since the place was named hundreds of years ago.

Kini-banek, "the long cut bank," seems the best interpretation of Kennebunk.

Mountequies Neck. In Arundel (Kennebunk).

Doctor Banks's notes give several references, all as "York Records," probably meaning *York Deeds*:

Mountequies (*York Records,* XII, ii, 265); *Mountekee* (*York Records,* XIII, 678); *Mountecaws* (*York Records,* XIII, 261).

Presumably *-tequies* stands for *-ticus,* a salt creek or small brook in the Arundel neighborhood; if there is one that is "dug out," deep in proportion to its importance, that may have given the name to the place.

Megankill River. An old map in *New Hampshire State Papers,* Vol. XXIV, gives this as the river next east of Josias's River in York. This would make it the same as Ogunquit River.

WELLS.

Ogunquit. A beach and river in Wells; formerly also a marsh and falls.

The spellings vary greatly. The fundamental reference is the grant of Gorges to Rev. John Wheelwright which Sullivan says was "the origin of Wells" (*History of Maine,* 408).

1642. "River *Ogornog* alijs *Ogoncog,* the great Marishe comonly called *Oguncug Marsh*" (*York Deeds,* I, i, fol. 6).
1643. *Ogunquick* Marsh—(*Ibid.,* I, ii, 28).
1643. *Ogunquett River*—Deed of Thomas Gorges to Rev. John Wheelwright, 17 April, 1643, "all that neck of land next adjacent to the marsh on the northeast of *Ogunquett* River." (Also *Ogungigg* and *Oganquett, ibid.,* I, ii, 28).
1645. *Obumkegg* River—(*Ibid.,* I, ii, 13).
1649. *Noguncoth*—(*Ibid.,* I, i, 28).
1650. *Agunquat*—Grant by the General Court to Rev. John Wheelwright for a sawmill "at the fales of *Agunquat*" (*ibid.,* I, i, 12).
1650. *Ogunquett* Marsh—(*Ibid.,* I, 1, 146).
1661. *Negunquett* Marsh—(*Ibid.,* I, 1, 146).

These records, taken in 1934, were twice verified, August, 1935, and March, 1940; yet they show surprising variations. The best form to work with would be *Obumkeag,* which indicates a sandbar, and particularly one which lay at the junction of a stream with a larger body of water. The deed to Wheelwright, locating the land as a "neck of land adjacent to a marsh" favors this, and we know that the Ogunquit River outlets wholly behind a long ocean beach and runs parallel with it for some distance. Therefore there seems a good reason to adopt Doctor Ganong's suggestion:

"The name comes rather close to the Micmac *Pog-umk-ik,* applied (with variants) to lagoons formed at the mouths of rivers by dune beaches driven by the wind" (Letter June 7, 1939).

Neguntequit. In Wells.

We find this also in the form *Negonquid,* 1720 (Maps and Plans, Vol. XXXIV, p. 8, in Massachusetts Archives); Mr. Cabot makes it the same as Ogunquit. On July 1, 1934, he wrote that *Neguntequit* meant "old abandoned fields," and November 6, 1934, that "Ogunquit means old fields." *Nganié* is "old, abandoned," and presumably that is the root used. We wish to offer no opinion except that the place is not the same as Neguttaquid River, which is in Berwick. *York Deeds* convey land between Neguttaquid River and the Epheford Branch of Great Works River (*York Deeds,* VIII, 266). The Berwick Sheet of the modern topographical map misprints this name as Neoutequid River, entering Great Works just below the village of North Berwick, which is not Neguntequit in Wells.

Nampscoscocke. The names in Wells are early, and the forms of them numerous; but they are beyond guessing. When the Indians themselves seem not to know what was the name of a place or had too many for the same place, later comers might as well "give one bubbling cry and sink."

The Indian deed of Thomas Chabinocke, sagamore of *Nimscoscoke,* to John Wadleigh, October 18, 1649, conveys the tract of land now Wells and Kennebunk—but not Kennebunkport, and lacking the western part of the present Wells. "This extended from the sea up to the great falls on Cape Porpoise (now Mousam) River and from Negunket to Kennebunk River" (Williamson, *History of Maine* (1832), I, 294 n.)

There are various recorded papers of the date of 1649 which give a bewildering number of names.

Thomas, the sagamore, belongs to *Nimscoscocke* and to *Newscossecke;* his land is called *Nampscoscocke,* below *Naguncoth* and Kenebunke" (*York Deeds,* I, part 1, fol. 128). It is also "called by name of *Nischasset,* bounded between *Ogunquit* and Kennebunke" (*ibid.,* III, fol. 65), where it is also *Nimschasset* (as in *York Deeds,* I, fol. 124). In *Suffolk Deeds* (XI, 245) it is *Namscascock,* "between Naguncoth and Cennybunke."

More names might be added from Doctor Banks's notes, but the foregoing are sufficiently irreconcilable. The best of these, *Nampscoscocke,* might be from *amk,* "sand," *kask,* "comes out," *auke,* "place"—"comes-out-sandy-place"; but then we have not disposed of the initial *N,* persistent in all forms. To the eastward, initial *n'* means "going up"; it implies an ascent in a straight line, like going up a ladder, or fish migrating up a stream, and it seems not to combine very well with *kask,* an outlet word; and *namps* is not the same as *nisch* or *newsc,* and instead of trying to reconcile the forms we may take refuge in Lincoln's dictum about the disadvantages of knowing "too many things that ain't so."

Webhannet River. A small stream in Wells, entering back of a sand beach, probably important in early days because, though only about four miles long, it had a fall of over a hundred feet, making it desirable as a millstream. In languages to the westward, *-hanna* is the root for a stream with a good current; but we do not undertake to explain the word.

Mousam River. "Formerly Cape Porpoise River or Maguncook" (Preface to *York Deeds,* II). The modern pronunciation of Mowsam is proved correct by an entry in *Province Records* (II, 353, dated 1679), about "Mowsum Mills lying in Wells," which Mr. C. T. Libby corrects to Kennebunk. We have no clue to the meaning of the name.

YORK.

Cape Neddick. A prominent rocky headland in York, between the Long Sands and the Short Sands. Its noteworthy feature is a small, high island off the tip which is called The Nubble, and is separated by a deep tidal strait.

Among Dr. C. E. Banks's Indian notes, turned over to the writer after his death, were fifteen dated forms of the word, from 1638 to 1747, chiefly from *York Deeds.* All of these begin with the word "Cape." The outstanding variations are:

1638. *Cape Neddock*—(*York Deeds,* VIII, 121).
1649. *Cape Neddicke*—(*Ibid.,* I, i, 14).
1651. *Cape Nodacke*—(*Ibid.,* I, i, 64).
1687. *Cap Nadick*—("Probate Records, D. 26").
1689. *Capenudock*—(*York Deeds,* VIII, 176).

The variations contain nothing significant. Though Ballard makes the word from *nitauke,* "my place" (*Coast Survey,* 1868, 254), and Judge Potter from *netegoo'ike,* "clear land," their findings are not impressive.

Doctor Ganong, on the other hand, in correspondence with Doctor Banks in 1926, remarks: "The word seems to stand complete. This may be a parallel to Chivarie Split at Minas Basin, Nova Scotia, where a rock forms a little island, or nubble, like that at Cape Neddick. It is called in Micmac NAEAD'CH (Rand, *Reading Book,* p. 86). A Suggestion. It is possible that the NAE is root NAOO meaning *solitary,* as a single object, a single tree. In place-names in Micmac *k* is often elided in the middle of words: hence it seems possible that NAEAD'CH is simply a form of NAOO(K)TAJ, a solitary object, in allusion to the upstanding island." A little later Dr. Ganong wrote: "My dear Col. Banks: Re Neddick. Browsing through my notes I find this:—in Passamaquoddy: 'A standing square sandstone pillar [a 'pulpit' rock] isolated on a point above Elmolgook (on Perry coast) is *P'lok-ma-na-dwk.* Looks as if we were on the track of Neddick (Nedock) all right."

That is, while the "Cape" is English, and well applied to the bold headland, "Neddick" was the name of the Nubble where the lighthouse stands, and was of Micmac or Maliseet origin.

Agamenticus River. A salt creek in York, now called York River. It is but seven miles long and is characterized by wide marshes which are flooded at every tide.

From among many slight variations, we may select a few with good early authority behind them:

- 1614. *Accominticus,* a region, Capt. John Smith, *Description of New England,* printed 1616, p. 8; a harbor, Capt. John Smith, *ibid.,* p. 25.
- 1623. *Aquamenticus,* "the river called Aquamenticus," Christopher Levett, *Voyage into New England,* printed 1628.
- 1630. *Aquamenticus,* "near Aquamenticus," John Winthrop, *Journal,* I, 46.
- 1640. *Accamenticus*—Thomas Lechford, *Note Book* (MS., printed by Massachusetts Historical Society, 1885) pp. 339 and 408.
- 1650. *Agamenticos*—Father Druillettes, letter to John Winthrop, saying he had been there.

The word is purely a river name; for *-ticus* means a salt creek or a brook. It cannot apply to the mountain some miles away, now called Mount Agamenticus, or to the little lake at its foot, now called Chase's Pond. So small a stream should have an interpretation from features comprehended at a glance. Yet authorities are in entire disagreement about the meaning.

Dr. C. E. Banks thought it referred to the tidal submergence of the marshes, "where the tidal stream overflows the marshes" (Letter, 1931); but his analysis is far-fetched.

Dr. J. H. Trumbull (Connecticut Historical *Collections*, II, 10) calls it " 'the small other-side river'—a name first given (as *Agamenticus* or *Accomenticus*) to York Me., from the 'small tidal-river beyond' the Piscataqua on which that town was planted." (We may remark that York nowhere touches the Piscataqua, and how could the little river be 'beyond' the great one, if one were facing westward?)

Mr. W. B. Cabot expressed several opinions, but gave no judgment. Dr. Ganong quoted others and said, "I have nothing to add to this." Dr. Ballard called it "the snowshoe river," from the shape of the pond at its source. Unfortunately, York River is purely a tidal creek, with no pond tributary; the pond in question is four miles away upon another river; it is not a natural pond, but one made by damming the outlet; and it is *not* shaped like a snowshoe. This is as near as Dr. Ballard got with most of his Indian interpretations. Father O'Brien has tentative forms, "river on the other side," "stream across the river"— but what river? *This* is the river itself.

The way to settle the matter was to look at the place as an Indian would have done in old times. I went carefully up and down both sides of the river at different stages of the tide and out upon the neck (once a half-tide island) where the Marshall House stands, to see, if I could, what an Indian would have seen when there, how he would have named the place.

We must remember that rivers and streams were ordinarily named from some feature at the mouth. York River, trending seaward, turns sharply west and then east, with a crooked, obstructed channel (hard to navigate on an ebb tide or with a high sea and strong wind outside), as it works its way around the west end of the old bar-island which blocks its mouth. The bar eastward is now built up into a causeway, but in old times, by taking a few steps across it at any time of tide, an Indian could have easily gone from the sea into quiet water above the Marshall House. This half-tide island was the feature no other river had at its mouth. It would be natural to call it "river over across (the island)," "other-side-island river," "river-other-side."

In Father Aubéry's Dictionary, is the word *Aganmen-oket,* "land over across." Change the ending, and we get *Aganmenticus,* "river over across." Nudenans bears this out. He has *Agamen8ki* for "land over across," that is, Europe. Across what? The sea! By a perfect parallel Agamenticus is the "little river over across." Across what? Why, the island which lies in its mouth. It is "the little river which lies behind an island in its mouth."

Wannametoname. A hill in York commonly caled Tonemy Hill.

Doctor Banks gave the full form and inquired whether it might not mean "red paint." I thought *wanname* might be the *n*-form of our *wullamon,* or *oulamon,* "vermilion." A friend of Doctor Banks investigated for him and reported an abundance of both red and yellow ochre at the hill, hematite and limonite.

Doctor Banks questioned whether the *-eton* might not be *etn,* "a hill," "mountain," the whole being "red-paint-his-hill"; but considering the difficulty of disposing of the remainder of the word, it seems better to suggest the possibility that the last part of the word is related to the Natick *tannegan, adtannegen, dtannegan* (*Natick Dictionary,* 157), "it produces, brings forth" (as the earth brings forth plants, the trees, fruits). *Wunnamdtannegin,* "it produces red earth," would be reasonable provided the language, of which we have no vocabularies, was nearer Natick than Abnaki.

Tatnock, Totnock Marshes. In York.

In 1659 "Certen Marshes (comonly called *Tottnocke* Marshes)" near the town line of Kittery and Wells are mentioned. These most likely were fresh marshes, notable in a region of salt grass, but perhaps they were "shaking meadow." The root seems to be *tatagou,* "shake." The Chippewa has *tatogana,* for a trembling piece of ground in a marsh.

Fagotty Bridge. In Wells. Twice mentioned in early records.

It is spelled *fagattie* and *fagatie* as well as *fagotty*. Once it is mentioned as of Berwick at Great Works, and again, in 1678, the Selectmen of Wells are to lay out "a highway between Mr. Naylers brooke and the sea Wall and fagatie bridg." The word may refer to nothing but bundles of brush thrown into wet land to build up a causeway; yet, if it is the name of different places, there is a chance of Indian origin.

Yeapskesset River. Place unknown.

In 1639 Vines deeded to Wadlowe "land at *Yeapskesset* River" (*York Deeds,* I, ii, 12). Since *-apskesset* means "near the rock," *Ye* may have been intended for *Che,* "big"—"near the big rock."

KITTERY.

Amiciskeag Point. "Fish Point," now Kittery Point.

Gorge's grant to Francis Williams and his wife Helena, 13 November, 1635, was of land "on N.E. side of Pascataguach over against Tompson's Point, wch is bounded ... with blacke creek next adjoining to Sagamore Runacwitt's old planting ground on the north and from thence alongst said River to run Downe towards the harbor's mouth into a creek or cove adiacent to *Amiciskeag point* so called by the natives ... about 1000 acres."

The creek is Spruce Creek; the point, Kittery Point. *Amiciskeag* is plainly *Namayskeag,* "fish point."

Godmorrocke. The name of a small grant between Brave-boat Harbor and York River, a word found once only and supposed to be English (*York Records,* III, 97 and 98).

BERWICK.

Monnebasa Pond, "alias Humphrey's Pond" (*York Deeds,* XVI, 810).

Humphrey may have been Humphrey Chadbourne, who in 1668 was conducting lumbering operations on Great Works Stream; in which case this pond may have been Cox's Pond of recent maps. In analysis, the *Monne* may undergo the *n, l, r* change and we get *molle,* "deep." This, telescoped with the next syllable, would give *nebes,* "water." The topographical map shows that Cox's Pond, though one hundred feet above Salmon Falls River, is still in a hole; for the hills rise above it to 140 feet, making the rather narrow pond seem to be in a ditch or ravine—which is precisely the meaning of *mola* or *mona* (as in Molunkus).

Massabesic Pond. "Now Waterboro, Maine" (editors of Jeremy Belknap's "Tour to the White Mountains").

"Big water," "large pond"—a very common place-name, though in Maine *Sebec* or *Sebago* is found oftener.

Bunganut Pond. On the Middle Branch of the Mousam River in Lyman (U. S. Topographical Map), but known only from this recent map and Joseph Sayward's Scout Report of 1733. We find in documents *Bunganuc Pond* in Cumberland, *Bunganut Pond* in Alfred, *Bungernuck* Pond and Stream in Hartford, besides this in Lyman and *Bungamug* in Brunswick; it is presumed that they share the idea of being boundaries of some sort.

Osabeg Hills, Palmasicket Hill. Known only from William Gerrish's Scout Report, 1755. He says: "From upper Salmon Falls Pond, N.E. to *Osabeg Hills* and over one of the highest of the hills called *Palmasicket.*" *Osabeg* is probably for *Ossipee.*

Anunket Pond, and Obnask Pond. In York County, but known only from the Scout Report of Joseph Sayward in the fall and winter of 1733. "Searched up the river (Mousam) and came to the carrying place to *Anunket Pond.*" From there Nov. 26 to White Oak Pond, the 27th to *Tobaskick Falls,* the 30th "Moved out for head of Salmon Falls River, Came to *Obnask* Pond and afterwards to a branch of Salmon Falls River"; Dec. 2, "Got to York" (Massachusetts Archives, 38 A, p. 45). Someone familiar with the country might be able to place these old names.

Assabumbedock Falls. In South Berwick.

> 1650. *Assebumbedock,* or Quamphegon Falls—(Suffolk Court House Calendar, Indian Col., I, 208). A wrong identification apparently, not Quamphegan.
>
> 1669. *Assabumbedock*—"the ffalls in Newichewanick river comonly cald Assabumbedock ffalls" (*York Deeds,* VI, folios 46, 102, 104, 106, and 129).

1669. *Assabumbeducke* River—"at Newgewanacke" (*ibid.*, II, fol. 69).

1720. *Asacubedoc* falls, "otherwise called Great Works in Berwick"— Deposition of Hannah Hobbs that about sixty years before, Roger Plaisted had a sawmill at *Asacubedoc Falls* (*ibid.*, XIV, fol. 102).

If the writer knew this section intimately, the name would perhaps explain itself; from inspection alone it looks as if the first part might be either *awassa*, "on the other side," "behind," or *asawa*, "sloping," "smooth," with the second element containing the idea of sand, as we get it in Bumbahook on the Kennebec, for a sandy shoal.

Bonnebeague Pond. In Sanford, on Great Works River, an easterly branch of Salmon Falls River, entering the latter in South Berwick.

The modern topographical sheet for Kennebunk shows Bauneg Beg Pond and Mountain; but this is not a mountain name. We get it in many forms. *Bonbisse, Bonnebisge* (1676, in *Province Records*, II, 32), *Bonnebeege* Hills (1752), but the best is

1731. *Bannabeague*—(*New Hampshire State Papers*, XXIV, 773).

Here the roots are clear—*panna*, "spreads out," *begat*, "still water"; or *pan* and *nebeak*, "lake," with the same meaning. It is the term so commonly applied to the first expansion of a stream as one ascends it—such as Banook, Pawnook, and even Saponic. It is Indian, not Scotch.

Squimonk Pond. On Great Works River, near Berwick.

The word is found in the winter scout of Joseph Sayward, in 1733 (Massachusetts Archives, 38A, p. 45). The pond must be Bonnabeg Pond and the chance is everything to nothing that the original word was *Mesk8amig8,* Rasles' name for a salmon, since this was on a branch of Salmon Falls River.

Tombegewoc Pond. Deering Pond in Lebanon.

The identification of the place is from Edwin Emery's *History of Sanford, Maine, 1661-1900* (Fall River, 1901): "On an old plot of Lydston's grant, the Indian name of the pond is given as *Tombegewoc,* and the name of the outlet as Salmon Falls River."

Now Tombegewok cannot be the name of a pond, since its chief root is *idj*, "rapids"; it was probably the name of some rapid on the outlet.

Tobaskick Falls of Sayward's scout probably were near by, and *Squimonk*, already noted, may have been Salmon Falls Stream, if the final *-unk* was our eastern *-hunk*.

Newichawannock, "between the rapids" (at a fork). The junction of the Salmon Falls and Cocheco Rivers, on the western boundary of Maine.

The variations of the name are many, but generally recognizable, the forms in deeds being much better than those in probate and court records. Characteristic forms, including the earliest, are:

> 1633. *Newichewanock*—Jenness, *Early Documents relating to New Hampshire.*
> 1634. *Neghechewank*—William Wood, Map, *New England's Prospect.*
> 1646. *Newichwannock*—Deed of sale of "the fishing Ware (weir) at the falls of the great river Newichwannock, reserving personal rights to get alewives for eating and planting" (*York Deeds*, I, i, 6).
> 1667. *Newgewanacke*—(*Ibid.*, II, fol. 27).
> 1676. *Niwichewanacke*—Deposition of William Seavey (Jenness, *op. cit.*, p. 63). This shows beautifully the root *niwi*, "between."

Doctor Trumbull devotes some space to the word, giving the meaning "at the fork," or confluence of the two rivers, and making it from a word for fork, which he does not give, and the more western *-hanna*, a river (Connecticut Historical Society *Collections*, II, 12). The general idea is right, but the derivation isn't. *Newichawannock* comes from *niwi*, "between," and *idjuan*, "rapids," with a land-locative *-ok*, "land" or "place." It is the point of land between the rapids on two rivers which unite just below it. It may be that *idjuan* will resolve into *idj-*, "rapids," and *-hanna*, "river"; but in Maine it is one compound word of definite application and we are not sure that we have *-hanna* (as in *Susquehanna, Lackawanna,* and other place-names).

We can hardly pass by Judge Potter's masterpiece. He makes *Newichawannock* from *nee*, "my," *week*, "house," and *owannock*, "come"! (*History of Manchester*, p. 28).

Quonechewanick Falls, of New Hampshire State Papers, is a different word and different place; it means "long rapids."

Quamphegan Falls, "dip net falls." Salmon River Falls, South Berwick.

"At the head of the tide in the river Newichwawanick we meet the falls of *Quampeagan.* The natives gave this appellation to the place, because fish were there taken in nets" (Sullivan, *History of Maine* (1795), p. 20).

The oldest references bear out Sullivan's statement. In 1643, Roles, Sagamore of Newichawanucke, gave a bill of sale to Humphrey Chadbourne of "half a mile between the little river and the great river" except a parcel of ground called by the name *Comphegan (York Deeds,* I, i, 6). In 1646, he gave a deed of "My Right of the Ware at the Fales of the Great River of Newichawanucke known by the name of Little John's Fales ... excepting so much small Alewives to fish Ground [*sic*] as I my H[eirs] or Exec[rs] shall have Occasion to make use of for Planting from Time to Time & likewise Fish for to eat & also Half y[e] great alewives that shall be taken at that Ware from Time to Time forever" (*York Deeds* I, i, fol. 6).

Quamp-hegan is well understood by modern Indians as "an instrument (*hegan*) for dipping fish" (that is, a net).

Mr. Cabot found among the modern Penobscots the word *Wussquamhegonsett,* "dip net falls" (though it was not located). The root is found in Natick, Cree, Ojibway, and other languages, from the verb *quompham,* "he dips (it) up" (*Natick Dictionary,* p. 141), or the similar Cree *kwoppahum,* "he scoops or ladles it out" (Howse).

We would call attention to the fact that two sorts of fishing went on near here. The weirs would have to be within the reach of the tide; the dip nets would be used above, probably on the steep, rocky falls between South Berwick and Rollingsford, New Hampshire.

CHAPTER SIX

PENOBSCOT BAY: THE EASTERN SHORE, AND THE COAST EAST TO SCHOODIC POINT

The Indian place-names in Hancock County are few. The original inhabitants were Maliseets, who were largely destroyed by the great plague of 1617-1618 and by invasions of the Micmacs. Though the survivors came back, there is very little documentary reference to them, and they seem to have left the country before English settlers came into it, following the Peace of 1763 with the French, so that we have no Indian names for the numerous lakes, ponds, and streams within this county. There were no Indian deeds here, no early maps of importance, no records that could have preserved them.

The list which follows includes all we have found as far east as Narraguagus River. In the Castine region so many long accepted historical opinions have been challenged that it has seemed necessary to present our conclusions, based upon the root-meanings of the place-names, at considerable length.

VERONA.

Nalagwem'-menahan'. Given without explanation by Father O'Brien as the name of Verona Island.

Ah-lur-meh'-sic, "spawning island." Given by Joseph Nicolar as Verona Island.

This is clearly the same as Alamoosook, now restricted to the lake on Orland River, which enters the Penobscot from the east behind this large island. Both these names for the island will be considered at the close of the discussion of the difficult words associated with Orland.

It might be remarked that until a recent period, Verona was called Orphans' Island, because it was a large part of what was left to Gen. Henry Knox's children after the wreckage of his fortune.

ORLAND.

Alamoos'-ook. A large lake on Orland River, noted for its fisheries.
This name has proved a very difficult one. We have found no

early occurrences in print or in documents, and Father O'Brien could get no explanation from his Indians, who tried to make it from *aleme,* "to step," "one's gait in walking." Abbé Maurault interpreted it as "the country of the little dogs," from *alemoos,* "dog." In a list of words obtained from Penobscot Indians, Hanson (*History of Gardiner,* 1852) has *"Allamoosic,* good for nothing" and *"Narramissic,* hard to find." It is plain that all these Indians were merely guessing. Even Nicolar's name cannot refer to an island; for no fish would resort to an island to spawn and no migratory fish would stop in salt water for the purpose.

It is a safe conclusion that the word *alamoosook* belonged to the lake, only two miles from salt water but enough higher in level not to be affected by the tide. It was one of the greatest resorts for fish known, particularly for bass, shad, and alewives, especially the last. The prehistoric Red Paint people lived upon the fish they caught at the outlet, and even today the industry of smoking alewives is carried on extensively. It should not be a bad guess that the original name had something to do with fish. It might come from *n'ahmaysak,* "fishes," or from *anmeswak,* "alewives," but most likely it was from a word in one of the earlier languages, because no one can explain it. The Maliseet word *adlemetit,* "spawning bed," which Mr. Cabot got of Governor William Neptune in 1922, opens up a possible solution, if we had some early printed forms to bridge the gap with *alamoosook.*

Narramissic. The name of the Grange Hall at Orland, also said locally to be the name of Orland River. We are unable to get any documentary or Indian information about the word, but it seems to connect well with our next, is certainly long established in this place, and is Indian. *-Amissic* is not too far from *-amoosook* to be the same word.

Rameson. Probably an old name for Orland.

An ancient French document, *"Accadia portefeuille, 128"* (associated with the "Memorial from Acadia, 1686"), evidently intended to accompany a map bearing corresponding numbers, has one note numbered Seven, which reads: *"Une terre plate, où il y a quantité de Chesnes fort aisée à Cultiver qui faict l'embouchure de la rivière de Rameson sur les bords de laquelle* on peut placer plusieurs d'bitans [des habitants] il y a aussi quantité de Chesnes et de beau bois où y peut faire grand pêche de bare, D'aloize et de Sardines et de Casparot, et il y a mouillages pour des navires."

Since this paper was endorsed "Description de la Rivière et Terre de Pentagouet et lieux circonvoisins," the location of *Rameson,* a place of many oaks, good woods, and quantities of sea-bass, shad, smelts, and alewives, with good anchorage for vessels, could have been nowhere but at the mouth of Orland River. If *Rameson* is not *Narramissic,* what else can it be? For the form of it shows that Rameson is not a perfect word, since it begins with an R. In the longer word, when we make the usual change of *r* to *l,* we get Nalamissic. If *nala-* means "below," as it usually does, and *-amissic* is *añmessoo,* an "alewife," in the locative, then the Orland Grange name meant "below the alewife place," which would be Alamoosook Lake, where alewives thronged in countless numbers to spawn. By adding the word for an island, we get Joseph Nicolar's name for Verona, "the island below the spawning place."

This word *Rameson* is in "Documents Collected in France," about 1844, by Ben Perley Poore, now in a manuscript copy in the Massachusetts Archives. It was reprinted in the Maine Historical Society *Collections* (Documentary Series, IV:425).

Ramassoc. The next form we find is in a German map, based on the Jefferys of London, 1755, also in the Massachusetts Archives (Maps and plans, II: 3, #716), which has *"Ramassock, où Penobscot où Pentagouet Rivière,"* which further identifies and locates the word.

The German maps of this period were pirated from better maps and are full of ignorant blunders; but this *Ramassock,* so definitely bound to Penobscot and Pentagoet, is the link between *Rameson,* which we have located and the *Ramassoc* of Purchas, 1623, in that maddening list of the nine rivers ruled over by the great chief Bashaba, or Betsabes, or Bessabes, whom Champlain met on the site of Bangor in 1604 and Father Biard saw at Castine in 1611. Purchas says that the river Ramassoc was less than a day's journey from the home of this chief, and Orland River was about midway between the two places where we know he was seen by white men. We hardly need question whether Purchas's *Ramassoc* was not the same as *Rameson;* we note that it was more than forty years earlier and had an Indian ending.

Without claiming too much, we may point out that *Ramassoc, Rameson, Narramissic,* and *Alamoosook* are very closely associated, if not identical, and all contain the root *-am,* found in Indian words for "fish," whether as *namesak,* "fishes" in general, or *aïmesswak,* "alewives." Mr. Cabot writes: *"Ramassoc* runs into a pretty revealing word for dried fish!"

Nalagwem-menahan, the name given by Father O'Brien as Verona Island, provides a possible interpretation for Nicolar's name. Dr. Ganong says that in Maliseet, *"Gwimek* is a place where salmon lie side by side in a smooth rapid"—that is, a spawning-bed. If we had the word in the Penobscot dialect, *nalagwem* might mean "below the spawning-beds"; but this is purely conjectural.

PENOBSCOT.

Wallamatogus. A hill (height 460 feet) in Penobscot, Hancock County, generally called Mount Wallamatogus.

Early forms of this name are lacking entirely; therefore there is no assurance that it more than approximates the original. The only other occurrence known is in Pittston on the Kennebec, where Togus Stream and Ponds are tributary; an old map in the Massachusetts Archives (Roller #976, date 1790, gives the name as Worromontogus Stream and Ponds.

Since *l* and *r* are largely interchangeable, *Worromontogus* and *Wallamatogus* would appear to be the same word, especially since the *nt* was probably a nasal compound, sounded very much like the corresponding syllable of the second word.

If they are the same, the words could not have been applied one to a stream and the other to a mountain; and as the ending *-togus* is a water-ending, equivalent to *-ticus,* a brook, the name dating to 1790 in documents would be the one correctly used as a water-name. We may rest assured that this name never belonged to the mountain.

If *Wallamatogus* was not the mountain name, to what did it apply? In 1935 Mr. Chester Versteeg of Los Angeles asked the Smithsonian Institute for the meaning and was told "probably 'small vermilion Inlet' in Abnaki Algonquin."

If that was the meaning, there should be such an inlet near. Inquiry of residents of the locality revealed no knowledge of any such place, though one said that water from a certain well along the Penobscot road left white clothes boiled in it of an orange-yellow tint.

In 1931 I had inquired of Mr. Herbert Hutchings of South Penobscot, grandson of the last Revolutionary soldier; and he said that Wallimatogus meant "spring under the mountain" and was named for a great spring near the foot of the mountain where the Indians used to take out their canoes when they were carrying them across to Penobscot Bay. Yet anyone who knew anything of the region and of the maps would see that the Indians would never select that course as a carrying place to Morse's Cove on Penobscot Bay.

There was one locality which seemed to me the reasonable place for a carry, a short course, over good ground, ending above the tide-falls of the Bagaduce River. In 1935, Mr. William H. Dunbar of North Castine, who lived within sight of this place, said his father could remember when the Indians used to camp there. Near there a little brook came into a small cove above the falls. If Wallamatogus should be a corruption of *Waliniticus*, the meaning would be clear, the application perfect—"Brook Cove," the place where the carry across the greater Castine peninsula began or ended, a place which needed a name.

Walini is a cove; *-ticus* is a brook or stream. Mill Creek in South Orrington has the same name, *Walinetuk*. And we note also that the characteristic of Togus Stream is that the stream ends in a cove before it enters the Kennebec River.

The conclusion from acquaintance with the locality and analysis of the word is that the name does not belong to the hill but to the cove just above Bagaduce Narrows and the meaning is "brook cove," a cove with an entering brook.

CASTINE.

Pen·tag·oet'. This French form was most often used of Castine and the vicinity, but sometimes it was extended to the Penobscot River.

The word is commonly printed with a dotted o and the accent on the second syllable; but since *-öet* is only the French form for *-wet,* the word has but three syllables instead of four and is accented upon the last, Pen-tag-wet'. It means "falls of the river," or as we would say, "at the falls," referring to the tide falls on the Bagaduce River.

The analysis is simple—*pen-,* "descending"; *-tegwe,* "river"; *-t,* locative.

Map-makers were by no means agreed upon the locality to which this name belonged. A few typical citations will show how uncertain was the application:

1607. *Pentagoet*—Champlain, on his first map of all, now in the Library of Congress. The name is placed at Castine; it seems to refer to the junction of Penobscot and Bagaduce Rivers.

1699. *R. Pentagouat*—Guillaume de Rozier map (Parkman Collection, Massachusetts Historical Society, Boston). He puts the name upon the main Penobscot River.

1715. *R. de pentagouet ou pantagoué*—Father Joseph Aubéry map (French Archives, Paris). He puts the name upon the headwaters of the West Branch of the Penobscot, and *Pentagouet* across Penobscot Bay, with no name at all upon the main river.

1749. *Penobscot ou riviere de pentagouet*—Jean Baptiste de Couagne, map (French Archives, Paris, reproduced in *Acadiensia Nova,* 1935, William Inglis Morse). This is the Penobscot River, but on the same map is *La petite R. pentagouet,* which is plainly Bagaduce River.

1755. *Penobscot ou R. de Pentagouet, Petit Pentagouet*—Bellini, Map of Eastern New France (Massachusetts Archives, Maps Collected in France, II:12). Petit Pentagouet is the Bagaduce River.

The conclusion we draw is that *Pentagoet* was first used of the Bagaduce region; later the name was extended to cover the whole Penobscot, and later still, it was so firmly fixed in its first location that there were two Pentagoets, the Big and the Little.

Since the word definitely means "the falls," it must have been settled on the tide-falls of the Bagaduce and the tide-falls at Bangor (Pemjedgewok). While the Abbé J. A. Maurault (*Histoire des Abenakis,* XV) made many bad guesses about Maine names, there was something in his definition of *"Pen-*

tegoet, de Pôteg8i, endroit d'une rivière où il y a des rapides." This is perfectly descriptive of Bagaduce Narrows, and since *Pôt* (*Poⁿt, Bahn,* etc., meaning a waterfall) comes from the same root as *pen-,* "a descent," *Pentegoet* does not "come from" *Poteg8i,* but is the same word.

Majabigwa'-duce, Bagaduce'. "The big tideway river." Bagaduce River.

This word, variously spelled, with little to choose among most of its forms, the very worst excepted, has long been applied to the Castine peninsula. It has been said to mean "bad bay" (Ballard), "bad water to drink" (Vetromile), "bad landing place for canoes" (Penobscot Indians), and "at the small bad shelter place" (Dr. J. Hammond Trumbull).

An intimate acquaintance with both land and water about Castine and Cape Rosier has convinced the writer that the name was not originally applied to the Castine promontory; that it was not Abnaki Indian; and that the meanings are bad guesses, or wrong conclusions from misunderstood premises.

I believe that the original word, replaced by an Abnaki form, was Micmac Indian; that it meant a big tidal salt bay; and that it referred to the whole Bagaduce River, so called, not merely to Castine Harbor.

If there were no stronger objections to the meanings given in books, there is one which covers all of them: they are pointless. An Indian would not have given this name to Castine Harbor merely because the shore was hard to land upon—there are too many such places on the Maine coast; or because it was a poor harbor for sailing craft in a sou'wester—he could pick up his canoe and carry it up the bank and "let it blow"; or because the water was salt—like the rest of the Atlantic Ocean; nor would he or anyone else who had ever seen the spacious roadstead of Castine have described it as a *"small* bad-shelter place." Not one of these meanings serves to identify the locality.

Yet if Majabigwaduce is the right name, the Indians were correct in their interpretation; and Dr. Trumbull is correct in his translation of *Matsibig8ad8ssek,* given by Father Rasles in his dictionary (under "Noms," p. 358) as *"la rivière, où est Mr. de St. Gaustin";* and Father Rasles has given a faultless Abnaki form and located it so precisely that there can be no dispute, unless it centers upon the place where Castine was living. There is here a discrepancy between the name of the place and the place itself.

To demonstrate just what has happened, one should know the topography of the entire region, the archaeological and historical background of the natives and their white successors, as well as the documentary and philological history of the place-names. This cannot be done in a brief summary, if proof of assertions is demanded.

The topography of this section is too involved to be understood without a map, but it may be said that the Bagaduce River, if we are ascending it, begins in the harbor before the present town of Castine and continues about three miles as a tideway running northeast to the Narrows, where there are three sets of tide-falls. At the head of these falls, navigable at high tide for sailing vessels of considerable size, but wholly impassable for everything on the wrong tide, the great salt bays open out—on the left the Northern Bay, on the right the South Bay—through which the river proper trends southeast for several miles, then turns southwest for two miles more and finally, after falls and rapids, heads in the fresh pond called Walker's Pond, two miles long, and so close to the sea that a half-mile carry brings one out at the Punch Bowl on Eggemoggin Reach. The whole course of the river, along the town line which separates Brooksville on the west, from Castine, Penobscot, and Sedgewick on the north and east, is about fifteen miles, without reference to the great Northern Bay, three miles long—all of it salt water except Walker's Pond—which twice each day is emptied and filled again through the Narrows. So great is the pressure of one tide flowing in while another beneath it is still drawing out that in passing through the Narrows on the top of the flood, when the surface is smooth, a stout motor boat will drum and tremble all over. This is a tideway indeed.

Here, too, was the proper home of the Indian, in a country full of fish, shellfish, fowl, moose, deer, and beaver, with its portals easily guarded, and lying out of the way of roving enemies.

Here, too, was the region which the oldest map-makers, before the towns were organized, called Majabagaduce. The name was not applied to Castine town until it grew into prominence. The name belonged to the salt river.

Because the French fort was on the Castine peninsula, in a place well suited to European communications and defence, it has been taken for granted that the Indians were here also, settled in numbers about the fort. But anyone acquainted with Indian life and its necessities could see that this was no place for Indians; for it provided neither food, shelter from weather, nor safety from enemies. Archaeological research warrants the statement that they never were here in numbers, unless for trade or upon special occasions. Dr. Moorehead found little evidence of Indian occupation in his exploration of the whole surrounding territory and located but two Indian villages on his map (*Archaeology of Maine,* Andover, 1922, p. 161)—one of them on the eastern side of the North Bay, the other at the foot of Walker's Pond, where occurred the battle with the whites mentioned in the Introduction. Governor Pownall's map of 1759, for the west bank of the Bagaduce River, puts the sign of an Indian town near the Narrows, but has only the word "Casteen" upon the baron's fort. It is probable that there was an early Indian settlement upon the great point above Hatch's Cove; for an old map in the French Archives, dated only by a remark about the Flemish pirates having burned Castine's fort, has a legend at this place, "Habitacion de Mr. St. Castain," as if he had taken refuge with his Indian friends at a place commanding the carry across Castine Neck. That there was a large Indian population near is proved by Father de la Chasse's census of 1709, which gives their names (MS. in Ayer Collection, in Newberry Library, Chicago), but they were not living where they have been assumed to be.

The foregoing resumé is not wholly irrelevant, if we are to understand Father Biard's story in *Jesuit Relations* (Thwaites ed., II:47-49). Coming eastward from the Kennebec in 1611, the Frenchmen reach the *Pentagoet,* "a very beautiful river" which "has many islands and rocks at its mouth; so that if you do not go some distance up you will take it for a great bay or arm of the sea. . . . When we had advanced three leagues or more into the current of the river, we encountered another beautiful river called *Chiboctous,* which comes in from the northeast to discharge its waters into the great Pentegoet. At the confluence of these two rivers there was the finest assemblage of savages that I have yet seen. There were 80 canoes and a boat, 18 wigwams and about 300 people. The most prominent sagamore was called Betsabes [Bashaba of the English], a man of great discretion and prudence. . . . As for us we were very glad to be in a country of safety; for among the Etchemins, as these are, and the Souriquois (Micmacs), as those of Port Royal, we are no more obliged to be on our guard than among our own servants."

The Pentegoet here is Penobscot Bay. Biancourt and Biard had landed at Metinic Island and from there struck across the bay for Castine, meeting the strong ebb tide, which pulls hard past Cape Rosier, and coming to anchor at the present town of Castine, where they were met by a great concourse of Indians and their most important chief, Bashaba. The time was early November, 1611. Though they had wigwams, this was no sign that they were resident there; for birch-bark pointed wigwams were as easily transferred from place to place as tents, and the weather was cool. The very large number of canoes, all where they could be counted, is almost proof that the Indians, who were Maliseets, had gathered by appointment to meet the French at the mouth of a "beautiful river called *Chiboctous,* which comes in from the northeast."

There is no mistaking the place, or that the Maliseets called by the name of *Chiboctous* the salt river which has long been known as the *Majabigwaduce.* Upon this single occurrence of the word rests our chance to prove that the latter name is an interloper, not belonging to the place.

We may trace the history of the word in a few characteristic forms:

> 1611. *Chiboctous,* "the Big Bay"—Father Biard (*Jesuit Relations,* II:49; analysis follows).
> 1625. *Chebeguadose,* "the Big Bay"—Purchas (*Pilgrims*). From *k'chi,* "big," and *a^{n}baguatus,* "cove," "bay."
> 1644. *Matchebiguatus,* "the Bad Bay"—Edward Wislow, in a quit-claim deed of August, 1644, to John Winthrop and others, of a storehouse and goods which d'Aulnay de Charnizay had appropriated two years before. (Winthrop, *Journal,* Savage's ed. II:221, n.) By this time the word has shifted from *k'chi,* "big," to *matchi,* or *marjee,* "bad."

1724. *Matsibig8ad8ssek,* "the Bad Bay"—Rasles (*Dictionary,* 493). Translated by Dr. Trumbull as "at the small bad-shelter place" (Connecticut Historical Society *Collections,* II:39).
1762. *Majebequadeaux*—Johnson and Holt, Survey (Massachusetts Archives, Roller Map #478). They took the name to be French, which probably marks the beginning of the folktale about the French "Major Biguyduce."
1765. *Maggebagaduse*—Map of Seacoast and Islands of Penobscot Bay (Massachusetts Archives, Roller #764). *Magge-* probably pronounced with both *g*'s soft, *majee-,* "bad."

Father Biard's statement that the people he met were Maliseets, and the word he gives, which is pure Micmac, and may also have been Maliseet, prepare us for the change in this word; for Purchas's form, only a few years later, is Abnaki. They have the same meaning, "big bay." The modern Micmac name for Halifax is *Chiboctook,* "the great Harbor." But with Edward Winslow begins a new slant upon the name: it is no longer the "big bay," but the "bad bay"—and yet Father Biard distinctly says the name was that of the *river* which flows into the harbor. This name also is Abnaki. It is possible that the Pilgrim Fathers, whose larger business was upon the Kennebec River, used Abnaki interpreters in dealing with the Maliseets of Castine and that these Indians made over the word into their own dialect. Though Father Rasles refined the form of it to impeccable Abnaki, he was not responsible for the change, which had begun a century before.

It will be immediately asked concerning Father Biard's *Chiboctous,* if it could not have referred to the great Smith or Lawrence Bay across from Castine, very properly called a "great" bay; also why, if the word for Halifax means a great harbor, this does not refer to Castine Harbor itself.

The questions are pertinent, but the answer is more so. The Micmac word does not permit either interpretation, quite aside from Father Biard's statement about the name belonging to the river now called Bagaduce. The word has in it a Micmac root which means a "tideway," which was especially applied to salt bays which are filled through a tidal channel. Halifax is such a harbor; Wiscasset is another; the Great Bay of the Piscataqua is precisely similar to the great bays of the Bagaduce. All of them are protected inland harbors connected with the sea by longer or shorter tide-channels, "great salt bays."

Of the second element of the word *Chiboctous,* Dr. Ganong (speaking of a Canadian name) says: "Evidently the *Boog* is identical with the root *book,* meaning a bay or inlet (of salt water) ... thus *boogwek* signifies collectively an inlet of salt water forming a river" ("Organization of Indian Place Names," Second Paper, 1912, 184-193). In letters, Dr. Ganong not only approved our interpretation, but first suggested it though he did not know the locality. "The big tidal river" and the "the big salt bay" equally well carry the idea, for a salt bay has to have a tide. It might be remarked that one reason why such places were great Indian resorts was that the tide brought food-fishes and the water was always open the year round.

In rendering the later form of the word as "bad bay," we have been strictly orthodox, not opposing the authorities; but there is in Maine a root, not known to Dr. Trumbull, which would align the later forms with Father Biard's. *Bigwek* is the Penobscot word for a tideway, or channel—as in *Pitowbigwek,* "between two channels," the name for Long Island (Islesboro). *Matchebiguatus* might conceivably be "the bad tideway" and still be both Abnaki and applicable, if we understood the final syllable to stand for *-tegwe,* "river," though this does not work out for Rasles' improved, academical form.

We have no hesitation in saying that Majabigwaduce could not originally have belonged to either the harbor or the headland of Castine; but that it was the name of the great tidal river now known as the Bagaduce, with the signification already explained.

Penobscot. A name often applied to the Castine promontory in early times, probably specifically to Dice's Head.

In early times nobody seemed to know where the Penobscot River began, and the names Penobscot and Pentagoet were applied without reference to their root-signification. Though Capt. John Smith mentions Penobscot River, his list of names makes Penobscot the equivalent of "Aberdeen," and on his map Aberdeen is planted squarely upon the Castine peninsula. This was the general custom for a long time: when anyone went to Penobscot, he went to Castine. Bradford's *History of Plimouth Plantation* repeatedly uses Penobscot as the name for Castine (pp. 309, 326, 333, 350, and 395). Ashley, he says, was landed in 1631 at the place "caled Penobscote, some 4 score leagues from this place

[Plymouth]," and in 1635, Monsieur d'Aulnay, "coming into ye harbore of Penobscot," took possession of the Pilgrims' trading house, which we know was at Castine, or near by. In a letter to his Majesty Charles II, dated 5 October, 1676, about the Dutch pirates taking Baron Castine's fort, Edward Rawson, Secretary of the Commonwealth, speaks of the "fforts Penabskop and St. John, belonging to the French and scituate upon the River Pentagouet" (Maine Historical Society *Collections,* Doc. Ser., VI:131).

This usage seems to indicate that regardless of the Penobscot River, or any of the other places called Penobscot, the aborigines themselves might have applied the name "at the descending rock" to Castine. There was no place along the coast better entitled to it than the abrupt Dice's Head, where the lighthouse sits, a landmark from all sides. In Indian nomenclature a name did not have to be unique—it was used as often as it described a place, provided it was not too near another of the same name. There is no good reason why the falls section of the river at Bangor should have prohibited the use of the same name at Castine, forty miles away.

Apanawapeske.

Purchas His Pilgrims, 1623, detailing the discoveries by English travelers between 1602 and 1609 in Maine, has a confused medley of Indian names of rivers, towns, and chieftains, many of them recognizable as to form but not as to place. Among these is *Apanawapeske,* upon which tract is a town called *Chebegnadose.* Dr. Trumbull identified the town as a misprint for Chebeguadose and called the river Penobscot (Connecticut Historical Society *Collections,* II, 1870, 39).

In this Dr. Trumbull was mistaken. The Penobscot River was not called *Apanawapeske.* Above Old Town Falls, where the river valley spread out, the section next to Penobscot, "the rocky part," was called *Pannawampskek* (*q.v.*), and as a *word* this is identical with Purchas's name, in which the initial *A* is a not-understood preliminary to many forms of words, chiefly tribal names and place-names found in Maine. Purchas also has inserted an extra *e* near the end, making the root *p'ske,* "split," instead of *-apsk'-,* "ledge"; otherwise the words are the same, except for the locative, which it was permissible not to use when one was *at* the place named, but was used for places apart from the speaker's location.

Where Purchas's river was it would be useless to inquire, but where his word could have been fittingly applied is another matter. Its association with the known Chebeguadose (Majabigwaduce) leads the hunt for a suitable location to the Castine region. And there we find precisely the spot which it would fit. We have located Pentegoet as the appropriate word for the tide-falls at Bagaduce Narrows, below where Chiboctous, "the great bay," expands; and at the head of the Narrows is the place aptly described by such a word as *Pannawampske,* "opening out upon the ledgy place," not a river but a point which marks the expansion of the river. Except for this being upon a tidal stream, the conditions are so parallel to those at Old Town above the falls that we need not hesitate in saying that this is the one word which the Indians would have used in naming the place, one which was important because it guarded two carries, the one past the falls and the long carry to Morse's Cove on Penobscot Bay.

We cannot demonstrate the point, but if we had been Indians naming this region, we should have called Castine *Penobscot,* the Bagaduce Narrows *Pentegoet,* and the great bays above *Chiboctous,* or an Abnaki equivalent—or in English usage, the Head, the Falls, and the Great Salt Bay.

M'd'aⁿgamak, "his snowshoes." Dice's Head, Castine.

The M' is the personal possessive pronoun referring to Glusgehbeh, the demi-god of the Abnaki, the Glooscap of the Micmacs; *añghemak* (pl.) is "snowshoes" (Rasles, 429).

Near the lighthouse at Dice's Head there used to be marks in the ledge which the Indians believed were made by Glusgehbeh when he leaped across Penobscot Bay in pursuit of a moose. They were greatly venerated by the Indians, but the whites have destroyed them, so Indians have told me. Clara Neptune said you could "see his snowshoe prints *plain* till white folks spoil 'em."

The legend is that at Moosehead Lake Glusgehbeh killed a large moose, which became Kineo, and then pursued the calf. He threw down his kettle upside down, which now is Kokadjo, "Kettle Mountain," or Little Spencer Mountain. Then he threw down his pack, which is Sabotawan, or Big Spencer Mountain.

With his dog, Glusgehbeh pursued the moose to Penobscot Bay and when the moose took to water near Searsport or Belfast, Glusgehbeh, on snowshoes, leaped across Penobscot Bay, landing at Castine. On Cape Rozier he killed the calf, whose body may still be seen (see *Moos-i-katch-ik*).

Father O'Brien's notes give *Mosemadega* as at Searsport, and the word would seem to mean "moose's snowshoes," an absurdity probably accounted for by the unwillingness of the Indians to talk with him about their traditions. The Douglas-Lithgow Dictionary has "Madagamus Hill, near Belfast, Waldo County, 'the trace of the snowshoes.'" This is a rather incorrect rendering of Hubbard, who gives the legend in *Woods and Lakes of Maine* (23-26). The place was not Belfast, but Castine. Father O'Brien also has *Madagam'issek*, "snowshoe mark."

Dr. F. G. Speck heard the tale from Wawenocks in Canada ("Wawenock Myth Texts," 43rd Annual Report, Bureau of Ethnology, 189); and Joseph Nicolar tells it in *Life and Traditions of the Red Man* (Chap. III). None of our Maine Indians has ever mentioned *Pukdjinsquess*, the old witch, following Glusgehbeh, as the Wawenocks told Dr. Speck.

CASTINE NECK.

Several names, all recent and of little importance, have been found for the marshy stretch across which the British dug their trench. Before this was dug, the Indians, to avoid going around the whole peninsula with its strong tides and winds, used to carry across the Neck into Hatch's Cove and located the place by several descriptive names, in which *edali* is only "the place where."

Edali-sibac'lemuk, "where they waited for the tide" (Clara Neptune). *Siba-* probably is from *sebes*, indicating a narrow place, "almost through,"; we do not catch any tide-idea.

Edali-andalach'simem'ook, "place where you would have to rest, or resting place; might be Castine Neck" (Lewis Ketchum). By waiting for the tide to rise, the carry here was much shortened.

Edal-skowasi'muk, "where you would have to wait" (Ketchum). The root *sko-* shows that this would be a watching-place, a look-out.

Eti'da-waskika'sik, "grassy down there" (Ketchum). He also gave

Eti'da-waskigas'sik. The root is *-esk,* grass. The Neck is still a notably grassy place for the Maine coast.

BROOKSVILLE.

Moos-i-katch'-ik, "the moose's rump." Cape Rosier.

A ledge on the shore of Cape Rosier, between Harborside and the Tip of the Cape, at about half tide strongly resembles the hinder part of a moose when lying down. It was thought to be the calf moose killed by Glusgehbeh.

Osquoon', "the liver," is a large rock of a reddish color which is near by.

Oo-lagh'e-see, "the entrail," seen close by, is a vein of white quartz which runs under the sea to Ilesboro, coming out in a bluff between Ryder's Cove and the point below. The legend says that Glusgehbeh's dog was sitting on Long Island when he killed the moose and as the dog's share of the game, Glusgehbeh threw him the entrail which is still seen under water as a streak of white quartz.

The legend of Glusgehbeh's moose hunt was one of the tales most often told by campfires. John Soctomer, a Passamaquoddy of Machiasport, told me a similar legend of the Maliseets associated with Moosebec Reach.

Musikuc'ik (the *c* sharp, *tch*) and *Pembotchick,* "moose's hinder part, rump," are found in O'Brien's notes.

Mose-ka'-chich, "signifying moose's rump" and the legend, as given by A. W. Longfellow, in 1868, are in Wheeler's *History of Castine* (p. 16).

Edali-chichiquassik, "where there is a very narrow place." The short carry across Cape Rosier from the head of the creek at Goose Falls into the bay on the south side of the Cape.

Chichi is reduplicative, from *tse, tchi,* or *se,* "narrow."

Ooneganoosis, "the short carry," another name for the same.

The "big carry" was from Castine to Blue Hill, which in later years was made by team.

Minnewo'kun, "the many-directions-route." The route by Bagaduce River from Castine, through Walker's Pond, to Eggemoggin Reach.

The word, as nearly as I can recall, was heard many years ago from a summer visitor at Bucks Harbor, who got it from another summer visitor. Since then it has been submitted to several Penobscot and Passamaquoddy Indians, who accepted it as a good Indian word.

The best definition was that of John Soctomer of Machiasport, who said: *"Millewankan, Milheganew,* turn about good many different ways." This precisely describes the route, which following the irregular Bagaduce River, is very angular.

O'Brien has *Milankigan,* "very crooked."

The regular change of *l* for an *n* shows that *minne-,* the first element, is the same as *milli,* in words like Millinocket, meaning "many." The last part of the word is *wokun,* a "bend." In Rasles this would be *wanghigen,* but farther east the Micmac form remains. *Minnewokun* is an old Micmac or Maliseet survival. The word for a route is not expressed.

Winne-ag'wam-auk. Said to be an old name for Walker's Pond at the head of the Bagaduce River.

The word is given in Wheeler's *History of Castine* (Bangor, 1875, 55 n.), where it is said to mean "the beautiful water place" and to be compressed into *Winnewag.* The word is poor, manufactured Indian. Indians are not likely to use the ending *-auk* (*aki,* "land," "earth") in the name of a lake, and "beautiful water" means nothing during the six months when a pond is locked in ice, nor does it enable anyone to recognize the lake on seeing it. *Winne-* is not common in Maine place-names and it does not mean "beautiful," but usually "round about," "in the vicinity of," or else it is some form of *ounigan,* "a portage," as in Winnegance.

The word may be a mere corruption of *Minnewokun,* the "many-angled route," or it may be meant for *Ouniganek,* or *Winneganek,* "the carrying place," and refer to the short but very important carry from the head of Walker's Pond into salt water on Eggemoggin Reach.

SEDGWICK.

Sep'sis-edal-apskitahan'sit, "where a bird is drawn on the granite near Fox Islands," (O'Brien).

Father O'Brien is wrong in his location. The "stone figure

of a bird" was near the entrance of the Punch Bowl, a little round harbor on the Sedgwick shore. It was much venerated by the Indians, but the whites knocked off its head.

Sepsis, "a bird"; *edal,* "where there is"; *apskit,* "punched in the rock." O'Brien's list of related words is worthy of record:

Abskit, punched, the outline in holes.
Nudabskitahiget, stone-cutter.
Sukskapskitehemen, to punch without order.
Assobapskitahemen, to smooth.
Skukskalalagitemen-abasi, to punch wood.
Alakussemen, to carve.
Mamalhakussemen, to carve ornamentally.

SEDGEWICK-BROOKLIN.

Eggemoggin Reach. The eastern channel of Penobscot Bay.

The name means "the fish-weir place," but originally it must have had a much more limited application. It would have been the narrow passage between Great and Little Deer Isles, just below the present long bridge from the mainland.

    1686. *Archimagau, Larchisnagam* (the difference in endings a misprint). The French "Memorial on Acadia, 1686" and the legend to accompany a large scale map, probably the Franquelin-De Meulles map of 1686, give the two forms, reprinted as above in Maine Historical Society *Collections,* Documentary Series, IV:42, 429.

        Archimagau, "*l'isle apellée Archimagau six lieües plus Est qu Pentagoüet.*"

        Larchisnagam, "*L'isle et le fort de Larchisnagam où les terres sont bonnes et où il y a quantité de Chesnes et des prairies qui ninnonde pas.*"

        Good land, many oaks, meadows which never were overflowed were attractive, a place desirable enough to be lightly fortified. Six Frenchmen lived here as early as 1686. The place was an island about twenty miles by sea easterly from Castine. Roughly estimated this would be near the thoroughfare between Great and Little Deer Islands, and the Indian word strengthens the supposition.

    1726. *Agemogen, loc. non cit.*
    1762. *Algomongan Reach*—Survey of Johnson and Holt.
    1770. *Edgamoggan*—Journal of Capt. William Owen, R.N.
    1780. *Algemogin*—Calef, of Castine (Wheeler, *History of Castine,* 1st ed., 312).

1832. *Edgemaroggan*—Williamson, *History of Maine*, I, 74, who says it was pronounced Edgemorgan. In the writer's childhood it was called Egg-moggen, and in Indian *g* before *e* is hard.

A-mog'-en was the Maliseet word for fishing; *a-mog-en-esk'* was a "fishing place" (Ganong, *Monographs of Place-nomenclature*). *Seet-mok-an'gan* is the word the Maliseets gave Mr. Cabot for a brush fish-weir, and Lewis Ketchum gave me the same as the Penobscot word, *seek-mook-kan'gan*. The word is from *siti*, "shore"; *-amaug*, "fish" (in composition); *kangan* (or *higen, -higan*) the usual word-ending for anything man-made, a tool, instrument, or contrivance. A fish-weir is a "fish-catching contrivance on the shore." It is a fence of stakes interwoven with brush, which begins at the shore and leads out to a pound, made similarly of stakes and brush, which encloses a net.

Anyone who knows the locality would at once perceive that the channel between the two Deer Islands, with its wide, soft mud-flats, would be an ideal place for pounding down the stakes for a weir, as well as being a natural passage for fish in great numbers, which, following the shore, would encounter the fence and by keeping along beside that, would be guided into the pound.

The early French name *Archisma'gan* is a short form for *K'chi-siti-mokan'gan*, "the Great Fish Weir." In *Larchismagan* the initial *L* is probably only the French definite article *le* or *l'* before the vowel.

BROOKLIN.

Naskeag Point, "the end," "the extremity." This long point marks the eastern bound of the entrance to Penobscot Bay.

The name is one of the simplest, yet no Penobscot Indian asked has been able to define the word. Rasles has *8anask8i8i*, "*le bout, au bout*" (p. 42) and Nudenans gives *8nask8k8k, ad extremitatem acuminis, summo acumine*, "the tip" of anything. Dropping the first syllable, we get our word *Naskeag*. It is quite possible that the full word was not *Wanaskookook*, but *Kwinaskeag* (or *-kookook*), the Long Point. In a letter dated May 12, 1895, Mr. Roland E. Robinson, of Vermont, wrote, "The Wabanaki called the Point [in Shelburne] 'Quinaska,' the

Long Point." He also said that the stream near by was called Quinaskatook, Long Point Stream, as he was informed by John Wadso, "the most intelligent man of his tribe I ever met." This is important as showing that the St. Francis dialect has the stem -*ask,* meaning a "point," although no Penobscot could explain it.

The word *Naskeag Point* is found as early as 1703 (Massachusetts Archives, 8:285).

BLUE HILL.

Awan-adjo, "small hazy mountain" (Newell Lyon to Mr. Cabot). Blue Hill, in the town of Blue Hill.

Though not high, Blue Hill is a notable landmark, as it can be seen on all sides from very far away, so that it is characteristically blue from the distance. Whether the English name is a translation of the Indian, or the opposite, it is impossible to tell. *Awan* is "fog," "mist," and *-adjo* is a shortened form of *wadjo,* "a lone hill of the sugar-loaf type."

The chance that this is the aboriginal name is somewhat increased by Lyon's telling Mr. Cabot that *K'chi-awan-adn-ock* was "the big hazy mountain." In this word he used a different stem, *-adene-,* the inseparable for a mountain, instead of *-wadjo.* The name would apply very well to Old Lead, or Humpback, Mountain, far to the northeast of Blue Hill, also a landmark.

Neither word has been found in documents, which may mean that they are quite recent.

Kolle-jedj'-wok, "the salt-fresh falls" (lit. "mixed rapids") (O'Brien).

Kulad'am-itch'wan, "mixed rapids" (O'Brien). Blue Hill Tide Falls.

Though slightly different, the two words have the same meaning and refer to the same place. Both come from Father O'Brien's notes, but both have been revised in form, the first to bring out the roots, the second to get the sound. What Father O'Brien wrote was: *"Kollegedgewock.* Blue Hill. *Kuladiewak,* mixed stream of salt and fresh water. *Kuladamicwan."*

The word comes from *k8rade* (Rasles), "mixed," and *-idj-,* the root for rapids, which in the second word is written in full, *-itchwan,* or *-idjuan.* It was first printed by Mr. Willis as *Kollegewidgewock,* with the location but no meaning.

The Tide Falls are three miles from the center of Blue Hill, at the eastern end of the salt strait called Benjamin River, which cuts across the head of the great Brooklin peninsula from the Penobscot to Blue Hill Bay. When the tide is running out, so much fresh water comes in from tributary ponds that the "river" is much less salt than the ocean; when the tide rises, the stream is salt again—whence the appropriateness of the name. This quiet thoroughfare was a favorite Indian short route, avoiding all exposure to the open sea and affording a good food supply.

BAR HARBOR.

Man-es-ayd'ik, "clam gathering place" (Ganong). "The Indian name for Bar Harbor."
"The word *manes* or *menes* means to collect clams; *es* (pl. *esak*) 'clam.' This is an item there is no doubt about. I have it from several sources" (Ganong, Letter).

Al-es-an'uk, "clam-bake place" (O'Brien). *Ais* (*es*), the common soft-shelled or long clam.

Ah-bays'-auk, "clambake place" (Ballard). The word for a clam occurs in the second syllable; the third is -*auk,* "place."
Dr. Ballard said that Hon. E. M. Hamor told him of great piles of shells at Somes Sound, Hull's Cove, Indian Point, and Bar Harbor, which marked spots where the Indians used to bake clams. These were then dried by smoke and kept for winter use.

P'ais-unk, B'ais-ahgan, "Mt. Desert Island, but especially Bar Harbor"—John Soctomer, Passamaquoddy, 1931.

P'sahn, or Besahn, "Mt. Desert Island, especially Bar Harbor"—Lewey Mitchell, Passamaquoddy, 1930.

Abes-sah, or Abnessan, "clam mountain, signal place, light or smoke"—Governor William Neptune, Passamaquoddy, to Mr. Cabot, 1922.
The meaning is impossible; Governor Neptune probably unconsciously used the wrong root and then undertook to translate it. Instead of *Abnessah* (with the *bne, tn,* "mountain" root) he thought he was saying *ablusam,* the Maliseet for "where you go clamming."

ELLSWORTH.

Wech-ko-te'-tuk, Union River.
Admittedly a very hard word although there are several forms.

    1686. *Houestotagois* (Westotagwak)—Found in a French document, evidently the legend to accompany the numbers on a map; located by its relation to other numbered places as probably Union River, and apparently the same as Dr. Ganong's Maliseet word.

    1868. *Wichacowick*—Ballard, "a name applied to Ellsworth River and falls," showing that it was the name of the mouth of the river, in the city limits of Ellsworth. His meaning of "place of pine tree cones," on the supposition that *-co-* is from *koa,* a pine tree, is wholly indefensible.

    1890. *Wec8kantegwek*—O'Brien, "coming towards." (The *c* is the sharp *tch,* making the first element *wetchu,* "from," "out.")

    1919. *Wishtotokwac*—Ganong, who said it was a weak form of the above, given him by a Machias Indian.

    1930. *Wechkotetuk*—Lewey Mitchell; no meaning given, but probably the same word as above in Maliseet form.

The word is very puzzling. The last part of it means a "river." The first element is *wetchi,* "from," "comes out," which we found in Sunkhaze. The difficulty is with an element which can be represented as *co, kan, kot, tot,* and still mean anything when combined with *wetchi.*

The location possibly presents a solution, even though rather forced as an explanation.

Union River discharges into the bay with a rapid, partly tidal, and a little above is a sharp bend in the river, around which was a very considerable fall, now covered by the high Bangor Hydro Dam. In the old days, when the country was wooded, this natural fall was probably much more concealed than at present, and one came upon it suddenly in passing the bend—a natural and insurmountable barrier, facing the canoeman. We have here the ideal *wetchi* situation, where the current comes round a bend which shuts off further view. There is a possibility that in this place, the second element might come from a word found in Nudenans, *k8e, g8e,* (very much like the word for a pine tree) which he defines as *caput, vultum, sive anterioram partem capitis,* "the face." From this base an Indian could easily make a word meaning "facing," even though we cannot find it in our limited vocabularies. "Comes-out-facing river" might be his idea, which Father O'Brien's "coming towards" seems to justify. No other river that we remember has just this sort of outlet into the sea. At the very mouth of it one was confronted by an impassable barrier.

Appeumook River, Union River. A name found only in Joseph Chadwick's Survey of 1764, but unexplained.

Le Chock River, named by Governor Phipps in a letter to Capt. Jabez Bradbury, 3 April, 1751 (Maine Historical Society *Collections,* Doc. Ser., 23, 378).

Le Jok River, on a German map based on Jefferys' map of 1755. None of these last has been deciphered.

MOUNT DESERT ISLAND.

Pem·et'·ic (for *Pem-etn-ic*), "a range of mountains." The Mount Desert Hills.

Pemetic is the old word given by Father Biard in 1611. Either accidentally or by error of a copyist or printer, the necessary *n* of the root *etn-, -adn-,* "mountain," was dropped. It is the name for Mt. Desert as seen from the sea, where the hills rise in a long saw-toothed range.

Some Indians have defined the word as meaning "mountains seen at a distance," but "at a distance" is *pemigak* (from *pem-,* "extended," and *-mighe-,* the inseparable root for "land").

Dr. Shea's remark, "The Indians called Mount Desert Pemetig (Biard) and the country Pemetigouek, corrupted into Pentagoet, the English Penobscot" (Charlevoix, *Works,* I, 253 n.) is incorrect—the three words are entirely different.

Winsk·eag. Otter Creek Point.

The late Dr. William Otis Sawtelle located the home of Cadillac and his wife as on the western side of Otter Creek Point below the new bridge across Otter Creek. A note on the writer's topographical map puts the date when they were known to be here as May 10, 1688.

The name is probably a somewhat corrupted form of *Kwinaskeag,* "the Long Point," from *kwini-,* "long," and *-ask-,* "end," "termination," with a locative.

HANCOCK-SULLIVAN.

Adowauk'-eag, now known as *Waukeag.* Falls Point, in Sullivan.
By cutting in half the great tidal stream from Sullivan Harbor which twice a day has to fill Flanders and Egypt Bays above, Falls Point causes tide-falls and whirlpools second only to those at Cobscook Narrows on Quoddy Bay. The place and the name are of historic interest, because until the Indian word had been identified and located, no one knew what were the bounds of De la Mothe-Cadillac's grant, which old documents called Donaquet and Douaket, in great variety of spellings.

Though *Adowaukeag* is a land word and, strictly speaking, is Falls Point, where the glacial kame crosses the river, it is, by extension in common use, a section of the river itself regarded as a boundary. In both Penobscot and Maliseet *adowaket* is the name for a "horseback," or glacial kame. Meanings given by Indians do not vary essentially.

1916. *Akedowaukek,* "sloping downwards, down hill"—Lewis Ketchum.
1920. *Adoahaneek,* "height of land"—Newell Lyon to Mr. Cabot.
1922. *Adowakeag,* "rising ground from the water"—Governor Neptune, Passamaquoddy, to Mr. Cabot.
1930. *Adowakeag,* "a knoll"—Lewey Mitchell, Passamaquoddy.
1932. *Adowaukeag,* "a horseback"—John Soctomer, Passamaquoddy.

Some early examples of the forms are:

1674. *Douakesc Bay*—Capt. George Manning's account of his fight with the Flemish pirates who burned Castine's establishment (Maine Historical Society *Collections,* Documentary Series, VI, 42).
1675. *Adouake Bay* (*ibid.,* 86), *Adowaket* (*ibid.,* 88), the last a perfect Indian form.
1688. *Douaquec*—Cadillac's Grant, *"lieu appele Douaquec"* (*Acadian Seignories,* IV, 53).
1692. *Douaquet*—De la Mothe-Cadillac, "Memoir of Acadie."
1697. *Adouaquet*—Sieur Hautville's Grant, *"au-dessoûs d'Adouaquet"* *Acadian Seignories,* IV, 138). This would be in, or near, Sorrento.

What fully settles the identity of the names is Captain Manning's Journal, in which he tells of chasing an enemy ketch, August 7, 1674, "up into a great river." "We bore vp vpon her & she claped close vpon the wind & shott into a Cruell & most formidable place, that if we had shott a Cables lenght more on head we had lost Ketch & men, but we came too & had a stout scurmighs wth them..." (Maine Historical Society *Collections, volume cit.,* 183). Anyone who knows the locality will recognize this as the tide-falls above Mt. Desert Ferry, where every now and then, on the ebb of the tide, the great "Cellar Hole" gapes below the white sheet of the falls.

A Passamaquoddy form of the word, found by Mr. Cabot, may be worth noting. *Adowaukeskeag* was given by Governor William Neptune, in which we note not only the idea of a slope, but also *-weskat,* "the tide runs out," giving the picture of a horseback in a place where the tide runs out very strong.

GOULDSBORO.

Schoodic Point (pronounced skoo'-dik). The end of the great Gouldsboro peninsula now a part of Acadia National Park.

This long, rocky, and also hilly, point is a prominent feature of the Maine coast. Its name has been left for study by Dr. Ganong. There are at least three roots, quite unlike in meaning, which are covered by the English word Schoodic. They may be called the "fire-Schoodic," the "trout-Schoodic" and the "point-Schoodic" names.

The root *skut,* "fire," has given names to many places, the most important being Calais and the great Schoodic lakes upon the international boundary. In 1798, Francis Joseph Neptune, the Passamaquoddy chief, told the Commissioners who were studying the boundary line, that *"Scoudiac* meant a great clear place, because all the country had been burnt" (Kilby, *History of Eastport* (1888), 113).

The root *sko'tum,* "trout," is in the name of Schoodic Lake on the Piscataquis and in other Maine words.

Finally, the Micmac *eskwodek,* "the end," is so aptly descriptive of Schoodic Point in Gouldsboro that it seems as if it must be the aboriginal name for it. It is hard to think that the natives would have depended upon a purely transitory name, like "the burnt place," for the end of this great point, "The Point" of the east, as Pemaquid was "The Point" of the west coast. Des-Barres, in his *Atlantic Neptune* map of April 24, 1776 (reprinted by Dr. W. O. Sawtelle in his "Sir Francis Bernard"), has *Scuttock Point,* which might come from either the first or the third root.

CHAPTER SEVEN

THE EAST COAST: WASHINGTON COUNTY

Realizing that Doctor Ganong's great study of Maliseet and Micmac place-names is not yet finished and that when done it will be published in Canada and probably not easily obtained by American students, we extend our list eastward, beyond the limits originally planned, by including many names, largely Maliseet, found in Eastern Maine. For the most part, these were obtained from Indians upon the sites named; and their forms and interpretations are given without critical comment. We follow the shore eastward in the order of the incorporated towns, and up the Machias River; but in the wilderness a river is followed to its head, branch by branch. As most of these have strings of lakes upon them which go by number, and as the Indians are rather poor geographers, we are not always sure of getting the right name upon the right number, though fortunately we know the headwaters of most of these rivers through woods camping upon them many years ago. Returning to the coast, we follow it eastward by towns and then up both branches of the St. Croix River.

CHERRYFIELD.

Narra-gua-gus (Narraguay'gus). The river which flows through Cherryfield. The meaning of the name has not been ascertained.
 This is one of the most difficult words we have and its meaning has not been established. Indians seldom undertake to give a meaning—and those who do are wrong. The following are samples of the definitions found:
 Hubbard has "something breaks and you cannot fix it"— *Nallagwagis.*
 Vetromile (MS.): *"Nallaguegus,* a river entering a cove, about the middle of the cove." (But it doesn't!)
 Maurault: *"Nar8ikg8s, c'est embrouillé, ce n'est pas clair.* There are so many islands and bays that it is hard to find the mouth of the river"—certainly not a helpful definition for recognizing the place when one arrives there!
 O'Brien has *"Nulagweguissek,* 'that way,' 'facing that way'! Narraguagus River at Cherryfield, right opposite Passadum-

keag River—that way." Evidently an Indian statement, but not satisfactory to the present writer, who knows the country and the many routes by which one goes from the Passadumkeag to other river systems by the carries. Besides, the word, by its history, plainly belongs to the mouth and not to the head of the river.

Ballard: "The Indians do not explain this word."

Willis gives the word without comment.

Springer (*Forest Life and Forest Trees,* 1855, 184) says: "The true Indian orthography seems to be *Na-la-gue-guess* and signifies palate, stream, or river. To use the precise language of my interpreter, opening his mouth wide and thrusting his finger down his throat, 'It means all one, jus' if I open my mouth and never run down my throat into mine belly.' Whether there is any peculiarity about the river, or the form of the bay into which it falls, to originate such a name, I am unaware." The only place where such an explanation could possibly mean anything seems to be the long and rather narrow point of land between the East and West branches above the town; but the historical application of the name has been below the town.

Ganong, in letters some years since, suggested that it might be from *nalla* (*nalek,* "split"), adding that *"waakus* (*guagus*) was a limited spot, quite frequently applied at the mouth of a branch of a river" by Micmacs—"The idea is a piece split off."

Cabot offers a series of southern New England names in which words allied to *-gwegis* indicate marsh-land, and cites Tooker for *Gueguss* (*Indian Place-names on Long Island,* 67) used in a deed of 1696 for a neck of land "commonly called or known by ye English by ye name of ye Litell necke by ye Indians *gueguis."* Mr. Cabot explains that there is some salt marsh along the shore and up inlets near here.

Lewey Ketchum said it was a Quoddy word, and would undertake no explanation.

Henry Lorne Masta, St. Francis, wrote that it is from *Nallaguagus* and means "irregular" (*Abnaki Indian Legends,* p. 92).

Lewey Mitchell, Maliseet, gave the form *Nul-gue-quisk-took,* in writing, but no explanation.

John Soctomer, Maliseet, said *Narraguagwess* was "narrow creek"; and said he was "sure of the meaning." But it is not a creek and it is not narrow.

Thus thirteen authorities have bogged down in a slough from which it seems useless to try to extricate them. We may, however, review some of the historical entries of the word, with the preface that we have found none which we recognized in any French source.

    1769.   "This is a plan or Description of the Mill Privilege at *Arroguagus*.... surveyed by me July 6th 1769. Daniel Merrill, surveyor."—(Lincoln County Records, XV, fol. 97). This was at Steuben or Milbridge

    1773.   "Joseph Wallace of a place called *Arroguagus* to James Grace ... land and marsh beginning at the Hay Road coming from the Flatt Bay and so running up Cole's Creek." 19 October, 1773.—(Lincoln County Records, XV, 97.)

    1775.   "Land on the Northeasterly side of the *Narraguagus* or *Allaguagus* River in Township no. 5." September 8, 1775. (Lincoln County Records, XII, fol. 276.)

           (These references printed as found, not verified.)

Of "Ancient Narraguagus," Col. Joseph W. Porter says (*Bangor Historical Magazine,* VII, 1891, p. 162): "All that part of Cherryfield lying south of the mills on the first or lower dam was, prior to 1826, a part of Steuben, and was called Narraguagus to distinguish it from the settlement at the southwestern part which was called 'Head of the Bay,' and the postoffice at Cherryfield was called 'Narraguagus' until within some twenty-five years past."

By a broken boundary line the topographical map shows clearly that the portion of Steuben set off in 1826 was on the west shore of the river between Milbridge, "the head of the bay," and the town of Cherryfield—it was the tidewater portion on Narraguagus River, the Lower Narraguagus. This section of the river runs in a straight channel, unbroken by rocks or islands, with alluvial shores bordered by more or less grassy tide-marsh, not enough to be conspicuous, yet sufficient to provide cattle-feed for the earliest settlers.

The word divides itself into two parts, the prefix *nala-*, which offers the variations *alla-* and *arra-* for comparative work, and the main stem *guagus* or *gwegis*.

Guagus is found elsewhere in Maine. *Guagus Stream* is a tributary to Brandy Pond on the West Branch of Union River; we know it from travel on it, a long dead stream through meadowy marshes.

In New Brunswick, Dr. Ganong lists *Guagus Lake,* "a typical New Brunswick woods lake, shallow, with boggy margin on the west and boulder margin on the east." Also *Little Gaugus Lake,* "also typical of the region, shallow, boggy and bouldery." "The Micmacs said that Guagus meant 'rough stream.' "

In Maine we have *Quakish Lake* on the Penobscot West Branch. The writer remembers this before Millinocket was projected, as a shallow expansion of the river, rimmed with spruce trees draped with *usnea,* the counterpart of Dr. Ganong's lakes. Early surveys show that formerly it had several islets, later submerged or blasted out by lumbermen. Lewey Ketchum said there was an Indian tradition that about two hundred years ago the lake sank, though like most Indian history, this probably was invented to account for a name not understood. Hubbard gives no explanation.

The consensus of actual examples cited points to these names' being associated with lands more or less marshy or under water, and to these perhaps we may add the word Lewey Ketchum gave for the small islands below the bridge in Orono, *Ellalagwagawaysek,* "a sort of flooded place," because on high freshets they were sometimes overflowed. The root *-gwa-,* found in the words for a canoe, a landing place, an otter slide, and other words, indicates close connection with low places near water.

ADDISON.

Wass-quagos. Pleasant River.

The name was found in old French documents by Dr. Ganong, who knew nothing about it at the time he wrote. The ending bears a resemblance to *Narra-guagus,* perhaps only accidental.

JONESPORT.

Moosabec Reach. A protected inland passage between islands and the main, much used by sailing vessels.

The word is generally supposed to mean "overflowed"; but

no one has explained how a tidal passage *can* overflow its banks. You cannot fill a barrel when both ends are out—and a reach is practically that. Though Tooker explains the word learnedly (*Algonquian Series,* Vol. II, pp. 39-42), he did not know the place; neither did Hubbard, Willis, or Ballard. John Soctomer was outspoken. "It had nothing to do with *mispaak,* 'overflowed'; that was Micmac; it was land, not water. It was an island outside the Reach; rock, seen at a distance, looks like a moose's head—*Moospayechick.*'"

We have had no chance to investigate either the place or the word, but Soctomer believed that it was connected with a moose, and knowing something of the number of times in which the story of Glusgehbeh killing the moose is associated with coastwise places, we think it very likely that this is another, perhaps similar to *Moosekatchik,* "the moose's rump," at Cape Rosier. If Soctomer had inserted a *k* in his word (as he may have done the next time he spoke it!) he would have had *Moospaykechik,* close to the earliest forms we find.

- 1675. *Muspeka Rache* (misprinted *Racke*)—Capt. George Manning's statement that "after wee sett saille ffrome Adowaket to Aplaisse called Muspeka Rache," June 17, 1675 (Maine Historical Society *Collections,* Documentary Series, VI:88).
- 1770. *Mispecky,* or *Mispecki Reach*—Capt. William Owen, *Journal,* p. 770 (printed for Victor Paltsits by Ganong).
- 1777. *Mispecki*—Col. John Allan, (Kidder's *Military Operations,* etc.).

K'mokad'ich, "trying out porpoise oil"—John Soctomer, 1930; given as the name of some spot in Moosabec Reach. *Kadich* is *kañntti,* indicating abundance, with the final *ch* soft, like *sh,* approaching the Penobscot locative in *s* instead of *k*. *K'mo* was not explained.

Seguin Island, and Seguin Passage, near Jonesport. (Blount's *Coast Pilot,* 1864.)

The name occurs elsewhere only at Seguin Island, off the mouth of Kennebec River. Dr. Ganong, many years ago, interpreted Seguin as meaning "turtle," *checquenocks* (*siguenoc*). It seems more likely that both instances may be a form of *segan,* a "hump," —*ahassonsegan'al* being a horse's withers.

Humalatski-hegon, "many carvings on rocks" (Lewey Mitchell). Roque Bluffs.

Mitchell wrote that this was "on an island near Roque's Bluffs, called South Island," which we have failed to identify. There were many marks on rocks here, supposed to have been made by *Wanagameswak,* or fairies, "a little human being, very seldom seen, but seen their works." It seems to be an eastern, or Maliseet, duplication of the markings at Hampden Narrows. These old Indian myths and traditions are found repeated in different localities about far enough apart to mark early occupation by different tribes.

Eskwiwamigek. Spruce Island. No explanation.

Soctomer said there was a beach there a mile long. The Indians said that long ago two men in love with the same girl, agreed to run a race here, the winner to have the girl. One of the runners dropped dead just as he finished the course.

MACHIASPORT.

Squa-zo'-dek, "the watching place" (Soctomer). Clark's Point.

Here John Allan's Indian scouts watched for British vessels during the Revolution. Just above the tide-mark, on a smooth, sloping ledge, many small figures of men and animals are chipped in the ledge; these are commonly believed to be prehistoric pictographs with a meaning which some have tried to decipher. In 1931 I examined this place in company with Mr. Decatur, who owned the property, Mr. Frank S. Ames of Machias, and John Soctomer, the Maliseet, who lived at Machiasport. From what the Indian said and what could be seen on the spot as likely to happen there, the figures appeared to have no meaning but to be only "doodlebugs" made by Allan's scouts as they lay lazily at ease watching the seaway for English ships and chatting with one another, head to head, as they stretched out in the sun on a ledge with a double slope, like the roof of a house.

MACHIAS.

Ma-chi'-as (second syllable sharp, *tch,* accented), "bad little falls" (Indian informant). The name originally of the steep, rough little fall on the West Branch of the Machias River, in the heart of the town, later extended to branches of the river and to lakes far away.

The name as given by Lewey Mitchell is *Mecheyisk,* "bad," "rough," of which the first part is plainly *matchi,* "bad," but the syllable *-yisk* may include considerably more than appears. The *-k* is the locative sign; the *s* probably stands for "little," and the *-yi-* we suspect is the old Maliseet root *ya-, -ia, -ha* (in more modern use *wee-o, ee-o-ee*), "a run of water" (Ganong, "Organization of Place-Names," Third Paper, 1913, p. 83) related to the Micmac *-jooik,* "to pour, to run swiftly," thus warranting the popular interpretation of "bad little falls."

Of great importance to historical students are the many forms of the name which are found in documents. Without some knowledge of these it is almost impossible to locate many references in old papers. We note the following:

1675. *Maythijas*—Capt. Petrus Roderigo, a Dutch pirate, "a place where we had a trading house" (Maine Historical Society *Collections,* Documentary Series, VII:63).
Mathias—(*ibid.,* p. 54); *Matchias* (*ibid.,* p. 82); *Mechias* (*ibid.,* p. 85).
1683. *Magos, Mages*—*Inventaire des Concessions* (Quebec Archives, III, 241).
1688. *Mageis*—"*Douaquet proche de Mageis*" (*ibid.,* IV, p. 33).
1695. *Majais*—"at Majais" (*ibid.,* IV, p. 108) and, 1692, De la Mothe-Cadillac.
1715. *Macseies*—Father Aubéry's Map (French Archives, #254); also *Markiseug*—map #253 (French Archives, Bureau de la Marine), error of a foreign map-maker, no doubt.
1746. *Mechisses*—map of Cyprian Southack, in *American Pilot;* a favorite form of the word.
1777. *Mechios*—Des Barres, picture of Mechios Mills, in Massachusetts Archives (copy in Machias, probably in Public Library, with another picture of the town at that time).
(For the French references, 1683-95, we are indebted to Dr. Ganong.)

Indian attempts to explain the name are sometimes fantastic. Dr. Gatschet gives it from *"matchiess,* partridge" (*National Geographic Magazine,* January, 1897); but *m'tchiess,* the Maliseet name of the ruffed grouse, means "bad bird." To the writer John Soctomer told a story of the old chief Kokohass, "the barred owl," often called Cougougash, trying to set fire to an English vessel stranded in Machias River by the tide; he failed in his attempt, on account of which he was said to be *matchio,* "clumsy"—whence the name of Machias River!

We would suggest a probable connection between the word Machias and *Matchiwisis,* Great Works Falls on the Penobscot.

Kawopskitch-wak, "rough, rocky falls." West Branch of the Machias River.

Originally this was the name of the fall in the town, probably modern Abnaki crowding out the older Maliseet *Machias,* which, however, maintained itself by being adopted as the town name. Mr. Cabot found *Kawapjkitchwock* in the Massachusetts Archives on a map dated 1792 (#1618); and the Osgood Carleton map of 1802 has the form we give, which comes from *kah,* "sharp," "splintery," "rough"; *-apsk-,* "ledge"; *-idj-,* "rapids."

Coupcheswick. Col. John Allan's rendering of the above (Kidder, *Military Operations,* 125).

Sibeheganuk, "a passage." Cross Island, near Machias; so called, says Soctomer, because the Indians used to carry across it to avoid the sea outside.

EAST MACHIAS RIVER.

Kebumkewis, "Sandy Lake" (Soctomer). Second Lake of the whites on East Machias River.

One would suppose this meant "little sand-bar lake," but we do not know the place.

Gay-way'-sik. Given by Soctomer as Pokey Lake (Crawford Lake), on East Machias River and defined as "big body of water." He said it was an old camping ground for Indians, and Old Joe Benwit, the magician, used to live there before he went to Gardner's Lake.

Sobag-wa'gum, "lake near salt water" (Soctomer). Hadley Lake, on East Machias. The lake is very near the salt water, and shows the two roots *sobag-,* "the sea," and *-guagum,* a "lake."

Other forms are *Subecwangamook* (Vose's list), and *Sobequeskagn* and *Subeguagem* (Lewey Mitchell).

Nem'damas-sua'gum, "sucker lake." Gardner's Lake on East Machias. This was a great resort for suckers and the name is found in many variations.

Nemdamwuk-wagam, "from *nemdamwuk,* 'swim up' " (Lewey Mitchell).

N'damisguagum, "sucker lake" (John Soctomer), "great place for suckers."

Nemadamas-swagum (Soctomer). In this we see the *madamas* which we found elsewhere as an alewife; *-swagum* is one of the many Maliseet endings for a lake.

Nemdomwook; from *m'dom,* "sucker" (plural *n'domwock*); "*N*' means 'going up' " (Lewey Mitchell).

Numdemociss Stream, "where suckers go up to spawn" (Hubbard).

The usual Maliseet name for a sucker is *kikamkw;* the present word, so near to the alewife name, indicates a migratory fish, and has reference to the breeding habits of the sucker instead of to its physical peculiarity, the "outward turning mouth," noted by the Penobscots in their name, *abodumk'n.*

Num'che-nug'ma-wis, "lake one-sided," that is, with the inlet and outlet on the same side of the lake, a lake where you go "straight up." Second Lake on East Machias, according to Soctomer (but see *Kebumkewis,* above).

Necon-aug'amook, Round Pond, Third Lake on East Machias River, if Soctomer's location was correctly understood.

Bahkahsok'sik, "long straight deadwater" (Soctomer). The big meadows above Third Machias Lake on East Machias.

Menik-padik, "place to get cedar bark" (Lewey Mitchell).

This was the old name for Poke-moonshine Lake at the head of the East Machias River, say the Indians. In a letter Mitchell wrote, *"Munikpadik,* place where they had cedar bark. This bark used by Indians like rope for tye the Bundles or many different purposes."

Caribou Lake on the West Branch of the Penobscot had the same name, *"Mahnekebahntik,* where they used to get cedar bark for packs" (Hubbard, *op. cit.,* 199).

Father O'Brien has *"manigeke,* bark or rind, of basswood (braid)." The word would do for any flexible, tying bark—

basswood, cedar, elm, or the very tough wicopy (*Dirka palustris*) preferred to all others for the finer strings.

Poke-moonshine Lake. A corrupt form of the Indian name for the large lake at the head of the East Machias River.

Both Soctomer and Tomer Sebattis denied that the word was Indian, giving the old name *Menikpadik* and the English name Shiner Lake, so called for the small bait-fish in it. However, the word must have had an Indian basis, and in 1937 Peter W. Ranco, one of the best informed of the Penobscot Indians, told me that originally it was not the name of the lake but belonged to the outlet where by flowage from a dam the trees were killed and there was a large area of "dry-ki," or dead standing timber, which later became stumps standing in shoal water. From this it was called Stumpy Brook, *Pokwajanak-i-tagook*. Though I have been unable to confirm the accuracy of this statement, it is reasonable, and I know that almost a century ago *Bocaganak*, "stump," was the nickname of a Penobscot Indian, who was called Newell Stump.

This accounts only for the first part of the word, which might easily be turned into *poco* (Pocomoonshine was the older form). After this was well established for the brook, *maquozsebem*, "lake," might be added to extend the term, which American humor could twist into "moonshine." However, the case is conjectural, and lacking any documentary evidence, may be all folk-etymology.

THE MAIN MACHIAS RIVER.

The Main Machias River has various branches, each with its lakes and names and numbered systems, making it not always easy to identify an Indian name unless one knows the country or has a good map. It divides into Old Stream, to the east, and Main Machias west; and the latter, after receiving Mopang Stream and its lakes, divides again into East and West Branches, with the Machias Lakes on the East or Main Machias, and the Sabaos on the West Branch of the Main River. The two lower lakes on the East Branch of the Main Machias are not known to the writer and their names were not obtained or have been misplaced with those of the East Machias

River, though Soctomer, the informant, knew the country thoroughly and is believed to have been understood. Concerning the following there is no question of correct identification.

Egol-bayik, "long, narrow lake" (John Soctomer). Third Lake Machias, on the Main River.

Given as *Egolpake* by Tomer Sebattis (the same word), and as *Adolpewicke,* by Lewey Mitchell, which may or may not be the same. Lewey was well over eighty years old, long past his days in the woods, and his geography was of much the same sort as his history—it had seen better days. *Acalpewick, Adopewicks,* and *Adolphewick* were his alternate forms, in writing.

K'tolbewik, "big turtle lake" (Lewey Mitchell). Fourth Lake Machias.

This name is a reconstruction of the word given by Mitchell in the four ways mentioned above and defined as Turtle Lake. Remembering the huge mud turtles with which both Fourth and Third Lake abound, it seemed as if his definition were correct, but his word is a confusion with the properly descriptive *Egolpake* of Third Lake, which is long and narrow. Accordingly, I suggest *K'tolbewik,* the name of the great snapping turtle, as the probable name; the *K'* standing for *k't* or *keght,* "principal," "biggest"; *tolbeh,* "turtle," and *-ik,* the locative ending. The *w* merely replaces the final *h* sound.

Katekwysip (Lewey Mitchell). Unknown Stream, tributary to Fourth Machias Lake. No meaning given. The ending *-sip,* or *sebou,* means "stream."

Ba-a-kosk', "end of the lakes" (Soctomer). Fifth Lake Machias. *Bayekosk* was the form used by Tomer Sebattis.

WEST BRANCH OF MAIN MACHIAS.

Sab'ao, "passage." The name given to a string of lakes on the West Branch of the Main Machias. They are four in number and the river passes through three of them, terminating in Fourth Sabao, or Upper Sabao (on the topographical map, unfortunately, as Big Machias), only two miles from Nicatowis Lake on Penobscot waters.

The word is related to *Sebayik, Sebasticook, Sibangan,* and other words indicating a passage or "almost through."

Wiscogo-sis'icook, "lakes in a string" (Soctomer). Another name for the Sabao Lakes.

Wiscogo'sis, given by Soctomer as the name of Lower Sabao, the first in the string, formerly, and properly, called Big Machias since it is much the largest of the series.

Umsquasquos'pem, "first lake," Big Machias, or Lower Sabao, from *umsquas,* "first," and *quospem* "lake," a translation of the English name (Soctomer).

Mopang. A lake tributary to the Main Machias from the west.
The word is said by Lewey Ketchum to be a Maliseet word, but he gave no meaning.

Escutnagen, "trout lake" (Lewey Mitchell). Mopang Lake; from *scotum,* "trout."

Apskikek, "lonely lake." Mopang Lake; the name given Mr. Cabot in 1922 by Governor William Neptune of Point Pleasant; no explanation. The lake stands far off from the others.

LUBEC.

Kepam'kiak, "bar of gravel." Lubec, near the ferry to Campobello. "*Kep,* meaning 'closed,' from the word *kephig'n,* 'dam,' *kephaso,* 'shut close'," wrote Lewey Mitchell. *Amkiak* is a well-known word for a gravel bar, found in Micmac, Maliseet, and Abnaki. "*Kebamkeak,* 'stopped by a sand-bar'," wrote Rand of the Micmac; and *Kebumcook,* commonly called "The Hook," on the Kennebec below Gardiner is another instance, while Mattawamkeag shows the same root, *amkiak.*

Unagan'-ek, "at the carry" (Gatschet). An ancient portage over a mile long at low water, where the U. S. Life Saving Station stood in the last century (Gatschet).

Wusus'-ek, or **Wusosis'ek** (the diminutive), "an old nest" (Lewey Mitchell).
An old word for West Quoddy Head. *Was* is a nest (*8asesé,* in Rasles). Probably an eagle, raven, or fishhawk, all of which

make bulky nests and resort to the same locality many years in succession, marked the place before there was a lighthouse here.

Minnicops'cook, "many rocks" (John Soctomer). Sail Rock, near West Quoddy Head.

In 1770, Capt. William Owen of the Royal Navy, in his Journal, spoke of *Seal Rocks* instead of *Sail Rock,* and his plural is borne out by the Indian interpretation. Though Dr. Charles T. Jackson (*First Report on the Geology of Maine,* 1837, 31) speaks of this as Sail Rock, and shows a picture of it, it may be questioned whether, considering the importance of the seal to Indians and the certainty that this would be a location where they were found, the name was not originally Seal Rocks, as given by Captain Owen—pronounced, as we have noticed in the Introduction, as "sile," and then changed to "sail."

Pessak'enew-ag'enek, "at the lighting apparatus" (Gatschet). West Quoddy Light.

Perhaps a better form would be *Pessaken-i-higanek. Pessakwe,* "light," "brilliancy," possessive *i,* and *-higan,* the ending meaning a contrivance, tool, instrument—the ordinary name for a lighthouse.

WHITING.

Keght-nigan'-ish (John Soctomer). Whiting's River.

Though Soctomer gave no meaning, it is entirely clear—*keght-,* "principal"; *nict,* "crotch," "fork," with the softened locative *-ish,* meaning the larger of two streams which meet in a crotch.

EDMUNDS.

Ehkaps-ak (Soctomer); **Acrups-ak** (Mitchell). Hobart Stream (Mitchell), Little Falls Stream on topographical map.

"Rocky bottom," said Mitchell—and the stream looks it as the tide runs out of its lower part near Dennysville.

Kenalclin. Given by Lewey Mitchell for Edmunds.

One of the earliest settlers was Colonel Crane, who lived near the old Indian carry from Cobscook Bay to Machias and had a mill on a brook still marked Crane Mill Brook on the topographical map. The mill is marked as Col. Crane's Mill on the old Indian map made by Francis Joseph, July 12, 1798, for the Boundary Commissioners. It was done in pencil; and "the lines followed afterwards with Ink, as nearly as possible" is the Commissioners' endorsement of the original in the Maine Historical Society. Dr. Ganong could not make out the all but illegible names, so that his tracing in *Evolution of the Boundaries of New Brunswick* (*Monographs*) Map No. 4, only approximates the word. It was meant for "Colonel Crane," which the Indians pronounced *"Kenalclin"* and still occasionally call by that name. (See *Georgekeag*.)

Swankwahig'-anus (Lewey Mitchell).

Swakwa-higanus'-isk (John Soctomer). Bell's Place, in Edmunds.

The name translates to "little chimes." Mitchell's attempt to explain it when on the spot was wholly unintelligible, but Soctomer made it clear. Bell was an early settler whose name still marks Bell's Mountain in Edmunds. He was a small man and was called "Little Bell." The Indians in passing from St. Croix to Machias waters by the carry used to say, "Let's stop at Little Bell's." They even translated his name, possessive case and all, into Indian. According to Nudenans *Sawank8ehigan* is a "bell." Since *-higan* is the ending for a tool or contrivance, the *h* belongs with the third syllable; *-us* is the diminutive; *-isk* a soft locative.

DENNYSVILLE.

Ket-h'nik, K'thenis. Cathance River in Dennysville (Lewey Mitchell).

Ket-h'nik is the form as Lewey Mitchell spoke it; he wrote it *"Kett h'sikham,* main brook or stream," probably made from *keght,* "principal," and *-nik,* "fork," "branch."

The name, said Lewey, properly belongs to the larger branch of the Denny's River, but the whites transferred it to the lesser branch, destroying its aptness as a name. Cathance (pronounced Cat-hance) is found again in Topsham (where Dr. Ballard says the Indian form of the word was pronounced *kat-hah-nis,* as here) and the application is the same; it means the larger branch of two, uniting into one stream—and not "crooked," as Dr. Ballard says.

PEMBROKE.

K'chi-punahmaquot, "where tomcods come to spawn" (Lewey Mitchell). A brook at the head of Sipp Bay.

The word is made from *pun-e-me-kwa-nuk,* "fish spawn" (Montague Chamberlain, *Maliseet Vocabulary*).

Posseps-caugamock. Cathance Lake (Peter E. Vose's list, 1886).

On Francis Joseph Neptune's map of 1798 the name is given as *Posses-caugum* (which Dr. Ganong misprints as "Lake Scaugum," Map No. 4, *loc. cit.*). The meaning of the name is unknown.

Pemmaquan. Lake and stream, outletting in Pembroke.

(Location of lakes and streams is only approximated by the town names given—for they may lie in several different towns.)

The name applies to either the lake, by transfer, or to a rockmaple ridge beside it where the Indians used to go to get maple sap and make sugar. If written *Penmaquan,* we have *pen-,* "descending," *maquan,* "maple sap," or "sweet," and it means a sloping ridge of maples. If *Pennamaquan* (*panna-,* "extensive," "opens out"), the idea is of the area covered by the trees. If *Pemmaquan,* then it is "extended" and we see a long ridge. The form does not matter—all are or have been used. We have little idea of the amount of maple sugar made and eaten by the Indians. Joseph Chadwick the surveyor, says in his Journal, in 1764, of Passadumkeag, "hear the Indians make Maple Sugar nere Equel to single Refined—in SundreWeigwoms they have 3 or 400 wat which thay say is only a Stock for one year in there famelys." (Massachusetts Archives, Vol. 243, pp. 85-103.)

Dr. Gatschet gives the form *Imnakwan-agum* for the lake, but we have never heard it without the *P*. Even on Francis Joseph's undecipherable map it seems to be *Penmeone,* or as Ganong reads it conjecturally, *Pomnean.*

Pewagon, West Branch of Pemmaquan River (Kilby).

Probably from *piwi,* "small."

EASTPORT.

Passamaquoddy. More correctly *Peskutam-akadi*, "pollock-plenty-place."

The great bay at certain seasons throngs with pollock feeding upon the smaller fish. The name comes from *peskutum*, "pollock"—"jumping," "breaking water," said Lewey Mitchell and others, evidently connecting the word with the root *piske*, "something split off." The fish leap entirely out of water, reversing at once so that the bay seems full of fishes standing on their heads, while innumerable screaming gulls, thick as snowflakes, dive upon both the larger and the smaller fishes. One who has seen such a sight knows that there can be but one explanation for the name Passamaquoddy.

Cobscook. The labyrinth of salt streams and bays back of Eastport Island, between Perry and Lubec.

Kapscook, "water-falls," is the usual interpretation. But these are not ordinary waterfalls; they are the boiling tide over unseen rocks on the bottom, creating whirlpools, changing with every foot of the tide. Moses Greenleaf gave perhaps the best meaning for the word when he remarked, in his *Letter* that *opscook* meant a "rock under water."

Epukunik'ek, "something you would have to go around." Harrison's Island, near Eastport.

Word and meaning were given Mr. Cabot in 1822 by Governor William Neptune. The first element is probably only a variation of the name for Campobello, combined with the inseparable *-naghe*, "island."

Ebagwid'ek, "floating between" (Gatschet). Campobello Island.

Dr. Gatschet makes the word from *eba*, "between," and *gwiden*, "floating," the stem we get in *akwiden*, a birch canoe. (*National Geographic Magazine*, VIII, 16-24, January, 1897.) The name occurs in several different spellings. *Ebaghuit*, "lying between" (Lewey Mitchell); *Ebaw'huit*, "island lying between or near the main land" (C. G. Leland, *Century Magazine*, September, 1884).

Closely similar are *Epagwit*, "it lies on the water," the name of Prince Edward Island, and another form of the same, *Eppaygeit*, "anchored on the wave" (Murdock, *History of Nova Scotia and Acadia,* 1887, I :534).

Wabig'-enek, "at the white bone" (Gatschet). Kendall's Head, Eastport. From *wabigen,* "white bone"; so called from a white ledge on top.

W'skidabs'kek. The Friar's Head, Campobello. A pillar rock on the western shore which stands alone apart from the cliff, usually called The Old Friar.

Lewey Mitchell said that *"W'skidabes* was a dishonored man, no warrior, because he was conquered by a woman long ago in the prehistoric age" (C. G. Leland, *Century Magazine,* September, 1884, 676, has *Skidapsis-penabsqu',* the stone manikin).

PERRY.

Se-bay-ik', the "passage." Indian Village at Point Pleasant, which was often called *Tchaibayik,* "at the narrows."

The name applied specifically to the back passage from the Indian village past Quoddy Village and Eastport to Cobscook Bay.

Sebes'kiak. The narrow neck of land connecting the Indian village with the main, a place where at very high tide the water goes "almost through," and the Indians can cross from water to water with little trouble.

The name was given me by Lewey Mitchell as we crossed the narrowest part of the neck; he waved his hand and said "Sebeskiak." It is obviously related to *Sebascodegan, Sebestiguk,* and other words with the root *sebe* or *tchaibai.*

Wajos'es, "little mountain." Pigeon Hill, near Point Pleasant.

In winter the Maliseets used to withdraw from their exposed summer home on the Point to this warmer place not far away where firewood was more plentiful. From *wadjo,* "mountain"; *sis,* "little."

Ut-losk'-es, the Little River, a small stream, the outlet of Boyden's Lake, its lower part a tidal creek. Meaning unknown.

Pil'-squess, "the virgin." A pillar rock, now gone, which used to stand on Carlow's Island, next Pleasant Point.

Name given in 1937 by Benedict Francis, Maliseet, grandson

of Governor John Francis. *Pil-,* in composition is "new," "chaste," and *-squess* is a suffix denoting a female, animal or human.

Dr. Ganong says that there is, or was, a Pilsquess on Campobello and another on Grand Manan.

Wek-wa-bigek', "head of the tide" (Gatschet). The head of the tidal part of Little River, Utloskes.

Ne-say-ik', "muddy lake." Boyden's Lake, about four miles from Point Pleasant.

Ne'seyik, "the muddy lake" (Dr. J. D. Prince); *Nesseyik* and *Nesseik,* "at the roiled water" (Dr. Gatschet).

This lake was the scene of the legendary encounter between Old John Neptune, the magician, in the form of an eel, and a Micmac chief in the form of a dreaded water-monster called the Wiwiliamecq'. Neptune killed the Micmac and ever since the water in the lake has been roily.

ROBBINSTON.

Mekwamk'-es'k, "at the small red beach" (Gatschet). Red Beach. Red granite appears here on the shore, making it a landmark.

Wabasgach', "white boards" (Lewey Mitchell). Mill Cove, Robbinston.

This was an old Indian camping-ground, and a saw-mill here, with its piles of white boards, served as a good landmark. Peter E. Vose's list of 1886, reprinted in the Bangor *Daily Commercial,* February 14, 1918, gave this name as *Waboos'-sagosh.*

Qua-wejoos, "dirty mountain." Devil's Head, a corruption of D'Orville's Head. The name "dirty" was given it after it had been burned over. Gatschet gave the word as *Kwagustchus'k,* from *kwagweyn,* "dirty"; *tchus,* "mountain"—that is, *wadchus'is.*

Meddybemps. A lake in Alexander, tributary to Dennys River.

Said by both Gatschet and Lewey Mitchell to be from *medembess'm,* "horned pout." This may be; but Francis Joseph's map of 1798 calls the lake *Madambontis,* as nearly as it can be read, and this looks very much like Madamiscontis, "plenty of alewives." At least, the lake abounds in alewives, and very recently they were taking alewives there and shipping them to Lubec to be smoked.

Megurrewock Lakes. Two lakes back of Robbinston, outletting into the St. Croix River.

These were properly the *Magalwok Lakes*. At these lakes, said Lewey Mitchell, the wind draws through a valley and makes the snow drift in as if it had been shovelled in; whence the name *magulwok*. Nudenans has *"magarebin, amovere nivem, 'to remove snow',"* and Rasles gives for a shovel, *"Pele p'r ôter la nége, magañrask8añdi (magalaskwahdi)."* The Maliseet name for a caribou is *megaleep,* "the shoveller," because he uses his broad forefeet in pawing the snow off from his favorite reindeer moss. *Magalewak* would be a better form than the one used on maps at present.

CALAIS (pronounced "Cal'-lis").

Skudek, "at the burned place" (Lewey Mitchell).

An opening in the forest in old times was usually the result of a fire; hence clearings, camp-grounds, and farms were named *skudek* or *pemskudek,* "burnt land," "extensive burns."

Calais and St. Stephen were favorite campgrounds, and Soctomer says that *Pemskudek,* "the extensive burned place" was used of Calais, while *Skudek* was the name of Machias. However, in general use, both were names for Calais, and the St. Croix River was called *Skudenteguk,* "the burned river" (O'Brien).

ST. STEPHEN, NEW BRUNSWICK.

K'tchi Medabiaught, "great landing" (Gatschet).

This was the first landing made by the Indians when returning from seal and porpoise hunting. It had good fresh water and a large beach (Gatschet, *Eastport Sentinel,* September 15, 1897). (See *Bedabedek* and *Catawamtek.*)

ISLANDS IN ST. CROIX RIVER AND BAY.

Eduki-m'ninek, "deer-his-island" (Gatschet). Deer Island, New Brunswick.

The name is a translation of the English. This large island would hold the eastern end of power dams in case the International Power Project were adopted.

Mutchignigos. Indian Island, formerly called Lutterell's Island, a small island off the lower end of Deer Island.

"Named from the rough, strong tides all about it," said Lewey Mitchell—*mutchig'n,* "bad," *nigos,* for *naghe,* "island." We do not accept Dr. Gatschet's interpretation from *Misiknigus,* "at the tree island" (*Geographic Magazine, loc. cit.*). In 1793, Boyd, a resident, gave the name as *Jeganagoose,* which certainly is not "tree-island," though *jegan-* might easily be *mutchnigan,* "bad." Gatschet's *misik* is properly an inseparable suffix denoting a certain species of tree, and should not be used as a prefix denoting trees generically. It is also probable that, having lived all his life a few miles from the place, Mitchell knew what he was talking about.

Mus-elenk, "Moose Island." Eastport (Gatschet).

A mixture of Indian and English; *elend'k* is only the English word "island."

Muttoneguis, Dochet Island, and **Muttonegwenish,** Little Dochet Island.

On Dochet Island, De Monts and his companions wintered in 1604-5. In 1797, the Indians told the Boundary Commissioners that these islands were used for the storage of articles deposited upon them and had "a name describing that as its use" (Kilby, *History of Eastport,* 1888, 113-115). The form given by Dr. Ganong is *Mut-an-ag-wes.*

PRINCETON.

Memada'kamioguk, "a point of land."

Said by Dr. J. Dyneley Prince to be the Penobscot name for Princeton.

Mdakmiguk, "on the rising soil" (Gatschet). Princeton.

Mda, "high," *kmigu* (*katakamigu*), "high land." The same word as Dr. Prince's.

Wapskeni'gan, "white rock carry," that is, "granite carry."

On the topographical map as Wapsaconhagan Brook, entering the St. Croix in Woodland.

Soctomer gave a historical story about it. He said it meant "carrying rocks out of a brook"; that during the Revolution, the English would not let the Indians go down the St. Croix River; so in the night they took all the rocks out of the stream and cleared a passage into Pocomoonshine Lake and thus took their families down the East Machias River. (To be believed by those who cannot see that *wapsk* means "white rock" and *enigan* stands for *ounigan,* a "portage.")

THE ST. CROIX LAKE SYSTEM.

On the Boundary, above Calais, the St. Croix River divides. Both branches have very large lakes with names so similar that without care in identification it is easy to confuse Big Lake and Grand Lake of the St. Croix Lakes, or Grand Lake of Schoodic and Grand Lake of St. Croix. In addition, some of them are known by several different Indian names with a number of forms each. We do not undertake any analysis or close work here, as Doctor Ganong had full information.

Elli-tegway-gamek, "between two lakes" (Soctomer). The thoroughfare between Lewey's Lake and Big Lake on the St. Croix system. The word may be connected with Rasles' *ermitegwe,* "river or lake which enters into another" (*rivière,* 523).

Matta-miquot, Peter Dana's Point on the above thoroughfare.
Given by Lewey Mitchel in a letter, but not explained.

Chi-men'as-sag'anum (Soctomer). Big Lake on the Schoodic system. *Genesaganargum,* on Kidder's Map, 1867.

K'chi-p'sag'anum (Tomer Sebattis). The same.
The two words have quite different interpretations. Soctomer said that the word came from the piles of stakes used in making eel-weirs, which were taken up each year to be used over again the next fall. We should guess that the word meant something like a big pile of sticks, *k'chimenas* (heaped up, collected)— *saganum* (related to *sagoshk,* "boards"); but it was not analyzed. The ending is *-aganum,* "lake."

When Tomer Sebattis gave his word he was facing the place itself, the thoroughfare between Big Lake and Lewey's Lake; and he said that the word came from *p'saganic,* "shoeing canoes to drag them over gravels at low water in the thoroughfare." The custom is described fully in Hubbard's *Woods and Lakes of Maine,* and the word contains the root *p's,* "split," and apparently the *sagosk,* for boards, meaning the rifted slats used in shoeing the birch canoes.

Menas-saganag'anis, the diminutive of Soctomer's word.

P'saganag-um, the diminutive of Sebattis's word.

This pair of words, corresponding to the foregoing, was given by the same men for Lewey's Lake, smaller than Big Lake.

Willeguaganum. The usual word for Grand Lake of the St. Croix system.

Chilnucook. Grand Lake on the St. Croix.
    1802. *Chihnucook* Lake—Maps and Plans #1618, Massachusetts Archives (Cabot).
    1816. *Chilnucook*—Joseph Whipple, *Acadia,* p. 26.

Ausomaugoit. A lake name found on an old map (Massachusetts Archives Roller #1618), almost illegible, placed above Grand Lake and below Pocumpus. *Ansaquoit* on Kidder's Map.

Pukamkes'k', "at the thoroughfare" (Gatschet in *Eastport Sentinel,* September 5, 1897). Pocumpcus Lake lies next above Grand Lake. This name was not originally that of the lake but of its inlet, a short, sandy thoroughfare between the lake and Lower Dobsy, or Sekledobscus Lake. *Puk-,* "narrow," and *amkes,* "little gravelly place"; with locative *k.* *Pakompcus* on Kidder's Map, 1867.

Beetsbaygesk', "long pond" (Soctomer). Given as a tributary to Grank Lake.

Amilk'esk, the ordinary name for a place where provisions are cured or stored. Given by Tomer Sebattis as a place at the head of Big Lake, and of another at Princeton. John Soctomer also gave *Amilkesk-wagamook* as "middle ground between the eastern and western arms of Crawford Lake."

Malec-uni'gan-ess, "lazy carry." The short carry at the thoroughfare between Pocumpcus Lake and Sekledobscus Lake. So named because, being very short, canoes often were not fully unloaded, but carried across right side up, partly filled.

Dr. Ganong says that in 1797 a surveyor put the name upon a short portage at the Point of Rock on Magaguadavic River, and Lewey Francis translated it as "lazy portage," making it from *malec,* "lazy," *ounigan,* "portage," and the diminutive ending. Our Merriconeag Island has the same word, Maleconegan, "lazy carry," *l* and *r* being interchangeable.

Sekled-obsc'-us, "shark-shaped rock" (Lewey Mitchell). Lower Dobsy Lake, usually known as Sisladobsis, which is a corruption of the name.

The whole lake is rocky, but in the outlet at the thoroughfare is a great rock, with the channel on one side and shoal water on the other, which stands up like a shark's fin. The name comes from the Maliseet *seklun* or *siglat,* a dogfish (a sort of small shark), and *-apskek,* the locative of a rock. The word is old.

 1776. *Sycledobscus*—Col. Jonathan Lowder, during the Revolution (*Bangor Historical Magazine,* VI, 1890, 296).
 1802. *Sekledobscus*—Osgood Carleton's map. Also used by Frederic Kidder in the map to his *Military Operations,* 1867.
 1930. *Sikladapskesk*—Lewey Mitchell, "shark-shaped rock." This form shows the roots best, but the preceding has a long tenure on good maps.
 1930. *Sigayo-opscus*—Tomer Sebattis, who defined it as "split rock."
 1931. *Sigladobskesk*—John Soctomer, "rocky lake." He also used the ending *-scus.*

The word Sisladobsis is a corruption of the correct name and often is given with added diminutives, even to the humorous perversion *Sis-sis-ladobsis-sis,* supposed to show the extreme of diminution. The word is impossible, even if there had been a pond to put it on, yet in Doctor Ballard's correspondence in Vetromile Papers, we have the form *Sisladobsissis* in his own handwriting. This should be discredited; the real name ends with *-scus,* not *-sis.*

Deekeewens'kek, "end of the river" (Soctomer). Upper Dobsy Lake.

The word was not explained. *Deekee* may stand for *tegwe,* "river," while the rest of the word is the locative for "the head of"; more likely it is "river-his-head," the second *ee* being a possessive sign.

Messagosq'uel, "marshy river" (Soctomer). Musquash Stream.

Messa-gosq'uel-ag'amook. Musquash Lake (Soctomer).
Messa, "much," *gosquel* (*eskal,* plural), "grass"; *agamook,* "lake."

THE SCHOODIC LAKES.

The Schoodic Lakes were left wholly to Doctor Ganong, and having no acquaintance with that country, I am unable to comment; yet Doctor Ganong's untimely decease makes a few words necessary at the risk of blundering.

These great lakes lie upon the Boundary and are commonly called Grand Lake (the upper) and Spednic (the lower). The Indian name *Cheputneticook* would translate as "big hill stream," transferred to the lake. In a letter Doctor Ganong wrote, December 10, 1916: "Big Fork River, traced out historically, nobody knew before." O'Brien gave *Skudentequek* "Burnt Land River" as Lake Chepednek, and Springer has a comment, with the form *Chepetnacook* (*Forest Life and Forest Trees,* p. 179).

Grand Lake on the Schoodic system was given as *Ktchikwispam,* "the biggest lake," by Governor William Neptune (Cabot). It is only a translation of the English name.

The old Indian name meant "Gull Lake" and came from the name of the herring gull, *kaak* in Penobscot, *kiakw* in Maliseet. It has a long history and varied forms.

    1715. *Kaouaksaki*—Aubéry, Map.
    c.1723. *Kaouakkiousikki*—French Map #253.
    1755. *Kousaki*—Mitchell's Map.
    1798. *Kioxakiek*—Chief Francis Joseph's Map.
    1802. *Kawakusike Lake*—Massachusetts Archives (Maps and Plans 57:8—Cabot).
    1922. *Ki-yaku-sakik*—Governor William Neptune (Cabot).
    1930. *Ki-yakus-wakeag*—Lewey Mitchell, Letter.

North Lake on the Schoodic was on early maps as *Omquememkeag* (Map 1793, Massachusetts Archives, Vol. 20, p. 32) and *Omquemenikeeg,* in report of Alexander Campbell, 1794, on a survey of 1792 (*Bangor Historical Magazine,* VI, 263). The name is said to mean "lake of unripe cranberries."

To these should be added *Baskahegan,* a large lake tributary to Penobscot waters by the Mattawamkeag, but an important part of the old travel route from the Penobscot River to the St. John. Capable Indians are entirely disagreed as to the meaning, but the best interpretation seems to be that it comes from *peske*, a "branch." This would seem to have been a guide word, indicating that in going up the Mattawamkeag, one turned off at a branch which entered at an acute angle.

APPENDIX

JOSEPH NICOLAR'S PENOBSCOT PLACE-NAMES

Though quoted regarding every place mentioned in it, this document, contributed to an obscure Old Town newspaper, well deserves reproduction entire, partly because of its extreme rarity, partly because of its authority, but also in a measure because the writer was well worth being held in remembrance.

Joseph Nicolar (as he spelled his name) was the son of Tomer (Thomas) Nicolar, of Norridgewock stock, and Mary Malt (Martha) Neptune, daughter of Lt. Gov. John Neptune, a hereditary chief. He was born February 15, 1827. By his own statement, he attended schools in Rockland, Warren, Brewer, and Old Town, thus having perhaps the best education of all the Indians of his time. He had a natural gift for oratory and writing, and during the eighteen-seventies often contributed news items and brief articles to the newspapers under the pen-name of "Young Sebattis." A few years later he wrote, for an Old Town newspaper of so brief a life and so small a circulation that no copy of it ever has been found, some articles upon his tribal arts, crafts, and history. Of these the present writer has been able to find but two, which had been copied by larger newspapers. Unquestionably all were valuable; for no other man in the Penobscot tribe was so well qualified to write out what at one time all of them knew—but no one recorded. Mr. Nicolar's last writing, *The Life and Traditions of the Red Man,* was a book copyrighted in 1893. Unfortunately most of the small edition was burned.

It seems fitting to add some reminiscences of Mr. Nicolar written by his daughter, Mrs. Florence Nicola Shay. "He did not have very much of an education, but what he did acquire served him well. His grandfather was one of those who escaped the massacre at Norridgewock, and was taken in by a friendly white family by the name of Lovell. [A grandson of "Half-arm" is probably meant.] He lived with them until he was about eighteen years old, then went to his own people at Old Town, Indian Island. My father was born in the year 1827 and lived to be 67 years old. His father died when he was nine years old and his mother was left with six children to support. In the fall of 1839, two years after the death of her husband, she took her family in a canoe down the river to Rockland, from Brewer where they had lived, to seek fields where she could best support her large family. Fortunately she came in contact with a Mrs. Thomas who took a great interest in her and who was very good to her, loading her with all kinds of food. She then made her husband order his man to move them back into the country to a forest where they would be able to get all the ash they needed to work with. There they met a Mr. Samuel Packard who was also very good to them, letting them have their food at half price and coming to visit them every Friday evening to give them a little concert on a violin that he had. It was through Mr. Packard's influence that my father was allowed to attend his first school and that was his greatest ambition. From there he went to grammar school but was not able to finish as his mother died and he was left to help support his brothers and sisters. A few years before his death he wrote a book on the Life and Traditions of the Red Man, which is very interesting. He was chosen by the tribe eighteen times to serve as representative to the Legislature. The advice of both my father and mother was always sought when there was anything of importance to discuss in the tribe."

The article on place-names here reproduced was originally printed in the *Old Town Herald,* of unknown date. It was signed "Y. S." and is evidently one, but neither the first nor the last, of a series of contributions to this local paper. The copy here reproduced was in a scrap book found in rubbish abandoned in an old house. A dating based upon the contents of the scrapbook indicated that it was made a little before 1890, and the arbitrary date of 1887 has been assigned to the paper because about the middle eighteen-eighties all the larger towns in Penobscot County hatched ephemeral weekly newspapers with "patent insides" and an outer coating of local news. The *Old Town Herald* is unknown to old newspaper men, but the article was probably copied into the short-lived *Bucksport Clipper,* in a broken file of which were found two other articles signed "Y. S." Identification of the signature was made by searching the files of old Bangor dailies and finding that their reporter from Indian Island was "Young Sebattis," after which the substance of his contributions made it easy to name him.

The following is a full transcript of Mr. Nicolar's article. Long paragraphs have been divided for easier reference, and a few typographical errors in the English, such as "bedge" for "ledge," have been corrected. Indian words, even when misprinted, have been left unchanged. The letter *r*, which occurs often, is not a rolled *r* but a determinant of the vowel preceding it.

THE SCRIBE OF THE PENOBSCOTS SENDS US HIS
WEEKLY MESSAGE

*Some of the Names that the Indian Has Bestowed—Quaint and Old—
Our Indian Correspondent Continues the Legends of his Race.*
[Old Town Herald]

Formerly members of our tribe on their annual trip to salt water for the purpose of fishing, etc., gave names to a number of places along the bay and river, which may prove of some interest to many persons living in those places.

Commencing at "Coo-cook-har-want-buk," "Owl's Head," we will ascend the west side of the river to our village. The name "Owl's Head" or the Indian name meaning the same, was applied to that promontory, now so well known to all entering Rockland harbor from the south and was so called from its resemblance to the neck and head of an owl when viewed from the north side. About two and a half miles north of this place is "Ca-tar-gwan-tic," "Grand Landing," now known as the city of Rockland. This was always used as a landing place for those who were going south. Canoes were generally taken out and carried across, that the "boisterous White Head" might be avoided, for the way around White Head was considered dangerous, also by carrying across into George's River two miles, a trip of fifteen miles was saved.

"Matar-kar-mi-co-suk," "High Land," was the name given to Camden on account of its mountains. Lincolnville was called "Mar-kurn-ta-quick," "Water ready for waves." The old Indians assert that the little bay is full of waves from whatever quarter the wind blows.

"Pa-qua-tan-ee," "out of the way," was applied to the spot where Belfast City is now located. This place was considered out of the regular course of travel. Sears Island, on account of a little sandy beach which can be seen from far away in the southern direction, was called "Warsumkeag," "Bright sand."

Now we come to the celebrated "Ar-quar-har-see-dek," "Stepping Ashore," now known as old Fort Point, where hundreds of pleasure seekers during the summer months enjoy the cool sea breeze, but in the olden times when members of the tribe visited here, they only stopped long enough to make the sign of their visit, showing which direction they were going, the number of their party and canoes, etc. On account of its being a marking place no one was ever allowed to mar or deface its outline by using it for a camping ground.

The reason for selecting this for a marking place, was because of it being the last prominent point, from entering the river from the bay, or going out into the bay from the river, and coming or going from the eastern or western shore all stopped here and made their marks. All the families of our tribe were known by a mark. Some were represented by animals, fish and reptiles, and others by well-known implements, the moon, sun, etc. Each mark showed the number in the family and the direction taken.

"Asick," "Clam-bed," is situated a little west of Fort Point now known as Stockton and was always noted for being the first place where good clams could be found on going down river.

Verona Island was known by the name of "Ar-lur-meh-sic," spawning island." The small river that flows into the Granite Quarries between Prospect and Frankfort, "Que-que-mis-we-to-cook," "Duck River."

Our next stopping place was "War-li-ne-tuk," "Cove Brook," on the east side of the river north of Winterport. Then we crossed to the west side, landing at "Et-ta-li-tek-quan-ki-lur-nuk," meaning "a place where everybody runs up." Here we have a sort of high bluff, slightly sloping, produced by land slides. A cove is located on the one side, and at the base of the bluff there was a fine pebbly beach. This was always a noted sporting place and here they left the cramped position made necessary by the canoe of those times, and exercised by running up the steep sandy side of this bluff. It was always considered a great feat to run up to the top of this sandy-sided bluff without stopping, as the sand gave way under the feet, and the steepness of the incline taxed the wind-powers of the runner to the fullest extent. This was also a popular sporting place for all who wished to test their strength as well as a general race ground. And often large parties chose sides at "Kur-des-keag," put up a large amount of wampum and other valuables to be contended for as a wager, and started very early in the day that a large amount of time might be given to sports and that the superiority of the different factions might be decided. Thus a great amount of wampum and valuables here changed hands.

The name "Toul-bunt-bus-suk," "Turtle Head," was applied to what is now known as "High Head." Hampden River was called on account of a "slanting ledge" "Su-war-tep-skark." Then we stopped at "Kur-des-keag," "Eel River" upon which at its junction with the Penobscot river is now located the City of Bangor. The river now retains the old Indian name somewhat Anglicized into Kenduskeag.

Up the river a short distance, at what is now known as the Red Bridge, was the "Devil's Track," "Majah-hundo-pa-mumptunque." Also here the Hathorn Brook was called "Pem-jedge-wock," "Current raggedly dropping down."

But returning to the Penobscot, at the water works, where so many beautiful salmon are taken every year by the sportsmen, the "So-ba-quarps-cook," "Sea-rock" was applied, and farther up, near Veazie we have "Wee-quer-gar-wa-suk," "Head of the tide." "Steep Hill," "Ar-quer-kek" was applied to Veazie, and what is now known as Basin Mill, was called "A-ne-quer-sar-sa-suk," "Ant heap."

"Mur-lur-mes-so-kur-gar-nuk," "Alewive catching on the way," is now known as Stillwater Falls, and just above we have "Mar-tarmes-con-tus-sook," "At the young shad catching," and the next rips were called "War-sar-sump-qua-ha-moke," "Slippery ledge rips," and further on, at the bend of the river just before reaching Greatworks is "Bet-cum-ka-sick," "Round bend shoal." Then comes "Wag-ge-we-sus-sick," "Bad gall," now known as Greatworks. An old Indian once killed a sturgeon here, and finding a very large gall in the fish thought he must be bad.

Just before reaching Oldtown is "Tar-la-lar-goo-des-suk," "a place of painting," now known as "Shad Rips." Here the women were allowed to stop and paint themselves before entering the village.

Now we arrive at "On-ne-gar-nuck," "At the carry," on the Oldtown side; here it was always necessary to take canoes out and carry by what is known as Oldtown fall before paddling across to their village.

As there were but few stopping places on the east side of the river we will briefly mention them. Returning to the bay we have "See-bur-es-suk," "At the sea thoroughfare," now known as Vinalhaven; the "Cas-cu-nar-cook," "Crane Island," now known as Mark Island, opposite Camden, and "Pit-tow-be-gook," "Inland sea island," now called Long Island. Last, but not least was "Margi-bee-guar-do-suk," which the white man calls Castine. If we have not tired the readers of the HERALD this week with Indian names, we will give a few more in the course of two or three weeks. Next week we hope to interest them in a few more of our amusements.

Y. S.

BIBLIOGRAPHY

The list which follows resembles a proper bibliography only in being a summary of authentic material which the writer has used and personally commends or disparages. It has the wholly practical aim of saving the time of beginners, specialists, and librarians by calling attention to what they can get, if they think they want it; what they cannot use, even if they think they want it; and occasionally, some library known to contain a needed title. The number of pages in a volume and the number of copies printed are given not as bibliographical details but to show the relative importance of a title or the chances against being able to secure it, and also the advisibility of saving it should a copy turn up among those printed discards in which the rarest items are often the least prepossessing. (Housekeepers and those clearing out old attics are hereby warned never to throw away any Indian pamphlet, even if in poor condition, merely because they cannot read it!)

This is a working list, for workers; and books, instead of being arranged alphabetically, are roughly classified for convenience; however, it is not for beginners only. It does not include recent publications by the Government, the periodicals of learned societies, the latest privately printed books and pamphlets. Librarians know about these items, the larger libraries generally contain them, and the small libraries can secure them by inter-library loans for the low cost of book postage. In Maine, the State Library at Augusta specializes in this service. The State Library, the University Library in Orono, the Bowdoin College Library in Brunswick, the especially richly provided Public Library in Bangor, and the fine collections of the Maine Historical Society in Portland offer convenient centers for work and excellent facilities for students.

A. General Works Easily Accessible

Bureau of Ethnology—*Forty-eighth Annual Report: Index to the previous reports, 1879-1931.* Washington, 1933. Pp. 1220.
    A very complete index to all previous reports, covering all topics relating to Indian life.

Douglas-Lithgow, R[obert] A.—*Dictionary of American-Indian Place and Proper Names in New England.* Salem, Mass., 1909. Pp. 400.
    An elementary book, assembling many forms of New England place-names without critical comment as to their value or meaning.

Hodge, Frederick Webb—*Handbook of American Indians North of Mexico.* Bulletin 30, Bureau of Ethnology, Washington. 2 vols. Part 1, 1907, pp. 972; Part 2, 1910, pp. 1221.

    Popular and practical, always worth consulting, but meagre in details of New England Indian life.

Pilling, James Constantine—*Bibliography of the Algonquian Languages.* Bulletin 13, Bureau of Ethnology, Washington. 1891. Pp. 614.

    Minute details of all books, up to date of printing, which contained even a few words of the Algonkin dialects, with biographies of writers of importance; much information about manuscripts. In all libraries which have Government reports.

B. Books Fairly Accessible in Libraries

a. New England and Canadian Place-Names

Alger, Abby Langdon—"A Collection of Words and Phrases taken from the Passamaquoddy Tongue." A paper read before the American Philosophical Society, February 6, 1885. About 550 words and phrases.

    A few author's reprints known from *Proceedings,* Vol. 22, 240-255. Rare but good.

Ballard, Edward—*Geographical Names on the Coast of Maine.* Report of the Superintendent of the Coast Survey, 1868. Appendix No. 14, pp. 243-259. Washington, 1871. Also published separately.

    One of the few easily available printed sources; but full of errors, because Dr. Ballard, though painstaking, relied upon incompetent informants. To be quoted with great caution.

Chamberlain, Montague—*Maliseet Vocabulary.* Cambridge, Mass., 1899. Pp. 94.

    The only useful book we have thus far on the Passamaquoddy dialect. Few place-names.

Ganong, William Francis—1. *Monographs of the Place-nomenclature, Cartography, Historic Sites, Boundaries and Settlement Origins of the Province of New Brunswick.* (*Contributions to the History of New Brunswick,* Nos. 1-7). Transactions of the Royal Society of Canada, Ottawa, 1895-1906.

    The second Monograph (1896, New Series, II: sec. ii, 175-289) contains many place-names duplicated in Maine; but it is an early work and some decisions must be revised. (A copy in Bangor Public Library.)

——————, 2. *An Organization of the Scientific Investigation of the Indian Place-names of the Maritime Provinces of Canada.* Transactions of the Royal Society of Canada. Third Series, sec. ii, seven papers. Ottawa, 1912-1928.

    Predominantly Canadian, these papers also contain detailed discussions of many Maine names, especially those of Maliseet and Micmac origin. (Copies in State Library, Augusta, Bowdoin College, and Bangor Library.)

Gatschet, Albert Samuel—"Indian Place-names in Maine."

National Geographic Magazine, January, 1897. Takes up Maliseet names near Eastport. Continued in

Eastport Sentinel, Sept. 15, 1897. (Copies of both in State Library, Augusta).

When completed, Dr. Ganong's great study of place-names will cover all this ground and much more in Maine.

Greenleaf, Moses—*Indian Place-names... on the Penobscot and St. John Rivers in Maine.* (Hereafter, referred to as "Letter.")

The full title is nearly as long as the pamphlet, informing us that it is "Taken from a Letter from Moses Greenleaf, Esq., to Rev. Dr. [Jedidiah] Morse, D.D. First General Report of the American Society for Promoting Civilization and General Improvement of the Indian Tribes of the United States. New Haven, 1824." The rare original of the "Letter" we have not seen. It was reprinted by the De Burian Club in *Moses Greenleaf, Maine's First Mapmaker* (Bangor, 1904, 200 copies privately printed. Fifty copies of the Letter, twelve pages each, were struck off for Edgar Crosby Smith). On account of its early date and local character, it is one of our most valuable sources.

Hubbard, Lucius Lee—*The Woods and Lakes of Maine... to which are added some Indian Place-names and their meanings now first published.* Boston, 1884.

Pp. 191-226 are on Indian place-names in the Maine woods. Fifty copies were issued separately. One of the best sources of information.

Pacifique, Rev. Father—1. *Etudes Historiques et Geographiques.* Extrait du Bulletin de la Societé de Geographie de Quebec (Cover title).

Three papers printed as pamphlets in 1928, 1932, and 1934, in all pp. 145.

——————— 2. *Le Pays des Micmacs...* Sainte Anne de Ristigouche, Quebec, 1935.

The preceding number, with the addition of a title-page and an introduction by Dr. Ganong, assembled as one volume; no changes. (Copy in the University of Maine Library.)

The most complete list of place-names ever assembled and the base of Dr. Ganong's unfinished work—2,500 geographical names in the Maritime Provinces, with full historical and geographical notes and five regional maps.

In French, upon Micmac names, always difficult and spelled with peculiarities which greatly increase their unpronounceability, these valuable papers are the court of appeal of the specialist. There is in manuscript an alphabetical arrangement, in both Micmac and English translation, prepared by Mr. W. B. Cabot, from whose original the present writer has typed two copies, direct and carbon, one in her possession, the other in Dr. Ganong's.

Rand, Silas Tertius—*A First Reading Book in the Micmac Language.* Halifax, Nova Scotia, 1875. Pp. 126.

Pp. 81-104 are Micmac place-names, with meanings. Rand is one of the best Micmac authorities.

Trumbull, James Hammond—"The Composition of Indian Geographical Names." *Collections* of the Connecticut Historical Society, Vol. II (1870), pp. 3-51.

The basic essay on place-name study.

Wright, Harry Andrew—*Indian Deeds of Hampshire County, Massachusetts.* Springfield, 1905. Privately printed, 100 copies.

The many names in the Connecticut Valley are much nearer the Maine Indian names than are those of Eastern Massachusetts.

b. NAMES OUTSIDE OF NEW ENGLAND

Beauchamp, William M.—*Indian Names in New York, with a Selection from Other States and Some Onondaga Names of Plants, etc.* Fayetteville, N. Y., 1893. Pp. 128. Privately printed.

Though chiefly dealing with the Iroquois, the book includes many Mohican names, allied to Maine names; many were obtained from Indians by the author. The plant names are particularly good.

Boyd, Stephen G.—*Indian Local Names with their Interpretation.* York, Pennsylvania, 1883. Pp. 70. Privately printed.

The names are largely Lenni-Lenâpé (related to Maine names) or Iroquois (wholly unlike); not scholarly, but helpful.

Kelton, Dwight H.—*Indian Names of Places near the Great Lakes.* Detroit, Michigan, 1888. Pp. 55.

The names, chiefly Ojibway, are analyzed scientifically. The best of the brief books, useful in Maine.

Tooker, William Wallace—1. *Indian Place-names of Long Island and Islands Adjacent with their Probable Significations.* Edited by Alexander F. Chamberlain. New York, 1911. Pp. 314.

A sound and useful book for consultation.

———————— 2. *The Algonquian Series.* 10 vols. New York, 1901.

Very small volumes of about 75 pp. each, in an edition of 250 copies, reprinting newspaper and other discussions of a few Indian names of New York and Long Island. Sound in scholarship and stimulating.

C. DICTIONARIES

(This list includes printed lexicons in the Algonkin language which might be useful in the study of Maine dialects.)

Baraga, Frederic—1. *A Dictionary of the Otchipwe Language.*

———————— 2. *A Theoretical and Practical Grammar of the Otchipwe Language.*

Two good books, in several editions, between 1850 and 1878, in the Ojibway or Chippewa language; useful for work with cognates. (Copies in Maine Historical Society Library, Portland).

Brinton, D. G., and Anthony, A. S.—*A Lenni-Lenâpé Dictionary....* Philadelphia, 1888. Pp. 236.

A useful low-priced dictionary, new copies usually selling for about two dollars. Lenni-Lenâpé is close enough to Maine Indian for this to be helpful to a well-grounded student.

Cotton, Josiah—*Vocabulary of the Massachusetts (or Natick) Indian Language.* Massachusetts Historical Society *Collections*, 3rd Series, Vol. VIII, 1830. Also separately published, 1829. Pp. 121.

Edited by John Pickering, who also edited Rasles' *Dictionary.* This is still a useful book, especially in connection with Rasles and Trumbull.

Cuoq, Jean-Andre—*Lexique de la Language Algonquine.* Montreal, 1886. Pp. 446.

Indian-French, rather rare, but very useful to the serious student.

Edwards, Jonathan, Jr.—"Observations on the Mohegan Language." Massachusetts Historical Society *Collections,* 2nd Series, X, 81-160. Boston, 1823. Notes by John W. Pickering.

The most available reprint of this paper, originally printed in 1788. As the work of a highly educated man who had spoken the language from childhood, this, like Williams's, Mayhew's, and Cotton's papers, has a high value for students.

Lacombe, Albert—*Dictionnaire de la Langue des Cris.* Montreal, 1874. Pp. 713.

French-Indian and Indian-French. A rare book, but very helpful. Cree is fundamentally like Maine Abnaki.

Lemoine, George—*Dictionnaire Francais-Montagnais. With Montagnais-English Vocabulary and a Montagnais Grammar.* Boston, 1901. Pp. 63 and 281.

Printed by William Brooks Cabot and Philip Cabot, to whose oversight it owes much. A modern, useful book, though the language is superficially less like Abnaki than are several other Indian tongues.

Mayhew, Experience—1. *Observations on the Indian Language... Now published from the Original MS. by John S. Fogg,* etc. Boston, 1884. Pp. 12. 100 copies.

─────────── 2. "Letter of Experience Mayhew, 1722, on the Indian Language. Communicated by John S. Fogg, M.D., of South Boston." *New England Historical and Genealogical Register.* Vol. 39, pp. 10-17. Boston, 1885.

The same text in both, but the latter more easily accessible than the first title. Brief but informative, chiefly grammatical; of high value because the work of an educated man who had spoken Indian from his childhood.

Rasles, Sebastian—*A Dictionary of the Abnaki Language, in North America, By Father Sebastian Rasles. Published from the original manuscript of the author. With an Introductory Memoir and Notes by John Pickering, A.A.S. Memoirs* of the American Academy of Arts and Sciences. New Series. Vol. I. Cambridge, Mass., 1833. Pp. 204.

A phrase-book in French-Indian rather than a dictionary, and never completed by the author. Very important for the scholar but of little use to the casual inquirer.

Trumbull, James Hammond—*The Natick Dicionary.* 25th Annual Report of the Bureau of Ethnology, Washington, 1903. Pp. 347.

Based on Eliot's Indian Bible in the Natick language of Central Massachusetts, this scholarly dictionary is the most useful single book the beginner in the Indian languages can have, even though the dialect is not so close to Abnaki as are some of the western Algonkin tongues. It is sold, in good cloth binding, by the Superintendent of Documents in Washington for a dollar and is much the cheapest and best Indian language book procurable.

Williams, Roger—*A Key into the Language of North America; or, an Help to the Language of the Natives of that Part of America Called New England.* London, 1643; Rhode Island Historical Society *Collections,* Vol. I, 1827 (Third Edition), and other editions, particularly the Fifth Edition, reprinted from the original, with an Introduction by Howard M. Chapin, for the Rhode Island and Providence Plantations Tercentenary Committee, Inc., Providence, 1936. 500 copies.

This delightful book, still very useful and readable, is a practical introduction to Indian life as well as to the Narragansett dialect.

D. INDIAN GRAMMARS

(There are many Indian Grammars, some of them more difficult than helpful; but most of the Dictionaries have some brief introduction into the inflections and modifications of the languages. Baraga for the Ojibway, Lemoine for the Montagnais, have been mentioned; Henry Masta and Joseph Laurent will be named later. The following are the most useful treatises):

Howse, Joseph—*A Grammar of the Cree Language with ... an Analysis of the Chippeway Dialect.* London, 1844. Pp. 324.

Though an old work and now rare this book by a man who had a practical mastery of Indian ways of thinking is still an excellent authority.

Jones, William—"Some Principles of Algonquian Word-Formation." *American Anthropologist,* New Series, Vol. VI (1904), No. 3. Also a few author's separates, pp. 42.

A Columbia University doctoral thesis, submitted by an Indian scholar. Brief, informative, with the authority of a native Indian behind it, this paper heads the list of helpful imprints.

Michelson, Truman, and Jones, William—"Grammar of the Fox Dialect," in *Handbook of American Indian Languages.* Edited by Franz Boas. Part I. Bulletin 40, Bureau of Ethnology, Washington, 1911.

A posthumous work of Dr. Jones, revised by Dr. Michelson, this is the most thorough, as well as the most accessible work we have on Algonquian grammar and word formation. The Fox language is quite similar to Abnaki.

Michelson, Truman—"Preliminary Report on the Linguistic Classification of Algonquian Tribes." *28th Report,* Bureau of Ethnology, Washington, 1906-1907 (printed 1912).

By showing the lexical correspondences of the Algonquian dialects, this paper harmonizes the vocabularies of dictionaries cited above. Micmac, Maliseet, Passamaquoddy, and Penobscot form a group "very intimately related to Fox and Shawnee; next to Cree-Montagnais; not closely to Ojibwa; and remotely to Delaware and Natick" (p. 288).

O'Brien, Michael C.—"The Abnaki Noun." Maine Historical Society *Collections,* IX (1887), 259-294.

The first of two projected papers upon Abnaki grammar, based upon Rasles' Dictionary. The second never was printed.

Pacifique, Rev. Father—*Leçons grammaticales theoretiques et practiques de la langue Micmaque.* St. Anne de Ristigouche, Quebec, 1939. Pp. 243.

A practical grammar by a priest long settled among the Micmacs. (Copy in University of Maine Library.)

E. BOOKS WRITTEN BY INDIANS

Laurent, Joseph—*New Familiar Abenakis and English Dialogues....* Quebec, 1884. Pp 220.

A good, small compilation (in English) of lexical and grammatical material of the St. Francis dialect. The place-names, pp. 205-222, are, like most Indian philological work, sometimes good, but not dependable.

Masta, Henry Lorne—*Abenaki Indian Legends, Grammar and Place Names.* Victoriaville, Quebec, 1932. Pp. 110.

A useful book in the St. Francis dialect. Place-names pp. 81-102, show the usual Indian failings, some good, some wholly guess-work.

Nicolar, Joseph—*Life and Traditions of the Red Man.* Bangor, 1893. Pp. 147.

The best account we have of the Indian epic of Glusgehbeh (Glooscap of the Micmacs), though far from lucidly written. A grandson of Lt. Gov. John Neptune, Joseph Nicola (as the whites wrote his name) came from a line of shamans and inherited the old lore; he was also a man of intelligence, education, and probity. This book contains few place-names, but the newspaper contribution reprinted here in the Appendix is the best record we have of Indian place-names on the lower Penobscot.

Teneslas, Nicola—*The Indian of New England and the North-eastern Provinces*, etc. [Edited by Joseph Barratt], Middletown, Conn., 1851. Pp. 24. (Copy in Maine Historical Society.)

A rare pamphlet which contains about 300 words in both Maliseet and Micmac, listed by Pilling under Barrett. It contains also a reproduction of the earlier pamphlet "Key to the Indian Language of New England," pp. 8. (Middletown, 1850), in Barratt's name. (Copy in Newberry Library, Chicago, and University of Maine Library.)

Wzokhilain, Peter Paul (also called *Osunkhirine*)—*Abnaki Spelling Book.* Boston, 1830. Pp. 90.

The best word-book in the Penobscot dialect, but now very rare. (Copy in Newberry Library, Chicago.)

The author, at one time a student at Dartmouth College, taught an Indian school in Old Town. For an account of the man, see Pilling's *Bibliography*, pp. 539-540. Kidder, Crawford, and others have given partial lists from this little book. (An account of his son Silas in Hubbard, *Woods and Lakes of Maine*, pp. 32-33.)

F. MANUSCRIPTS

(Some of the best Indian material available has never been printed. It is mentioned here because it has formed a large part of the best source material used by the writer.)

Aubery, Joseph, S. J.—"Abnaki Dictionary." Original in the Archives of the Roman Catholic Church at Pierreville, Quebec. The "second edition," dated and signed by the author, August, 1715, was copied by The Very-Rev. M. C. O'Brien, and is in the Maine Historical Society Library. A photostat of this, 490 pp., was made for Mr. William Brooks Cabot. Thus there are three copies in existence, besides the short list of words compiled by the present writer from the photostat.

Father Aubéry was at one time a priest in Maine and knew perfectly the Abnaki dialect. His book, in French-Indian, is well alphabetized and is the most scholarly Jesuit compilation the present writer knows, much more usable than Father Rasles' manuscript. Pilling has an account of Aubéry and his work, *Bibliography*, pp. 18-19.

Cabot, William Brooks—1. "Vocabularies," taken down from Penobscot and Passamaquoddy Indians, *circa* 1920; alphabetized. Mr. Cabot generously permitted the writer to copy and use these papers.

——————— 2. "Massachusetts Vocabularies," compiled by Mr. Cabot from original manuscripts of his forbears John and Josiah Cotton and of Samuel Danforth. In Massachusetts Historical Society Library. (A copy typed by the writer.)

——————— 3. "List of New England Place-names," compiled from maps and documents. In the Massachusetts Historical Society Library. (A copy typed by the writer.)

Nudenans, Jean Baptiste—"Radicum Wabanakkaearum Sylva," etc. ("A Garden of Abnaki Roots, Collected and Arranged in Alphabetical Order from Various Codexes of Old and More Recent Manuscripts by J. B. Nudenans, in the year 1760.")

The original, in the Archives at Pierreville, Quebec, was copied by the Very-Rev. M. C. O'Brien and is among his papers in the Maine Historical Society. It is the Indian-Latin part of the original listed by Pilling in his *Bibliography* (p. 375). This Mr. Cabot had photostated in 217 pages, and from his copy the present writer made two typed copies. The direct copy, translated, is retained; the carbon, without translation, was given to Dr. W. F. Ganong. Thus there are four known copies of this work, which Pilling says was prepared by an Indian educated by the Jesuits. The original was occasionally annotated in French by someone signing himself as "M," who may have been Abbé Maurault; a few other glosses are by Father O'Brien.

O'Brien, Charles Michael, S. J.—"Manuscripts," chiefly independent field notes, taken while the writer was pastor of the Indian Church at Old Town; intended to be the base of a modern re-issue of Father Rasles' dictionary, with additions from other Church manuscripts. Bequeathed to the Maine Historical Society.

At his death Father O'Brien was bishop-elect of Maine and our finest Indian student, but too busy to follow out his Indian studies. The notebooks contain much valuable material, which is of little use to any but an expert. Most of it has been copied and verified by the writer but not alphabetized. The date of 1890 is arbitrary, as the notebooks must cover at least twenty-five years.

Rasles, Sebastian, S. J., edited by Frederick S. Dickson, Ph.S., Yale, 1871. "Abnaki Dictionary" (1724), alphabetized and translated into English in 1918.

A work of great labor, which exists in two forms, neither ever printed. Four copies are known. The corrected copy, revised by the author, location unknown; the uncorrected, original copy, owned by Mr. W. B. Cabot; and two copies, direct and carbon, typed by the present writer from Mr. Cabot's. These copies are unabridged except for the omission of the first-personal forms of the verbs (all beginning with *n*), about 200 pages of the original. The copies list between 6000 and 7000 words.

Vetromile, Eugene, S. J.—Manuscripts, in Maine Historical Society Library.

Not recommended to either beginner or expert unless for studying Vetromile's contributions to Dr. Ballard's work.

H. Printed Documents

(For place-name work some of the best material is found in printed documents, particularly in deeds, which date and locate each word and make possible securing sequences of changes in forms. As land changed owners, new forms and new dates appearing side by side, the gap between early Indian forms and later corrupted ones is often bridged. The following may be used profitably on certain names.)

York Deeds—Eighteen printed volumes of Maine deeds, covering land from the western boundary of Maine almost to the Penobscot, chiefly coastwise. In the beginning, York was the only county in that part of Massachusetts which became the State of Maine. These records began with the earliest, often with the Indian deeds, were on the whole very well kept, and are invaluable in close work upon particular words of early date.

Probate Records, even if printed, less often yield material than do the deeds.

The Massachusetts *Deeds of Suffolk County* and the *Historical Collections of New Hampshire* both printed, give some Maine material; but the greatest amount, as would be expected, is found in the Maine Historical Society *Collections,* particularly in the *Documentary Series* of twenty-four volumes. Unfortunately, the papers, most of which come from the Massachusetts Archives or from *Documents Relative to the Colonial History of New York,* are often badly copied, badly proofread, and too inexact for close work, and the location of the originals is not given.

In the Massachusetts Archives, the Suffolk Court House in Boston, and the State House in Augusta are great stores of unprinted material bearing upon these place-names.

I. Books Containing Some Maine Indian Place-Names

(Many books, particularly town histories, have Indian information, often very good, including lists of place-names and Indian words.)

Purchas, Samuel—*Purchas His Pilgrims.* A very old and standard work but usually reprinted with the omission of matter of special interest, a list of Indian words taken down from the Indians captured by Waymouth near Thomaston, carried to England, and later returned to Maine. This earliest known list of Maine Indian words, says Dr. Frank T. Siebert, who called the writer's attention to it, is good Abnaki, with a few exceptions. It is retained in the edition called *Hakluytus Posthumus; or Purchas His Pilgrims,* printed by James MacLehose and Sons, Glasgow, 1906, on pp. 358-359, Vol. XVIII. (A copy is in the State Library, Augusta.)

The earlier *Hakluyt,* 1613, also edited by Purchas, contains a list of place-names and chieftains which is the despair of historians.

Wood, William—*New England's Prospect.* London, 1634, and various later reprints.

A delightful book, by a young man who came over in 1629 at the age of twenty-three and wrote of what he saw in New England. It closes with a list of nearly three hundred words from the Merrimack River region "whereby such as have In-sight into the Tongues, may know to what Language it is most inclining and such as desire it for an unknowne Language onely may reape delight, if they can get no profit." There is still no book so good about New England Indians.

Kendall, Edward Augustus—*Travels through the Northern Parts of the United States in the Years 1807 and 1808.* 3 vols. New York, 1809.
>About sixty pages of the last volume are upon his travels in Maine. His remarks on Indian place-names are uncommonly good.

Coffin, Paul—"Missionary Journeys in Maine, 1796-1800." Maine Historical Society *Collections,* 1856, Vol. IV.
>Good place-names, taken down from Indians.

Willis, William—Lists (already noted), Maine Historical Society *Collections,* 1856. Vol. IV.

Thoreau, Henry David—*The Maine Woods.* Boston, 1864. Appendix.
>Lists—those from Indians good; from books, poor; some misprints.

Chase, Mrs. Fannie S.—*Wiscasset in Pownalborough,* 1941.
>The name "Wiscasset" fully treated.

Eaton, Cyrus—1. *Annals of the Town of Warren.* Hallowell, 1851. Second edition, revised, 1877.

———————— 2. *History of Thomaston, Rockland, and South Thomaston.* 2 vols. Boston, 1865.
>Both histories contain excellent Indian material, which has been borrowed by other town histories.

Hanson, John Wesley—*History of Gardiner, Pittston, and West Gardiner.* Gardiner, 1852. Lists of words from Indians.

North, James W.—*History of Augusta.* Augusta, 1870. Pp. 450 to 455 are on the old name *Cushnoc.*

Rowe, William Hutchinson—*History of Yarmouth and North Yarmouth.* Portland, 1937.
>Local names in Appendix, by the writer of this study.

Wheeler, George Augustus—*History of Castine, Penobscot, and Brooksville.* Bangor, 1877.
>Local names treated in detail.

Williamson, Joseph—1. *History of Belfast.* 2 vols. Portland, 1877.
>P. 52 ff. gives the old name of Belfast.

———————— 2. "Castine; and the Old Coins Found There." Maine Historical Society *Collections,* VI (1859), 104.

The following, though often consulted as authorities, are not recommended:

Chute, J. A.—(Quoted in Wm. Willis's paper, above). To be quoted only when you know as much or more without the necessity of quoting.

Maurault, J. A.—*Histoire des Abenakis.* Sorel, Quebec, 1886.
>The author did not know Maine and his definitions of place-names are usually guesses, often bad ones, but occasionally helpful.

Potter, Chandler Eastman—"Language of the Abenakis." Maine Historical Society *Collections,* IV, (1856), 185. He knew nothing about it.

Vetromile, Eugene—*The Abenakis and their History.* New York, 1868.
>"In all matters that lay beyond his own immediate observation his book is quite untrustworthy" (Ganong).

J. MAINE INDIANS—GENERAL INFORMATION, SPECIAL EDITIONS

If a library catalogues several editions of a work, which should be preferred? What books will round out one's general information about the Maine Indians?

If the book is a standard, and there is any choice, take the best edited reprint, or the latest. For general information, go to the *earliest* travels and to the *latest* anthropological books. A book is no better for being expensive; and no worse for being readable. Prefer the man who saw the thing, did the thing, told his own story, to the mere compiler; but always invoke a special blessing upon the one who has done a piece of work so thorough that we do not need to resort to checking original copies and documents in archives to verify it.

In Maine and Canada, much of the best early information about our Indians, Abnaki, Maliseet, and Micmac, is found in the *Jesuit Relations* of the French missionaries. The only important edition is that of Reuben Gold Thwaites, with the original text facing the translation on each page. Sets in the principal Maine libraries, and at the Island Museum, Islesford.)

Of the early French travelers, such as Champlain, Lescarbot, Nicholas Denys, and others, the best edition is that of their *Works,* published by the Royal Society of Canada (Toronto) and edited by Dr. H. R. Biggar and other scholars, giving both French original and translation, with able annotation. (Sets at Augusta, Bowdoin, and Bangor.)

For Purchas, which contains Rosier's account of Waymouth's voyage, attention has been called to the MacLehose editon (in the State Library). Dr. Burrage edited a good reprint.

Captain John Smith's *Collected Works* are in the MacLehose (1906) edition, without annotation, and reprinted by Arber, 1884, with introduction and notes.

Of contemporary early books in English, our best accounts of the Indians are in William Wood's *New England's Prospect,* 1634, to which attention has already been called, Thomas Morton's *New England Canaan,* 1637, ("a graceless author" but good reading), and John Josselyn's two books, *New England's Rarities Discovered,* 1672, and *Two Voyages to New England,* 1675. Morton and Josselyn both resided in Maine long enough to give their books local flavor. All these exist in enough reprints to be easily located in libraries.

The foregoing books tell of the Indian ways of life when Europeans first settled among them. For an understanding of what is known of the prehistoric Indians and of the arts and crafts of a later date, the best book is Dr. C. C. Willoughby's *Antiquities of the New England Indians* (Cambridge, Mass., 1935), a fully illustrated, carefully prepared account by the former head of the Peabody Museum of Archaeology of Harvard University. There is nothing else as good. It covers the whole field from the Stone Age to modern times.

Handicrafts of the Modern Indians of Maine (Bulletin III, Abbe Museum, Bar Harbor, 1932) by the present writer, is a brief description (72 pp., 26 plates) of the recent crafts, basket-making, canoe-making, bark work, quillwork, and the like.

Penobscot Man, by Prof. Frank G. Speck (Philadelphia, 1940) is the latest and by much the fullest account of the life, customs, amusements, and organization of the modern Penobscot tribe. It is very fully illustrated and contains authentic Indian music.

Much legendary lore of the Maine Indians has been preserved and most of it is easily accessible. Aside from contributions to periodicals like the *Journal of American Folk-lore,* we have in books, *Algonquin Legends of*

New England, by Charles Godfrey Leland (Boston, 1884), *In Indian Tents,* by Abby Langdon Alger (Boston, 1897), and *Kuloskap the Master,* by Charles Godfrey Leland and Dr. J. Dyneley Prince (New York, 1902), as well as the privately printed *Life and Traditions of the Red Man,* by Joseph Nicolar (Bangor, 1893), already listed.

From such of the foregoing titles as are available to him, the interested reader should be able to build a background for this more specialized study of the Penobscot place-names.

K. INDIAN INFORMANTS

The amount of information credited to Indians in the books listed is considerable, and much of it is excellent; but we observe that the best of it names the Indian giving the information. Thus we know that Pierpole, Sockabasin, Sebatis, John Neptune, and Captain Francis, to whom the Reverend Paul Coffin, William Willis, Cyrus Eaton, and W. D. Williamson went, were reliable men. Thoreau and Lucius L. Hubbard also took pains to name their informants, and their John Neptune, Joseph Polis, Nicolai, Steven Stanislaus, John Penwit, and others—all of them known to the writer's family—were competent. There is, however, much material not as yet printed which was secured from individuals not very intelligent or else too eager to be paid for their information, which in the future may get into print and do harm. Hereafter the name of the Indian authority should be a part of the record.

Among the Penobscots, the writer has consulted almost exclusively her old friends Mrs. Clara Neptune and Lewis Ketchum. Mrs. Neptune, who died in 1922, aged about 88 years, was born a Mitchell (of the Bear family), a niece of Joseph Polis (who was also a Bear); and after the death of her father she was adopted by her uncle, Dr. Sebattis Mitchell, known as "Sebattis Lobster." At the age of fourteen she married Joseph Orono, a descendant of Chief Joseph Orono, for whom the University town was named. She traveled as far as New York and Philadelphia, taking part in the primitive vaudeville shows of Indian life. "We ben marry mos' ebry man dere" was her remark about the scene of an Indian wedding; and again: "Boot', Boot' what kill it Lincoln, he fix it my hair"—that is, she was at some time on the stage with J. Wilkes Booth. After her first husband's death, she married as second wife, Mitchell Neptune, grandson of Lieutenant Governor John Neptune. Left a widow again, she worked with courage and gayety to maintain herself and an adolescent great-grandson by selling baskets, telling fortunes, and gathering folklore—a brave old woman.

Lewis Ketchum, a valued friend from the writer's earliest childhood, was the son of a high-ranking officer in the English army, stationed in Woodstock, New Brunswick, during the eighteen-thirties, and of a Penobscot Indian girl, daughter of Newell Peol Tomer, descended from "Half-arm Nicola," who lost his left fore-arm in the Norridgewock Fight, in 1724, and escaped to Penobscot. A man of fine intelligence, courage, endurance, and skill, Lewis Ketchum was one of the best hunters, woodsmen, and watermen we ever had; he could also sail a canoe and hunt seal and porpoises as well as the Passamaquoddy Indians. He died in 1922, aged eighty-eight.

Among the Maliseets, Lewey Mitchell of Point Pleasant, who had been C. G. Leland's chief informant fifty years before, and who was better acquainted with his tribal history and legendary lore than any one else in his tribe, not only wrote me much about his people but went with me to visit many places between Grand Lake Stream and Machias, explaining the place-names and their meaning. In Machias, John Soctomer, also a Passamaquoddy, proved a ready and intelligent helper, and with him I went to several places to note the application of the names. At Peter Dana's Point in Princeton, Tomer Sebattis explained some local names.

A small amount of information was obtained from Mrs. Sylvia Stanislaus, the oldest woman in the Penobscot tribe, and from her son Francis, both now deceased. Others occasionally contributed a little, but before this work was undertaken, the old friends of early years had been gathered to their fathers and what has been saved is only a fraction of what should have been preserved.

L. ABNAKI SCHOLARS

It would be ungracious in a study of this sort, dependent upon the labor of others, not to mention some whose work has commanded recognition, even though they have contributed nothing directly. Dr. William Ruggles Gerard, Professor Alexander F. Chamberlain, Dr. J. Dyneley Prince, and Prof. Frank G. Speck deserve mention by name as Algonkin scholars; as do Dr. Albert S. Gatschet, whose work about Eastport has been quoted, and Dr. Frank T. Siebert, a rising scholar of Abnaki, who has been personally helpful. It is wished that Dr. Nathaniel Tuckerman True, of Bethel, Maine, one of our early Indian students, who developed a method in advance of his time, could have been given suitable recognition; but his contributions, largely to newspapers, are too ephemeral for reference or are buried in the files of newspapers and periodicals.

Again we would mention with respect the work of the Very-Reverend Michael Charles O'Brien and would salute those tried and generous friends, Mr. William Brooks Cabot and Dr. William Francis Ganong, without whose comradeship and encouragement this study would not have been undertaken.

ERRATA AND ADDITIONS

Page 126, for *scow,* read *skow.*

Page 131, Arrowsic Island.

The missing deed has been found, not in *York Deeds,* but in *Suffolk* (Mass.) *Deeds.* It was given in April, 1649, by Robin Hood of Negwasseg, Indian, to John Richards of Weymouth, Mass., "One Island, whereon now the said John Richards Inhabits," and was recorded by Edward Rawson, September 21, 1654. On August 5, 1654, John Richards sold Clark and Lake of Boston the island "called Arrozick formerly, now called Richards Island" except 100 acres formerly sold to John Parker. (*Bangor Historical Magazine,* III (1887), 41).

Page 141, for *Point Agreeble,* read *Point Agreeable.*

Page 201, add *Madagamus Hill,* located at Moose Point, Searsport.

Add to Chapter II:

Piscataquis River. Tributary at Howland to Penobscot River.

From *piske,* "branch." The final *s* is not a diminutive, but the softened locative.

Bet-cum-ka-sick, "round bend shoals." Placed by Joseph Nicolar at the bend in Penobscot River just below Great Works in Old Town. If he had divided it as *Betc-unk-asick,* we should recognize the roots *petk* (*petek*), "bend"; *unk,* "sand," "gravel"; and *essek,* locative; and that the word meant "round bend with a gravelly bottom," like Patagumpus.

Chebeague Island, Casco Bay. Substantially the same as Sebascodegan. The Jordans, in 1680, deeded to Walter Gendall (*York Deeds,* XVI, ii, 240) half of an island "called Jabeque or Gaboag.... The sd Island being at High Water as two Islands yet altho comonly called Little and Great Gaboag or Jabegue yet is but one Island." This shows a passage through the parts of the island, and is one of the *sebes,* "almost through," words; or a *tchaibi,* "separated," word. Father Aubéry's *Sibambes* for it indicates *sebes.*

VITA

Mrs. Fannie Hardy Eckstorm was born June 18, 1865, in Brewer, Maine, the daughter of Manly and Emma F. (Wheeler) Hardy. As a girl she traveled and lived much with her father among the Maine Indians and woodsmen. She was graduated from Smith College in 1888, and married five years later the Reverend Jacob A. Eckstorm. Their two children were Katharine Hardy (deceased) and Paul Frederick. She has published, separately or in collaboration, several works dealing with Maine history, folklore, and balladry. Among these are *The Penobscot Man* (1904); *Minstrelsy of Maine,* with Mary W. Smyth (1927); *British Ballads from Maine,* with Phillips Barry and Mary W. Smyth (1929); and *Handicrafts of the Modern Indians of Maine* (1932). Mrs. Eckstorm died December 31, 1946.

INDEX

Bold-type entries are towns in which Indian names are found. Names in parentheses are those of towns or approximate localities in which the Indian name is found.

Abagaduset Stream and Point (Merrymeeting Bay), 141
Abahos Stream (Mattamiscontis), 52
Abamgamok, West Lake (Nicatowis Lake), 49
Abessah (Bar Harbor), 207
Abomazeen, Indian, 129
Abonegog, Back River (Boothbay), 122, 123
Abonegog, Ebenecook (Southport), 124
Acrupsak, Hobart Stream (Edmunds), 224
Addison, 217
Adowaukeag, Waukeag (Hancock-Sullivan), xx, 210
Agamenticus Mountain, 180
Agamenticus River (York), 179, 180
Agguahega (Damariscove Is.), 66, 108
Aguahadongonock, "portage" (Bath), 66, 134
Aguahassideck, "landing place," Fort Point (Stockton), 63, 65
Aguncia, Aggnncia, Agoncy, 15
Ahbasauk, "clam place" (Bar Harbor), 207
Ahlurmehsic, Alamoosook (Orland), 187
Akweekek, "steep hill" (Eddington), 21
Alamoosook Lake (Orland), 187, 188
Alesanuk, "clam-bake place" (Bar Harbor), 207
Alnambi-i-menahan, Indian Island (Old Town), 38
Alnambi-kwaysahwayk, Indian Point (Bucksport), 3
Allan, Col. John, 217
Ames, Frank S., of Machias, 217
Amgopilasig, Cambolassie Pond (Lincoln), 55
Amiciskeag, Fish Point (Kittery), 182
Amilkan, Amilkesk, 149
Amilkesk (Big Lake, St. Croix), 233
Amirkangan, Lisbon Falls, 149
Amitgonpontook, Lewiston Falls, 149
Ammacongan Falls (St. George River), 92

Ammadamast (Enfield Grange), 49
Ammecungan River (Presumpscot River), 160
Amobscot (Muscongus), 91
Andros, Sir Edmund, xv, 122
Androscoggin River, xv, 147
Anmessokantisis (Muscongus), 90
Ant Island, Basin Mills (Orono), 37
Anunket Pond (York County), 183
Apanawapeske (Castine), 199
Aponeg (Sheepscot River), 124, 125
Appeumuk River (Union River), 209
Appowick (Damariscotta River), 108, 125
Apskikek, "lonely lake" (Mopang Lake), 223
Aquadoctan (The Weirs, N. H.), 66
Aquehedongonock (Bath), 66, 134, 140
Argyle, 40, 46
Argyle Boom Islands, 40
Arnold's Trail (See Short Route), 11, 145
Arramopsquis, Arrimonscus (Muscongus), 91
Arrowsic, Arousick, Arusuk Island, 131
Arumpsunkhungan Falls and Island (Old Town), 131
Arundel (Kennebunkport), 174
Asnela, Orson Island (Old Town), 39
Assabumbedock Falls (Berwick), 183
Assa-i-menahan, Orson Island, 39
Atkinson, Theodore, of Portsmouth, 68
Atlantic Coast Pilot, 124
Attean, Orson, Indian, 69
Attebemenock, Choke-cherry Island (Penobscot River), 43
Aubéry, Father Joseph, 22, 77, 107, 145, 151, 162, 180
Aucocisco, Back Bay, Portland, 169
Augusta, xvi, 144
d'Aulnay, Charles, 196, 199
Ausomangoit (St. Croix System), 233
Awanadjo, "misty mountain," Blue Hill, 206
Awassawamkeak, "shining shore," Sears Island (Searsport), 68

Awassoos Island, Bear Is. (Penobscot River), 42
Ayer, Joshua, of Orono, 26
Ayer's Rips (Orono), 26, 27

Bahkahsoksik, Third Machias deadwater, 220
Back River (Boothbay, Bath), 130
Back Way (Stillwater Branch, Penobscot River), 32
Bagaduce, Castine, xvi, 193
——— Narrows, 194
——— River, 194
——— (See Majabagaduce)
Bailey, Rev. Jacob, of Pownalboro, 143
Bakungunahik, Crooked Island (Penobscot River), 43
Bald Hill Cove (Winterport), 5
Ballard, Dr. Edward, xvi, 51, 67, 76, 78, 95, 99, 115, 117, 124, 136, 140, 141, 148, 152, 153, 154, 157, 164, 175, 180, 193, 207
Bangor, 14
Banks, Col. Charles Edward, M.D., 85, 105, 121, 127, 128, 129, 163, 170, 175, 178, 179, 180, 181
Bar Harbor, 207
Barry, Phillips, 16, 26
Barter's Island (St. George's River), 125
Bashaba, Betsabes, Etchemin (Maliseet) chief, 121, 125, 130, 189, 196
Basin Mills (Orono), 26, 37
Bath, 134
Battie, Mount (Camden), 74, 75
Bauneg Beg Pond (See Bonnybeague)
Baxter, Hon. James Phinney, 80, 82n., 86, 133, 150, 168, 170
Baxter, Rev. Joseph, missionary, 131, 138
Bay-a-kosk, Fifth Lake Machias, Main River, 222
Beaver trade at Negew, 24
Beaver-tail (Belfast), 70
Bedabedek (Rockland), 76, 78
Belfast, 67
Bell, Gertrude, xii
Bell, "Little," of Edmunds, 225
Bemidjiwok, Treat's Falls (Bangor), 17
Benjamin River (Brooklin-Blue Hill), 207
Bennet Brook (Bernardston, Mass.), 27
Benwit, "Old Joe," Indian Shaman, of Machias, 219
Berwick, 177, 218

Biard, Father Pierre, 15, 98, 195, 196, 197, 198, 209
Big Lake (St. Croix), 232
Bigwatook, Pushaw, 33
Birch Island and Stream (Penobscot River), 41
Black Island, Little Hemlock (Penobscot River), 39
Blackman Stream (Bradley), 25
Bliss, Mr., 165
Bliss Island (Letete, N. B.), 155
Blue Hill, 206
Boiling Rock (Kittery), xix
Boiling Rocks, xix, 21
Bombazine Island (Sagadahoc River), 129
Bonnyneague, Bannabeague, Bauneg Beg Pond (Sanford), 84
Bonython, John, of Saco, 133
Boom Islands (Penobscot River), 40
Boothbay, 131
Bordman, Andrew, of Woolwich, 133, 137
Bosquenahgook Islands (Penobscot River), 40, 41, 42
Boyden's Lake (Perry), 229
Bradbury, Capt. Jabez, 132
Bradford, Rev. Alden, of Wiscasset, 120
Bradford, Gov. William, 198
Bradley, 25
Bradshaw, Richard, of Spurwink, 150
Brastow, Miss Julia T., 8
Bremen (see Bristol and Waldoboro)
Brewer, 18
Brewer, Col. John, 18
Brigadier's Island (Sears Island), 67, 68
Bristol, 88, 102
Broken Island (Penobscot River), 40, 41
Brooklin, 204, 205
Brooksville, xi, 202
Brown University Library, 25
"Brunovicus" (Dr. Edward Ballard), xvi
Brunswick, xx, 150
Brunswick Falls, Pejepscot, xix, xx, 114, 150
Buck, Col. Jonathan, of Bucksport, 3
Buckstown-i-menahan, Verona Island, 3
Bungamug Brook, Brunswick, xix, 152
Bunganut Pond (Lyman), 183
Burlington, 16, 49, 50
Burnt Land Island (Penobscot River)

Indian Place-Names of the Maine Coast 259

Burrage, Dr. Henry, 114, 130 150, 166
Burying Ground Islands (Penobscot River), 40
Cabot, William Brooks, xii, xxvi, xxviii, 20, 32, 47, 54, 61, 96, 98, 103, 104, 108, 111, 113, 117, 120, 123, 129, 141, 149, 157, 163, 177, 180, 186, 188, 190, 205, 206, 210 213, 219.

Cadillac, Sieur de la Mothe, xi, 210
Calais, 230
Cambolassie Pond (Lincoln), 55
Camden, 73
Cammock, Thomas, of Scarboro, 170
Campobello Island, N. B., 121
Capanawagen, 124
Cape Bonawagon (Southport), 121
——— Harbor (Southport), 124, 125
——— Jellison (Stockton), 65, 66, 68
——— Neddick (York), 178
——— Newagen (Southport), 123
——— Porpoise (Kennebunkport), 174
——— ——— River (Mousam River, Kennebunk), 178
——— Rosier (Penobscot Bay), 201, 202
Capissic River (Portland), 165, 167
Cargill, Capt. James, 65, 75, 119, 124
Caribou, habits of, 56, 230
Caribou Lake (West Branch Penobscot River), 220
——— Lakes (Megurrewock, Washington Co.), 56, 230
Carlow Island (Perry), 121
Castine, xvi, 191
——— Baron, xi, 195
——— Census of Indians, 1709, 195
——— French fort, 199
——— Neck, 201
Casco Bay, 168
Catamawawa (Winterport), 5
Catawamteak, "grand landing" (Rockland), 77, 83
Cathance River (Dennysville), 140
——— (Topsham), 140
——— Lake (Washington Co.), 226
Chadbourne, Humphrey, of Berwick, 182, 186
Chadwick, Joseph, surveyor, 8, 9, 10, 24, 42, 226
Chamberlain, Montague, xviii, 121, 226
Champlain, Samuel, 3, 36, 76, 98, 128, 130, 173, 189

Chase, Mrs. Fannie S., 110
Chasse, Father de la, 195
Chaubunagungamaug (Mass.), xix
Chebatigosuk, "the crossing" (Levant), 8, 13
Chebattis' place, 12
Chebattiscook, 12, 13
Chebeague Island, Saco Bay, 255
Chebeguadose (Castine), 199
Chebogardinac, "big hill place" (Camden), 75
Cheemahn Island, "big island" (Penobscot River), 42
Chegewannussuck Falls (Waldoboro), 95
Chegony Island (Sagadahoc River), 129
Chemo Lake, "the big bog" (Clifton), 25, 26
Cheputneticook (Grand Lake, Schoodic), 235
Cherryfield, 212
Chevacobet (Sheepscot River), 117
Chewonki Neck (Wiscasset), 117
Chibanook, "big opening" (Saponac Lake), 89
Chiboctook, "the big bay" (Halifax Harbor), 197
Chiboctous, "the big bay" (Castine), 195, 196, 197, 198, 200
Chickawaukee Lake (Rockland), 78
Chilnucook (Grand Lake, St. Croix), 233
Chimenasauganum (Grand Lake, St. Croix), 232
Chisapeak Bay (Merrymeeting Bay), 138
Chops of Merrymeeting Bay, 66, 135, 140, 143
Chouacouet (Saco River), 173
Church, Capt. Benjamin, xi, 79, 81
Chusquisak (Yarmouth), 157
Chute, Dr. A. J., xv, 142
Clark's Point (Machiasport), 217
Cleeve, Cleaves, George, of Portland, 165, 166, 168
Clifton, 26
Clives, Cleaves, Thomas, of Wiscasset, 116
Cobbossecontee (Gardiner), 69, 144
Cobscook (near Quoddy Village, Washington County), 227
Coffin, Rev. Paul, missionary, 13, 72, 74, 102, 106
Colburn, Jeremiah, of Orono, 26
Cold Stream (Enfield), 48
Connecticut River, 108
Cook, The (Old Town), 34

Cotta, John, Indian, 106
Cotter, Sarah and Peter, of Brunswick, 106
Cougougash, Kokohass', "the barred owl," Maliseet Revolutionary chief, 218, 219
Cousins, John, of Yarmouth, 158
Cousins River (Yarmouth), 158
Cowesisek River (Newcastle), 111
Cowsigan, Cowsegan Narrows (Sheepscot River), 116
Crane, Col. John, of Whiting, 84
Criehaven, 99
Crockett, David, 86
Crockett's Point (Rockland), 77
Crooked Island (Penobscot River), 43
Crowne, John, 24, 25
———, William, 3, 24
Crowne's Point (Negew, Eddington Bend), 23
Cromwell, Oliver, 23
Cushnoc (Augusta), xvi, 144

Da Costa, Rev. B. F., 114
Damariscotta, 28, 105
Damariscove Island (Boothbay), 104, 121, 122
Damazee, Indian, 129
Damerell, Humphrey, 105, 106
Davis, Capt. Sylvanus, 83, 94, 140
Decatur, Mr., of Machiasport, 217
Deekeewenskek, Upper Dobsy Lake (St. Croix), 234
Deer Island, N. B., xxi
Dehanada, Indian, 130
Denys, Nicholas, xviii, 70
Dennysville, 225
Des Barres, *Atlantic Neptune*, 211
Devil's Arm-chair (Bangor), 18
——— Foot-prints (Bangor), 18
——— Head (Calais), 229
——— Rush River (Dresden), 143
Dice's Head (Castine), 199, 200
D'Orville's (Devil's) Head (Calais), 229
Douaquet, Donaquet, Douaket (Waukeag in Sullivan), 210
Douglas-Lithgow *Dictionary*, 137, 148, 201
Drake, Samuel A., 80
Dresden, 143
Druillettes, Father Gabriel, 131, 138, 174
Drummond, Hon. Josiah, 152, 153
Dummer, Lt.-Gov. William, 81
Dunbar, William H., of North Castine, 191
Dunnack, Dr. Henry E., 65

Dyer's Neck and River (Newcastle), 112, 113

Eagle Island (Merrymeeting Bay), 140
Eagle Island (Penobscot River), 41
East Machias River, 219
Eastport, 227
Eaton, Cyrus, 72, 77, 78, 79, 82, 83, 84, 85, 93, 97, 99
Ebaghuit, Ebagwidek, Prince Edward Island, 121, 227
———, Campobello Island, 121, 227
Ebenecook Harbor (Southport), 124
Edali, "there is," "a place where":
——— -andalachsimemook, "where they waited and rested" (Castine Neck), 201
——— -chichiquasik, "where it is very narrow" (Cape Rosier), 202
——— -q'saga-holdemuk, "where one crosses over" (Prospect Ferry), 3
——— -sibach'lemuk, "where they waited for the tide" (Castine Neck), 201
——— -t'wakilamuk, "where they run up hill" (Bald Hill Cove, Winterport), 5
——— -wikek-hadimuk, "where there is writing" (Hampden Narrows), 6
Edala-wikheegedit (Hampden Narrows), 6
Edal-skowasimuk, "where you would have to wait," 201
Edawi-manwik, "where you go down stream either way" (Hermon Pond Inlet), 8
Eddington, Eddington Bend, 20, 21, 22
Edjida-waskodek, Marsh's Farm (Orono), 28
Edmunds, 224
Eduk-m'ninek, Deer Island, N. B., xxi, 230
Eels, habits of, weirs for, 16
Eggemoggin Reach, 194, 202, 204
Egolbayik, Third Machias Lake, Main River, 222
Ehkapsak, Hobart Stream (Edmunds), 224
Elaware Rips (Winn), 56
Ellala-gwaga-waysik Islands (Orono), 37
Ellitegway-gamek (St. Croix), 232
Ellsworth, 208
Emery, Edwin, 184
Emmetinic, Matinicus Island, 98

Enfield, 48, 49
Enikus-wassissek, "the ants' nest," Basin Mills Island (Orono), 37
Epagwit (See Ebaghuit)
Epituse, Fisherman's Island (Boothbay), 121
Epistoman, 121
Eptidukes (Grand Manan), 121
Epukunikek, Harrison's Island (Passamaquoddy Bay), 121, 227
Erascohegan, "watching place" (Georgetown), 126
Escutassis, "trout brook" (Burlington), 50
Escutnagen, Mopang Lake (Machias River), 223
Eskiwiwamiguk, Spruce Island (Jonesport), 217
Eskumunaak, N. B., "look-out," 126
Eskwiwobudick, N. S., "look-out," 126
Essak, "clams," 66
Essick, "clam place" (Stockton), 66
Etchemins (Maliseets), xxvi, 15, 117
Etna, 10
Etna Pond, Parker Pond, 10

Fagotty Bridge (Wells), 182
Falmouth, 160
Farmer, John, xxiii n.
Field's Pond (Orrington), 19
Fifth Lake, Machias Main River, 222
First Falls, Penobscot River (Eddington Bend), 17, 21, 22, 23
Fisherman's Island (Boothbay), 121, 122
Five Islands Rapids (Winn), 57
Folk etymology, xvi, 30, 75
Fort Halifax (Winslow), 145
———— Knox (Prospect), 4
———— Point (Eddington Bend), 23, 68
———— ———— (Stockton), 65, 67, 135
———— Pownall (Stockton), 65
———— St. George (Thomaston), 78, 80
Fourth Lake, Machias Main River, 222
Fox Islands, 95
Fox Island Thoroughfare, 95
Francis, Joseph, Penobscot Indian, 63
Frankfort, 4
French Island (Old Town), 37
Fryeburg, xxiii

Ganong, Dr. William Francis, x, xi, xii, xiii, xxviii, 1, 2, 3, 4, 6, 17, 19, 23, 36, 51, 52, 63, 73, 75, 76, 80, 84, 96, 101, 103, 104, 106, 109, 110, 115, 117, 120, 121, 126, 133, 134, 139, 141, 142, 144, 154, 155, 158, 163, 164, 168, 169, 175, 177, 179, 180, 190, 198, 207, 211, 213, 215, 218, 225, 229, 234, 235
Gardiner, 144
Gassobeeis Lake (Nicatowis), 49
Gatschet, Dr. A. S., xxi, 2, 31, 73, 78, 223, 224, 226, 227, 228, 229, 230, 231, 233
Gaulin, Mons., of Sears Island, 68
Gaywaysick (Pokey Lake, Machias), 219
Georgekeag (Thomaston), 84
Georgetown, 126
Gerrish, William, scout, 183
Glusgehbeh (Glooscap of Micmacs), the Indian demi-god (see Indian legends)
Godmorrocke (Kittery), 182
Goldthwait, Capt. Thomas, 70, 71
Gorges, Sir Ferdinando, 165
————, *Brief Narration,* 121
Gouldsboro, 211
Grand Landing (Rockland), 76, 78
———— (St. Stephen, N. B.), 230
Grange at Burlington, 50
————, Enfield, 49
————, Orland, 188
Great East Pond (Sebasticook Lake, Newport), 10
Great Works (Berwick), 182
Great Works Falls (Old Town), 29
Greenbush, 44
Greenland River (Muscongus), 94
Greenleaf, Moses, 14, 21, 22, 25, 29, 33, 40, 41, 46, 55, 56, 162
Guagus Lake, Little, N. B., 215
Guagus Stream (Township 40), 215
Gutch, Robert, of Bath, 136, 137
Gyles, Capt. John, xxii, 129, 143

Hadaway, Bertha M., 175
Hadley's Lake (Machias East River), 219
Hahkik-watpuk, Seal Head (Fox Islands), 95
Halifax, N. S., 197
Hallowell, 144
Hampden, 6; Narrows, 6
Hammond Pond (Hermon), 8
Hancock County, 187
Hanol-menahanol, Five Islands Rapids (Winn), 57

Hanson, John W., 188
Harpswell, 154
Harraseeket River (Freeport), 161
Harrison's Island (Passamaquoddy Bay), 121
Hatch's Cove Island (St. George's River), 80
Hathorn Brook (Bangor), 18
Hazel-nut Island, Sears Island (Searsport), 68
Heath, Capt. Joseph, surveyor, 66, 134, 137, 141
Hedgehog Island (Penobscot River), 42
"Helfenstein, Ernest," pseud. Mrs. Elizabeth Oakes Smith, 16
Hell Gate, Upper and Lower (Arrowsic Island), 133
Hemlock Island (Old Town), 41
Hermon, 8
Hermon Pond, 8
Herrick, Capt. Israel, 12
Hewes, Elihu, surveyor, 27
Hiawatha, 153
High Head (Bangor), 14
Hobart Stream (Edmunds), 224
Hobbomocka, Hockomock Point (Arrowsic Island), 133
Hogamockook Point (Muscongus), 93, 94
Hogarth, Dr. D. G., xiii
Hook, The (Hallowell), 144
Hubbard, Dr. Lucius Lee, x, 27, 29, 32, 33, 52, 55, 60, 63, 201, 212
Hubbard, Samuel, historian, 131
Humolatskihegon, "many carvings on rock" (Rouqe Bluffs, Machiasport), 217
Hutchings, Herbert, of Penobscot, 191
Hypocrites, Hypocras, Hypocrist, ledges off Boothbay, 122

Indian Island (Old Town), 38
Indian Town (Muscongus), 94
Indian village, Point Pleasant (Perry), 228
Inventaire des Concessions, Quebec, 80
Isle au Haut, 99
Isles of Shoals, 127
Islesboro, 67, 202
Indians:
  Camp-grounds, 19, 20, 23, 46
  Legends
    Glusgebheh (Glooscap), xxix, 162, 202, 203, 216
    historical, 215, 217, 219, 228, 229, 232

Mythology
  dwarfs, 6, 27
  fairies, 6, 217
  magic of cat-tail, 143
Pictographs
  Jonesport, 217
  Machiasport, 217
Routes of travel, 11, 12, 48, 49, 54, 55, 76, 77, 78, 82, 92, 109, 110, 135, 167, 175
Language
  alphabet, xxiii
  inseparable roots, xxii
  interchange, p and b, xxiii
    m and n, xxiii
    l, n, r, in dialects, xxi, xxiii
  locative endings, xxi
  long and short vowels, xxiii
  plurals, xxi
  possessive pronouns, xxiv, 78, 95, 200
  roots and stems, xxv
  softened locative, 35, 51, 52, 58, 62, 63, 90
  sounds, xxiv, 53, 107, 137
  telescoping roots, xxii
Study of language
  folk etymology, xvi
  foreign influence, xviii
  lack of vocabularies, xix
  no fixed spelling, xx
  phonetics, xii
  syllabic analysis, xxv, xxvii
  understanding Indians, xix
  using Rasles' Dictionary, xxiv
  value of Indian information, xvii

Jackson, Dr. Charles T., 224
Jameson, Brig. Gen. Charles D., 32
Jamieson's Falls (Stillwater), 32
Jefferies, map maker, 76
Jenney, Judge C. F., 104
Jeremysquam (Woolwich), 137
Jockey Cap (Fryeburg), xxiii, 33
Joe Pease Rips (Old Town), 43
Johnson Brook (Eddington), 20
Johnston, Alexander, 117
———, John, historian, 88
Jones, Dr. William, 124
Jonesport, 215, 216
Jordan, Robert, of Scarboro, 170
Josselyn, John, xxi, 123, 162

Kaghsk-i-binday (Brewer), 20
Kah-no-nah-jik, Long Island (Penobscot River), 40
Kananghetne (Damariscotta), 108

Indian Place-Names of the Maine Coast 263

Kaoosi-menahan, Cow Island (Penobscot River), 43
Kaousaki, "gull lake," Grand Lake (Schoodic), 235
Kaskoonaguk, Mark Island (Islesboro), 96
Kassanumganumkeag Rips, 56
Katahdin, Tadden, Todden, Mountain, xxii
Katawamteag (Rockland), 83
Katewysip, Unknown Stream (Machias Main River), 222
Kawapskitchwak, "rough falls" (Machias), 219
K'chi-medabiaught, "great landing" (St. Stephen, N. B.), 78, 230
K'chi-mugwaak-i-menahan, "big bog island," Orson Island (Old Town), 39
K'chi-pasquahonda, "big guns," Fort Knox (Prospect), 4
K'chi-penabsq'-manaook, "big ledge island," Treat and Webster Island (Old Town), 38
K'chi-p'saganum, "big lake," Big Lake (St Croix), 232
K'chi-punahmaquot Brook (Pembroke), 226
Kebec (Merrymeeting Bay), 140
Kebumcook, Keedumcook, The Hook (Hallowell), 144
Keenaht-nassik, "steep island," Treat and Webster Island (Old Town), 37
Keene's Neck (Waldoboro), 94
Keght-niganish, "the principal fork" (Whiting River, Whiting), 224
Ke-kepan-naghliesek (Arrowsic Island), 132
Kemboeskisek (Newcastle), 113
Kendall, Edward Augustus, 114, 150, 157
Kendall Head (Eastport), 228
Kenduskeag Stream (Bangor), 15
Kenebis, Indian chief, 143
Kennebec River, xv, 142
Kennebunk, 174
Kennebunkport, 174
"Kennelclin" (Col. John Crane), 84, 224
Kepahigan, 123
Kepam, Cape Ann, 174
Kepamkiak, "bar of gravel" (Lubec), 223
Kessalogessomodik, Five Islands Rapids (Winn), 56
Ketakouan, Taconic (Waterville), 145
Ketchum, Lewis, xix, 5, 11, 15, 16,
17, 18, 20, 22, 28, 30, 37, 39, 45, 47, 48, 50, 53, 58, 67, 69, 83, 205, 213, 215
Ket-h'nik, Ket'h'nisq', "principal form," Cathance River (Dennysville), 140
Kiasobeak, Nicatowis Lake, 49
Kiasobeesis, Gassobeeis Lake, 49
Kinabskatnek, "steep rock mountain," Mount Waldo (Frankfort), 4
Kineo Mountain, 162, 200
Kinnicutt, Lincoln N., 104
Kittery, 182
K'mokadich (Moosabec Reach), 216
K'noon-nahgek, Argyle Boom Islands (Argyle), 40
Knox, General Henry, mansion of, 83
Kochisuk, "eel weir" (Passadumkeag), 16
Kokadjo, "kettle mountain," xxix, 200
Ko-ko-hass-wantp-ek, Owls Head (Rockland), 78
Kollejedjewok, Blue Hill Tide-falls, 206
Konkus, dry rot, 20
Kousanouskek, Wessawaskeag (St. George), 80
K'seusk-i-naghassik, Little Hemlock Island, 40
K'seuskis-menahan, Hemlock Island (Old Town), 41
K't-ahguamek, "grand landing," 78
K'tenis (Dennysville), 40
K'tolaqu'-wi-menahanuk, Orono's Island (Old Town), 39
K'tolbeh-i-ahmikenaqu'-nahgek, "snapping turtle shell island," Namokanok Island (Lincoln), 39
K'tolbewik, "snaping turtle lake," Fourth Lake, Machias Main River, 222
Kuladamitchwan, Blue Hill Tidefalls, 206
Kwaykwaynahmak, Long Reach (Old Town), 33
Kewedawi-manwik (Hermon Pond), 9
Kwelbedjwanosik (Stillwater), 32
Kwesahnouskek (St. George), 80
Kweshakamigus, "horseback," 83
Kwetahwamkituk (Old Town), 32
Kwi-kwi-mes-wi-ticook, "black duck stream," Marsh River (Frankfort), 4

Lake Champlain, 67

Laurent, Joseph, 120, 142
Lawrence, Col. T. R., xii, xiii
Lauverjat, Father, 86
Le Chock River (Union River), 209
Lefebvre, Lefebre, Lefaver, Thomas, interpreter, 80, 81, 86
Le Jeune, Father, 3
Leonard, Hon. Roger G., 42
Leonard's Pond, Chemo Lake (Clifton), 26
Lermond's Cove (Rockland), 77
Lescarbot, Marc, 3, 15, 142, 168, 173
Levant, 13
Levett, Christopher, 168, 170
Lewiston Falls, 149
Libbey, C. Trueman, 12
Lincoln, 52
Lincolnville, 71
Linekin, Bay, 106 n.
Lisbon Falls, 149
Littlefield, Ada, 5, 84
Locke, John L., 72, 73, 74, 75, 78
Long Island (Islesboro), 67
Long Reach (Kennebec River), 143
Lover's Leap, Bangor, 16
Lower Dobsy Lake (Sekledobscus Lake), 154
Lowell, 16
Lubec, 223
Lucerne-in-Maine, xvii
Lyon, Lion, Newell, 32, 33, 37, 40, 47

Machegony, Machegonne (Portland), 163, 164, 165, 166
Machias, xvii, 217
Machiasport, 126, 217
Machias River Systems, 219-224
McDuffie, Franklin, xvii
McKeen, John, 138
Machlich-nahgook, Hardwood Island (Penobscot River), 39
Mackworth's Point and Island (Falmouth), 161
Macwahoc Stream, "bog," 58
Madagam Lake (Lincoln), 54
Madagamus Hill (Searsport), 201
Madagaskal Stream (Burlington), 50
Madahumuck (Waldoboro), 92
Madakamigossek (Camden), 73
Madamaswok, Cold Stream (Enfield), 48
Madamascontee (Damariscotta), 106
Madamascontes (Mattamiscontis Plantation), 51
Madamiscontis, Blackman Stream (Bradley), 25
Madawaniganook, Carry (Old Town), 30

Madoamok (Waldoboro), 92
Madomcook (Friendship), 87
Madomock Falls (Waldoboro), 92
Madunkehunk Stream (Chester), 61
Madunkehunk Stream, Webster Stream (East Branch Penobscot), 61, 62
Magessemanussok, -sewanussuk, Falls (Waldoboro), 92, 94
Magurrewock Lakes (Washington County), 230
Magwintegwak, Lincolnville Beach, 71
Mahagantegwit, "choppy seas," Lincolnville Beach, 71
Maine Woods Songster, 16, 26
Majabagaduce, Castine, 193, 196
Malaga Island (Phippsburg), 127
———— (Isles of Shoals), 127
Malecuniganus, "lazy carry" (Magaguadavic River, N. B.), 154
Maliseets, xxvi, 15, 197
Mananis Island, 97, 104
Mananouze Island (Petit Manan), 97
Manaskek (-kong, -kous, -konkus), Arrowsic Island, 43, 131, 132
Manaskous Island, Green Island (Penobscot River), 43
Mandawassoe Island, Hedgehog Island (Penobscot River), 42
Manesahdik, "clam gathering" (Bar Harbor), 207
Manning, Capt. George, 210
Manokanok Island, "turtle shell Island" (Lincoln), 39
Manta wassuk, "inlet," Johnson Brook (Eddington), 20
Maple sugar, 226
Maps:
  Aubéry, 8, 10, 107
  Bellin, 36, 129
  Carleton, Osgood, 219
  Chadwick, Joseph, 8, 9, 21, 24
  Champlain, 36, 76, 169
  de Rozier, 36, 145
  Heath, Capt. Joseph, 137, 141
  Jeffreys, 76
  Johnston, 129
  Lescarbot, 142
  Maynard and Holland, 32, 39
  Neptune, Francis Joseph, 215, 226, 235
  Pownall, Gov. Thomas, 24, 195
  Simancas, 85, 98
  Smith, Capt. John, 198
  Treat and Marsh, xxiii
Mecadacut, "big mountain place" (Camden), 71, 74

Indian Place-Names of the Maine Coast 265

M'd'abiaught, "great landing" (St. Stephen, N. B.), 78
M'dakmiguk (Princeton), 231
M'd'angamek, "the snowshoe prints," Dice Head (Castine), 67, 200
Medambattek Pond, Chickawaukee Lake (Rockland), 79
Medambettox Mountain, Dodge Mountain (Rockland), 79
Meddybemps Lake (Alexander), 75, 79, 225
Medet, Meder, Hermon Pond, 8
Medombettick Bay (Rockland), 77
Medomac, Medomock (Waldoboro), 88, 92
Medumcook (Friendship), 87
Medway, 63
Meesokdowhok, Burnt Land Island (Penobscot River), 43
Megankill River (Ogunquit River), 176
Megunticook (Camden), 71, 72, 73
Megurrewock Lakes (Washington County), 230
Mekwamkisk, Red Beach (Robbinston), 229
Memada'kamioguk (Princeton), 231
Memeemeesitt Creek (Merrymeeting Bay), 140
Menahanisisicook, "very small islands," 40
Menasquasicook, Matinicus Island, 99
Meneer, Philip, son-in-law of Baron Castine, 68
Menes-saganaganis, Big Lake (St. Croix), 233
Meniekec (St. George), 81
Menikoe Point (Yarmouth), 125
Menikuk Cape Harbor (Southport), 125
Menikpadik, "getting tying bark," Poke-o-moonshine Lake (Washington County), 220
Micmac invasion, xxvii
Mikuswessak, "the dwarfs," 6, 27, 28
Milford, 44, 45
Mill Creek (Scarboro), 171
——— ——— Cove (South Orrington), 5
——— Cove (Robbinston), 229
——— River (Newcastle) ,111
——— ——— (Thomaston), 79, 83
Minnecopscook, "many rocks," Seal Rocks (or Sail Rock) (Lubec), 224
Minnewokun, "many bends route" (Brooksville), 202
Minstrelsy of Maine, 26

Mitaganessuk, "end of tide," Falls, (Eddington Bend), 22
Mitchell, Chaquot, Indian, 44
———, Lewey Maliseet, 11, 22, 42, 56, 120, 121, 155, 173, 207, 213, 217, 218, 219, 220, 222, 223, 224, 225, 226, 227, 228, 229, 230, 231, 234, 235, 254
M'kaza-ni-kuk-menahan, Black Island (Old Town), 40
M'n'adagahmis, Cold Steram (Enfield), 48
Moasham, 122, 125
Mohawk Island (Penobscot River), 43
Mohawk Rips, 52, 56
Mohawks, 27, 41, 43, 48
Molasses Pond (Franklin), 56
Molliconiganus, "lazy carry" (Pocumpcus Lake, St. Croix), 154
Molunkus Stream (Aroostook County), 57
Monhegan Island, 96, 103
Moniecook Island (St George's River), 85, 125
Monnebasa Pond (York County), 182
Monvel, Mons., French geologist, 82
Moorehead, Dr. Warren, 195
Moosabek Reach (Jonesport), 215
Moose Island, Eastport, 227
Moosehead Lake, 162
Moos-i-katchick, "moose's rump" (Cape Rosier), 202
Moospayechick, 216
Mosemadaga, 67, 201
Moshoquen, 166
Mount Agamenticus, 130
——— Battie (Camden), 74, 75
——— Desert Island, 209
——— Katahdin, xxii
——— Kokadjo, "kettle mountain" (Little Spencer Mt.), xxix
——— Sabotawan, "the pack" (Big Spencer Mt.), xxix
——— Sowanga, "eagle mountain" (Sowbungy Mt.), xxix
——— Sowangawas, "the eagle's nest" (on Seboois River), xxix
——— Waldo (Frankfort), 4
Mountequies Neck (Kennebunk), 175
Mountsweag Bay (Sheepscot River), 116
Mousam, Mowsam River (Kennebunk), 174
Mskutook, 33
Mskwamankanek, "salmon fishery" (Rochester, N. H.), xvi

Mugaleep-ahwangan, "the caribou trail" (Lincoln), 56
Mugurrewock Lakes, "caribou lakes," 56
Munanook, Monhegan Island, 97
Mundoouscootuck, "devil's rush river," Eastern River, Dresden, 143
Munolammonungan, "much red paint" (Piscataquis County), 46
Muscongus, 88
Mus-elenk, "moose island," Eastport, 231
Musikatchick, "moose's rump," Cape Rozier, 202
Muspeka Rache, Moosabek Reach (Jonesport), 215
Mut-an-a-gwes, Dochet Island, 231
Mutchignigos, Indian Island (Passamaquoddy Bay), 231
Muttoneguis, Dochet Island (Passamaquoddy Bay), 231
Muttonegwenish, Little Dochet Island, 231

Nadded, Hermon Pond, 8
Naguncoth, Noguncoth (Wells), 176
Nagusset (Woolwich), 141
Nahumkeag, Nehumkeag, "eel place" (Pittston), 143
Nalabongan, Newport or Sebasticook Lake, 10
Nalagwem-menahan, Verona Island (Orland), 187
Nallahamcongan (Bernardston, Mass.), 27
Nalumsunkhungan Rips (Orono), 26
Namadunkehunk, Webster Stream (Penobscot East Branch), 62
Namokanok, "turtle shell," Island (Lincoln), 43, 52
Nampscoscocke (Wells), 177
Nantucket Island, 121
Narraguagus River, 212
Narramissic Grange, Orland, 188
Naskeag Point (Brooklin), 68, 205
Nasket Point (Woolwich), 138
Nassaque, 138
Nassoemic (Newcastle), 112
Nassouac, Naxoat (Merrymeeting Bay), 138
Nawlombages (Etna Pond), 10
N'damas-swagam, Gardiner's Lake, East Machias, 219
Necadoram (Main Stream, Sebesteguk River), 9
Neconaugamook, "round pond," Third Lake, E. Machias, 220

Neganodenek (Old Town), 31
Negas, Negue, Negew, Neager (Fort Point, Eddington Bend), 23, 31
Nekounegan, Nekonigan, "the better carry" (Old Town), 30
Nekrangan, 126
Neguntequit (Wells), 177
Negunticook (Camden), 74
Neguttaquid (Berwick), 177
Negwamkeag (Waterville), 144, 145
Nehumkeag (Pittston), 143
Nemdamassuagum, "sucker lake," Gardners' Lake (East Machias), 219
Neptune, Mrs. Clara, xix, 4, 5, 16, 17, 18, 19, 20, 22, 30, 32, 34, 37, 39, 40, 41, 47, 200, 254
Neptune, Francis Joseph, Passamaquoddy chief, 211, 225, 226, 235
Neptune, Lt. Gov. John, Penobscot, 84, 86, 93, 99, 104, 159
Neptune, "Old John," the magician, 229
Neptune, Gov. William, Passamaquoddy, 11, 149, 188, 207, 210, 227, 235
Nequasset (Woolwich), 138, 141
Nesayik, "roily lake," Boyden's Lake (Perry), 229
Newagen (Southport), 123
Newberry Library, Chicago, 195
Newcastle, 111
New Meadows River (Brunswick), 135
Newichiwannock (South Berwick), 185
Newport, 10
Nexaongermeck, Stetson Pond, 9
Nicatow, "the fork" (Medway), 63
Nicatowis, "the little fork" of the Passadumkeag, 49
Nicatowis, Nicatous Lake, 49
Nichols Pond (Chemo Lake, Clifton), 26
———— Rock, Sobscook (Eddington), xix, 20
———— Stream (Johnson Brook, Eddington), 20
Nicolar, Nicola, Joseph, 4, 5, 16, 17, 21, 25, 27, 29, 30, 66, 68, 70, 72, 77, 78, 96, 106, 142, 188, 189, 201, 237-240
Nicola, Mrs. Mary Malt (Neptune), 79, 93
Nicola's Island (Penobscot River), 42
Nolatkeeheemungan, Freese Island (Penobscot River), 40, 46

Nonsuch River (Scarboro), 170
North Haven, 96
North Yarmouth, xix, 156
Norumbega, 15
Nubble, The, Cape Neddick (York), 178, 179
Nudenans *Dictionary,* 10, 14, 19, 20, 30, 41, 48, 55, 58, 66, 72, 135, 164, 169, 181, 205, 208, 225
Numchenumganis, "one-sided lake," Second Lake, East Machias River, 220
Nusalkchunangan, 86
Nutskamongan, 27

Oar Island (Waldoboro), 94
Obnask Pond (York County), 183
O'Brien, Rev. Michael Charles, xxi, xxii, 4, 7, 8, 9, 12, 14, 17, 19, 20, 22, 25, 29, 31, 32, 33, 35, 41, 44, 51, 57, 58, 62, 66, 67, 68, 72, 73, 75, 76, 90, 95, 99, 119, 157, 160, 175, 176, 180, 188, 190, 201, 202, 203, 204, 207, 209, 212, 220
Ogier, Lewis, of Camden, 73
Ogunquit, 176
Olamon, 46
—————— Island, 41
—————— Stream, 96
Old Town, 35
—————Falls, 30
Omquemenkeag Lake (North Lake, Schoodic), 235
Onawa Lake (Piscataquis County), 153
Oniganisek (Stockton), 36
Oolaghesee, "the entrail" (Cape Rosier), 202
Oolamonoosuk, 42
Ooneganissek, "short carry" (Stockton), 66
Ooneganissis, "short carry" (Stillwater), 32
Ooneganoosis, "the short carry" (Cape Rosier), 202
Opechee Stream (Searsport), 153
Orland, 187
Orono, 26, 43
Orono, Joseph, Penobscot chief, 26, 39
Orono Island (Old Town), 39
Orphans' Island (Verona), 187
Orson Island (Old Town), 38
Osabeg Hills (York County), 183
Osquoon, "the liver" (Cape Rosier), 202
Otter Creek Point, Mt. Desert, 209
Ounegan Block, Ounegan Mill (Old Town), 30

Ouneganek, "the carry" (Old Town), 30
Ouneganissis, "short carry" (Stillwater), 32
Ouneganissisikek, "the very short carry" (Stillwater), 32
Oven Mouth (Boothbay), 122
Owascoag River (Scarboro), 170, 171
Owen, Capt. William, 224
Owls Head (Rockland), 76, 78

Pa-am-tegwitook, Main Penobscot River, 1
Pacifique, Rev. Father, 11, 31, 32, 36, 55, 58, 61, 100, 166, 169
P'aisunk (Bar Harbor), 207
Palmasicket Hill (York County), 183
Pananke (Old Town), 36
Panawamskek-menahan, Indian Island (Old Town), 38
Pannawambskek (Old Town), 1, 2, 35, 39
Panouamske (Old Town), 38
Panoumke (Old Town), 36
Paquatanee (Belfast), 70
Parker's Island (Kennebec River), 126, 143
Pashipscot, Pashippscott (Sheepscot), xvi, xx, 114, 150
Passadumkeag, 16, 47, 48
Passagassawaukeag River (Belfast), 69
Passamaquoddy Bay, 227
Patagumkis, Pattagumpus Stream (Medway), 63, 64
Pateshall, Richard, 115, 121
Pawnook Lake (Saponac), 50
Pearse, Richard, John, Mary, 90, 91, 93
Pedcokegowake Carry (Newcastle), 109, 110
Pejepscot, Pejipscot (Brunswick), xix, xx, 114, 160
Pemaquid Point, xv, 102
Pematinacook, Pematinek (Lincoln), 55
Pembroke, 226
Pemetic, Mt. Desert Island, 209
Pemidjuanosick (Stillwater), 32
Pemjedjewock, Treat's Falls (Bangor), 17
Pemmaquam Lake (Pembroke), 226
Pemptegoet, Pemptegwit, the Main Penobscot River, 15
Pemskodek, Pemskudek, Marsh's Farm (Orono), 28, 37

Pemsquam-kutook, Birch Stream (Argyle), 41
Pemtegwatook, Penobscot Main River, 2
Penapsquacook (Prospect), 4
Penhallow, Judge Samuel, 68, 132, 139
Penobscot, 190
Penobscot River, 1
Penobseese (Waldoboro), 91
Pentegoet (Castine), 191, 192, 200
Pequawkett (Fryeburg), xxiii
Perham, Hon. David, 19
Perkins, Pateshall, 115
Perry, 179, 228
Pescedona, 148
Pessakenewaganek, West Quoddy Light (Lubec), 224
Pesutamesset (Brewer), 19
Petekamkes, Patagumkis (Medway), 64
Peter Dana's Point (Princeton), 232
Peticodiac, N. B., 109
Petoubougue, Petoobowk, Lake Champlain, 67
Pewagon, West Branch Pemmaquam River, 226
Phillips, Walter, of Newcastle, 110, 111, 112
Phillips Lake (Dedham), xvii
Phipps, Sir William, 80, 81, 87, 133, 137
Pierpole, Perepole, Indian, xix, 137, 139, 149
Pigeon Hill (Perry), 228
Piggsgut River (Scarboro), 171
Pigwacket (Fryeburg), xxiii, 33
Pigwaduk, Pushaw Stream (Stillwater), 33
Piks-him-menahan, Hog Island, 42
Pilsquess, "the virgin," or "the old maid," pillar rock, formerly on Carlow Island, Perry, 228
Pimiwamkikatook (Sugar Island, Penobscot River), 41
Piscataqua River (See Addenda), xvi, xix
Pita-witeguk, Stillwater Branch, Penobscot River, 32
Pitowbaygook (Islesboro), 67
Pittston, 143
Piwangamosis, "the little pond," Little Brewer Pond, now Field's Pond, Orrington, 19
Pleasant River (Addison), 215
Plymouth Company, 145; Purchase, 143, 144
Pocumpcus Lake (St. Croix System), 233

Podunk (Conn.), 167
Pogamqua River (Brunswick), 152
Pog-umk-ik (Ogunquit River, Wells), 177
Poke-o-moonshine Lake (East Machias River), 221
Pokey Lake (East Machias River), 219
Point Pleasant (Perry), Indian village, 228
Polis, Joseph, 117
Pomegobset, Hammond Pond, 9
Poore, Major Ben Perley, 189
Popham, Capt. George, 114, 130
Porter, Col. Joseph W., 16, 214
Porter, Rhoda, 16
Posseps-caugamock, Cathance Lake (Washington County), 226
Portland, 163
Potter, Dr. Chandler E., xv, 12, 79, 142, 148, 153, 185
Pownalborough (Wiscasset), 143
Pownall, Gov. Thomas, 21, 24, 65, 67, 68
Presumpscot River, 159
Prince, Dr. J. Dyneley, 2, 58, 120
Prince Edward Island, 121
Princeton, 231
Prospect, 4
P'saganagum, Big Lake (St. Croix), 223
P'sahn, Bar Harbor, 207
Psazeske, "muddy branch" (Topsham), 139
Psinkwandissek, Scalp Rock (Passadumkeag Stream), 48
Puggamugga River (Brunswick), 152
Pukhamkes'k, Pocumpcus, "thoroughfare," 233
Pumgustuck Falls (Yarmouth), 157
Punch Bowl (harbor in Sedgwick), 214
Pushaw, Stream and Lake (Stillwater), 33
Purchas, Samuel, 94, 108, 121, 124, 125, 189, 199
Purchase, Thomas, of Brunswick, 134

Quabacook (Merrymeeting Bay), 139
Quack (Portland), 170
Quahog, the round clam, 156, 170
Quakish Lake (West Branch Penobscot River), 215
Quamphegon Falls (Berwick), 186
Quantabacook Lake (Searsmont), 70

Qua-wejoos, D'Orville's Head (Calais), 229
Quebec, 140
Quisquamego Carry (Thomaston), 83
Quisquitcumegek (Thomaston), 83
Quoddy, xix, 21
Quohoag Bay (Harpswell), 156
Quonechewanock Falls (N. H.), 186
Quonenaghtuc (Connecticut River), 108

Raggertask Island (Matinicus group), 99
Ramassoc (Orland), 189
Rameson (Orland), 188
Ranco, Peter W., 59, 221
Rand, Rev. Silas T., xviii, 61
Rasles, Rev. Sebastian, xx, xxi; *Dictionary*, xviii, xxiv, 5, 14, 20, 21, 22, 29, 31, 32, 38, 40, 46, 47, 48, 50, 53, 57, 58, 61, 70, 72, 83, 86, 91, 121, 124, 132, 133, 134, 150, 169, 193, 205
Rawson, Edward, 199
Red Beach (Robbinston), 229
Red Paint People, 23, 31, 38, 188
Remobsquis, Remobscus (Musconcus), 90, 91
Richards, Elizabeth, "Betty," of Camden, 75
Robinhood Bay (Georgetown), 130
Robinson, Reuel, 75
Robinson, Roland E., 67, 205
Rockland, 76
Romer, Colonel, engineer, 173
Roque Bluffs (Jonesport), 217
Rowe, James H., 26
Rowe, William Hutchinson, x, 157
Roy, Pierre George, 80
Royall River (Yarmouth), 157
Rumfeekungus (Nallumsunckhungan, Orono), 26

Sabanoa, Sabino, 130
Sabao Lakes, West Branch Main Machias River, 222
Sabine, Lorenzo, 2
Sabotawan Mountain, "the pack" (of Glusgehbeh), (Big Spencer Mountain), xxix, 200
Saccarappa Falls (Westbrook), 162
Sachtalen, Socks Island (Penobscot River), 39
Saco River, 171
Sagadahoc River, 129, 172
Sagondagon (Sebasticook Lake), 10
Sagosset, 129
Sakadamkiak (Saco River), 173

Sail Rock (Lubec), 224
St. Georges River, 85, 130
——— Islands, 80
——— Fort (Thomaston), 81
Salmon Point (Bucksport), 3
Salmon Falls River (South Berwick), 186
Sandy Harbor (Friendship), 87
Sandy Isles (Penobscot River), 43
Saponac, Saponic, Pawnook, Chibanook Lake, 16, 49, 50
Saquaische (Sunkhaze), 45
Saquid (St. George's River), 85
Sasanow's Mount (Mt. Agamenticus), 130
Sasanow's River (Back River, Bath), 130
Sataylan, Shad Island (Old Town), 38
Saugus Island (Penobscot River), 42
Sawacook (Topsham), 153
Sawadapsek, Sowadabscook River, 6
Sawtelle, Dr. William Otis, 65, 211
Sayward, Joseph, scout, 183
Scalp Rock (Passadumkeag River), 48
Scarboro, 170
Schoodic Lake (Piscataquis River), 50
Schoodic Lakes (St. Croix River), 235
Schoodic Point (Gouldsboro), 211
Scitterygusset Creek (Falmouth), 161
Seaboard Paper Company (Bucksport), 3
Seal Head (Fox Islands), 95
Seals, xx n., 96, 224
Sears, Hon. David, 68
Sears Island (Searsport), 67
Searsmont, 70
Searsport, 67
Sebago Lake, 161
Sebasco Harbor (Phippsburg), 156
Sebascodegan Island, "almost through" (Harpswell), 154, 155
Sebasticook Lake (Newport), 12, 13
Sebasticook River (see Sebesteguk River)
Sebayek, narrows at Quoddy Village, 228
Sebec Lake (Piscataquis County), 162
Sebeskiak Neck at Point Pleasant (Perry), 228
Sebesteguk River, 11

Second Lake (East Machias River), 219
Sededunkehunk Stream (Brewer), 18
Sedgwick, 203, 204
Seebois River, "little river," 52
Segocket, Segoquet (St. George's River), 84, 85
Seguin, Satquin, Sutquin, Island (off Kennebec River), 127
Seguin Island and Passage (Washington County), 216
Seguski-menahanikkuk, Broken Island (Penobscot River), 44
Sekledobscus Lake (Lower Dobsy, St. Croix), 234
Semiamis (Cape Elizabeth, Portland), 166
Sennibec Pond (Union), 86
Seogoggunegabo (Brunswick), 135
Sepsis-edal-apskit, "stone bird carved in rock" (Sedgwick), 203
Seremobscus (Muscongus), 91
Sewadapskek Stream (Sawadapskek), 6
Sewall, Rufus King, xv, 111, 126, 137
Shay, Mrs. Florence Nicola, 237, 238
Sheepscot River, 113, 130
Sheepscot Farms, 117
Sheldrake, 160
Shelter Islands, 81, 86
Shirley, Gov. William, 145
Short Route to Quebec (Arnold's), 8 n., 11, 145
Sibeheganuk, Cross Island (Machias), 219
Sibley, John L., 79, 86, 87
Siebert, Dr. Frank T., 254
Siguenoc (Seguin Island), 128
Simancas Map, 85, 98
Sipp Bay (Pembroke), 226
Sipsisconta, Sipsaconta, 118
Sisladobsis Lake (Sekledobscus, Lower Dobsy), 234
Skeag (Brunswick), 153
Skeecoway Creek (Falmouth), 160
Skeenaylat, Skin Island (Treat and Webster Island, Old Town), 38
Skidwares, Indian, 130
Skitikuk (Stillwater Branch of Penobscot River), 32
Skowhegan, 126
Skudek, Schoodic, Calais, 230
Skukoal, "grass," Meadow Island (Penobscot River), 43
Skutahzin, Escutassis, Skutahzin Stream, "trout stream" (Burlington), 50

Slippery Ledge Island (Old Town Island), 14
——— ——— Rapids (Old Town), 28
Smelt Cove (Muscongus), 94
Smith, Capt. John, xv, xx, xxvii, 72, 74, 88, 94, 97, 99, 130, 138, 145, 166, 168
Smith, Elizabeth Oakes, 16
Smith, Walter B., archaeologist, 23
Sobagwagum, Hadley's Lake (East Machias River), 219
Sobscook Rock, Eddington, xix, 20
Socks Island (Penobscot River), 39
Soctomer, John, Maliseet, 95, 121, 203, 214, 215, 217, 218, 221
Sol-i-kuk (Isle au Haut), 99
Sorico (Solikuk), 99
Southack, Capt. Cyprian, 81
South Orrington, 5
South Thomaston, 80
Southport, 123
Sowangan, "bald eagle," 41, 140
Speck, Dr. Frank G., 5, 33, 96, 172, 201, 254
Springer, John S., 151, 213
Spurwink (Scarboro), 170
Squamanagonic (Rochester, N. H.), xvi
Squazodek (Machiasport), 126, 217
Squimonk Pond (Berwick), 184
Squitcomegek (Thomaston), 83
Stagomor (Portland), 166
Stanislaus, Francis, 10, 54, 61, 154
———, Mrs. Sylvia, 48, 49, 55, 56
Stetson, 9
Stevens, Thomas, of Brunswick, 66, 134, 135
Stillwater, 32
Stillwater Branch (of Penobscot River), 32
Stocemouo Point (Bremen), 93
Stockton Springs, 65, 66
Stone Bird (Sedgwick), 203, 204
Strachey, William, 84, 114, 130, 150, 166
Sturgeon, methods of hunting, 70, 144
Sturt, William, 122
Sugar Island (Penobscot River), 41
Sullivan, 210
Sullivan, James, xxiii, 137, 141, 170, 186
Sunkhaze Rips, 45
——— Stream, 44
Sunkheath (St. George's River), 85
Swango Island (Merrymeeting Bay), 140

Swankwahiganus, "little bells" (Edmunds), 225

Taconic Falls (Waterville), 145
Tagwesi-menahanol, Twin Islands (Old Town), 40
Tahanock (Thomaston), 85
Ta-la-godissek, "where they painted themselves," Treat and Webster Island (Old Town), 38
Tamescot (Damariscotta), 108
Tarentyns, Tarratines (Micmacs), xxvii, 74
Tatnock Marshes (York), 181
Tchebatigosuk, "the crossing" (Levant), 12
Teddon (Mt. Katahdin), xxii
Tegoak, "waves," The Cook (Old Town), 34
Tekebisuk, Cold Stream (Enfield), 48
Temple, Sir Thomas, 24
Tewksbury, John, 75
Thaxter, Mrs. Celia, 127
Thevet, Abbé, 15
Third Lake, East Machias River, 220
Third Lake, Main Machias River, 222
Thomaston, 82
Thorndike, James, 73
Thoreau, Henry D., 2, 45, 62, 117, 119, 160
Thoroughfare Islands (Penobscot River), 40
T'kopesuk, "the spring" (Bucksport), 8
Tobaskick Falls (York County), 183
Togus Stream (see Worromontogus)
Tolbuntbessek, Turtle Head (Hampden), 7
Tolman Pond (Rockland), 78
Tomah Island (Penobscot River), 42
Tombegwoc Pond (Deering Pond in Lebanon), 184
Tomer, Sebattis, Maliseet, 232, 233, 234
Tonemy Hill (York), 181
Toppan, Rev. Christopher, 112
Topsham, 153
Towessek, Tuessic (Bath), 136
Townsend Gut (Southport), 123
Townships 40 and 41, 49
Treat, Robert, of Bangor, xxiii, 17, 18
Treat and Webster Island, now French Island (Old Town), 30, 37, 126
Treat's Falls (Bangor), 17, 23

Treat's Falls (Stillwater), 32
True, Dr. Nathaniel Tuckerman, 69, 138, 139, 153, 163, 164, 254
Trumbull, Dr. James Hammond, xi, xx, 2, 51, 102, 141, 142, 168, 171, 180, 185, 193, 198, 199
Tucker, Richard, of Portland, 165, 166
Turtle Head (Hampden), 7
Turtle-shell Island, Namokanok (Lincoln), 52
Twin Island (Old Town), 40

Umsaskis Lake (Allegash), 55
Umsquaquospem, Big Machias Lake (Lower Sabao), 233
Unaganek, "at the carry" (Lubec), 223
Unknown Stream, Machias Main River, 222
Union, 86
Union River, 208
University of Maine, 28
Upper Dobsy Lake, Deekeewenskek, "end of the river" (St. Croix system), 234
Utloskes, Little River (Perry), 228

Vaudreuil, Gov. Phillipe de Rigaud, 81
Veazie, 22
Verona, 3, 87
Versteeg, Chester, 190
Vetromile, Rev. Eugene, xv, xvi, 12, 19, 38, 41, 54, 55, 117, 164, 193, 212
Vinalhaven, 96
Vose, Peter E., 226

Wabasgash, Mill Cove (Robbinston), 229
Wabeno-bahntuk, "white water falls" (Veazie), 22
Wabigenek, "white bone," Kendall's Head (Eastport), 228
Wachusett (Mass.), xxii
Wajoses, "little mountain," Pigeon Hill (Perry), 228
Wackquigut, "head of the bay," Back Bay (Portland), 169
Wa-ka-losen, Fort Knox (Prospect), 4
Waldo, Gen. Samuel, 21, 28
Waldoboro, 87, 92
Walinituk, "cove brook," Mill Creek (South Orrington), 5
Walkamigossek, "hollow" (Old Town), 31
Walker's Pond (Sedgwick), xi, 194, 202

Wallamatogus Hill (Penobscot), 190
Wambemando, Wombimando, "white devil," Micmac Indian, on Penobscot, 42
Wanagamesswak, rock fairies, 6, 217
Wannametoname (York), 181
Wannerton, Thomas, of Piscataqua, xi
Wapskenigan, "white rock carry" (Woodland), 231
Wasassabskek, Slippery Ledge Rapids (Old Town), 14, 28
Wasa-umkeag (Sears Island), 68
Wassamkihemuk, High Head (Bangor), 14, 29
Wassasumkwemuk, Slippery Ledge Rapids, 14
Wassoos-sumps-sque-he-mok, 14
Wassquagos, Pleasant River (Addison), 216
Wassumkeag, Sears Island (Searsport), 65, 67, 68
Waterboro, 183
Waterville, 145
Waukeag (Douaquet, Adowakeag) Falls Point (Sullivan), 210
Waylumkituk (Olamon), 39
Waymouth, Capt. George, xv, 80, 130
Webber Pond (Bristol), 90
Webhannet River (Wells), 178
Webster Place (Orono), 28
Wedebegek, 76
Wechkotetuk, Union River, 208
Weirs, N. H., 66
Wekwabigek, "head tide" (Perry), 229
Wells, 176
Wenkwidawiwiewak (Hermon Pond), 9
Wequ'agawaysuk, "head of the tide," Eddington Bend, 22
Wequahyik, "head of the bay" (Oak Bay, N. B.), 22
Wequash Pond (N. H.), 66
Wessaweskeag (Thomaston), 80, 82
West Bath, xv, 134
Westbrook, 160, 162
Westbrook, Col. Thomas, 31, 32, 162
Westgustogo, Yarmouth, 157
West Quoddy Head (Lubec), 223
Weswick, Whiskeag (Bath), 134
Wetchi-san-kessuk, Sunkhaze (Greenbush), 44, 80

Weymouth (Mass.), 157
Wheeler, Benjamin, of Hampden, 7
Wheeler, Dr. George A., 135, 138, 139, 140, 141, 202
Whiskeag (Bath), 134
White Man's Island (Penobscot River), 42
White Squaw Island (Penobscot River), 40
Whiting, 224
Whiting River, 224
Wichi-gask-i-taywick, 120
Wigwam Bay and Point (Brunswick), 135
Willeguaganum, Grand Lake (St. Croix), 233
Williamson, Joseph, xi, 68, 69
Williamson, William Durfee, 2, 19, 82, 99, 102
Willis, William, xiv, 87, 116, 148, 163, 206
Winn, 56
Winneagwamuk, 203
Winnegance (Bath), xv, 136
Winnegance (East Boothbay), 105
Winnepesaukee Lake, 138
Winskeag, Otter Creek Point (Mt. Desert), 209
Winslow, 145
Winslow, Edward, 196, 197
Winslow, Capt. Josiah, 86
Winslow Rocks (Sagadahoc River), 136
Winterport, 5
Winthrop, John, 196
Wiscasset, xxvi, 118, 119, 120
Wiscogosis, Lower Sabao Lake (Machias River), 223
Wiscogossisicook, chain of Sabao Lakes, 223
Wisqueg, Whiskeag (Bath), 134
Wood, William, xxi, 157, 250
Woolwich, 137
Worromontogus, Togus (Pittston), 190
Wskidabskek, Friar's Head (Campobello), 228
Wunnametonneme Hill (York), 181
Wususekm, Wusosisek, "the nest" (Lubec), 223
Wytopitlock, 57

Yarmouth, 157
Yeapskasset River (York), 182
York, 178

www.ingramcontent.com/pod-product-compliance
Lightning Source LLC
Chambersburg PA
CBHW051630230426
43669CB00013B/2241